About the Author

Andrew Ramdayal, PMP, PgMP, PMI-ACP, CISSP-ISSMP has over 15 years of project management experience in IT. He holds over 50 professional certifications in IT and accounting from vendors such as Microsoft, Cisco, CompTIA, and PMI. He also holds a Master Degree in Management Information System with a minor in project management. Andrew has worked on many ERP, IT Security, and computer networking projects over his career.

Andrew has been teaching the PMP exam prep for over 10 years to thousands of students all over the world. His unique teaching methods have allowed his students not only to pass the exam but also to apply the concepts in real life. He is currently the CEO of the Technical Institute of America which provides training to thousands of students every year in IT and medical courses.

About Technical Institute of America

Technical Institute of America (TIA) is a nationally accredited school headquartered in New York City with locations in Arlington, VA, and San Francisco, CA. TIA is a PMI Registered Education Provider #3333. TIA provides online and in-person classes in most IT certifications and short term medical courses.

PMP® Exam Prep Simplified

Andrew Ramdayal, PMP, PgMP, CISSP-ISSMP
Editor: AJ Mercier BS, MS, MBA, PMP

Project Management Professional (PMP) is a registered mark of the Project Management Institute, Inc.
PMBOK is a registered mark of the Project Management Institute, Inc
Materials in this course are taken from *A Guide to the Project Management Body of Knowledge (PMBOK® Guide) – Sixth Edition*, Project Management Institute Inc., 2017

By Andrew Ramdayal, PMP, PgMP, CISSP-ISSMP

Forth Printing: March 2021

ISBN-13: 979-8-59028-804-5

PMP, CAPM, PMI-ACP, PgMP, PMI-RMP, PMI-SP, PMBOK, Project Management Professional, Certified Associate in Project Management (CAPM), Project Management Professional (PMP), PMI Agile Certified Practitioner (PMI-ACP), Program Management Professional (PgMP), PMI Risk Management Professional (PMI-RMP), PMI Scheduling Professional (PMI-SP), A Guide to the Project Management Body of Knowledge (PMBOK Guide), The PMI R.E.P Logo are registered marks of the Project Management Institute, Inc.

Technical Institute of America has been reviewed and approved as a provider of project management training by the Project Management Institute (PMI). As a PMI Registered Education Provider (R.E.P), Technical Institute of America has agreed to abide by PMI established quality assurance criteria.

Technical Institute of America

545 8th Ave

New York, NY 10018

Phone: 212-564-2351

Fax: 800-490-7341

E-mail: info@tiaedu.com

Web: www.tia.edu

Thank you for the purchase of "PMP Exam Prep Simplified"!

To access your 35 hours of Project Management education **E-learning course** follow all the directions on the **last page** of this study guide.

For Live Authorized PMP Bootcamps checkout
Technical Institute of America: **www.tiaedu.com**
Contact us: **info@tiaedu.com** or **212-564-2351**

Join me **Live on Youtube** for my PMP Questions and Answer Sessions and additional PMP resources

www.youtube.com/c/AndrewRamdayal

Table of Contents

Chapter 1
Introduction

The PMP exam is one of the world's most recognized and well-respected certifications in Project Management. A PMP certification generally means better pay and more esteem from your peers. Getting the certification will not be an easy task to accomplish. The exam is difficult, and even the application process is challenging.

Over my 12-plus-year career of teaching toward this exam, I have developed many tips and tricks that have allowed thousands of students to pass this exam on the first try. I believe if you follow the tips and guidance I present throughout this book, and especially the exam tips in the last chapter, you can successfully pass this exam the very first time.

When I decided to write this book, I didn't want to write an 800-plus page guide for students to slog through. I wanted to write a condensed book featuring just the information that you need to know to pass the tests. I also wanted to include lots of practice questions to give students a good sense of the actual PMP exam. I've written this book from a first-person perspective as if I were actually teaching a class. That means that I will address you, the reader, as my student.

I know that preparing for a PMP exam is an enormous undertaking that will require many hours of studying and countless other sacrifices in order to achieve. But the rewards are worth it. A PMP certification can open many doors and can lead to a significant pay increase and/or career opportunities.

The Current PMP Exam

This guide is written for students taking the most current PMP exam, which was released on Jan 2, 2021. This exam, unlike the previous PMP exams, will incorporate not just predictive project management but also agile and hybrid approaches. In this guide, I will be covering all three approaches.

It is important to realize that as a certified PMP, you should be able to manage any type of project, whether that is a traditional waterfall-based project to an agile project. In many businesses today, companies will even combine traditional project management methods with agile to create a hybrid approach.

It is also important to note that PMI uses many different resources to create the contents of a PMP exam. On their website, they have something called the PMP reference list that outlines about 10 different books that were used in the creation of the PMP exam. Books such as the PMBOK® Guide 6th Edition and Agile Practice guide were used along with others. No worries, you do not need to read all 10 different books to get your PMP; this study guide will be more than sufficient for you to ace your PMP on the first try.

One document in particular that we will be reviewing in the last chapter of this guide will be the PMP Examination Content Outline (ECO). The ECO will list a variety of tasks that are mapped to three different domains. The examination questions will come from these tasks and domains. Check the last chapter of this book for a detailed review of all of the tasks within the ECO for the current exam. It is important to note that the ECO is not listed in any particular order; rather, it describes roles and activities that a project manager should be doing on a project. So, when we have completed all of the different parts, processes, and terms within a project, we will then review the ECO in detail to ensure we get a full understanding of what will be covered on the exam.

PMBOK® Guide and Other Materials

While the current PMP exam has been updated to support other methods of project management, it is still heavily dependent upon the PMBOK® Guide 6th Edition. PMBOK® Guide, which stands for Project Management Body of Knowledge, is a book of best practices for managing a project. It outlines all of the processes that a project will follow from beginning to end. The exam also uses a variety of other books, including the agile practitioner guide.

What many people fail to understand is that the PMBOK® Guide is not an exam study guide.

There are many topics that we will cover in this book that are not in the PMBOK® Guide. The PMBOK® Guide does not have any practice questions or exam tips. This book will cover the PMBOK® Guide in detail and include everything you need to know to pass the exam. This book does not waste time on topics that won't show up on your exam.

The PMBOK® Guide is a very difficult book to read. Most of my students have a hard time understanding it and making sense of what is in there. If you are looking to simply pass your exam, then this book is what you need. You can attempt to read the PMBOK® Guide, but I will congratulate you if you can get past the first five pages without falling asleep. It is probably the world's best sleeping aid.

While the PMP exam will not be based solely on the PMBOK® Guide, most of the questions will use the PMBOK® Guide as a reference. As such, this study guide's chapters will be structured in the same way as the PMBOK® Guide. Since the PMBOK® Guide doesn't include all of the topics you will need to know for the exam, I will be adding more to these chapters to ensure you understand the different components of agile and hybrid project management. The PMBOK® Guide is mostly concerned with a traditional waterfall-based project management method, so studying the PMBOK® Guide alone would only give you about 50% of the exam content.

Application Process

The PMP exam has quite a few requirements and a lengthy application process, not challenging, but time-consuming. Here are the current requirements.

The PMP exam requires:

- 35 hours of project management education. You can get this from any registered PMI education provider. You can search for it on the PMI website. For example, my company, Technical Institute of America, offers boot camps and online classes that will satisfy this requirement. You can also use a CAPM certification substitute for the 35 hours of project management education.

- A number of years of project management education dependent on your highest level of education as follows:

  - A four-year degree:
  - 36 months of leading projects

  OR

  - A high school diploma or an associate's degree (or global equivalent):
  - 60 months of leading projects

One question I keep getting over and over from students is, "does this experience qualify as 'leading projects'?" PMI does not go into detail on the exact definition. Most people that have led projects, or even specific parts of projects would qualify. You do not need to have the title of 'project manager', but you do need to have done the job of leading a team through all parts of a project. For example, if you are working on a large software development project and you are managing only a few team members, but your title is lead programmer, you will qualify to take the exam.

You have to fill out an online application at www.pmi.org in order to see if you qualify to take the exam. In this application, you have to document the start and completion dates for your projects. You also have to write a description of a few hundred words about each project. This study guide comes with supplemental videos where I will be reviewing with you how to write the descriptions to apply for your exam.

Let's take a look at the steps to apply and get your PMP:

Here is the general process you will follow to pass your PMP exam:

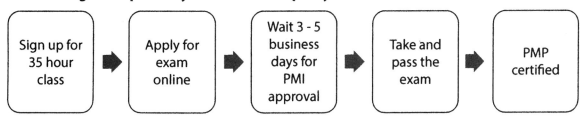

These are just the basic steps you will need to take to get the actual certification. You will also need the 35 contact hours. This should come from a project management course. Apply for the exam online and submit the application. PMI will take about a week to approve the application. After you get approval, you can then schedule the exam at any Pearson Vue testing center (www.pearsonvue.com). You cannot schedule this exam without first getting approval from PMI.

Exam Stats

- **180 questions.**

- **230 Minutes.** This is just enough time to complete the exam. Most people will need the

- entire 230 minutes to finish it. Two 10-minute breaks will be allowed while taking the exam.

- When you complete the exam, you will be informed right away if you passed or failed. The exam does not give a numerical score. It's either pass or fail.

The exam is broken down as follows:

Domain	Percentage of Items on Test
I. People	42%
2. Process	50%
3. Business Environment	8%
Total	100%

Every few years, PMI conducts what is known as the Job Task Analysis (JTA), where they do interviews with many current project managers to learn about what's happening in the real-world environment of project management. It's from this JTA that they create the PMP examination content outline (ECO). The ECO for January 2021 documents three domains. People, process, and business environment.

The domains are high-level knowledge areas that are essential to managing any project. When conducting a project, you will have to manage people following processes in a particular business environment. The ECO documents that within each domain, there are certain numbers of tasks, and each task has a certain number of enablers. For example:

Domain 1: People

- **Task 1: Manage conflict**
  - Interpret the source and stage of the conflict
  - Analyze the context for the conflict
  - Evaluate/recommend/reconcile the appropriate conflict resolution solution

As you can see in this example, this task is about managing conflict on a team. You will be required to understand the source of the conflict, analyze the conflict, and come up with the correct solution.

In the chapter titled "examination content outline review and project management mindset," we will be reviewing all of the tasks listed in the exam outline, and I will present a brief summary of each. This will be a great way to review all of the concepts that you will have learned throughout the study guide. Be sure to review this chapter thoroughly before taking any mock exams or your real exam.

Taking the actual exam

At the time of this writing, the PMP exam is being given as a proctored online exam or in-person exam at a Pearson Vue testing center. When you schedule the exam, you will have the option of choosing either one.

If you select the proctored online exam, you will need to have a Webcam on your computer and a quiet room in order to take it. This exam can be done at home or at work. You will be monitored for the entire duration of the exam from your Webcam.

If you select to take the exam at a Pearson Vue testing center, you have to physically go to the center and sit down for four hours and take the actual exam on one of their computers. You can take breaks as needed throughout this exam but, same as the online exam.

Types of Questions

The PMP exam will contain a few different types of questions, as follows:

- **Multiple-choice**: These are standard questions where you will have to select one choice from a series of four different choices. These types of questions will generally contain at least 2 'correct' answers, and you have to choose the best of these two choices. You will also get questions where you have to select multiple responses. For example, you may have to select two or three of the five or six choices presented.

- **Drag and drop**: These are questions where you have to match multiple things up. For example, they may give you a question where you have to match what tools may be used in what process or match what conflict resolution method would work in certain scenarios.

- **Hotspot and a few fill-in-the-blank questions**: These questions will require you to click on a spot of a diagram or graph.

As you can see, the exam contains a variety of question formats.

Secret to Passing

My students often ask me, "Andrew, is there a secret to passing this exam?" The answer is yes. There are two main secrets you will need to apply in order to pass this exam.

1. Understand the concepts and don't memorize them

2. Do not apply your work experience

All too often, students feel they have to memorize so many different processes, terminologies, and tools only to come to find out that the exam doesn't want you to memorize any of them. This exam is about understanding the concepts of best practices in a predictive and Agile project management environment. Memorizing these different processes and tools while failing to understand when we can use them is unlikely to be a successful strategy. The questions on this exam are scenario-based and generally have multiple correct answers. So, if you fail to understand these processes and tools and how to apply them as per best practice, your chances of passing are very low. When going through the study guide, try to understand when it would be best to use particular processes and tools.

One other issue I often see students encounter is that they attempt to apply their work experience to the questions. WHEN TAKING THIS EXAM, DO NOT APPLY YOUR WORK EXPERIENCE. This exam is based on best practices and not the practices your organization follows. Sometimes what we do within our personal work experience may not always be considered best practices. The best thing that a student can do is to forget all they have done in project management in the real world and try to understand it from the "PMI" world. I would suggest from this moment on that as you go through the study guide, clear your mind of every type of project you have ever worked on and start with a blank mind as if you have never managed the project before.

After Becoming Certified

Passing the PMP exam means you have committed hours to studying for, and almost an entire day to take an exam. Right after you finish the exam on the computer, it will tell you if you passed or failed. If you pass, you are certified from that moment. If you fail, you will have the chance to retake the exam. You can retake the exam up to two more times after the first attempt. After that, you must wait one year before resubmitting your application.

Once you pass, you are instantly certified-but you will need to do more work to hold onto the certification. You will need to maintain the certification, or you could lose it after 3 years. You will be required to earn 60 PDUs (Professional Development Units) every 3 years, or you could lose your certification.

Earning PDUs is done in the following ways:

- Taking classes relating to project management. These can be live classes or online classes. Most people will get them this way. Generally, for every hour of class, you will get 1 PDU.

- Attending PMI chapter meetings. Every month, the local PMI chapter will hold a meeting with its members. If you are a member and attend, you can get about 1-2 PDUs.

- Reading books or articles.

- Volunteering at PMI or other nonprofit organizations.

I know you're not currently worried about renewing your PMP certification since you are not certified yet, but it's good to keep this in the back of your mind. Three years will go by very fast, and no one wants to retake this exam.

Chapter 2

Key Project Management Terms

PMBOK® Guide and Agile Practice Guide

Originally published in 1996, the PMBOK® Guide is currently in its 6th edition. It has been consistently updated every four to five years. When you get certified in one PMBOK® Guide, you do not need to be certified in another; all you have to do is maintain that certification.

The PMBOK® Guide was written by a large body of very smart folks who came together to write common standards for project management. One has to ask: Do all projects from different industries follow a standard set of processes? The answer is yes, they do, and that's what each PMBOK® Guide maps out. If we were to take 10 random employees from different industries, sit them down, and tell them, "I want you guys to write a book that standardizes the way all projects are managed," what would that standard be? What would those processes be? The goal of the PMBOK® Guide is to answer these questions. It is just a book that's written by a lot of different individuals from many different industries to standardize the way a project is actually managed.

Another famous guide that your exam will use heavily is the Agile Practice Guide. This guide will outline many of the agile concepts, processes, and terminology you will need to know on your exam. Although 50% of your exam is still based on the PMBOK® Guide, you should expect to see questions on agile practices. Review our dedicated chapter on Agile to learn more about this guide in all the different terms you will need to understand what Agile is.

Project

A temporary endeavor to create a unique product, service, or result. A project by definition is temporary; it can be either short or long. A project could be something as simple as painting a room, a task that will last for a few days, or something long-term, such as building a complex application, which could require two to four years to complete. The key point is that all projects must be temporary, and they have a start date and an end date. The output of the project has to be unique, and it must be unique to the customer. In other words, the customer hasn't done this before. Even though a project is unique and temporary, the output of the project, the main deliverable, will be around for a very long time, such as constructing a large building that will be used for hundreds of years.

Examples of projects can include:

- Building a house.
- Creating new software.
- Installing a new computer network.
- Redesigning a process in a company.
- Merging different organizations.

Operations

Operations are the opposite of projects. Operations deal with the day-to-day work of a business. One of the main differences between projects and operations is that one is temporary, and the other is ongoing. Operations have no start date or end date. An example would be sales: that's something you do every day. It's never finished. Providing IT support is also an operation. If you're building cars on an assembly line, that is also an operation because the output is not unique, and there is no start or end date. The main difference for your exam is: projects are temporary and unique, whereas operations have no start date, no end date, and are not unique.

Progressive Elaboration

Progressive elaboration involves discovering greater levels of detail as the project moves toward completion. This is also known as "rolling wave planning." The easiest way to think of it is that as time progresses, things get more detailed. At the beginning of a project, you may not know the specific details of what you want to do. Example: I want to build a house for my family in the suburbs of New York City but do I know which specific address I'm building on? It could be upstate or part of Connecticut or Long Island. I may know a high-level, approximate cost, but not a detailed cost. As the project progresses, things will become more elaborated. A few weeks into this project, I may know exactly where I want to live and how big the house will be.

Project Management

Project management is the application of knowledge, skills, tools, and techniques to meet the project requirements; it's about managing people to accomplish the scope of the project in the given constraints of time and costs. All projects are limited as to time, cost, and scope. In project management, our goal is to get work done within a specific budget and a specific timeframe. Example: If I were to paint a room, what activities would I need to do? I'd need to buy the paint, remove the furniture, paint the walls, and put the furniture back. By accomplishing the project activities, you're finishing the actual project requirements.

The PMP exam will look at three different approaches to managing a project. The approaches are:

- Predictive: a predictive project, also known as a traditional waterfall, or plan-driven is a project where much of the planning is done upfront at the beginning of the project, and then the rest of the project would be to execute the plan to complete the actual work. This is more of a traditional project, such as building a house. You would plan for a few months on what the design would be and how it would be built, then execute and actually go out and build this house with very few changes in planning throughout the rest of the project.

- Agile: An Agile project is known as adaptive or change-driven, where the product is built in small increments versus being built all at once as you would in a traditional project. The agile project allows more customer interactions as small increments are being built. For example, on a software development project, you could bill certain modules and deploy these modules to the users so they can start using the product right away and give their feedback. Agile projects also support changes throughout the entire project, allowing customers to add requirements without having to go through a change management process as you would on a traditional project.

- Hybrid. A hybrid project is when an organization combines the use of both predictive and agile methods for managing projects. This can be done in a variety of ways, in which case, a part of the project can be done using a traditional predictive approach while another part is done using agile methods.

Value of Projects

The main reason a company does a project is to derive value from the output of that project. Upon the completion of a project, a company should gain some kind of value from it. Value can be tangible, such as money, or intangible, such as brand reputation. No company wants to spend money doing a project that does not return any value.

One of the main tasks of the project manager is to ensure that the project and its completed deliverables are always adding value to a business. These values are mostly driven by changes within a company. In order for a company to grow, it must change, and that usually results in a new project being started. That change, for example, can be a new sales management system or the development of a new product.

Processes

Processes have inputs, tools and techniques, that are combined to execute a specific activity on a project and create a specific output. Many processes are performed multiple times. Do not think of them as being performed sequentially or discretely in their iterations. Everything we do in life follows some kind of a process. We execute a process because we want the output.

Every process has inputs, which are things that are needed to start the process. Tools and techniques are things that help you to execute a process. Output is what you get out of the process. In this particular book, we have 49 processes that projects will go through in order to go from start to finish. Each process is performed multiple times within a project. Inputs, tools and techniques, and outputs (ITTO) will be covered for each process in this book.

EXAM TIP: ITTO is an acronym that will be mentioned throughout this study guide. ITTO stands for Input, Tools and Techniques, and Output.

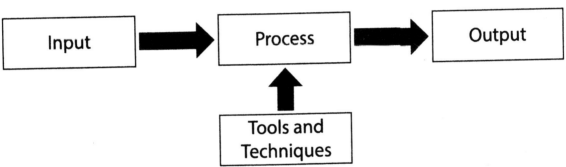

All processes have inputs, tools and techniques, and outputs

Phase

A phase is a division within the project where extra control is needed to effectively manage the completion of one or more deliverables. Phases are generally concluded and formally closed with the acceptance of a deliverable. Each phase has all five process groups of initiating, planning, executing, monitoring and controlling, and closing.

Phase gates (AKA phase reviews, stage gates, and kill points) are held at the end of each phase of a project to determine if the project is meeting its goals and if the project should continue.

Deliverable

A deliverable is a part of the product that is presented to the customer or stakeholders for acceptance.

Phases are used to complete deliverables. How do we know if a deliverable is good after the project team has built it? We have to get that deliverable accepted by the customer or sponsor. How do we know when a phase is done? It is done when the deliverable is accepted by the customer or sponsor. A project could have many phases; the project manager determines the phases of a project. Every phase within a project will create a specific deliverable or deliverables. These deliverables are taken to a customer for approval. Outputs from one phase will become inputs for another phase. The 49 processes that are explained in this book take place in each phase of the project.

For example, installing a new phone system will have a number of phases. First, selecting the phone system; second, testing it; third, installing it; fourth, training users to use it. Who created the phases? I did as the project manager. Each one of these phases has a particular deliverable. The first phase of selecting the phone system has a deliverable of knowing what phone system you want to install. The deliverable of the testing phase will be the test results. The third phase deliverable will be having the actual phone system on the user's desk. The fourth phase deliverable will be trained users who can use the phones effectively. As we complete each phase of the project, a customer or sponsor will formally accept each deliverable.

Process Group

A process group is used in project management to group a set of processes the project manager maybe doing at a certain time. The five process groups are initiating, planning, executing, monitoring and controlling, and closing. A process group is not a phase, but all phases on a project will contain these five process groups. We will explain this in more detail in chapter 3.

Knowledge Areas

A knowledge area is a certain set of processes that are usually defined by the knowledge needed to manage that area. In project management, there are 10 knowledge areas: integration, scope, schedule, cost, quality, resources, communications, risk, procurement, and stakeholders. For example, the scope knowledge area will require a project manager to have skills and knowledge about project scope in order to complete the processes within that knowledge area. These knowledge areas make up the chapters of this book and the PMBOK® Guide. We will be covering each of these knowledge areas in more detail throughout the rest of this book.

Development Life Cycles

The project life cycle is the series of phases a project will go through from start to finish. Most projects will have more than one phase, and they need to be completed in order to be done with the project. Different projects have different life cycles. A life cycle can be predictive or adaptive.

- A predictive life cycle is where the scope, time, and cost are known early in the project. The project manager will try to complete the project scope within the given time and cost. For example, you might be renovating a kitchen where the customer knows exactly what they wanted, how much they wanted to spend, and how long it should take.

- An iterative, incremental, or adaptive life cycle is when the scope is known early, but the time and cost will be refined as the project is progressing. This is done using iterations of the product. For example, some projects use different prototypes to get customer feedback as the project is progressing. This means the product is built in increments versus being built as a whole.

- Some organizations might use both a predictive and adaptive life cycle for a project. This can be done for projects where certain parts are well known before the work is started, and other parts will be developed incrementally.

Projects, Programs, and Portfolios

We must understand the differences between projects, programs, and portfolios. A program is a collection of projects containing a common goal managed by a program manager. A portfolio is a collection of projects and programs that are implemented to achieve a strategic business goal, and are managed by a portfolio manager. For example, building a skyscraper is a very large project. If you are building a 60-story skyscraper, it could take years to do and will take an incredible amount of money and manpower to get the job done. It would be better to break up this project into smaller projects and then manage them individually. Getting a permit could be a project. The excavation of the site could be a project. Later, you can roll all those smaller projects into one large program. Tasks like building a skyscraper, building bridges, or redesigning a car are very large projects that could be considered programs. So, a program is a collection of projects with a common goal and is generally used for larger endeavors.

Portfolios include projects and programs that are created to achieve a strategic business goal. Portfolios identify, prioritize, authorize, manage, and control a collection of projects and programs to meet a strategic business goal. The portfolio aggregates all of the resources of the projects and programs to accomplish the strategic goal. A strategic business goal is generally a three-to-five-year goal that a business wants to accomplish. An example would be a company that wants to be the top provider selling widgets. This would be a long-term goal, as it will take at least three years to become a top provider of a product. The company would need a program to create the product. It would also need a project to train the sales team and a project to advertise the new product.

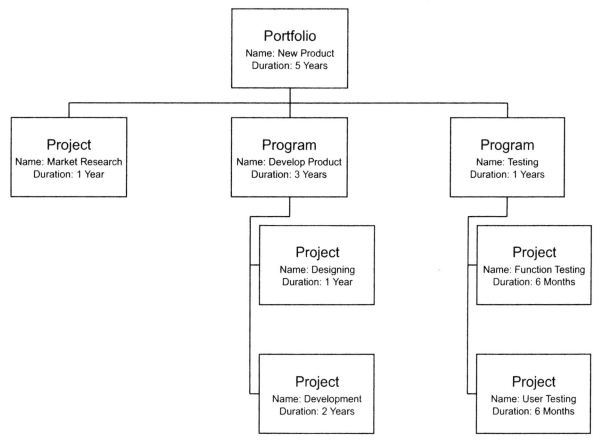

Five-year portfolio to develop a new product.

Baselines

There are three baselines on all projects; scope, time, and cost. A baseline is an original plan plus any approved changes. All projects are measured against these three baselines. When you have finished planning a project, you will come up with the three baselines for that project. During planning, you create your cost baseline, also known as your budget; your schedule baseline for your schedule; and the scope baseline of what work needs to get done when the project is executed. You then measure the performance of the project against the three baselines as the project is being executed. Without baselines, it is impossible to actually measure the performance of the project. When you say that the project is doing great, this means that you have to compare what's currently happening to what you hope will happen. What you hope will happen is your baselines. The status of the project is reached by comparing the actual work against the planned work, i.e., the baselines.

For example, painting the server room has a scope baseline of painting the walls white, a schedule baseline of three days, and a cost baseline of $2,000. You start working on the project, and by the middle of day 2, you have completed half the work and spent $1,000. This is going great. The project is on scope, time, and cost. The sponsor comes into the room and says it looks great so far, but he now wants you to paint the hallway. He is adding more to your scope. You will ask the sponsor for a formal change request. This way, you can assess the effects of scope on time and cost. After your assessment, you determine that you will need an additional $1,000 and one more day. You take this back to the sponsor for approval, and he does approve your request. You update the baselines with this approved change. Now you will paint the server room and the hallway. Baselines are the original plan plus all approved changes.

Historical Information

Historical information records what has been learned from previous projects. This can include things like templates and lessons that were learned from previous projects. Historical information is covered under the term "Organizational process assets" in the PMBOK® Guide. It is one of the most common inputs to many of the 49 processes we will be covering in this guide.

Lessons Learned

As a project is progressing, you will learn new and better ways of completing various tasks and apply those methods to the remaining tasks on the project. Lessons learned are recorded at the end of every project or phase. We examine lessons learned to ensure that the next time you do something, you do it better. This involves updating the lessons learned register as the project is being executed. When a project or phase is completed, the stakeholders should have a lessons learned meeting and determine what they did correctly and incorrectly on this project. This will be useful for the next project.

Regulations

Regulations are official documents that provide guidelines that must be followed. Regulation is something that must be followed, generally imposed by law. An example could be regulatory compliance, such as following HIPAA compliance in medical offices. Not following regulations could result in fines or other serious penalties for a business.

Standard

A standard is approved by a recognized body that provides guidelines. Compliance with standards is common and generally encouraged, but not strictly mandatory. An example would include PMI's standards for project management (PMBOK®Guide). You don't need to follow a standard, but it is generally best to do so.

System

A system includes all formal procedures and tools put in place to manage something. All companies need a system to manage their businesses. A system would be needed in an accounting department to manage the payroll or to manage a project. Systems allow us to have formal procedures in place. This way, everyone working in that system knows what to do and how to do it.

Project Governance

Project governance is the framework, functions, and processes that a company will follow in order to complete a project. This is done to meet the organization's strategic and operational goals. Project governance is usually a framework that is developed internally in a business to complete its projects and make decisions about them. No two organizations have the exact same framework when it comes to project management. Every organization generally follows its own processes and procedures when it comes to managing a project.

Some companies have very specific processes when it comes to initiating a project, while some companies just initiate a project verbally. It's important to understand that every organization will tailor the processes in this book to meet its own needs when it comes to project management.

Project Management Office (PMO)

The PMO provides guidance and support for all project managers in the company. This office plays a big role by helping to ensure that all projects follow a standard set of processes from start to end. The PMO generally sets up the structure and framework that projects within a business will follow. These can include the processes and procedures that a project manager may follow to initiate and plan a project.

PMOs are generally broken into three types: supportive, controlling, and directive. A supportive PMO is just there to support the project manager by providing templates and training. A supportive PMO generally has low authority over the project. A controlling PMO will support the project manager by giving them a particular framework they need to follow and templates they will have to use. This PMO has moderate authority over the project. A directive PMO will direct the project manager on what they should be doing and is generally in control of the project. In a directive PMO, the project manager will report to the PMO, and the PMO is usually high in authority.

A PMO is an important stakeholder on a project and can help in the following ways:

- Provides training for project managers on project methodologies.
- Defines standards and the best practices for all projects in an organization.
- Provides templates for project managers to use.
- Helps with approvals or resource gathering.
- Defines the project management role.
- Provides assistant project managers with the resources needed to complete their projects.

Stakeholder

A stakeholder is any individual or business that may be positively or negatively affected by the project. 'Stakeholder' is a word that you will often see on the exam. It always refers to folks who are affected by the project. A key point to remember is that when the question mentions the word stakeholder, it is referring to anyone on the project. The project manager and the project team will identify all the stakeholders on the project. This is done when the project is initiated.

A stakeholder is affected positively when the outcome of the project helps him/her in his/ her personal life or business. For example, when a company installs a new application for the accounting department and the bookkeepers can now get income statements automatically rather than having to manually make one every time one is needed. This makes their work a lot easier.

A stakeholder that is negatively affected might be when someone loses his/her job because the new accounting application the company just installed means it does not need his/her skills or work anymore.

> *ExamTip: When you read a question, you have to be very careful when it uses the word stakeholder. When the exam mentions the word stakeholder, it means everyone that is affected by the project.*

Examples of project stakeholders:

- **Sponsor:** The sponsor may be internal or external, and provides resources and support to the project for the project's success. A sponsor is a person who pays for the project. The sponsor may help to initiate and authorize a project. A sponsor authorizes changes and approves the project deliverables.

- **Customers and Users:** Customers are the people who will use the project deliverables. Customers may also need to accept a deliverable. For example, when the project team has finished installing the accounting application, the customers will be the people who work in the accounting department and use the application.

> *Exam Tip: Deliverables are accepted by either the sponsor or the customers.*

- **Sellers:** Sellers (vendors) are companies that provide supplies or services to the project and are external to the organization hosting the project. For example, hiring a contractor to install a system.

- **Organizational Groups:** Organizational groups are internal entities that are affected by the project activities. These are entities such as sales, HR, legal, or finance.

- **Functional Managers:** Functional managers are individuals who are heads of different organizational functions. They are managers of the organization's groups, such as sales, HR, legal, or IT. Functional managers have control over organizational resources. When the project manager needs specific resources, such as a technician or programmer, he or she will need to ask and negotiate with the functional managers.

- **Senior Management:** These are individuals who are responsible for the strategic plans and goals of the company. They usually help to prioritize projects or resolve high-level organizational conflicts.

- **Program Manager:** Program managers are responsible for the programs they manage and for managing project managers.

- **Project Team:** The project team consists of the people who create the project's products, services, or results. The team is either full-time (dedicated) or part-time. These are the subject matter experts with the skills needed to do the actual project work. The project manager is always the leader of the project team.

- **Project Manager:** The project manager (PM) is responsible for the project outcome. PMs are always in control of the project and are authorized to use all project resources. PM's do the day-to-day management of the project team to complete the project deliverables. On an agile project, the project manager would sometimes be referred to as the scrum master or coach. On agile projects, the project manager would follow more of a servant leadership role, in which case, instead of actually directing the project team what to do, they will be more of a supporting manager. Review the chapter on agile concepts for more information on this.

- **Project Coordinator:** When working in a functional or weak matrix organization, the PM's role may not exist. In this case, a project coordinator may be used. He/she usually cannot make budget decisions but can assign resources. They have some decision-making power, but less than a project manager.

- **Project Expeditor:** In a functional organization where the project manager is part-time, an expeditor is used. An expeditor has less power over a project than either a PM or a coordinator. Expeditors just help to organize the project work and have no power or responsibility to follow a budget. They are usually staff with no formal authority.

- **Product owner:** The product owner is a role on an agile project done by a person who will prioritize the product backlog (list of features) on the project. Review our chapter on agile for a more in-depth explanation of this role.

Organizational Structure

The organization structure will help to determine the power and authority level of the project manager within a company. The structure of the organization will help to determine who controls the resources needed for the project.

Generally, the contention of power is between the project manager and the functional managers. Both of them need resources to conduct their activities. A functional manager will need resources to conduct the day-to-day operations of the business, and the project manager will need resources to conduct the project activities, such as painting walls or programming an application. The person who would be in charge of the resources is generally determined by the structure of the organization. Here are a few structures that you should know for your exam:

- **Organic or Simple:** Simple organization tends to involve a small business where the role of the project manager really does not exist. Project management is often part-time, and the organization owner or operator generally controls most of the budgets related to the different projects that are done. Expect most small businesses and startups to function like this.

- **Virtual:** A virtual organization is where project management is done virtually using different types of computer technology, such as virtual meetings and chats. The project manager's authority is low to moderate, and they will generally share the resources with the functional managers. Project management can be either full-time or part-time.

- **Functional Organization:** A functional organization is an organization where the project manager has very little power over the resources. The resources are controlled and managed by the functional manager. Businesses that are functional will have departments (IT, Accounting, Sales, Finance, etc..) with a functional manager as the head of it. Even the project manager reports to the functional manager. Project management is part-time and is something you do when you have extra time during the day. When the project is done, the team member goes back to his/her functional duties.

- **Project Oriented:** A project-oriented (AKA, projectized) business is where the project manager controls all of the resources. The PM has 100% control of the resources. This is a full-time position for the PM. A business like this might be a consulting business.

  In a consulting business, a contract is acquired to provide a consulting service to its customers. It will hire a PM, and the PM then hires all the resources needed to complete the project. In this case, the PM is in charge of everything until the project is completed. There are no functional managers. When the project is completed, the team members are either released from the company or reassigned to another project.

- **Matrix:** A matrix type business is a middle ground between the functional and the project-oriented. Here are the 3 types and their attributes:

  - **Weak Matrix:** In a weak matrix, the PM has a little more power than he/she did in the functional organization. His/her authority is still relatively low and is managed by the functional managers. This is still a part-time project management position.

  - **Balanced Matrix:** In a balanced matrix, the PM's power is almost equal to the functional managers for the control of resources. This is a full-time position. In this organization, the PM and functional manager will need to share the resources from a pool. The PM's power is low to moderate. Personnel generally leave operations to work on a project and then return to operations once the project is done. A balanced matrix has the highest likelihood of conflicts between the PM and the functional managers, since the power is even.

  - **Strong Matrix:** In a strong matrix, the PM has most of the power over resources. This is a full-time position. The PM's power is moderate to high. There is a functional manager, but with very little power. This is similar to a project-oriented company.

- **Hybrid:** A hybrid organization structure is when a company uses more than one of the different types of structures. A company may be functional when managing projects in its operational departments, such as sales and finance, while using a project-oriented style in research and development. Sometimes a functional organization may create a special unit with a dedicated team just to complete an important project, where everyone works full-time to complete the work. This would be a combination of functional and project-oriented approaches.

ExamTip: All questions on a PMP exam are generally based on a strong matrix unless otherwise noted in the question.

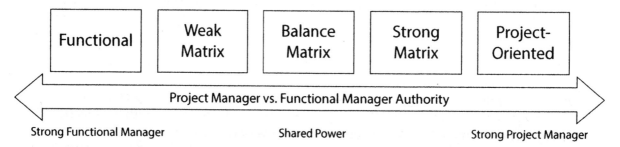

Name	Project Manager Authority	Who Controls the Resources	Project Manager Work Shift
Organic or simple	Little or none	Owner	Little or no time
Virtual	Low to moderate	Mixed	Full-time or part-time
Functional	Little or none	Functional Manager	Part-time
Project-oriented	High to full control	Project Manager	Full-time
Weak matrix	Low	Functional Manager	Part-time
Balanced matrix	Low to moderate	Shared	Part-time
Strong matrix	Moderate to high	Project Manager	Full-time

Constraint

One of the most basic concepts to understand in project management will be the constraints on a project. All projects are constrained by their scope, time, cost, quality, resources, and risk. What this means is that all projects are limited by these things. For example, all projects are limited by time and cost. All projects are also limited by the scope, as you cannot do work that is outside of the scope. Constraints also tend to affect each other as they are changing. For example, by increasing the scope of the project, you may also have to increase the budget and schedule.

Customer
Satisfaction
Project Constraints

Life Cycles

A life cycle is all of the stages or phases a project or product goes through from beginning to the end.

- **Product Life Cycle:** This is the life cycle that a product goes through from start to end. This will include buying the product, installing it, maintaining it, and disposing of it. One product life cycle may include many projects. A project will be needed to install it, add an update to it, and to dispose of it. In short, one **product** life cycle includes many **project** life cycles.

- **Project Life Cycle:** These are the phases that a project goes through from initiating the project to its closing. It is the breakdown of the work needed to complete the deliverable. This is sometimes referred to as the organizational methodology for managing projects.

Success

Projects, by definition, are temporary and create a product, service, or result. Project success is measured by finishing the project within the given limitations of scope, cost, time, quality, resources, and risk. The project manager will be responsible and accountable for ensuring that the project is completed within the approved baselines.

Key Terms and PM Processes Questions

1. You have been assigned as a project manager to implement a new and innovative smartphone application in a balanced matrix organizational structure. You may experience difficulties in obtaining and assigning resources to your project due to which one of the following factors?

    A. The power and authority are shared between you and the functional manager, and you do not have full authority over the project and its funding.

    B. Your role is like a coordinator or expeditor (communication coordinator or staff assistant).

    C. You have no real authority and power.

    D. The project budget is fully controlled by the functional manager.

2. A Project Management Office (PMO), which is a centralized organizational unit to oversee and coordinate the management of projects and programs under its domain throughout the organization, has all of the following functions EXCEPT:

    A. Identify and develop the organization's methodology, administrative practices, guidelines, policies, procedures, and rules.

    B. Establish and maintain templates, policies, procedures, best practices, and standards for project management methodologies.

    C. Monitor compliance with organizational project management processes, policies, procedures, and other items.

    D. Be involved heavily during project initiation as a key decision-maker and integral stakeholder to make recommendations, prioritize projects, terminate projects, or take other actions as required.

3. You are a project manager overseeing a web-based automation project in a weak matrix organization. You are playing the role of a communication coordinator with little power to make decisions and sometimes report to a high-level manager. Your role can be defined as a:

    A. Team lead

    B. Project coordinator

    C. Lead coordinator

    D. Project expeditor

4. Success in portfolio management, which can be generally described as a group of projects or programs and other works to achieve a specific strategic business goal, is generally defined as:

    A. Aggregate performance of all components.

    B. Control of changes to specific products and services.

    C. Compliance with schedule, budget, and specifications requirements.

    D. Realization of the business benefits and financial objectives.

5. You are overseeing the implementation of the internal website of your organization to view the company's event calendar. Your role is to coordinate activities, resources, equipment, and information on the project, but you have limited authority in making project decisions and have to negotiate with the functional manager to get the required resources for your project. Which of the following kind of organizational structures are you working in?

   A. Balanced matrix

   B. Composite structure

   C. Weak matrix

   D. Strong matrix

6. You are overseeing a complex project to implement a new wireless media streaming device. Due to the complex nature of the project, you need several highly skilled technical resources with very specialized expertise and domain knowledge. You obtain these resources from the organization resource pool and different departments, specifying the duration and bandwidth for which they will be required. You also commit to releasing these resources to respective departments once your needs are fulfilled. You are working in which kind of organizational structure?

   A. Composite structure

   B. Functional

   C. Projectized

   D. Matrix

7. A software firm is in the process of implementing a critical accounting application for a dentist's office. In order to implement the project, full-time staff from several departments are selected to create a special project team or task force. It was decided that the task force members would not report to their functional managers or work on their functional activities while working on this critical project. This type of organizational structure is called:

   A. Functional organization

   B. Hybrid structure

   C. Weak Matrix

   D. Balanced matrix organization

8. Which one of the following is NOT true about functional organizational structure?

   A. Project work is considered to be priority work in all functional groups.

   B. Similar resources are grouped by specialists.

   C. The project manager has little or no authority and could even be part-time.

   D. Multiple projects compete for limited resources and priority.

9. Which one of the following is the logical breakdown of what needs to be done to produce the project deliverables and is sometimes referred to as the performing organization's methodology for projects?

   A. Product life cycle

   B. Project life cycle

   C. Feedback loop

   D. Product development

10. The application of knowledge, skills, tools, and techniques to satisfy the project needs by establishing project objectives, identifying project requirements, managing stakeholders, and balancing project constraints (i.e., cost, time, quality, scope, risk, and others) is referred to as:

    A. Project management

    B. Project administration

    C. Project initiation

    D. Project coordination

11. All project phases conclude with a review of the deliverables and related work (phase exits or stage gates or kill points) for the purpose of:

    A. Determining if the project should continue and the next phase should be initiated.

    B. Detecting defects and correcting errors.

    C. Assessing project risks.

    D. Enforcing formal control procedure of the project.

12. The level of power and authority of a project manager may fluctuate due to various factors. Typically, how much power and authority a project manager will have depends on which of the following?

    A. The organizational structure

    B. The negotiation skills of the project manager

    C. Project management knowledge and technical competency of the project manager

    D. The relationship of the project manager with senior management, especially with the sponsor

13. Which one of the following descriptions is generally considered to be characteristic of operational works?

    A. It is a continuing endeavor that produces many identical or nearly identical products or provides repetition.

    B. It is temporary in nature and has a definite beginning and ending.

    C. It is completed when its goals and objectives have been met and signed off by the stakeholders.

    D. It is a unique undertaking.

14. You are overseeing a project to implement a new video game console. Since everything is not known upfront, you take the approach of defining and developing the product by incremental steps and continually reviewing and adjusting processes, assumptions, requirements, and decisions throughout the project life cycle as the project progresses. You are engaged in which of the following?

    A. Project selection

    B. Monitoring & Controlling

    C. Progressive elaboration

    D. Decomposition

15. Which one of the following is TRUE about the power of the project managers in different organizational structures?

    A. In a projectized organization, the project manager has no real authority and power.

    B. A strong matrix maintains many characteristics of projectized organization, where much of the authority rests with the project manager.

    C. In a weak matrix, the authority is shared between the functional manager and the project manager; the project manager does not have full authority over the project and its funding.

    D. A balanced matrix maintains many characteristics of a functional matrix; the project manager role is more like that of a coordinator or expeditor (communication coordinator or staff assistant) than that of a true project manager.

16. You are managing a group of related or unrelated projects or programs and other works to achieve specific strategic business objectives and goals. Which of the following best describes your role?

    A. Program owner

    B. Project manager

    C. Program manager

    D. Portfolio manager

17. As a project manager in a balanced matrix organization, how much authority do you have?

    A. Low to moderate

    B. Little to none

    C. High to almost total

    D. Moderate to high

18. You took over a software development project from another project manager who just left the company. You realize that the project is a mess as there is a lack of management control, and the previous project manager managed the project without much project organization. You decided to develop specific workplans for each of the 30 work packages and soon realize that the plan would help each phase, but would not control the integration of those phases into a cohesive whole. To your surprise, you also find out that there are no clearly defined project deliverables. You desperately need to organize the project as soon as you can. What will be the BEST course of action?

    A. Capture lessons learned as you progress and update organizational process assets.

    B. Report the poor condition of the project to management.

    C. Adapt a life cycle approach to the project.

    D. Develop a detailed description of project deliverables.

19. You just completed a critical data center project for your organization. Currently, the support team is conducting ongoing operations and maintenance to ensure that all routers, switches, firewalls, PCs, servers, and digital storage are operating as planned. A large portion of your project budget is allocated to maintenance and operations to run the data center smoothly. You will be sending out daily status updates and resolving issues, but there is no need for planning or providing documentation. These ongoing operations and maintenance are extremely important to the products of your data center project and should be considered as:

    A. Not a part of your project

    B. An entirely separate project

    C. A separate phase in your project lifecycle

    D. Activities in the closing process group

20. Steve is very concerned about all major constraints on his project as these constraints provide a framework for understanding trade-offs in managing competing project requirements. He identified scope, time, cost, quality, risk, resources, communications, and customer satisfaction to be the major constraints. Which one of the following is the prioritized order of all these constraints?

    A. Scope, time, cost, quality, risk, resources, communications, and customer satisfaction

    B. Time, scope, cost, quality, risk, resources, communications, and customer satisfaction

    C. Cost, scope, time, quality, risk, resources, communications, and customer satisfaction

    D. They all are of equal importance unless stated otherwise

21. The management framework within which project decisions are made is called:

    A. Project Management Information System (PMIS)

    B. Configuration management system

    C. Project management plan

    D. Project governance

Key Terms and PM Processes Answers

1. **A:** In a balanced matrix organization, the project manager is assigned full-time, and the authority of the project manager is usually at an equal level with the functional manager. This can result in conflict regarding resource assignments and priorities and in the general management of the project. The control of the budget is shared between the project manager and the functional manager.

2. **A:** The PMO identifies and develops the project management methodology, best practices, policies, procedures, and standards but not the organizational methodology, administrative practices, guidelines, policies, procedures, and rules.

3. **B:** Both the project coordinator and the project expeditor play a supportive role to the project manager. A project coordinator role is similar to a project expeditor role as they both act primarily as staff assistants and communication coordinators. However, unlike a project expeditor, a project coordinator has some power to make decisions and reports to a high-level manager.

4. **A:** Portfolio management encompasses identifying, prioritizing, authorizing, managing, and controlling the collection of projects, programs, other work, and sometimes other portfolios to achieve strategic business objectives. It is generally associated with the relationships between components in the portfolio, effective resource management to protect priority components and the aggregate results of the portfolio as they relate to strategic performance.

5. **C:** You are working in a weak matrix organization. Your role is that of a project expeditor or project coordinator, where you mostly act as a staff assistant and communication coordinator with limited authority and no control over the project's budget. You have to negotiate with the functional manager to get the needed resources for the project.

6. **D:** In the matrix structure, the personnel and other resources that a project manager requires are not permanently assigned to the project but are obtained from a pool and are controlled and monitored by a functional manager. Personnel required to perform specific functions in a particular project are assigned for the period necessary and are then returned to the control of the functional manager for reassignment.

7. **B:** Hybrid structure is a combination of functional, project-oriented, and matrix organizational structures. For example, a functional organization may create a special project team or task force to handle a critical project and may have many characteristics of projectized organization; it may include full-time staff from different functional departments with their own set of operating procedures, standards, and reporting structure.

8. **A:** In a functional structure, a project is given very little priority. Also, in a functional structure, similar resources are grouped by technical expertise and are assigned to one supervisor. Team members give more importance to their functional responsibility to the detriment of the project.

9. **B:** The project life cycle is the logical breakdown of what needs to be done to produce the project deliverables, and sometimes it is referred to as the performing organization's methodology for projects. On the other hand, a product life cycle consists of generally sequential, non-overlapping product phases determined by the manufacturing and control needs of the organization. For instance, as predicted by Moore's law, each year, a micro processor company introduces new models of processors that are faster and more powerful than their predecessors. Micro processors that are obsolete or do not sell well are quickly retired from production. This product life cycle begins in R&D, extends to manufacturing, and finally ends with phase-out.

10. **A:** Project management is the application of knowledge, skills, tools, and techniques to satisfy project requirements.

11. **A:** At the conclusion of a project phase, the project manager and team should assess the performance of the project and determine if acceptable conditions exist to support a decision to continue or terminate the project. If the decision is to move forward with the project, then the decision is also made about whether the next phase should be initiated or not. Risk levels will vary as the project progresses, and the end of a phase is generally considered to be a good point to reassess risk. Project control procedures should be enforced throughout the project lifecycle.

12. **A:** The authority of the project manager varies greatly depending on the organizational structure. In a projectized organization, the project manager has almost total authority. A strong matrix maintains many characteristics of projectized organization where much of the authority rests with the project manager. In a balanced matrix, the authority is shared between the functional manager and the project manager, and the project manager does not have full authority over the project and its funding. A weak matrix maintains many characteristics of a functional organization; the project manager's role is like that of a coordinator or expeditor (communication coordinator or staff assistant) than that of a true project manager. In a functional organization, the project manager has no real authority and power. Relationship, negotiation skills, and technical ability may affect the level of authority in some organizations, but managerial structure is generally the major factor.

13. **A:** Operational works are ongoing and support the day-to-day functions of an organization. Operational work differs from project work as operational work is any continuing endeavor that produces many identical or nearly identical products or provides repetitive services (e.g., frying burgers, manufacturing cars, and teaching algebra).

14. **C:** Progressive elaboration is defined as moving forward in increments and adding more detail as the project progresses.

15. **B:** The authority of the project manager varies greatly depending on the organizational structure. In a projectized organization, the project manager has almost total authority. A strong matrix maintains many characteristics of projectized organization where much of the authority rests with the project manager. In a balanced matrix, the authority is shared between the functional manager and the project manager; the project manager does not have full authority over the project and its funding. A weak matrix maintains many characteristics of a functional organization; the project manager role is more like that of a coordinator or expeditor (communication coordinator or staff assistant) than that of a true project manager. In a functional organization, the project manager has no real authority and power.

16. **D:** A portfolio can be generally described as a group of projects or programs and other works to achieve a specific strategic business goal. The programs may not be related other than the fact that they are helping to achieve a common strategic goal. A portfolio manager is usually assigned to manage these groups of projects, programs, and other works. Portfolio management encompasses identifying, prioritizing, authorizing, managing, and controlling the collection of projects, programs, other work, and sometimes other portfolios to achieve strategic business objectives. For example, the construction business has several business units such as retail, single and multifamily residential, and others. Collectively, all the programs, projects, and work with in all of these business units makeup the portfolio for this construction business.

17. **A:** A project manager has low to moderate authority in a balanced matrix organization.

18. **C:** Adapting a life cycle approach to effectively run the project will ensure overall control and successful completion of the deliverables. You may want to report the situation to management, but it will not really solve the issue. Capturing lessons learned will certainly assist with the subsequent phases, but would not really help with controlling the project. Developing a detailed description of the project deliverables would not improve control.

19. **A:** Operations and maintenance are not considered to be temporary as they are ongoing. A project is always unique and temporary in nature. Thus, these activities should not be considered as a project or even part of a project.

20. **D:** All major constraints are of equal importance unless stated otherwise. Senior management in an organization gets involved in setting priorities among these constraints directly or indirectly. The primary job of the project manager is to manage these different project constraints by assessing the situations, prioritizing competing demands, and analyzing the impact of changes on all the constraints.

21. **D:** Project governance is the management framework within which project decisions are made. The role of project governance is to provide a decision-making framework that is logical, robust, and repeatable to govern an organization's capital investments.

    This framework provides the structure, processes, decision-making models, and tools to the project manager and team for managing the project. It also provides the team with a comprehensive, coherent method of controlling the project and helps to safeguard project success by defining, documenting, and communicating reliable, repeatable project practices.

    The Project Management Information System (PMIS) consists of the data sources, tools, and techniques used to gather, integrate, analyze, and disseminate the results of the combined outputs of the project management processes. It is an automated system that can serve as a repository for information and a tool to assist with communication and with tracking documents and deliverables. The PMIS also supports the project from beginning to end by optimizing the schedule and helping collect and distribute information.

    The configuration management system is the subset of the PMIS that describes the different versions and characteristics of the product, service, or result of the project and ensures accuracy and completeness of the description.

    The project management plan is a single-approved document that defines how the project is executed, monitored and controlled, and closed.

Chapter 3

Project Management Processes and Role of the Project Manager

PMP Exam Prep Simplified

Knowledge Areas	49 Project Management Processes[1]				
	Process Groups				
	Initiating (2)	Planning (24)	Executing (10)	Monitoring & Controlling (12)	Closing (1)
Integration Management (7)	Develop Project Charter	Develop Project Management Plan	Direct & Manage Project Work Manage Project Knowledge	Monitor and Control Project Work Perform Integrated Change Control	Close Project or Phase
Scope Management (6)		Plan Scope Management Collect Requirements Define Scope Create WBS		Validate Scope Control Scope	
Schedule Management (6)		Plan Schedule Management Define Activities Sequence Activities Estimate Activity Durations Develop Schedule		Control Schedule	
Cost Management (4)		Plan Cost Management Estimate Costs Determine Budget		Control Costs	
Quality Management (3)		Plan Quality Management	Manage Quality	Control Quality	
Resource Management (6)		Plan Resource Management Estimate Activity Resources	Acquire Resources Develop Team Manage Team	Control Resources	
Communication Management (3)		Plan Communications Management	Manage Communications	Monitor Communications	
Risk Management (7)		Plan Risk Management Identify Risks Perform Qualitative Risk Analysis Perform Quantitative Risk Analysis Plan Risk Responses	Implement Risk Responses	Monitor Risks	
Procurement Management (3)		Plan Procurement Management	Conduct Procurements	Control Procurements	
Stakeholder Management (4)	Identify Stakeholders	Plan Stakeholder Engagement	Manage Stakeholder Engagement	Monitor Stakeholder Engagement	

EXAM TIP: *You will need to memorize this page. You should be able to write this entire page in about 5minutes.*

1   Project Management Institute, A Guide to the Project Management Body of Knowledge, (PMBOK® Guide) – Sixth Edition, Project Management Institute Inc., 2017, Page 25.

This chapter will review the framework that projects will follow in each phase. This includes the five process groups and 10 knowledge areas.

This exam will test your knowledge of the 49 processes extensively. This chapter will explain the basics of how they are structured and what their most common ITTO's are.

Project Management Process Groups and Knowledge Areas

There are five main process groups and 10 knowledge areas that we will cover in this book. Within the five process groups and 10 knowledge areas are the 49 processes. The remainder of this book will cover the 10 knowledge areas and the 49 processes in detail, starting in the next chapter, "Integration Management." This section will focus extensively on understanding the process groups and how they flow.

Here are the five process groups:

1. Initiating
2. Planning
3. Executing
4. Monitoring and Controlling
5. Closing

Here are the 10 knowledge areas:

1. Project Integration Management
2. Project Scope Management
3. Project Schedule Management
4. Project Cost Management
5. Project Quality Management
6. Project Resource Management
7. Project Communications Management
8. Project Risk Management
9. Project Procurement Management
10. Project Stakeholder Management

Project Management Process Groups

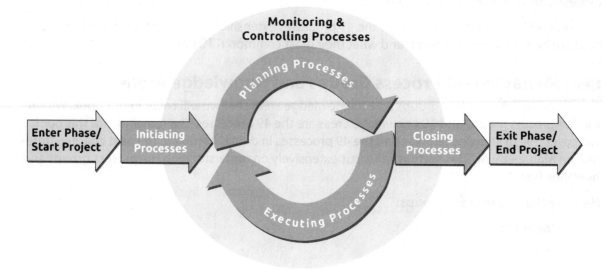

Understanding the flow of the process groups and how they relate to the phases in a project is a very important skill that you'll need to pass the exam. The life cycle of a project can span one phase or many phases, depending on the size and complexity of the project. For example, if you are installing a phone system for your organization, there will be a few phases that you have to go through. In phase 1, you will have to select the phone system; in phase 2, you will install it; in phase 3, you will test it; and in phase 4, you will train the users. As a project manager, you will create the phases for this project. Each phase of a project will contain the five process groups and have some kind of deliverable as its output. The five process groups are what create those outputs for each phase within the project.

For example, in phase 1 of our phone system project, the output will be having a phone system selected. To do phase 1, you have to initiate that phase, plan it, execute, monitor and control, and close it. To do phase 2, you also need to initiate, plan, execute, monitor and control, and close that phase also. The deliverable for phase 2 would be the installed phone system.

Phases can overlap. You can be initiating the next phase while still monitoring and controlling the previous phase. For example, while you are installing the phone system in phase 2, you can be initiating and planning phase 3 of testing.

Smaller projects, such as painting a room, will not have many phases. They will generally have one phase because the project is much smaller.

> **Exam Tip:** *The 49 processes are a part of every phase of the project. The goal of the 49 processes is to create a final product, service, or result.*

Tailoring the Processes

One of the most common questions I get when teaching this course is: Do we really need all 49 processes when working on a project or a phase? The answer is no, because every project is unique, and some projects may not need a certain process or do it according to how the PMBOK® Guide® describes it. This is understandable because the PMBOK® Guide is a very generic book that is written to work with all projects. What companies should do is tailor these processes to match their requirements and how they would like a project to be completed. This can be done with the help of the project manager and the project management office (PMO). Every company will develop its own methodology on how to conduct a project and generally customizes the 49 processes to match its requirements.

On this exam, we will assume that all projects will follow all of the 49 processes within each phase. Keep in mind that this is a PMI exam, and they're going to assume that every project will follow all of the processes. Don't think for a second that a process may not be needed on a project when it comes to answering an exam question. Again, all projects on your exam will assume all of the 49 processes will be in each phase of the project.

Initiating

Initiating a project or phase is about getting authorization to actually start that phase or project. Initiating has only two processes, making it one of the smallest of the five process groups. When you think of the word "initiating," think of authorizing. The main outputs of initiating the project are the project charter and stakeholder register.

Here are some key things you will do in initiating:

- Authorize the project to get started with the development of the project charter.
- Assign and set the authority for the project manager.
- Identify project stakeholders.
- Determine why the project is needed using business cases.
- Identify high-level estimates for time and costs.
- Determine high-level risks that can affect the project schedule or budget.
- Identify high-level constraints and assumptions.

Planning

Planning is done after the project has been initiated. The main output of planning is to create the PM's plan. This rather large document specifies how the project will be executed, monitored and controlled, and closed. Planning has 24 processes across all 10 knowledge areas. The processes are iterative and ongoing until the project management plan is created. It will identify the efforts and objectives needed to create the project deliverables.

Planning is very important in project management because without a comprehensive, well thought out plan, the project can fail. An old saying in project management is, if you fail

to plan, then you plan to fail. Let's take this saying to heart and make sure we do thorough planning.

Here are some key things you do in planning:

- Create the project management plan and all of its subsidiary plans.
- Create the three baselines of scope, time, and costs. This will be added to the project management plan.
- Collect requirements from stakeholders.
- Identify risk and create the correct response to it.
- Determine what components need to be obtained from outside sellers.
- Plan to meet the quality requirements.
- Obtain approval of the plan from designated stakeholders.

Executing

Executing is about getting the project work done. In this process group, you acquire a project team and bring it together to create the deliverable. This process group usually requires the most time and resources to complete. This is where project work is done. The main output

of executing is deliverable. It only has 10 processes, but it actually carries more weight and questions than planning does. You may have noticed that three of the 10 processes in executing fall under human resources. Expect to find quite a number of questions regarding human resources on your exam.

Here are some main things you do in executing:

- Satisfy project specifications.

- Implement all change requests, which include corrective and preventive actions, and defect repairs.

- Select and acquire the project team.

- Develop and manage the project team.

- Manage and resolve conflicts among project stakeholders.

- Conduct quality assurance for overall process improvement.

- Communicate project status with stakeholders.

- Select a vendor and award them a contract.

- Engage the stakeholders on the project, so they are aware of what's happening.

- Implement the responses to any risk identified for the project.

- Capture and document lessons learned.

Monitoring and Controlling

There are 12 processes in monitoring and controlling. They fall into all 10 knowledge areas. Monitoring and controlling ensure that the project stays on plan. It is about measuring, inspecting, monitoring, verifying, reviewing, and comparing the actual work to the planned work. In this process group, the project manager looks at the work that is getting done and compares it against the plan to see if they match. It's very important for the project manager to get these processes done correctly; if not, the project can very quickly go over its budget or fall behind schedule. If the project is off-scope, behind schedule, or over the budget, then the project manager will have to take some corrective actions and may need to initiate a few change requests to fix the project.

Here are some things you would do in monitoring and controlling:

- Check on the project work to ensure that it is with the scope, on time, and on budget.

- Check to make sure the quality requirements are met.

- Control risk to ensure it does not derail the project.

- Ensure vendors (sellers) are completing the work, as stated in the agreements.

- Ensure stakeholders are actually being engaged, as stated in the plan.

- If there are any internal deviations from the stated plan, then the PM should make corrections (use contingency reserve, if necessary).

- Get deliverables formally accepted so the project can then move into the closing phase.

- Manage changes to ensure they are either approved or denied.

Exam Tip: Keep in mind that "executing" and "monitoring and controlling" are parallel i.e., simultaneous, processes. After you have planned your project, you then "execute" and "monitor and control" at the same time. While you are executing a project, you will monitor and control that execution to ensure the project stays on plan.

Closing

Closing happens after the customer or sponsor has accepted the deliverables. Closing only has one process, but it will be covered heavily in the exam. When you have the accepted deliverables, the project manager will still need to do additional work, such as ensuring the contracts are closed out and lessons learned are documented. The project manager will also have to hand over (transition) the completed deliverables to the project customers or sponsors.

Here are some things you will do in closing:

- Contract closures and documentation.

- Archive project records.

- Document reasons why a project may have been terminated before completion.

- Update templates and knowledge bases.

- Transition deliverables to customers or sponsors.

- Create a final report on the project outcome

Common Inputs, Tools and Techniques, and Outputs (ITTO)

Across the 49 processes, there are 665 ITTO's. There are 239 inputs, 245 tools and techniques, and 181 outputs. Now you may be saying, do I need to memorize all of that? The answer is no. You will need to understand them and why an input may be used in a process or how a tool can help a project manager carry out the process.

Many of the processes have the same inputs, tools and techniques, and outputs. These will be covered in this section. The rest of the chapters in this book will cover the 49 processes and their most important ITTO's. As we cover each process, you might want to review this section.

Common Inputs, Tools and Techniques, and Outputs

Input
- Enterprise Environmental Factors
- Organization Process Assets
- Project Documents
- Project Management Plan

Process

Output
- Change Request
- Work Performance Data
- Work Performance Information
- Work Performance Reports
- Updates

Tool and Techniques
- Expert Judgement
- Data Gathering
- Data Analysis
- Decision Making
- Data Representation
- Interpersonal and Team Skills
- Meeting
- Project Management Information System

Common Inputs

Enterprise Environmental Factors (EEF)

This is one of the most commonly used inputs. It is an input to almost all planning processes. EEF are factors that are not under the control of the project team. EEF may have a positive or negative effect on the project outcome. For example, government regulation can have a negative effect on the project because it will take longer to get government approvals to begin selling a product to the public. EEF can be internal to the company, such as the software tools they use on a project, or they can be external, such as the regulations that a company may have to follow.

Enterprise Environmental Factors include, but are not limited to:

- Organizational culture, structure, and governance.

- Government or industry standards, such as regulations or quality standards.

- Infrastructure, such as facilities and equipment.

- Personnel and the way the company manages them.

- Stakeholders' risk tolerances.

- Company work authorization systems. This is a system that ensures work gets done at the right time and in the right sequence. The PM will need a system in place to authorize work to start.

- Information technology software that a company would use to manage the project. This can include the software tool that will help the PM to manage the budget, schedule, and requirements.

Organization Process Assets (OPA)

This is another one of the most commonly used inputs for most planning processes. OPA are the plans, processes, policies, procedures, and knowledge bases that are used by the organization; they are typically divided into processes, procedures, and knowledge.

OPA are things that can help a PM to manage the project more easily. For example, if you have to create a project plan, then getting a template or a previous plan from a past project can help you. Estimates from previous projects can also help.

OPA includes, but is not limited to:

- Previous project plans

- Templates

- Historical information

- Lessons learned

- Knowledge bases

- Software tools

- Organization procedures and policies

- Project management databases

- Project files from previous projects

Project Documents

Project documents are any documents that are related to the project. This is a very common input for many of the 49 processes. Project documents are additional documents that are created and used throughout the 49 processes that are not part of the project management plan. There are 33 different project documents as listed below. Check chapter 14 for a brief description of each of these documents.

When conducting a process, you may use one or multiple of these documents as inputs for the process. For example, for the process "define scope," which will create the project scope statement, one of the inputs is project documents because the project manager could use the "requirements documentation" when writing the scope statement.

While the PMBOK® Guide does list specific documents that could be used on a particular process, it does start the list with the statement: "including but not limited to." What this statement means is that any of the 33 documents could be useful on a particular process; it's just really up to the project manager to decide if that particular document will be useful in that particular process.

We will be reviewing each of these documents throughout this guide. You should be familiar with and understand the purpose of each document before taking your exam. Expect to see questions where you're asked what document is best used in a specific scenario.

Project Document	Knowledge Area Where Created
1. Activity attributes	Schedule Management
2. Activity list	Schedule Management
3. Assumption log	Integration Management
4. Basis of estimates	Cost Management
5. Change log	Integration Management
6. Cost estimates	Cost Management
7. Cost forecast	Cost Management
8. Duration estimates	Schedule Management
9. Issue log	Integration Management
10. Lessons learned register	Integration Management
11. Milestone list	Schedule Management
12. Physical resources assignments	Resource Management
13. Project calendars	Schedule Management
14. Project communications	Communications Management
15. Project schedule	Schedule Management
16. Project schedule network diagram	Schedule Management
17. Project scope statement	Scope Management
18. Project team assignments	Resource Management
19. Quality control measurements	Quality Management
20. Quality metrics	Quality Management
21. Quality report	Quality Management
22. Requirements documentation	Scope Management
23. Requirements traceability matrix	Scope Management

24. Resource breakdown structure	Resource Management
25. Resource calendars	Resource Management
26. Resource requirements	Resource Management
27. Risk register	Risk Management
28. Risk report	Risk Management
29. Schedule data	Schedule Management
30. Schedule forecast	Schedule Management
31. Stakeholder register	Stakeholder Management
32. Team charter	Resource Management
33. Test and evaluation documents	Quality Management

Project Management Plan

The project management plan is the single most important document in the entire project. The plan will define how the project is executed, monitored and controlled, and closed.

The project management plan is made up of 18 components, which will be used to guide the project manager on the different processes that will be executed in the project.

Expect to see the project management plan listed as an input for many of the 49 processes. Since the plan is made up of 18 components, any of those components could be used as a particular document needed in that process. The PMBOK® Guide once again uses the statement "including but not limited to." This means that when doing a particular process, you could use a particular document in the plan, or you could use whatever document the project manager feels is right for the process. For example, when doing the process "control costs," which is a process the project manager executes to ensure the work that is getting done is on budget, the input will be the project management plan. That's because the project management plan will contain the budget itself (cost baseline) and the cost management plan that details the steps the project manager will take to ensure the project stays on budget. As you can see, this particular process needs multiple components from the project management plan in order to be completed.

Here is a list of the documents that will be in the project management plan. Throughout the rest of this study guide, we will cover the details of how the plan is created and what these different documents do.

Project Plan	Process Where Made
1. Scope Management Plan	Plan Scope Management
2. Requirement Management Plan	Plan Scope Management
3. Schedule Management Plan	Plan Schedule Management
4. Cost Management Plan	Plan Cost Management
5. Quality Management Plan	Plan Quality Management
6. Resource Management Plan	Plan Resource Management
7. Communication Management Plan	Plan Communications Management
8. Risk Management Plan	Plan Risk Management
9. Procurement Management Plan	Plan Procurement Management
10. Stakeholder Management Plan	Plan Stakeholder Management
11. Change Management Plan	Develop Project Management Plan

12. Configuration Management Plan	Develop Project Management Plan
13. Scope Baseline	Create WBS
14. Schedule Baseline	Develop Schedule
15. Cost Baseline	Determine Budget
16. Performance Measurement Baseline	Develop Project Management Plan
17. Project Life Cycle Description	Develop Project Management Plan
18. Development Approach	Develop Project Management Plan

Common Tools

Expert Judgment

Expert judgment is one of the most common tools in the planning process. Expert judgment includes hiring an expert or subject matter expert (SME) to help you to plan a process or conduct a process. Experts can be people with specialized knowledge or training in a particular process, industry, or technology. For example, if you have to develop a project charter, but you're not sure how to do it, then hire an expert who can help you with the creation of the project charter.

Data Gathering

Data gathering is a tool that is used to do exactly what the name says; gather data about a particular process that you're working on. On certain processes, you will need to gather additional data before coming up with an output for that process. For example, when developing a project charter, you might sit down with stakeholders and brainstorm what should and should not be included in the project. Brainstorming is part of data gathering. It's just a technique that's used to gather information in a particular process.

Here are some of the techniques that you might be utilizing when using this tool. These techniques will be used on most of the processes that involve this tool, but there are other techniques that can be used, which will be discussed in those particular processes.

- **Brainstorming:** Brainstorming is when you bring together a group of stakeholders to get ideas and analyze them. Brainstorming sessions are generally facilitated by the project manager.

- **Interviews:** Any time you want to gather data from a particular group of stakeholders, one of the best methods is to just interview them. Ask them a series of questions and talk with them about their thoughts and views.

- **Focus groups:** A focus group is when you bring together subject matter experts to understand their perspectives and how they would go about solving problems.

- **Checklist:** A checklist is generally created by the organization and then given to potential stakeholders on a project for them to identify items they may or may not want on a project, and any success criteria they may have for the project.

- **Questionnaires and surveys:** Questionnaires and surveys can be given to stakeholders to better understand what they may be looking for on a project and to better understand their needs.

Data Analysis

Data analysis is used to analyze the data that has been gathered. During a process, a project manager and team collect different types of data and will then need to analyze that data in order to make decisions on the project. For example, in the process of "control schedule," you will gather data about the schedule, and then you will need to analyze the data to determine if the project is ahead or behind schedule.

Here are some of the techniques that you might be doing when using this tool. These techniques will be used on most of the processes that involve this tool, but there are other techniques that can be used, which will be discussed along with those particular processes later in this book.

- **Alternative analysis:** Alternative analysis involves looking at different options or ways to accomplish something. For example, by looking at a change request and then determine a few different ways we can implement the change. An alternative analysis is the most popular option in the PMBOK® Guide when it comes to doing data analysis.

- **Root cause analysis (RCA):** A root cause analysis is used to identify the main underlying reason for a particular event. For example, if there were defects in a deliverable, a project manager would use this technique to identify the main cause.

- **Variance Analysis:** Variance analysis is used quite often to find the exact differences between different things. For example, a project manager will use variance analysis to identify if a project is on budget by looking at the variance between the planned budget and the actual cost.

- **Trend analysis:** Trend analysis involves looking at data over a period of time to see if a particular trend is forming. For example, throughout the execution of the project, a project manager will be looking to see if the project is consistently on budget or over budget.

Data Representation

Data representation is used throughout the PMBOK® Guide to illustrate different ways that data could be shown to stakeholders. Methods generally include the use of charts, matrixes, and different types of diagrams. Certain processes will have unique methods to represent their data; we will discuss these in detail when we get to those processes.

Decision Making

In many processes, you will gather a lot of data and then have to make a decision on what to do with that data. Decision making is a tool that's used to come to a decision that can best serve the project.

Here are some of the techniques that you might be executing when using this tool. These techniques will be used for most of the processes that have this tool, but there are other techniques that can be used, which will be discussed with those particular processes.

- **Voting:** Voting is used by a group to determine whether to proceed, change, or reject something. Voting can be: majority wins, unanimity, where everyone agrees, or plurality, where a majority is not obtained, but the most popular decision is chosen.

- **Multicriteria decision analysis:** This is when you make a table (matrix) that lists different types of criteria and then evaluate an idea based on those criteria. For example, a project manager would use different criteria when selecting a team member, such as their availability, experience, education, and costs. For this example, you can make a table listing these criteria and potential team members.

- **Autocratic decision making:** This is when one person makes a decision for the entire team.

Interpersonal and Team Skills

All project managers need to have good interpersonal and team skills in order to manage the different stakeholders that will be on the project. In my opinion, this is the most important tool in real-life project management. Any project manager who does not have great people and team management skills is sure to have many problems on a project.

Here are some of the techniques that you might be executing when using this tool. These techniques will be used on most of the processes that have this tool, but there are other techniques that can be used, which will be discussed with those particular processes.

- **Active listening:** Active listening is understanding, acknowledging, and clarifying what others are saying to you.

- **Conflict management:** Anytime you bring a team together, you are bound to have conflicts on that team. A project manager will need to resolve these conflicts in order to move forward. We will be discussing different methods used to manage conflict in the "project resource management" chapter.

- **Facilitation:** Facilitation is the art of managing a group. This can include bringing the group together, generating ideas, solving problems, and dissipating the team. This is generally the job of the project manager when it comes to the facilitation of a project team. This will be a key skill in real-life project management, as you will have to facilitate groups of different stakeholders.

- **Meeting management:** Most projects will have many meetings involving different types of stakeholders. A project manager needs to be able to manage these meetings to ensure they're productive and meaningful to the project. Meeting management generally includes having an agenda, inviting the right stakeholders, setting a time limit, and following up with meeting minutes and action items.

Project Management Information System (PMIS)

The PMIS is an automated system that is used to help the project manager optimize the schedule or keep track of all the documents and the deliverables. It is usually the computer system that a given organization uses to manage its projects. It should include all the software and hardware tools that we need to manage the project from start to finish.

The PMIS includes the work authorization system and the configuration management system. The work authorization system is used to ensure work gets done in the right order and at the right time. The purpose of the configuration management system is to ensure the product gets the right settings and configuration. The configuration management system includes the change management system. This is used to ensure that changes to a project are documented, tracked, and authorized or denied.

Meetings

Meetings are used very often in the 49 processes. Meetings can be done face-to-face or virtually. Meetings frequently include all different types of stakeholders throughout the project. Here are some points to make meetings effective:

- Have an agenda and distribute it to all attendees before the meeting.
- Meetings must be timed, including having set start and finish times for topics and the entire meeting.
- Make sure that the meeting always stays on topic and does not go off topic.
- Ensure that all attendees have input on the topics.
- Distribute detailed meeting minutes once the meeting is complete.

Common Outputs

Change Request

A change request is one of the most common outputs in executing, monitoring and controlling, and closing. A change request is when a stakeholder, which may include a customer, sponsor, or project manager, needs to change a component of the project management plan. Changes can include a request to add or remove work from the scope, finish the project faster, or complete the project more cheaply. A change request implements corrective actions, preventive actions, and defect repairs. Corrective action is something that's taken to ensure that the project gets back on track. Preventive action is something you put in place to ensure the project stays on track. A defect repair is done to fix a broken component on a project, such as if an installed hardware component fails on a network upgrade project.

Work Performance Data

Work performance data is simply raw data. It is the status of the work that was done but did not have any analysis applied to it. It is not useful by itself. Work performance data are usually outputs of executing processes. For example, a painter might give work performance data such as, having painted the room with flat white paint, having completed the task in two days and having charged $500 for the task. Although this is good information, it really doesn't tell us the status of the project. Just the raw information of the work that was done so far.

Work Performance Information

Work performance information is the information about the work that was performed compared to the plan. It gives you the actual status of the deliverables. Unlike work performance data, work performance information is useful because it is the raw data that has been analyzed against the project management plan. Continuing with the room painting example, the work performance information should be that the room was painted in the correct color and on scope, the two days it took to complete is on schedule, and the cost of $500 is over the original budget of $400. Notice how work performance information is the comparison of the work performance data and the project management plan. Work performance information is usually the output of most monitoring and controlling processes.

Work Performance Report

Work performance report is the overall status report of the actual project. It takes all the work performance information and puts it together into one comprehensive document. The work performance report is usually all the compiled work performance information. For our painting example, it will read as follows: the project is on scope and schedule, but over budget. This report usually comes from the total of all monitoring and controlling processes.

> **Exam Tip:** You take the work performance data and compare it against the plan to come up with the work performance information. Then, you take all the work performance information and create the work performance reports. In short, data feeds info, and all the info creates reports.

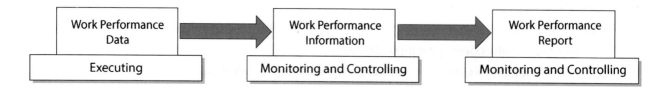

Updates (Project Management Plan, Project documents, EEF, OPA)

Updates is a catch-all term. When you complete many of the planning, executing, monitoring and controlling, and closing processes, you will need to update various documents and processes. Updates can include project documents, the project management plan, OPA, and EEF updates. Expect to see this output many times throughout the book. Most of the time, you will see this as an output of a process involving project management plan updates or project document updates.

Project management plan updates refer to some component or all components of the project management plan that had gotten updated when that process was done. For example, when working on a schedule, the process of "control schedule" should update the project management plan to reflect what work has been completed so far.

The other common output is project document updates, which would include an update to any of the 33 project documents. For example, if a project manager has just discovered a new risk in the process of "identify risk," he will then need to update the project document, in particular, the "risk register."

Role of the Project Manager

One of the newest chapters that was added to this PMBOK® Guide was chapter 3, "The Role of the Project Manager." This particular chapter deals with the skills and responsibilities a project manager must have on a project. We will cover this subject in this section. Although I know you will get questions on this topic, we will keep it short and cover just what you need to know for your exam.

The project manager's role is one of the most important roles on a project. The project manager is in charge of managing the project team to complete the project work and deliver the final product, service, or result for the business. The project manager is usually assigned by the sponsor, PMO, program manager, or portfolio manager to lead the project team to complete the project objectives.

Most stakeholders that are external to the project, such as the customers, tend to only see and interact with the project manager. That means that some of the main skills the project manager will need are good communication and soft skills.

Project managers usually get involved during the initiating section of the project or phase. They can help do the business case as to why a project should be conducted, and then they will also manage the resources to complete the project or phase. A project manager's role may be different depending on the organization. Some organizations may have a project manager that is in complete control of the project, while others may have a manager that is more dependent on a PMO to complete the project.

Completing the project is no easy task. A project manager has to complete the work given the many constraints of a project, such as time, costs, scope, and quality. The project manager will also have to manage conflicts while the project work is getting done. Conflicts may include team members having disputes over how to get work done or sponsors and customers disputing the requirements on a project.

The project manager's main skill will be communicating with the different stakeholders on the project. Almost all management positions require good communication skills, and this is no different. Good communication skills generally include:

- Having concise and clear writing and speaking skills
- Understanding stakeholders needs on a project
- Simplifying communications among stakeholders

- Giving and getting feedback from stakeholders

Keep in mind that a project manager will not only interact with the sponsor or customers of a project; they will also interact with other project managers in the organization. While working on a project, the project manager may want a resource that is already assigned to another project. The project manager will then have to negotiate and communicate with the other project manager to get that resource on their project.

One of the main things the project manager should do is to stay current with the latest information regarding their industry and how they can educate themselves to improve their skills. A project manager should attend continuous education classes in management, communications, and technical skills required in their profession, such as in engineering.

A project manager should also be an advocate for training other people within his/her organization on why following a well-defined framework for project management would lead to projects being completed faster, less expensive, and with higher quality.

PMI Talent Triangle

[2]One topic that you should be aware of is the PMI talent triangle. This talent triangle was created based on a study, and it outlines three specific skills a project manager needs to have. The PMI talent triangle outlines the skills of technical project management, strategic and business management, and leadership.

Technical Project Management Skills

Technical project management skills usually refer to skills that are related to the domains of the work on a project. These domains generally refer to different aspects of the project. For example, a project manager should know how to create a schedule and how to manage that schedule throughout the project. Another one would be creating a budget and knowing how to use earned value management to ensure the project stays on budget. A project manager should have strong skills when it comes to managing the many different processes the project will go through from start to finish. A project manager should also be able to customize the processes involved in each project to ensure success.

Strategic and Business Management Skills

Strategic and business management skills refer to skills related to the business and how to make decisions on a project that will benefit the business. It's important to understand that projects are done to ensure the business stays competitive and profitable. A project manager should be able to understand the business they are in and what it takes to succeed in that business. One important skill is knowing what products are sold by that business and who the business competitors may be. A project manager should also understand the mission of the business and the strategy needed to accomplish that mission. All project managers should strive to learn more about their strategic business objectives and how to accomplish them. This will lead the project manager to make decisions on the project that will benefit the organization's strategic goals.

Leadership

One of the main skills in the PMI talent triangle is leadership. Good leadership skills are vitally important to the success of any project. Leadership involves dealing with people. Project work is not done by hardware or software; it's done by people. If a project manager fails to lead the project team, then the failure of the project is imminent.

Good leadership skills generally involve negotiating, communicating, solving problems, and having good interpersonal skills. The more people on the project, the more complex leadership becomes. A bigger project team may lead to more conflict as the project is being executed. The project manager would then have to step in and solve these disputes.

Leadership skills should include:

- Managing relationships among stakeholders, such as building trust and finding consensus.

- Communications amongst all stakeholders, including giving feedback to customers about the status of the project and getting feedback from team members.

- Being respectful of all stakeholders.

- Learning continuously.

- Prioritizing the work that needs to be done.

- Being able to do critical thinking to ensure that problems are solved correctly.

I've come to learn that when it comes to leadership on a project, the more relationships you have with different stakeholders, the more likely you are to accomplish the task that was assigned to you. People like working with people they already know and have a good relationship with. I think it's important that all project managers work to improve their relationships with all members of the organization as you never know when you may need

to work with someone to accomplish a task. Politics within an organization, such as disputes between different managers, can really negatively affect a project. A project manager has to be able to work outside of those politics and to keep the politics away from the project team as they're doing the work.

Keep in mind; there is a difference between leadership and management. Management is more about directing people to get work done and maintaining what is there already.

Leadership is more about guiding and influencing people to accomplish a certain task while simultaneously developing new processes and procedures. Management is more about controlling people, while leaders tend to inspire people. Management focuses on solving problems, while leaders tend to motivate and create visions for their teams. A project manager might use management skills to control the project team to ensure work gets done according to the plan. They may use leadership skills to inspire that team to create new ways of developing a particular software. Both leadership and management skills will be needed on a project to ensure success.

The PMBOK® Guide includes a few different leadership styles as follows:

- Laissez-Faire: The project manager is hands-off, allowing the team to make their own decisions.

- Transactional: The project manager is more focused on the goals of the project and how to reward team members

- Servant Leader: The project manager focuses on removing obstacles from the team and giving the team what is needed in order to complete the work. This is mostly used in agile projects.

- Transformational: The project manager tries to empower the project team and motivates and inspires them.

- Charismatic: The project manager has high energy, is very enthusiastic, and influences the people around them.

- Interactional: This is a combination of different leadership styles, such as charismatic and transactional.

Integration

One of the main roles of the project manager is to perform integration, which we will cover more in the next chapter: "Integration Management." Keep in mind; the project has so many different subparts to it that integrating them can be complex. For example, the integration of the three main baselines, scope, cost, and schedule, are important for the overall success of a project. Having to manage the complexities of people, technology, and processes makes integration a very difficult task for project managers. For example, you may find your project team difficult to work with because they disagree with processes that have to be followed or dislike technology they have to use to do the work. Complexities within integration can be minimized with better training for the project manager, as well as his or her team.

Project Management Processes Questions

1. Which statement is FALSE regarding the initiating process group?

   A. Cost and staffing start low, increase toward the end, and drop rapidly near closing.

   B. Project risk is highest at the beginning of the project and reduces as the project approaches its end.

   C. Stakeholder influence is highest at the start and diminishes as the project proceeds.

   D. The project manager and team are always identified as part of the initiating process group.

2. All of the following will occur during project initiating EXCEPT:

   A. Creation of a project scope statement.

   B. Identification of internal and external stakeholders.

   C. Development and review of the business case and a feasibility study.

   D. Assignment of the project manager to lead a project.

3. Which of the following will occur only during the planning process group?

   A. Identify stakeholders

   B. Develop schedule

   C. Acquire project team

   D. Validate scope

4. Which of the following process groups includes the processes to complete the work defined in the project management plan and ultimately satisfies the project specifications and objectives?

   A. Planning process group

   B. Executing process group

   C. Initiating process group

   D. Closing process group

5. A knowledge area represents a complete set of activities, concepts, and terms that make up an area of specialization, project management field, or professional field. Each project management knowledge area is subdivided into which of the following?

   A. Best practices

   B. Policies

   C. Processes

   D. Guidelines

6. All of the following should be done during the closing process group EXCEPT:

   A. Formal sign-off and formal acceptance are received from the customers.

   B. Customer acceptance criteria are determined.

   C. Final versions of the lessons learned are compiled and made available for future projects.

   D. Completed project deliverables are handed off to operations and maintenance.

7. In which process group does the team track, measure, inspect, monitor, verify, review, compare, and regulate the progress and performance of the project; ensure that the plan is working; identify any areas in which changes to the plan are required; and initiate the corresponding changes?

   A. Monitoring & Controlling

   B. Closing

   C. Initiating

   D. Executing

8. You are overseeing a project for your organization to implement a web-based application for accessing pay and tax information online. Currently, you are in the process of implementing approved changes, corrective actions, preventive actions, and defect repairs in the project. You are in which of the following process groups?

   A. Executing

   B. Monitoring & Controlling

   C. Planning

   D. Closing

9. Which one of the following statements is FALSE about the executing process group?

   A. This process group usually takes the most time and resources.

   B. The processes in this process group measure and analyze the progress and performance of the project, ensure that the plan is working, identify any areas in which changes to the plan are required, and initiate the corresponding changes.

   C. Corrective actions, preventive actions, and defect repairs are implemented in this process group.

   D. This process group consists of processes to complete the work defined in the project management plan and ultimately satisfy the project specifications and objectives.

10. The sponsor has just signed the project charter and assigned you as a project manager to oversee a project to implement a simulator for a local golf club. What should you do FIRST as the project manager?

    A. Focus on identifying and classifying the stakeholders in the project.

    B. Start working on the project management plan.

    C. Develop the project schedule.

    D. Create WBS.

11. You have been assigned to manage a project to design a new type of vinyl-based resilient floor material. You came up with a few orders of magnitude estimates, high- level risks, constraints, and assumptions for the project. What project management process group are you in?

    A. Monitoring & Controlling

    B. Closing

    C. Initiating

    D. Planning

12. Which one of the following process groups consists of iterative and ongoing processes to establish the total scope of effort, to define the objectives, and to identify the course of action required to attain those objectives?

    A. Planning

    B. Executing

    C. Initiating

    D. Monitoring & Controlling

13. You are overseeing a construction project to construct a new fitness center at a local university. Currently, the team is working on collecting requirements and establishing estimates for the project. Which process group are you in?

    A. Initiating

    B. Executing

    C. Monitoring & Controlling

    D. Planning

14. Which one of the following is not an outcome when a project is initiated properly in the initiating process group?

    A. Authorizing the project manager to manage the project

    B. Defining the scope of the project

    C. Identifying the key stakeholders

    D. Understanding the goal, objective, and business need of the project

15. Which of the following is NOT a planning process?

    A. Create WBS

    B. Perform Qualitative Risk Analysis

    C. Estimate Costs

    D. Develop Project Team

16. Steve has been overseeing a project to implement a new wireless media streaming device for a local networking company. The team has completed all the technical work in the project. The senior management asked Steve to report on the remaining activities in the project. Which of the following will Steve report as the remaining work?

    A. Completion of the lessons learned

    B. Validation of the project scope

    C. Completion of the quality management plan

    D. Completion of risk response planning

17. You just finished creating your project charter. Which of the following will NOT be included in the charter?

    A. Detailed work package descriptions

    B. High-level roadmap and milestones

    C. Assumptions and constraints

    D. Authority level of the project manager

18. While working in the initiating process group, you are mainly focusing on creating a project charter and a stakeholder register. You will use all of the following as inputs EXCEPT:

    A. Organizational values and work ethics

    B. Project scope statement

    C. Configuration management knowledgebase

    D. Historical information and past lessons learned

19. Which one of the following is NOT a component of a change request?

    A. Corrective actions

    B. Preventive actions

    C. Defect repair

    D. Issue Log

20. While working on the operating system upgrade project, the project manager realizes that he cannot estimate the time needed to upgrade a particular server due to the complexity of its build. He enrolls the help of Mary, who has been working on servers for over 20 years. What tool or techniques is the project manager using?

    A. Subject Matter Expert

    B. System Administrator

    C. Expert Judgment

    D. Data analysis

Project Management Processes Answers

1. **D:** The project manager is assigned during project initiating, but some of the team members will be acquired during the executing process group.

2. **A:** The project scope statement is an output of the Define Scope process and is part of the planning process group.

3. **B:** Only Develop Schedule will occur during the planning process group. Identify Stakeholders occurs during initiating, Acquire Project Team occurs during executing, and Validate Scope occurs during monitoring & controlling.

4. **B:** The executing process group is intended to ensure that the work defined in the project plan is performed.

5. **C:** Each project management knowledge area is subdivided into specific processes, each of which is characterized by its inputs, tools & techniques, and outputs.

6. **B:** Customer acceptance criteria are determined during the initiating process group.

7. **A:** During the monitoring & controlling process group, project performance is measured and analyzed, and needed changes are identified and approved.

8. **A:** Usually, a project will enter the executing process group when the planning is completed, or the project management plan has been updated due to change requests, including defect repairs and corrective and preventive actions. The executing process group involves coordinating people and resources as well as integrating and performing the activities of the project in accordance with the project management plan. These approved change requests for corrective actions, preventive actions, and defect repairs are implemented in the executing process group.

9. **B:** The processes in the monitoring & controlling process group track, measure, inspect, monitor, verify, review, compare, and regulate the progress and performance of the project; ensure that the plan is working; identify any areas in which changes to the plan are required, and initiate the corresponding changes.

10. **A:** The project charter is created, and the project manager is assigned during the initiating process group. Stakeholder identification is also started during initiating and carried on throughout the project life cycle. It is essential to classify stakeholders according to their level of interest, influence, importance, and expectation at the early stage of the project as much as possible. Prior to planning, creating the WBS, and developing the project schedule, the project manager should focus on identifying and classifying the internal and external stakeholders in the project.

11. **C:** High-level risks, constraints, and assumptions are identified in the project charter, which is created during project initiating. Usually, orders of magnitude estimates are done during the initiating process group when not much information is available about the project.

12. **A:** The planning process group consists of iterative and ongoing processes to establish the total scope of effort and to define the objectives and to identify the course of action required to attain those objectives.

13. **D:** Requirements are collected from the customers and other stakeholders, and estimates on time, cost, resources, and other things are made during the planning process group.

14. **B:** Detailed project scope will be defined during the planning process group. The success of subsequent processes and activities greatly depends on the way a project is initiated. If a project is initiated properly, it would have a clear business need and feasibility, a clear goal, objective reasons for selecting this project over other possibilities, a clear direction for the scope, a project manager assigned, and a list of stakeholders for the project. On the other hand, if a project is not initiated properly, it could result in a limited or total lack of authority for the project manager as well as ambiguous goals or uncertainties as to why the project was initiated.

15. **D:** Develop project team is a process in the executing process group. All three remaining processes belong to the planning process group.

16. **A:** The lessons learned are usually done once the work is completed in the project. The quality management plan and the risk response plan are created during the planning process group. The validate scope process is done, not during closing, but in the monitoring & controlling process group.

17. **A:** High-level road map and milestones, assumptions and constraints, and authority level of the project manager should be included in the project charter. A project charter is created during initiating process group, but a project scope statement is created during the planning process group. The scope baseline will have the scope statement, WBS, and details on WBS work packages.

18. **B:** Organizational process assets such as configuration management, knowledgebase, historical information, and past lessons learned, as well as enterprise environmental factors such as organizational values and work ethics, are inputs in the initiating process group. Project scope statement is an output of the planning process group.

19. **D:** A change request consists of corrective actions, preventive actions, and defect repairs. Corrective actions are taken to bring the expected future performance of the project work in line with the project management plan. Preventive actions are taken to reduce the probability of risk items in the project. Defect repairs are taken to repair defects or entirely replace components that are faulty or dysfunctional. An issue is an obstacle that threatens project progress and can block the team from achieving its goals. An issue log is a written log to record issues that require solutions. It helps monitor who is responsible for resolving specific issues by a target date.

20. **C:** Expert judgment is a common tool used by most processes. It's where the project manager uses a subject matter expert to help with the process. Subject matter expert is not the name of a tool in the PMBOK® Guide.

Chapter 4
Agile and Hybrid Project Management

In this chapter, we will be reviewing all of the Agile processes and terms you're most likely to see on your exam. While you do not need to be an Agile expert in order to pass your PMP exam, you will need to be familiar with the entire Agile process and a few of the different terms. While most of the Agile terms and processes will be covered here, I will be reviewing additional Agile tools in other chapters in the guide as well.

Keep in mind, this chapter will only serve as an introduction to the world of Agile project management and will be more than sufficient to answer all of your PMP exam questions. If you are interested to learn more about Agile, please explore other certifications from PMI such as the PMI-ACP, Scrum Master, and many other certifications. There have been many books written about many different methods and forms of Agile. If you're looking to pass your exam, this chapter will be more than you need, but it will not make you an Agile expert.

In this chapter, the word traditional (predictive) project management will be used to represent a project that goes through the processes of initiating, planning, executing, monitoring and controlling, and closing. Predictive projects have a strenuous change management approach, and the project manager will generally be in charge of the entire project. The word Agile would be used to represent iterative(flexible) project management. This would include all of the different Agile methods that we are about to discuss.

One of the most important concepts to understand about the Agile framework is that it will build the product in increments versus being built as a whole. In a traditional project, the product is generally built in its entirety in one long execution phase. In an Agile project, the product is built in small increments allowing customers to give their feedback on each increment. Agile allows for more interaction with the customers and more empowerment to the team.

It is because of the frequent product delivery, customer interaction, and value being realized throughout the project that has made Agile one of the most popular project management methods, and that's why it's been included on your current PMP exam.

What is Agile?

Agile is an umbrella term that is used to refer to different types of iterative development. Agile methods include Scrum, Extreme Programming (XP), Kanban, lean development, and a few others. The PMP exam will not go into any of these particular methodologies in detail, but you will need to understand the Agile process and some of the terminologies from these methodologies.

Agile techniques have been used for at least several decades in various forms, and in 2000, a bunch of software developers met up and created what is known to be the manifesto for Agile software development. The Agile manifesto outlines 4 values and 12 principles. You will not need to memorize these values or principles; it's enough to have a brief understanding of them to really understand what Agile is about.

The four values are as follows:

1. **Individuals and interactions** over processes and tools
2. **Working software** over comprehensive documentation
3. **Customer collaboration** over contract negotiation
4. **Responding to change** over following a plan

While they are valuable practices on the right, in Agile, we value things on the left more.

The first value states that while it's important to have tools and processes on a project, it is more important to have competent people working effectively in order to get the work done. Remember, projects are done by people, not by tools and processes. The second value outlines that while comprehensive documentation is needed, customers are more interested in working software, not documentation. The third value states that while contracts are important, it will be more important to work with the customer to understand what they actually need on the project. The fourth value outlines that we need to be willing to accept changes and be willing to change our plan as the needs of the customer change. The willingness to accept changes at any point throughout a project is one of the main differentiating factors between traditional projects and Agile projects.

The 12 Agile principles are as follows:

1. Customer satisfaction by early and continuous delivery of valuable software.

2. Welcome changing requirements, even in late development.

3. Deliver working software frequently (weeks rather than months)

4. Close, daily cooperation between business people and developers

5. Projects are built around motivated individuals who should be trusted

6. Face-to-face conversation is the best form of communication (co-location)

7. Working software is the primary measure of progress

8. Sustainable development, able to maintain a constant pace

9. Continuous attention to technical excellence and good design

10. Simplicity—the art of maximizing the amount of work not done—is essential

11. Best architectures, requirements, and designs emerge from self-organizing teams

12. Regularly, the team reflects on how to become more effective, and adjusts accordingly

Here is a brief explanation of these 12 principles:

Agile is about continuously delivering increments of a product over a span of time. While a traditional project may take many months to a few years to deliver a working product, Agile would be able to deliver increments of that product in a very short period of time. The short period of time can be anywhere from a few weeks to a few months. This fast delivery method allows customers to realize the value of the product faster and allows the customer to fund the development of the product incrementally. In a traditional project, value will not be realized until the entire project is done and the product is delivered to the customer.

One unique aspect of an Agile project is the ability to accept and welcome change throughout the entire development process. Agile does not have a strenuous change management process that requires a formal change request and usage of a change management board. Customers are able to submit changes throughout the entire Agile project, and those changes will be accepted and inputted into the product backlog, which may get completed. This allows customers to feel more welcomed throughout the entire project. Agile projects will not suppress change management like on some traditional projects.

Since Agile is all about people collaboration, it is important for Agile participants to consistently be in contact with each other. This can be done using daily standup meetings with team members and also meeting with the customers during iteration reviews in order to review the product. This allows everyone to contribute and have a voice as the project is progressing. Agile promotes face-to-face interaction as the best means of communication. This means bringing together your teams into one central location (co-location) for them to work together. Humans are social creatures, and we work best under these conditions.

Agile projects are built around trust and motivation by the Agile project manager and the team members. This allows for transparent communication and a safe environment for constructive disagreement.

While it is important to give customer updates about the progress of a project, it is vital to understand that a customer will track the deliverables of your project as the primary means of measurement. Telling a customer that a project is 20% done does not mean much if they cannot actually use that 20%. Customers will track your progress based upon what you release to them and what they can actually use in order to realize value.

Agile tries to ensure that the project team is able to maintain a pace that is sustainable and predictable. This allows the team to accurately complete work in a predictable manner and at a pace that does not burn them out. Agile project teams are expected to not just maintain a sustainable pace but also to follow good technical excellence and design. At no point is it acceptable on any Agile or traditional project not to follow good coding practices or industry best practices.

One of the most complex things to do is to make things simple, and Agile tries to maximize simplicity by making things as simple as possible and focusing on the simplest things first. A simple process leads to more acceptance from your stakeholders and more people willing to comply with it.

Agile project teams are self-organizing and self-directed. Agile project teams are not dictated and managed by a project manager. An Agile project team determines what's best for the project, while the Agile project manager will serve as just a facilitator for the project team. This allows the teams to make decisions and resolve conflicts within themselves.

At the end of each iteration, the Agile project team will meet to do what's called a retrospective, which can be done on a monthly basis to reflect on what went wrong or what went right during that iteration. This allows them to improve and become more effective for the next iteration.

The Agile process

Before we get into the process, you should understand that the two most famous Agile methods that are being followed are Scrum and Extreme Programming (XP). Both of these methodologies follow a very similar process but use slightly different terms. For example, in Scrum, the work that is getting done is call a sprint, while in XP, it is known as an iteration.

Here is the set of terms we will be using as we go through this entire Agile process:

Product Owner – Designated person that represents the customer on the project

Agile Project Manager/Scrum Master – Manages the Agile project. Primarily acts as a facilitator.

Product Backlog – Project requirements from the customers.

Sprint Planning Meeting- Meeting done by the Agile team to determine what features will be done in the next sprint.

Sprint Backlog – Work the team selects to get done in the next sprint.

Sprint - A short iteration where the project teams work to complete the work in the sprint backlog, (1-4 weeks typically)

Daily Stand Up Meeting – A quick meeting each day to discuss project statuses, led by the Agile project manager. Usually, 15 minutes.

Sprint Review – An inspection done at the end of the sprint by the customers

Retrospective – Meeting done to determine what went wrong during the sprint and what when right. Lesson learned for the sprint.

Release – Several Sprints worth of work directed to operations for possible rollout and testing

For exam purposes Sprint = Iteration.

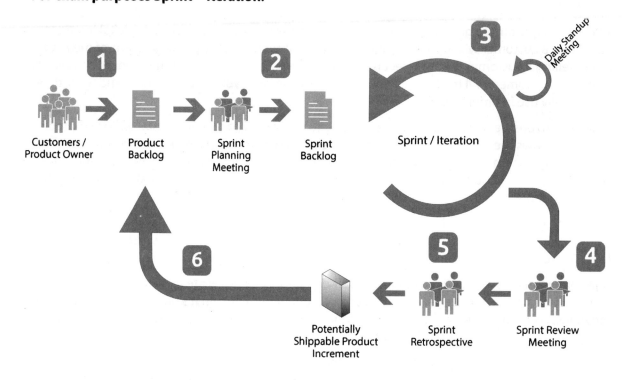

Here is a brief rundown of what the Agile process is:

1. The customers/product owner comes up with the requirements they would like to get done in the project. These requirements are stored in a document called the product backlog. The product backlog contains a list of all requirements that are needed for the project and is prioritized based on value by the product owner. Only the product owner can prioritize the product backlog. This means that items at the top of the product backlog would be considered more valuable to the organization than items at the lower part. For example, a company may prioritize completing the accounts receivable section of an accounting software over accounts payable. So, the top of the product backlog will have the accounts receivable section as being the first item.

2. Once the product backlog has been prioritized, the Agile project team then does a sprint planning meeting where they will determine what work they will do from the top of the product backlog in the next Sprint. They will then store these items that will be getting done in the next Sprint in another document called the sprint backlog. Keep in mind, a Sprint is only 1 to 4 weeks' worth of work. So, they will not be able to do all of the work in the product backlog but just a few items from the top. This means that the first few sprints in a project will complete the most valuable items on that project.

3. After the sprint backlog is complete, the team will then execute the sprint and begin the actual work. It is during the sprint that the team will actually code the application or build the server. During the iteration, the team will meet once a day to conduct what is known as a daily standup meeting. This meeting will have all team members answer

three questions, what did you do since the last standup, what will you do between now and the next standup, and what impediments or roadblocks are you facing currently. It is important to understand that while the sprint is going on, there should be no changes to the team members. This will ensure that the team can work at a sustainable pace. Adding or removing team members during the sprint could lead to the pace slowing down, as new people will need to learn procedures and the way the team operates.

4. After the sprint is completed, the customers will attend a Sprint review meeting. In this meeting, the customers will evaluate the work that has been completed during the sprint and give their feedback. The customers may say things such as the product is great so far or may outline what is wrong and what needs to be fixed.

5. After the customer has given their feedback, the team will then meet in a meeting that generally lasts about two hours and conduct a retrospective meeting. In a retrospective, team members will outline what they did correctly in the previous Sprint and what they did wrong. They will analyze things during the sprint that may have led to a defect and things that may have led to overcoming defects. This way, in the next iteration, they will know what to do to prevent these things. They will do things such as creating a list of things to do more of and things to do less of.

6. Once the retrospective is done, the team will then go back to the product backlog to complete the remaining work.

Once the team has completed the first Sprint, they may have a partial product that they could release all the way to production. While this may happen on a few projects, in general, it will take a few sprints before the team is able to release a product that is usable by the customer. So, it is not uncommon for a customer to wait anywhere from 2 to 4 sprints before they're able to get a minimal viable product (MVP). This is a product that may not have all the features but is still usable. The release of a partial product all the way to the customer is known as a release. The release is generally made up of one or numerous sprints; it just depends on the complexity of the product that is being made.

Value of Agile Projects

As you can see in our Agile process, the customers can start using a product within just a few months from the start of the project. This allows the customers to realize the benefits of that product without having to wait many months or years before it is delivered to them. During this process, you should've also noticed that the customers were involved right at the end of the sprint and gave their feedback. This means that the customers' input is given on a frequent basis. This allows the team to find and resolve defects or design issues at the very start of the project, rather than months or years in.

Also, keep in mind that the product backlog is prioritized based on value by the product owner. This means that the first couple of releases on an Agile project are generally considered to be the most valuable part of the product. That means the customers are able to use the most valuable part of the product just within a few months of the Agile project being started.

So, the next time you hear that an Agile project is all about delivering value, now you can understand why. And as you can see, customers would probably prefer to use Agile methods over traditional methods since there can be more people involved and they get a working product faster.

Inverting the triangle

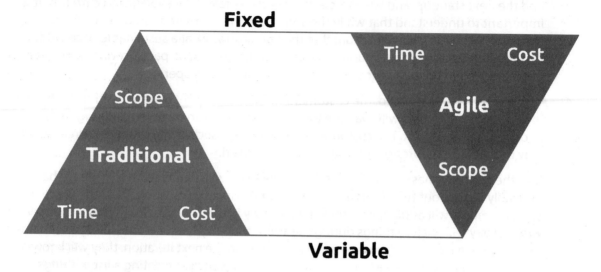

On a traditional project, you're expected to complete the scope while trying to keep time and costs fixed. Most traditional project managers will do what it takes to complete the scope, and this can include adding additional time or cost to the schedule or budget to finish that particular work. On projects with a fixed scope, such as constructing a large building, it is expected to do what it takes to finish the project scope. On this type of project, you cannot change the scope to remove a few floors from the building just to finish it within a fixed time and costs. In essence, the scope must be completed, while the time and cost will vary on the project.

Agile projects, on the other hand, will reverse this and invert the traditional triangle by keeping a fixed time and costs and varying the scope. This would apply more to software development projects where it might be okay to not complete all the features on the project. So, on an agile project, you would look to deliver the most valuable features within a fixed schedule and budget.

Roles on an Agile project

On an Agile project, there are three main roles you need to understand for your exam. They are as follows:

- Product owner: The product owner will represent the customer, and is responsible for the creation and maintenance of the product backlog. This includes changing the order of the product backlog based on value and adding and removing features from the product backlog.

- Agile project team: The Agile project team is a self-directed and self-managing team that does the actual work to build the actual product. Agile teams are generally considered small and are generally 3 to 9 members.

- Agile project manager (Scrum master, Agile coach): The Agile project manager is a servant leader who works to support the team by providing the team with the tools they need while removing any impediments.

Agile project team

On an Agile project, the team will be a small group of cross-functioning individuals that will generally manage their own work to create the product. They will have everything and everyone that is necessary to produce an increment of a product. The Agile project manager does not lead the project team but acts more as a facilitator to remove any impediments or any roadblocks they may be facing. The team will decide how much work they can get done in an iteration, and they will also decide how to do that work.

The team is made up of generalizing specialists. What this means is that team members have complementary skills so they can help each other in case one member needs help. When building the Agile team, select members with overlapping skills. This can help prevent bottlenecks that can occur on a project when team members are waiting on one particular member to finish a task, and no one else can help that person.

Agile team members should not be changed during a project, especially during the sprint. Changing a team member can lead to unpredictable results during the sprint. For example, replacing one member with a new member may result in work being delayed because the new member now has to learn the way the team currently works.

Agile teams will need to have workspaces where they can work and collaborate with each other. This generally means workspaces that are open where everyone can talk in an open and free environment. This is generally referred to as the "common" space. It will also need a quiet area or private space where they can work without any type of interruptions; this is known as "caves." It's important when designing the spaces to ensure that both common areas and caves are incorporated into the space. If the team is geographically distributed, then technology will have to enable more collaboration. This can include the usage of screen, video, and voice sharing software. Also, the use of digital whiteboards would be helpful.

Managing changes and the product backlog

Agile projects welcome change throughout the entire project. Any time a customer would like to add a feature to the product, they're welcome to add it to the product backlog. For example, if the product backlog currently has 20 features, and a customer would like to add another one, the product backlog would then hold 21 features. Once a feature is added to the product backlog, the product backlog is re-prioritized with that feature. So that means that a newly added feature does not automatically get placed at the bottom; if that feature is considered highly valuable, it may go right to the top of the product backlog. Of course, if that feature is not considered especially valuable, it may go all the way to the bottom or maybe the lower middle. Keep in mind, the product owner is the one that's prioritizing this product backlog based on value. Sometimes by adding a feature that is considered valuable, they may choose to remove features that are no longer valuable. This means that the number of features in a product backlog can change appropriately as the project is progressing.

This process of adding and removing, and re-prioritizing the product backlog is known as grooming the product backlog. This ensures that items at the top of the product backlog considered to be the most valuable to the project are what the project team should be trying to get done in the next Sprint.

Agile Methods

in this section, we will be exploring a few of the different methods that use Agile. Your exam will not need you to differentiate between these methods and will not ask you specific questions about these methods. They may test you on a few different tools and principles within these methods, but they will not ask you to specify to which tool it belongs or to which method.

Scrum and XP

In the previous section of the Agile process, what was covered was mostly Scrum and XP. These two methods are very closely related and basically follow the same process.

Several differences include:

- In XP, the sprint is known as an iteration.

- In XP, iterations are generally shorter; about two weeks long.

- In XP, the product owner is known as the customer.

XP has some particular principles that we should be familiar with for our exam:

- XP supports pair programming. Pair programming is when two programmers work together at one computer. One person writes the code while the other one observes and reviews the code as it's been written. While this may seem inefficient, this allows the code to be checked and reviewed as it's been written versus reviewing the code at the end. This generally leads to fewer bugs and errors in the code.

- XP supports collective code ownership. This is where any of the developers can improve or amend any code. This allows multiple people to work on all code, which can result in increased knowledge of the code. There will also be less risk if a programmer leaves the team since the knowledge is being shared between programmers.

- XP uses test-driven development. In this situation, the tests that the codes will need to pass at the end are developed first, and then the code is written to match the tests. While the initial test will fail since the code has not been written yet, when the code is written, it will be designed to pass the tests. This is a different way of thinking since traditionally, you would've written the code and then tested it.

Lean development

Lean software development comes from the lean manufacturing principles and practices used by the Toyota production system. Lean originated from manufacturing and is now used in software development.

Its main principles are:

- **Eliminate waste:** To maximize value, we must minimize waste. For software systems, waste can take the form of partially done work, delays, handoffs, unnecessary features, waiting, defects, and management activities.

- **Empower the team:** Rather than taking a micro-management approach, we should respect the team member's superior knowledge of the technical steps required on the project.

- **Deliver fast:** Quickly delivering valuable software and iterating through designs.

- **Optimize the whole:** We aim to see the system as more than the sum of its parts.

- **Build quality in:** Build quality into the product and continually assure quality throughout the development process

- **Defer decisions:** Balance early planning with making decisions and committing to things as late as possible.

- **Amplify learning:** This concept involves facilitating communication early and often, getting feedback as soon as possible, and building on what we learn.

When lean development is applied to software projects, it will help to decrease programming effort, budgets, and defects. Lean tries to eliminate as much waste as possible and build quality into the product. Empowering the team in delivering faster deliverables are some of the core concepts of Agile.

Kanban

Another famous Agile method is Kanban lean method. Kanban is the Japanese word for signboard or billboard. A Kanban approach limits the work in progress so that teams are not overburdened and able to focus on a specific set of work at any given time. Kanban is usually used in combination with other Agile methods, such as Scrum.

When using this method, you will create the eponymous Kanban board. The columns on the board that signifies work that is getting done will have a limit on them. As you can see in the diagram below, we have limited the number of cards that are currently in progress, and we have limited the testing. Each card is a task within that phase. By limiting the work in progress, you will have an increased indivisibility of issues and bottlenecks. This would allow the team to be focused on a certain specific number of passes that they can get done in a reasonable time.

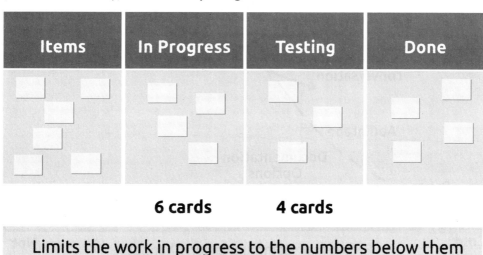

6 cards   **4 cards**

Limits the work in progress to the numbers below them

Another excellent feature on a Kanban board is the ability to visualize the workflow. Agile promotes the use of low-tech, high-touch tools, and this method, when done using an actual whiteboard and sticky notes, promotes more simplicity and interactions amongst team members. This will improve overall collaboration within the team.

Other methods

While there are many other Agile methods, which can include crystal methods, disciplined Agile, feature-driven development, Scrum of Scrums, and many others that are used in different industries, we will not need to know all of them for the exam. In fact, as I write this book, there are many other methods that are being developed and refined and will be coming out in the next few months to years as the world around us changes. That is a beautiful thing about Agile methods and practices; true to its values, it's always changing and improving.

Agile tools

In an Agile environment, the tools that should be used in order to conduct the Agile processes should always follow the concept of low-tech, high-touch. The tool should allow more collaboration and interaction among team members, customers, senior management, Agile project managers, and other stakeholders.

One such tool is a whiteboard with markers. Agile asserts that the best way to communicate is face-to-face with a whiteboard and a marker, as in the diagram shown below. Other Agile tools include a variety of different charts such as a burn-up and burn-down chart, which we will cover in the latter part of this guide, Kanban or task boards, and a wide variety of different software options.

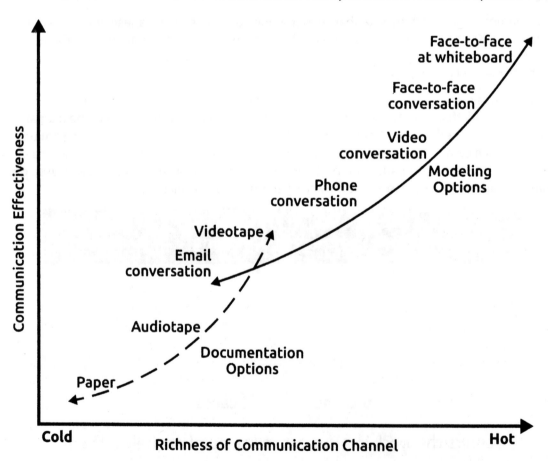

Agile tools would also be an information radiator. This means that any time you walk into a room or approach the tool, it will "radiate" information to you. Think of a Kanban board on the wall with all of the different cards that are getting done and what is left to be done. Information radiators can be hand-drawn, written, printed, or electronic displays, which the team will place in a location that is very visible to all team members as well as people passing by. This usually includes a large variety of different charts and graphs.

Servant leadership

One important concept to understand is the role of the Agile project manager. The Agile project manager will be a servant leader on the project. Servant leadership is about focusing on understanding and addressing the needs and growth of team members in order to ensure the highest possible team performance.

The main role of the servant leader is to be a facilitator for the project team. Do not try to control the project team, help them, and coach them to succeed with their task. As a facilitator, the servant leader will encourage team members to participate in meetings through conversations and collaboration. As the facilitator, the leader will ensure that more inclusive tools are being used to ensure all team members are participating. For example, the usage of a whiteboard with markers would be more of an inclusive tool versus using a software where everyone sits at a desk by themselves.

Here are a few characteristics of a servant leader:

- Promotes self-awareness
- Effective listening
- Serving the team
- Helping people grow individually and as a team
- Coach the team and not control the team
- Encourage safety, respect, and trust

Servant leaders work to remove all impediments that are blocking the team. For example, if the team is having issues getting approvals and getting the product owner to participate, the servant leader would work with senior management and the product owner to ensure approvals are done quicker and the product owner is participating. This will allow the team to focus on the work and not be bothered by external factors that can cause interruption to the team's work.

On an Agile project, the project manager shifts from being the center as in a traditional project to actually serving the project team. Servant leadership encourages coaching, team collaboration, encourages the distribution of responsibility to the team because those are the people that actually have the knowledge to get the work done.

Hybrid Project Management

While Agile methods have many benefits, such as more customer interactions, it can be very difficult to implement on a project with a large team and many moving parts such as constructing a large bridge for a major city. Also, many companies that come from traditional project management methodology find it difficult to implement pure Agile. In these scenarios, companies implement what is known as hybrid project management. Hybrid includes both traditional methods and Agile methods. Combinations of these methods can be done in a few different ways.

One way is to have parts of the project done using Agile, and other parts done using a traditional method. For example, here at my company Technical Institute of America, when we created our internal student management system, the actual coding of the software was done using Agile, and the deployment was done using traditional methods. We created a small coding team that worked with all the company stakeholders to code the software, and after about 3-5 sprints, a release was done by another team to our locations following a traditional method of initiating, planning, executing, monitoring and controlling, and closing. This allowed us to have a very customer-centric approach to building the software and a more structured approach while deploying it.

When using this method, portions of the project with a lot of uncertainty, complexity, and risks will be developed using Agile, and parts of it that are more defined and repeatable will follow a traditional predictive approach. For example, when a software development project starts, gathering requirements and building the software will have a lot of uncertainty and will follow an Agile approach, while the rollout at the end of the releases will generally follow a more predictive traditional approach since the organization has done this many times.

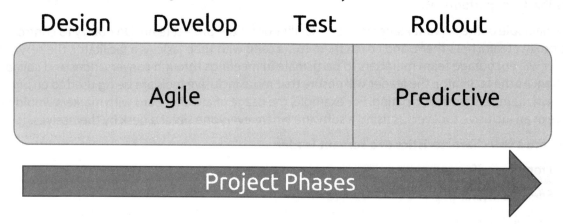

Another way hybrid could be done would be when companies incorporate both methods at the same time. While this may be more complex, it would allow traditional projects to have more customer interactions and welcome changes. They would also be using Agile practices such as incorporating daily standup meetings, short iterations, and retrospectives.

Organizations may typically do this when they're transitioning a traditional project style to be more Agile. Work would still be done using more upfront estimation and planning while they would use shorter iterations.

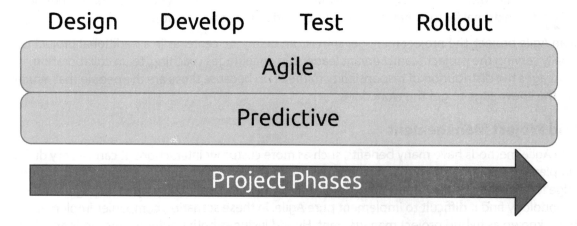

A few other ways hybrid can be done is when a project is using a predictive approach with a very small section using agile or an Agile project using a predictive method for a very small part. Here are 2 diagrams to illustrate this concept.

Predominantly Predictive approach with some Agile

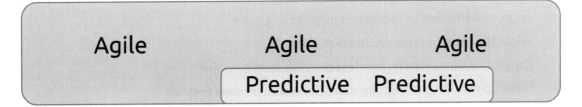

Predominantly Agile approach with some Predictive

Keep in mind that there is no right or wrong way to conduct hybrid project management. The hybrid method a company develops will generally be based on the specific project they're working on and the needs of the stakeholders on that project. A project that requires a high velocity of changes and refinements may have many of its phases done using Agile and only a few of them using traditional methods. A project that is more predictive and has been done many times, and has only a few phases with uncertainty would only use a little bit of Agile throughout the entire project lifecycle. This will vary greatly from company to company, and from project to project within those companies. As a PMP, you would just need to understand the overall framework for Agile projects and traditional predictive projects.

In 2019, PMI conducted a study in PMI's pulse of the profession global project management survey that found 60% of companies in the survey that are highly proficient in Agile project management use hybrid project management all of the time or most of the time.

Project management is all about delivering value, and if using a combination of the different Agile methods along with traditional predictive methods is what it takes to deliver value to your stakeholders, then that is the best method for the organization. As a PMP, you should not be resistant to trying different methods and mixing them. Sometimes the best method is not an extreme of one but a mixture of many.

Agile and Hybrid Project Managment Questions:

1. Which one of the following choices is a true benefit to following agile practices?

   A. Build the product all at once

   B. Do all planning upfront

   C. Build a product in increments

   D. Have any strict change management process

2. While following agile methodologies, which of the following decisions would an agile project manager make during an agile project?

   A. Allow stakeholders to request changes at any point

   B. Allow the team to prioritize the features

   C. Develop features that require less development time first

   D. Develop features that require more development time first

3. Which of the following is fixed on an agile project?

   A. Scope

   B. Time

   C. Customers

   D. Features

4. In the agile manifesto, we value responding to change over?

   A. Processes and tools

   B. Comprehensive documentation

   C. Contract negotiation

   D. Following a plan

5. While conducting an agile project, the agile project manager has implemented a new computer software that will allow this schedule to be auto-calculated. What agile value was not followed?

   A. Individuals and interactions over processes and tools

   B. Working software over comprehensive documentation

   C. Customer collaboration or contract negotiation

   D. Working software over following a plan

6. When conducting an agile project, what is the primary method by which customers will measure the agile project progress?

   A. On a percentage scale

   B. on cost scale

   C. how much of the software is working

   D. how much of the budget is left

7. What is the primary output of the sprint planning meeting?

   A. Product backlog

   B. Sprint backlog

   C. Sprint register

   D. Product register

8. After the team has completed prioritizing the features in the product backlog, the project manager has informed them of the following:

   A. They should have used a numerical scale

   B. They should not have prioritized the features

   C. They should have prioritized the features based on value

   D. They should have prioritized the features based on costs

9. Which of the following agile tools help all stakeholders to see the maximum amount of work the team will be doing in each phase of the development cycle?

   A. Kanban development

   B. Lean development

   C. XP programming

   D. Verbal discussions

10. Which of the following is an example of servant leadership?

    A. Dictating what processes the team should use when resolving problems

    B. Holding individual team members accountable for issues

    C. Continuously communicating the project vision

    D. Communicating the methods the team should use when developing software

11. As an agile project manager, you have encountered many issues with the product owner. The product owner has refused to prioritize the product backlog, stating that all items are equally important. After educating the product owner about the value of prioritization, he still refuses. What should the agile project manager do?

    A. Continue to educate the product owner

    B. Prioritize the product backlog for the product owner

    C. Have the team prioritize the product backlog

    D. Replace the product owner

12. After speaking with the outside application testers, the agile project manager has been informed that the application has passed the test and is ready to be installed into production. How should the agile project manager inform the team?

    A. Email them the test results

    B. Tell them in person

    C. Tell them in a conference call

    D. Send it to them as a memo

13. When implementing Kanban development, which of the following should be done?
    A. Create it using custom software on a large screen
    B. Create it on a whiteboard with erasable markers
    C. Only have the team create it using software
    D. Only have the agile project manager create it using software

14. The product owner has informed the project manager that all items in the product backlog are valuable and they should all get done. How should the agile project manager respond?
    A. He should agree with the product owner and try to complete as much of the items as possible
    B. He should educate the product owner on the benefits of prioritizing the product backlog
    C. He should inform the project team that all items should get done immediately
    D. Should prioritize the items himself

15. Where will the customers have the ability to give feedback on a completed increment of the product?
    A. Sprint planning meeting
    B. Sprint retrospective
    C. Sprint review meeting
    D. Sprint product meeting

16. While discussing the benefits of agile with three of the organization's key stakeholders, what would be seen as the main benefit of conducting the project using agile methodology versus traditional methodology?
    A. Agile delivers value incrementally
    B. Traditional delivers values all upfront
    C. Traditional delivers value at the beginning
    D. Agile project requires funding upfront

17. Which of the following is an XP practice where programmers work together in order to write one set of codes?
    A. Dual programming
    B. Peer programming
    C. Pair programming
    D. Double programming

18. Which of the following would be considered a waste on a project?
    A. Value-added features
    B. Value-added processes
    C. Completed work
    D. Waiting

19. The product owner has added three new changes to the product backlog. The agile project manager has met with the team, and they have immediately decided how to implement these new changes, although these changes will be implemented three iterations from now. The product owner informs the agile project manager that he is not happy about this. What should the agile project manager do?

    A. Ask the team members to implement the change right away

    B. Ask the product owner when he would like the changes to be implemented

    C. Inform the product owner of the potential risk of each change

    D. Tell the team they should not have committed to doing these changes until they were ready to implement them

20. While building the agile space for a new agile team, which of the following tools should the project manager ensure is available to all of them?

    A. A big screen monitor with the latest Kanban software

    B. A whiteboard

    C. A network-enabled project management software

    D. Private offices with virtual meeting software

21. Who is in charge of managing the work during the iteration?

    A. Agile project manager

    B. Team

    C. Product owner

    D. Senior management

22. The agile manifesto values working software over?

    A. Processes and tools

    B. Comprehensive documentation

    C. Contract negotiation

    D. Following a plan

23. The agile manifesto contains how many guiding principles?

    A. 4

    B. 10

    C. 11

    D. 12

24. Who should determine the work that should be placed in the iteration backlog?

    A. Product owner

    B. Agile project manager

    C. Team

    D. Senior management

25. While a Sprint is currently being done, which of the following should not be performed?
    A. Adding work to the product backlog
    B. Reprioritizing the product backlog
    C. Changing the team members
    D. Changing methods of communication with stakeholders

26. To have an effective daily standup meeting, which of the following should not be done?
    A. Limit the meeting to 15 minutes
    B. Try to hold the meeting at the same time everyday
    C. Try to hold the meeting at the same place everyday
    D. Allow team members to discuss personal issues

27. Which of the following is the characteristic of a high-performing agile team?
    A. A team of specialized skills
    B. A team of generalizing specialists
    C. A team that uses the latest in communication software
    D. A team of extremely knowledgeable programmers

28. When following XP practices, what is the concept of collective code ownership?
    A. The codes are collectively owned by the team and can be improved or amended by anyone
    B. The code is owned by a single person
    C. The code can only be amended by a single person at a time
    D. The code should be collected and amended by a single person

29. During the daily standup meeting, the team members are required to answer how many questions?
    A. 3
    B. 4
    C. 5
    D. 6

30. What is critical on an agile project for it to be successful?
    A. Being a servant leader
    B. Stakeholder satisfaction
    C. Very thorough change control process
    D. Having a well-defined project management plan

Agile and Hybrid Project Management Answers:

1.   **C.** Building a product in increments is an agile practice that allows for more customer feedback and interactions while the product is being built. All other choices are related to traditional project management.

2.   **A:** On an agile project, change is welcome and encouraged at all points throughout the project. The product owner, not the team, will prioritize the features on the product backlog. The team will develop features based on their value, not the amount of time it takes to develop them.

3.   **B:** In agile, the concept of inverting the triangle is to have a fixed time and cost while having a variable scope.

4.   **D:** One of the four values in the agile manifesto is to respond to change over following a plan.

5.   **A:** The value of individuals and interactions over processes and tools will guide the agile project manager to get people more involved and interacting versus using a software tool.

6.   **C:** The agile guiding principle #7 states, working software is the primary measure of progress.

7.   **B:** The output of the sprint planning meeting is the Sprint backlog, it will contain the work and methods to complete the work for the next Sprint.

8.   **B:** The product backlog is prioritized by the product owner based on value, not the project team.

9.   **A:** One of the core principles of Kanban is to limit the work in progress (WIP).

10. **C:** One of the characteristics of being a servant leader is to communicate and re-communicate the project vision continuously throughout the project.

11. **A:** One of the core tasks of being an agile project manager is to educate and promote the values of agile practices even when stakeholders are reluctant to follow the principles.

12. **B:** Agile values face-to-face conversation over any other methods of communication. This leads to more engagement and overall communication satisfaction.

13. **B:** When managing an agile project, it is important to use low-tech, high-touch tools such as a Kanban, which is created on a whiteboard with erasable markers.

14. **B:** Part of being an agile project manager is to be an advocate for agile processes. This includes educating and teaching stakeholders on the benefits of agile. Agile principles state that only the product owner can prioritize the product backlog.

15. **C:** During the Sprint review meeting, customers will have the ability to evaluate the completed increment that was done in that Sprint and to provide their feedback.

16. **A:** One of the main benefits of using agile over traditional project management is that agile delivers value incrementally versus getting value only at the end of the project.

17. **C:** The concept of Pair programming is when developers work in pairs to write and provide real-time reviews of the code as it's been written.

18. **D:** Waiting is considered waste on a project, as it represents the time when no work is getting done.

19. **D:** One of the core principles of agile is to defer decisions. What this means is to hold off on making decisions about potential changes or features until the very last minute.

20. **B:** The use of high-touch, low-tech tools such as a whiteboard is vital in an agile environment to ensure collaboration and engagement of all team members.

21. **B:** Agile project teams are self-organizing and self-directing, and manage their own work throughout the Sprint. The agile project manager will be a servant leader that provides the environment and the support they need to succeed

22. **B:** The agile manifesto values working software over comprehensive documentation

23. **D:** The agile manifesto contains 4 values and 12 guiding principles

24. **C:** While the product owner will prioritize the product backlog, the agile project team will determine what work they can do in the next iteration, which they will store in the iteration backlog

25. **C:** During an iteration, changes of team members should not be allowed as that will change the velocity of the team. All other choices could change while the iteration is taking place

26. **D:** A daily standup meeting is a time box event that is limited to 15 minutes and should be held at the same time and place every day. Personal issues should not be discussed during this meeting.

27. **B:** An agile project team should be a team of generalizing specialists to help reduce bottlenecks by sharing the workload and knowledge.

28. **A:** XP uses the practice of collective code ownership to specify that the code is collectively owned by the team and can be improved or amended by anyone.

29. **A:** During the daily standup meeting, all members should answer three questions: what have you done since the last meeting, what will you be working on today, and do you have any impediments

30. **B:** On an agile project, the aim is to have as much stakeholder engagement as possible, which will lead to more satisfied stakeholders.

Chapter 5
Integration Management

Before we get started with this chapter, we have to understand what integration is. Integration management is the unification of all of the other knowledge areas. It could be thought of as the combination or summary of the other nine knowledge areas. For example: Let's take a look at the process "Develop Project Management Plan." In order to develop the project management plan, you will need to perform the other 23 planning processes, which can be viewed on the process table at the beginning of Chapter 3. By doing the other 23 processes, their outputs become the main input to the project management plan.

The processes that are listed under the integration knowledge area roll up to create the integration knowledge area. Another example: In the integration executing process of "direct and manage project work," you would need to complete the other nine processes listed under it. Once more, refer to the process chart at the beginning of Chapter 3.

This is an important concept for you to understand for your exam, as most students will not understand why we need an integration knowledge area. This knowledge area is probably the most important of the 10 knowledge areas, as it incorporates and summarizes all of the work the project manager will need to do in order to successfully complete each phase of a project. The project manager's main job is to perform integration, and that means the integration of all the other knowledge areas such as scope, time, cost, and quality. As you work on a project, you will integrate different knowledge areas in different sequences depending on the project, such as using the information we gather from the project scope to create the schedule and budget.

If you work on an agile project, the concept of managing a project in this knowledge area will not change. You will still be in charge of initiating, planning, executing, monitoring and controlling, and closing. The only difference may be that the project team will be more involved and making more decisions than the project manager. In a traditional project, in integration, the project manager will play more of a central role with the project team reporting to them. On agile and hybrid projects, the project manager will play more of a servant role, in which case they will support the team members to conduct many of the processes listed in this knowledge area. Also, in agile, you should expect more changes throughout each phase and the project as a whole.

Expect to see quite a few questions on the exam about the processes covered in this chapter. It's very important not just to know the processes but also to understand why an input is needed, how a tool can be used in that process, and the main outputs from each process.

Process Name	Process Group	Main Output
Develop Project Charter	Initiating	Project Charter, Assumption Log
Develop Project Management Plan	Planning	Project Management Plan
Direct and Manage Project Work	Executing	Deliverables, Work Performance Data, Issue Log, Change request
Manage Project Knowledge	Executing	Lessons Learned Register
Monitor and Control Project Work	Monitoring and Controlling	Work Performance Reports, Change Requests
Perform Integrated Change Control	Monitoring and Controlling	Approved Charge Request
Close Project or Phase	Closing	Final Product, Service, or Result Transition and Final Report

Develop Project Charter

This is the process of developing a document that formally authorizes the project or phase and documents initial requirements to satisfy the stakeholders. The project charter establishes the partnership between the performing organization and the requesting organization.

This process is what you do at the very beginning of a project or phase. The charter is senior management written approval to start the project. When you think of the project charter, think of the authorization of the project manager and the project itself.

The charter is usually developed by the project sponsor while working with the project manager. The charter will contain high-level information that senior management will review in order to determine if the project should proceed. So, the information that is collected to create the charter is critical in that it outlines the cost, schedule, scope, and benefits.

Once the project charter is approved, the next step would be to identify your stakeholders and get started planning the project. You should complete the two initiating processes of "develop project charter" and "identify stakeholders" before you start planning the project.

On agile and hybrid projects, you will also have a project charter. Although the project charter may not be as detailed as it would be in a traditional project, it will still have some of the high-level requirements so the project can be authorized. An agile project charter generally contains a very high-level scope since most of the project will be unknown when the charter is being written.

Inputs

Business Documents

Business documents are documents that contain specific information as to why a project should be initiated. There are two main documents; the business case and the benefits management plan.

Business Case

A business case basically says why a business should do this project. Businesses usually do a cost-benefit analysis to justify the money being spent on the project. There are a few reasons why companies initiate a project, and they include:

- Market demand, such as introducing a new product to the market that has a need.
- Organizational need, such as reducing overhead to improve profits.
- Customer request, such as improving a product to meet a customer request.
- Technological advance, such as installing the latest operating system for better security.
- Legal requirement, such as new regulations that a business needs to implement.
- Environmental impacts, such as cleaning up toxic waste sites.
- Social need, such as a project to reduce crime in certain areas.

Selecting a project can be a complex task. Here are a few methods that can be used to select a project.

- **Benefit-Cost Ratio (BCR):** This is the ratio of benefit to cost. For example, a BCR of 2.5 would be if a project returns $5,000 but costs $2,000. $5,000/$2,000 = 2.5. You are making $5 for every $2 that you spend. The larger the ratio, the better the project.

- **Internal Rate of Return (IRR):** This looks at the return of the project investment as an interest rate. The bigger the interest rate, the better the project. An IRR of 20% is better than an IRR of 10%.

- **Opportunity Cost:** This is an economic term that represents the value of what you choose not to do in order to do something else. For example, if project A will return $20,000 and project B will return $30,000, what is the opportunity cost of selecting B? That would be $20,000 of the entire value of project A. We give up option A to pursue option B.

- **Payback Period:** This is how long it will take to return the investment capital in the project. The shorter, the better. The faster the business gets its money back, the faster it can start another project.

- **Economic Value Add (EVA):** This looks at the net value of a company over a period of time. It is equal to profits after tax minus the average cost of capital. A business is only profitable if it creates value for its shareholders. A formula is not needed for the PMP exam; you just need to understand it.

- **Present Value (PV) and Net present value (NPV):** This is the term that means money will lose value over time due to inflation. $10 now will not worth $10 in the next 5 years. It will be worthless. The NPV includes the expenses of the project. The bigger the PV or NPV, the better.

- **Return on Investment (ROI):** This is a percentage that shows how much money you will get back on the project. For example, if the company invests $1 million and the ROI will be 10%, then the return will be $100,000. The bigger the ROI, the better.

Project Benefits Management Plan

A project benefits management plan is used to describe the main benefits that the project will produce once it is completed. The project benefit could be the product, service, or result that the organization is looking to obtain after the project is done. This benefit would help to grow the organization.

Keep in mind that senior management will want to know the benefits this project will bring to the organization. Most of the time, this is probably expressed in financial terms, such as how much money the company can gain by selling a particular product that the project is creating or how it can reduce some of the organization's risk. It can also show how the output of the project is aligned with the strategic goals of the business. For example, it can show how the project deliverable will help to meet the organization's long-term goal of increasing its revenue by 50%.

This benefits management plan is generally created by doing a cost-benefit analysis of whether a project should proceed or not and using the different business cases as to why a project is needed. Keep in mind that this document must be continually maintained because as the project is progressing and more benefits are realized, the plan should be updated accordingly.

The flowchart below demonstrates how the business case and the benefits management plan will lead to the creation of the project charter, which will then lead to the creation of the project management plan.

Agreements

An agreement is another word for a contract. If this project is being done for an external customer, then an agreement will be needed to start the project for the contractor. The agreement should be signed before the project starts. Other forms of agreement can also include memorandums of understanding, service level agreements, letters of intent, or verbal and written agreements.

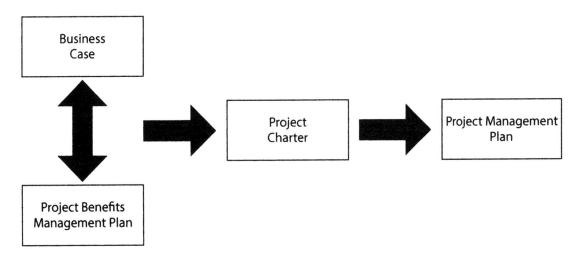

Enterprise Environment Factors – Covered in Chapter 3

Organizational Process Assets – Covered in Chapter 3

Tools and Techniques

Expert Judgment – Covered in Chapter 3

Data Gathering

Gathering data to create the project charter can include techniques such as brainstorming, focus groups, and interviews. The objectives here would be to gather the main requirements needed for the project. This can include requirements for scope, cost, and schedule.

Interpersonal and Team Skills

Expect to be doing a lot of facilitation among stakeholders while working to create the project charter. Also, meeting management techniques will be needed in order to ensure meetings are run properly.

Meetings – Covered in Chapter 3

Outputs

Project Charter

The project charter is a document that officially authorizes the project to get started. Here are a few things the project charter includes:

- Project justification and purpose.
- Name of the project manager.
- Assignment of authority to the project manager.
- Signature of the sponsor or others authorizing the project.
- High-level requirements, including scope, budget, and milestones view of the project schedule.
- High-level risks.
- Stakeholder list.
- Exit criteria (things that might cause the project to be canceled)

Assumption Log

The assumption log is simply a log of all the assumptions and constraints that are identified throughout the project. Think of this as the list of things that you perceive to be true (assumptions) and things that might constrain the project. For example, a project manager may assume that the project does not need to upgrade any of the computer hardware in order to install a new application. The project manager will then write this assumption of no hardware upgrades in the assumption log. As another example, a project may be constrained as to time because the work that is required may be too much for a short project schedule. A project manager would then list a constraint of time in the assumption log. This log is continuously updated throughout the entire phase or project.

Develop Project Management Plan

This is the process of creating the project management plan that includes all the subsidiary plans and baselines. The project management plan says how we will execute, monitor and control, and close the project.

When you think of the project management plan, don't think of something you create in an office application. It is much more than that. It includes all the baselines (scope, time, and cost) and all of the management plans that will be needed to manage each of the additional nine knowledge areas.

As you are doing all of the other planning processes, you will be creating many different types of documents that will be stored in this particular plan. The whole objective of all 24 of the planning processes is to create this plan. Without this plan, we will not know how to execute, monitor and control, and close the project. Once the plan is completed, you will then need it to get baselined, which generally means getting it approved by the project sponsor.

As you are doing the planning processes and changing or updating different components of the plan, there is no need for a change request as it has not been baselined. Once the plan is completed and baselined, only an approved change request that has gone through the process of "perform integrated change control" can be used to update the plan.

Exam Tip: Only an approved change request can change a plan once it has been approved.

When working on agile and hybrid projects, this plan may not be as detailed as it would be on a traditional project. While many of the components you're about to see below will mostly apply to a traditional project, agile projects can still use some of them. Also, while in many traditional projects, these plans may be given to the project manager from the PMO, on agile projects, the team will create them to best suit their needs.

Inputs

Project Charter – See the earlier process

Outputs from Other Processes

There are 23 other planning processes. Each of the planning processes will yield specific plans and baselines that will be needed to create the project management plan. In short, the output of the other planning process will serve as the input to this high-level process.

Enterprise Environment Factors – Covered in Chapter 3

Organizational Process Assets – Covered in Chapter 3

Tools and Techniques

Expert Judgment – Covered in Chapter 3

Data Gathering – Covered in Chapter 3

Interpersonal and Team Skills – Covered in Chapter 3

Meetings

While the project is being planned, you can expect to be attending lots of meetings. Utilize the meeting management techniques in the other tool, interpersonal and team skills. One meeting that you should be aware of is the project kick-off meeting. A project kick-off meeting is usually done when the planning is complete, and the team comes together to execute the project. There are times when the kick-off meeting might be done right after the initiating phase of the project. This is usually because the project is small, and the team is doing all the planning processes.

Outputs

Project Management Plan

The project management plan is a formal document that is used to describe how the project will be executed, monitored and controlled, and closed. This plan will be very important to the success of the project.

> **EXAM TIP:** *The project management plan is an input to all executing, monitoring and controlling, and closing processes since it describes how to do those process groups.*

Some important exam points about the project management plan:

- This is a document with 18 parts: 4 baselines and 14 subsidiary plans.

- This can be either summary or detailed; the more detailed, the better. Smaller projects might need a very simple plan in contrast to a large project, which might need a very complex plan.

- Once the project management plan is baselined, it may only be changed when a change request is generated and approved through the "perform integrated change control" process.

Here are the components of the project management plan and which processes create them:

Project Plan	Process Where Made
1. Scope Management Plan	Plan Scope Management
2. Requirement Management Plan	Plan Scope Management
3. Schedule Management Plan	Plan Schedule Management
4. Cost Management Plan	Plan Cost Management
5. Quality Management Plan	Plan Quality Management
6. Resource Management Plan	Plan Resource Management
7. Communication Management Plan	Plan Communications Management
8. Risk Management Plan	Plan Risk Management
9. Procurement Management Plan	Plan Procurement Management
10. Stakeholder Management Plan	Plan Stakeholder Management
11. Change Management Plan	Develop Project Management Plan
12. Configuration Management Plan	Develop Project Management Plan
13. Scope Baseline	Create WBS
14. Schedule Baseline	Develop Schedule
15. Cost Baseline	Determine Budget
16. Performance Measurement Baseline	Develop Project Management Plan
17. Project Life Cycle Description	Develop Project Management Plan
18. Development Approach	Develop Project Management Plan

While looking at this table, you might be thinking that it's a daunting task trying to understand what each of these components is. Don't worry; we will be covering all of them in detail. The project management plan is really broken into two components: management plans and baselines. A management plan is a plan that is used to describe how to do a particular component of a project. For example, the scope management plan will describe how to write the scope, baseline the scope, validate the scope, and ensure the project stays on the scope. A management plan is really a "how-to." When you think of a management plan, think of it explaining how you're going to manage that section of the project. A baseline is used to track the performance of the project. For example, the schedule baseline will tell you the planned schedule, and the cost baseline will tell you the planned budget of the project.

Most of the plans and baselines are created in other planning processes that we will be covering throughout the rest of this guide. There are a few plans that are created in this process that you should know about.

One of those plans is the change management plan. A change management plan will outline how change requests will be collected, assessed, authorized, and incorporated into the project.

The configuration management plan will outline how the various components of a project can be configured. For example, when installing a large software package across many computers, you will need a plan that describes how to configure each computer to ensure the software works correctly.

The performance measurement baseline is used to check the performance of the project as it is being executed. Anytime you see the word "baseline," think of what to measure against. The performance management baseline integrates scope, schedule, and costs into a single baseline that can be used to track the performance of the project.

The project lifecycle description outlines what type of lifecycle the project will be following. For an agile project, you would use more of an adaptive lifecycle, and for a traditional project, it'll be a more predictive lifecycle. This document would outline which of those lifecycles will be used on this project.

The development approach is a document that will outline how the product will be developed. For example, on an agile project that might be more iterative and developed in small increments. Meanwhile, on a project using a traditional, more predictive approach, you will develop the entire product in one shot.

We will cover the other parts of the project management plan in more detail as we review the processes where they are created.

Direct and Manage Project Work

This is the process of performing the work defined in the project management plan to create the project deliverables. The project manager leads the project team to actually build the deliverables and incorporate all approved changes. Keep in mind that this is an integration process and represents the rollup of the other nine executing processes.

Since this is an executing process, you are expected to do the project work as defined in the project management plan. The project manager will be training and managing the project team that is assigned to the project to ensure that the deliverable is built according to the plan.

As the project manager is doing this process, he/she is also collecting data on the work that is getting performed, in other words, the work performance data. The work performance data will be output here but will be used as input to all monitoring and controlling processes.

On agile and hybrid projects, this would be when the sprint starts and the project team begins to work. This process would only last for a short time on an agile project, anywhere from 1 to 4 weeks as they create that increment of the product. This is vastly different than it would on a traditional project in which this process can last for the entire duration it takes to build the actual deliverable. In a traditional project, this process can take months to years.

Inputs

Project Management Plan

The project management plan will describe the steps needed to build the deliverable. The plan also tells the project manager how to execute, monitor and control, and how to close the project. The more detailed this plan, the more successful the project execution will be.

Project Documents

While executing a project, the project manager will use many different project documents to ensure that the deliverable is getting created according to the plan. Documents can be things such as the project schedule, risk register, risk report, or milestones that will be used throughout this process.

Approved Change Requests

If a change is formally approved, the project manager will then execute that change in this process. An approved change request can just be a customer request for a change, as well as a corrective or preventive action. For example, if a customer requested to change the color of paint in a room on a renovation project and the change got approved, then the project manager should execute that change by changing the paint color in this process. Approved change requests are outputs of the process "perform integrated change control."

Enterprise Environmental Factors – Covered in Chapter 3

Organizational Process Assets – Covered in Chapter 3

Tools &Techniques

Expert Judgment – Covered in Chapter 3

Project Management Information System – Covered in Chapter 3

Meetings – Covered in Chapter 3

Outputs

Deliverables

The most important output of this process is the deliverables. Deliverables are the products or parts of the products that are given to the customer for acceptance. When the project team has completed the execution of the project, they should have a deliverable. For example, on a "paint the room" project, the deliverable would be a completed painted room.

This deliverable will become the input to the process, "control quality." From there, it would be checked for quality requirements and then be passed on to the "validate scope" process to be given a formal acceptance by the stakeholders. After it's been formally accepted, the project may move on to the "close project or phase" process.

Work Performance Data

This is another very important output. Work performance data is the raw information about the work that was performed. It can include things like how long the work took or how much it cost. This output is something that you get continuously as the project is being executed. Using this output, the project manager will analyze the data alongside the plan to create the work performance information, which would give him/her the status of the project. This work performance data will be used as an input to many of the monitoring and controlling processes.

Issue Log

As a project is being executed, you can always expect to encounter a variety of problems, conflicts, and issues. An issue log is where you will keep the list of all the issues on a project. As they arise, add them to this log. This document will be vital to ensure that issues are described, assigned, prioritized, and addressed. It will also keep track of who raises the issue and when they did. Keep in mind that this log must be updated continuously throughout the project.

Change Requests

As a project is being executed, you can expect to have changes, throughout. Changes can come from customers, sponsors, team members, or senior management. Changes can also be requested because of preventive actions, corrective actions, or defect repairs. Once a change has been requested, it would then be passed over to the process "perform integrated change control," where it would be assessed.

Project Management Plan Updates – Covered in Chapter 3

Project Document Updates – Covered in Chapter 3

Organizational Process Assets Updates – Covered in Chapter 3

Manage Project Knowledge

This particular process is new to PMBOK® Guide. It's a process that ensures the knowledge that is gained before, during, and after the project is used for the organization's benefit. Knowledge is power, and if utilized correctly, can greatly benefit an organization. Knowledge management is the main objective here, so the project manager can use the knowledge that is gained throughout the project for the benefit of the project and organization.

Knowledge can be either explicit or tacit. Explicit knowledge has a tangible form, which would include documents, procedures, or manuals. Textbooks are good places to get explicit knowledge. Tacit knowledge is difficult to transfer between people by just speaking to them. Tacit knowledge is gained by doing the work and is sometimes referred to as "know-how." In this process, the project manager will try to ensure that the knowledge, both explicit and tacit, is managed correctly for the benefit of the project.

The project manager will have to ensure that the knowledge that will be gained from the project is used correctly with stakeholders to ensure the project is successful. The main output of the lessons learned register is where the project manager will keep a repository of all the main knowledge that is learned throughout the project.

On agile and hybrid projects, the team will conduct a retrospective at the end of the sprint to capture the project knowledge and any other lessons that are learned during the sprint. They will then use these lessons in order to enhance their performance during the next sprint.

Inputs

Project Management Plan – Covered in Chapter 3

Project Documents – Covered in Chapter 3

Deliverables

Deliverables are the products or parts of the products that are given to the customer for acceptance. When the project team has completed the execution of the project, they should have a deliverable. Deliverables are the objectives of the project.

Enterprise Environmental Factors – Covered in Chapter 3

Organizational Process Assets – Covered in Chapter 3

Tools &Techniques

Expert Judgment – Covered in Chapter 3

Knowledge Management

Knowledge management is about the sharing of generally tacit knowledge between stakeholders on a project. Each project is different, and the interaction between the stakeholders might change from project to project. It will be up to the project manager to ensure that stakeholders are sharing knowledge with each other. This can be done using a variety of different methods, such as networking, meetings, discussions, seminars, workshops, and training. The method that is chosen will be dependent upon the project and the people working on the project.

Information Management

Information management is about ensuring that information is available to the stakeholders when needed. While projects are unique, most will use a similar method to get information to the stakeholders. These can include using websites, libraries, articles, and documents. It's important that the project manager works to ensure that information is widely available to his/her team as the project is progressing.

Interpersonal and Team Skills – Covered in Chapter 3

Outputs

Lessons Learned Register

The moment a project executes, the project manager should start to gather the lessons learned. Lessons learned are gathered throughout the project, not just at the end. The lessons learned register is where the project manager will store all of the lessons learned as the project is being executed. This is a living document that will be consistently updated every time you recognize new knowledge within the project. For example, if a team member discovers a new method to code faster, then the project manager should add that method to the lessons learned register. When the phase or project is completed, the lessons learned register would then be given over to the organization's PMO to be stored in the lessons learned repository that will be used for future projects within the organization.

Project Management Plan Updates – Covered in Chapter 3
Organizational Process Assets Updates – Covered in Chapter 3

Monitor and Control Project Work

This is the process of tracking, reviewing, and reporting the progress of the project work. The goal of this process is to keep the project on plan. As the project is executed, it is the responsibility of the project manager to ensure that the project is on plan. If the project is falling behind schedule or budget, corrective or preventive actions in the form of a Change Request may be needed.

Monitoring and controlling a project includes looking at the work that was done and comparing it to the plan to see if they line up. If they do not, you will need to implement the necessary changes to fix it. Keep in mind that the monitoring and controlling processes are performed in parallel to the executing processes.

The main outputs of this process will be the work performance reports (status report), which will give the stakeholders an understanding of what's currently happening on the project and also if the project needs any kind of corrections or repairs via a change request.

On agile and hybrid projects, the monitor and control project work is generally done by the team themselves. In traditional projects, the project manager takes on the role of monitoring the work, ensuring that it gets done according to the plan. Monitor and control project work is generally done throughout the sprint on an agile or hybrid project.

Inputs

Project Management Plan – Covered in Chapter 3

Project Documents – Covered in Chapter 3

Work Performance Information

This is the information on the performance of the work that was done on the project. It gives the status of the deliverables and is made by comparing the work performance data with the project management plan. Work performance information is the output of all "Control" processes, such as "Control Scope," "Control Schedule," etc.

Agreements

An agreement is usually a contract between a buyer and a seller for work. It generally includes the work that needs to get done, terms, conditions, pricing, or penalties. Agreements will be used in this process by the project manager to monitor the contractors' work while the project is being executed. We will discuss more specifics about agreements in the procurement management chapter.

Enterprise Environmental Factors – Covered in Chapter 3

Organizational Process Assets – Covered in Chapter 3

Tools and Techniques

Expert Judgment – Covered in Chapter 3

Data Analysis – Covered in Chapter 3

Decision Making – Covered in Chapter 3

Meetings – Covered in Chapter 3

Outputs

Work Performance Reports

While you are monitoring and controlling the project, you will create reports on the status of the project, such as if it is on schedule or budget. Sometimes this is also called a status report. The work performance report is what we will use to update the stakeholders on the progress of the project. The input to this process is the work performance information, and the output will be the work performance report.

Change Requests

While the project manager is monitoring and controlling the project, he/she may need to implement corrective actions, preventive actions, or defect repairs. For example: if the project is 20% over budget, the project manager will need to get a change request for additional funds to complete the project (corrective action). Once the project manager has initiated a change request, he/she would then follow the process of "perform integrated change control" to get that change approved.

Project Management Plan Updates – Covered in Chapter 3

Project Documents Updates – Covered in Chapter 3

Perform Integrated Change Control

This is the process of reviewing all change requests and approving or rejecting them. Once a project management plan is approved, any subsequent changes to it will need to go through this process to be updated. Changes may be requested by any stakeholder. A sponsor may want you to finish the project faster or more cheaply. A customer may want to add something new to the scope. The project will need a system to document and manage changes throughout the project. This is done using the change and configuration management plans which specify the steps to manage changes.

All documented change requests need to be approved or denied by the correct authority. All changes need to be evaluated and approved correctly. Changes can be authorized by the project manager, sponsor, or change control board. A change control board (CCB) can be used to review, evaluate, approve, or reject changes. The project manager should be influencing the factors that affect change in order to prevent unnecessary changes.

This process is a key topic for the exam. You are almost guaranteed to encounter questions on how to manage changes such as, what will we do first or next when a change is requested?

What we do first is to assess the change and see how it impacts the overall project. Then, we come up with the options for how to implement the change. Next, we will get the change approved. Once a change is approved, you can execute the changes. If a change request is rejected, then a project manager should communicate that back to the original stakeholder that requested the change to let him/her know the change will not be implemented. Do not approve or deny a change without assessing the actual change. The diagram below gives you a quick outline of a simple change management process.

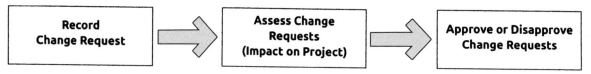

ExamTip: Never take action without an assessment and never reject a change without an assessment on a traditional project.

The diagram above mostly applies to a traditional project, in which case you would have a well-documented defined change management process. On a traditional project, no changes should be made to any of the project management plans without submitting a change request and getting it approved.

On an agile and hybrid project, change management is less process-oriented and more welcoming. Generally, when a stakeholder wants to add a feature to an agile project, it just gets added to the product backlog. The product backlog is then re-prioritized based on value to incorporate this new feature. The product owner would be in charge of re-prioritizing the product backlog and determine if it's something that should be added to the product backlog. So, most of the change management power on an agile project is given to the product owner and not the change control Board. Agile projects do not have well-documented change management processes as a traditional project would.

Exam Tip: On an Agile project, changes are generally added to the product backlog that is then re-prioritized by the product owner.

Inputs

Project Management Plan

The project management plan contains details about how to process, monitor, and control changes in a project.

Project Documents – Covered in Chapter 3

Work Performance Reports – Covered in Chapter 3

Change Requests

A change request is an output of most of the executing and monitoring and controlling processes. Change requests are evaluated in this process.

Enterprise Environmental Factors – Covered in Chapter 3

Organizational Process Assets – Covered in Chapter 3

Tools and Techniques

Expert Judgment – Covered in Chapter 3

Change Control Tools
Change control tools are manual or automated tools used to manage the change request. The tools will help to identify, document, and track the changes. The tools' main objectives are to help the CCB make a decision on whether to approve or disapprove the change.

Data Analysis – Covered in Chapter 3

Decision Making – Covered in Chapter 3

Meetings – Covered in Chapter 3

Outputs

Approved change requests

Once a change has been approved, it becomes an input to the "direct and manage project work" process. This is where the approved change request is executed. For example, someone requested a change to the color of paint on a renovation project; this change was submitted to the change control board, the change control board approved the change. Now the approved change request is passed to the next process of "direct and manage project work," where it will be implemented by the painters actually changing the color of the paint. An approved change request will trigger the Project manager to update the project management plan and its associated project documents.

Project Management Plan Updates

Once a change has been approved, it is then time to update the project management plan. Any of the 18 plan components can be updated with an approved change request. For example, if the stakeholders requested that the project is to be completed faster and that change got approved, then the project manager should update the schedule baseline to reflect the earlier finish date and maybe the cost baseline to show the additional costs associated with finishing the project sooner.

Project Documents Updates

As with the project management plan, any of the additional 33 project documents could be updated with an approved change request. One document, in particular, that would need to be updated is the change log. The change log records the status of the changes throughout the project, which can include if the change was approved or disapproved. For example, if stakeholders requested more work to be added to the scope and that change got approved, then the project manager needs to update the change log to reflect the newly identified change to the project.

Close Project or Phase

This is the process of formalizing all activities and overall project management process groups to formally complete the project, phase, or contract. This process also establishes a process to investigate and document the reasons a project is terminated early.

In this process, the project manager reviews the scope baseline and the completed work to ensure all the work was in scope and was done correctly. The project manager will transfer the deliverable to productions or operations, successfully capture lessons learned, and finally release the project team. Updating templates and knowledge bases is also done in this phase. Closing generally should follow these steps.

Closing a contract can include things such as having the seller sign off that all fees were paid and the buyer sign off that all work was done. Keep in mind that even if the contract is not successfully completed, it must still be formally closed in this process.

It is very important to understand that if a project is terminated before completion, the project manager will still have to formally close the project. You will get questions on the test where they will tell you that the project was terminated before completion and will ask you what you should do. The answer is to follow the closing procedures. All projects must be formally closed before moving on to the next phase or project. Also, if a project is closed and the customers want to add new requirements, then you might have to start a new project.

On agile and hybrid projects, the close of the project is generally done when the work in the product backlog has been completed. On agile projects, the team will need to tie up loose ends and handover the product operations. The agile teams will need to ensure that the different documents and tools that they were using will be archived in the documents and will be organized for future use on other projects. They will also need to ensure that they correctly hand over the product to operations to be maintained. They will then need to conduct a final retrospective for the team to focus on the lessons learned throughout all the different sprints on the project. Then finally, celebrate!

Inputs

Project Charter

The project charter is created in the initiating section of the project. It's a document that's used to authorize the project and the project manager. The project manager may want to refer to the project charter to ensure that all components of its scope were accomplished in this project or phase.

Project Management Plan

Expect to use the entire project management plan to close a project. All 18 of its components are generally used to ensure the project is successfully closed down.

Project Documents

Most of the 33 project documents would generally be used in this process to ensure that the project is closed successfully.

Accepted Deliverables

Before a project or phase can be closed, the sponsor or customer will need to formally accept the deliverables. The deliverables are formally accepted in the "validate scope" process, which we will cover in the Chapter, "Scope Management."

Business Documents

The two main business documents that the PMBOK® Guide usually refers to are the business case and the benefits management plan. The project manager may want to look back at these two documents to ensure that the project will benefit the business and that it was cost-efficient.

Agreements

An agreement is usually a contract between a buyer and a seller for work. It generally includes the work that needs to get done, terms, conditions, pricing, or penalties. It will be used in this process by the project manager to monitor the contractors' work while the project is being executed. We will discuss more specifics about agreements in the procurement management chapter.

Procurement Documentation

Procurement documentation usually refers to the documents used to bid on a project, such as an RFP, the procurement statement of work, contract, or source selection criteria. We will cover the specifics of these documents in the procurement management chapter. In this process, the project manager will collect these documents to be indexed and filed. This would be part of closing out a contract.

Organizational Process Assets – Covered in Chapter 3

Tools and Techniques

Expert Judgment – Covered in Chapter 3

Data Analysis – Covered in Chapter 3

Meetings – Covered in Chapter 3

Outputs

Final Product, Service, or Result Transition

This is the transition of the final output of the project or phase. After a deliverable has been accepted by the customer or sponsor, it will be given over to them in this output. For example, handing over the keys of a newly painted room to the customer. Another example would be the programmers handing over the completed application to the system administrators to install it on all company computers.

Final Report

The final report will give you the overall performance of the project that will then be filed with the organization. It will give you a summary of what took place on the project and how successful the project was. It should include the following:

- High-level description of the project or phase
- The objectives (scope) of the project and whether they were accomplished.
- The techniques that were used to measure the quality requirements and whether the requirements were met.
- The budget of the project, how it was measured, and whether there were any variations.
- Whether the project accomplished its real-world problems that it had set out to achieve and the benefits of this project to the organization.

Project Documents Updates

When a project or contract closes, you can expect many of the 33 documents to get updated. One of them, in particular, would be the lessons learned register, which documents all of the lessons learned that were accumulated during the project or phase. This would then be passed on to the organization to be added to the lessons learned repository.

Organizational Process Assets Updates

Upon closing the project, the project manager will update many of the organizational process assets, such as templates, knowledge bases, and lessons learned to help with future projects or phases.

Project Integration Management Questions

1. You recently took over a project in the middle of executing from another project manager who left the organization. You became extremely worried to find out that a substantial amount of new change requests are coming from your key stakeholders, customers, and even your manager. You are anxious that the changes will drastically increase the cost and time of the project, and you are not sure about how to process these incoming change requests. What should you refer to for any kind of help in this situation?

    A. The previous project manager who can provide guidance and relevant information

    B. The project charter

    C. The project requirements document

    D. The project management plan

2. John, the project manager, is in the process of Develop Project Charter to develop a document to formally authorize a project or a phase and identify the business objectives and needs, current understanding of the stakeholders' expectations, and the new product, service, or result that it is intended to satisfy. Which one of the following is NOT an input to this Develop Project Charter process?

    A. Project benefits management plan

    B. Business case

    C. Agreements

    D. Project management plan

3. Which one of the following is FALSE about change management in a project?

    A. "Influencing the factors that affect change" means determining the source of changes and fixing the root causes.

    B. Whenever there is a change request, the project manager should evaluate the impact on project objectives such as scope, time, cost, quality, risk, resources, and other factors.

    C. The project manager should make all the effort to prevent unnecessary changes in the project.

    D. The project manager should make the change happen as soon as possible to meet and exceed customer expectations.

4. Which one of the following statements is NOT true about the project management plan?

    A. It is a single-approved document that defines how the project is executed, monitored and controlled, and closed.

    B. It is developed through a series of integrated processes.

    C. It is progressively elaborated by updates and controlled and approved through the Perform Integrated Change Control process.

    D. It provides project inputs, tools & techniques, and outputs to be used on the project for the purpose of managing the product of the project.

5. You are a technical specialist and domain expert working on an IT project to implement a new video game console. There is a change control process in place, and the project scope is already signed off by the sponsor and key stakeholders. While having a casual conversation with one of the stakeholders, you realize that a simple change in the design will add a great feature to the project. Since there is no visible impact, you made the change to the project without informing the project manager. What kind of reaction should you expect from the project manager?

   A. The project manager should simply ignore the change since it had no visible impact.

   B. You should be informed that your action was inconsistent with the change management plan, and this kind of unauthorized action should not be repeated again.

   C. The project manager should get the customer sign-off on the implemented change.

   D. You should be recognized for exceeding customer expectations without affecting the project cost or schedule.

6. You are approaching the end of your project and have been asked to release the resources so that they can be assigned to other projects. Before releasing the resources, you want to make sure that you have completed the necessary actions. Which of the following is the correct order of actions that you take during the closing process?

   A. Get formal acceptance, write lessons learned, release the team, and close the contract.

   B. Get formal acceptance, release the team, write lessons learned, and close the contract.

   C. Write lessons learned, release the team, get formal acceptance, and close the contract.

   D. Release the team, get formal acceptance, close the contract, and write lessons learned.

7. While overseeing the implementation of a new computer infrastructure at the local hospital, you notice that a substantial amount of change requests have originated from one single key stakeholder. The stakeholder is also insisting that all of his requests should be implemented as soon as possible. What will be your BEST course of action?

   A. Ask the sponsor to have a discussion with the key stakeholder and ask him not to request so many changes to the project.

   B. Call the stakeholder and request him not to send any more change requests.

   C. Have a meeting with the stakeholder to review the change process in the project and determine the causes of his changes.

   D. Assign a team member to work solely with the stakeholder to understand his needs and expectations.

8. Which one of the following statements is FALSE about the Project Management Information System (PMIS)?

   A. It can be electronic or manual.

   B. It is an automated system that can serve as a repository for information and a tool to assist with communication and with tracking documents and deliverables.

   C. It consists of the data sources and the tools & techniques used to gather, integrate, analyze, and disseminate the results of the combined outputs of the project management processes.

   D. It defines how the project is executed, monitored and controlled, and closed.

9. Ashley is overseeing an IT project to implement a payroll system for a local doctor's office. The project has twelve team members and nine stakeholders, and it is supposed to be completed in six months. Ashley was unaware that a modification request to the product specifications by one of the stakeholders was immediately implemented by the project team. During the final testing, Ashley was surprised to find out that there was a major variance between the actual test results and the planned results. Which one of the following is a contribution to this kind of adverse consequence?

    A. Poor quality management plan

    B. Lack of commitment to the change control process

    C. Poor definition of the test plan

    D. Lack of adherence to the communication plan

10. You just received a change request from the customer, which will require an additional

$2,000 and will also delay the project by two weeks. The customer mentioned that they were okay with the delay and were willing to pay for the extra amount as the new change will drastically improve their business automation. As per your organizational policy, you are supposed to get the project office's approval for any change that will extend the project duration by more than a week. What should you do in this situation?

    A. Discuss the change with the project office.

    B. Do not allow the change since it would extend the project duration by more than one week.

    C. Allow the change and ask a team member to implement it since it will drastically help the customer, and the customer is paying for the change anyway.

    D. Advise the customer to take the change request to the project office and explain to them the importance of the change and his/her willingness to pay for it.

11. The Project Management Information System (PMIS), such as an automated system that can be utilized during the Direct and Manage Project Work process, will include all of the following EXCEPT:

    A. A tool & technique to identify the internal and external stakeholders.

    B. An information collection and distribution system.

    C. A configuration management system.

    D. A scheduling software tool.

12. One of your colleagues recently took over a project and expressed her concern to you about the new changes that may be streaming in from various sources. What is the best piece of advice you can offer her regarding changes and where she should devote most of her attention?

    A. Implementing changes as accurately as possible

    B. Tracking and recording all changes as accurately as possible

    C. Preventing unnecessary changes in the project as much as possible

    D. Informing the sponsor about all changes

13. You are a project manager at a dairy farm that offers several dairy products to its clients in different states, especially on the West Coast. You have sent a few of your team members to China to get specialized training on a spectacular dairy food processing equipment recently introduced in the market. The team members just completed the training, and this is one of the work results you have collected and recorded. This output describes which of the following in the Direct and Manage Project Work process?

    A. Deliverables

    B. Work performance information

    C. Change requests

    D. Project management plan update

14. All of the following statements are true regarding assumptions EXCEPT:

    A. Assumptions are factors used for planning purposes and may be communicated to a project team by several different stakeholders.

    B. Assumptions are generally considered to be true, real or certain, and nonfactual.

    C. Assumptions are absolute and non-negotiable.

    D. Failure to validate assumptions may result in significant risk events.

15. You are one of the members of the project prioritization and selection committee in your organization. The selection team is debating between two projects, which are both considered to be very important. The organization has to make an initial investment of $250,000 with expected cash inflows of $75,000 in the first year and $25,000 per quarter thereafter for the first project. The second project has a payback period of thirty-five months. Based solely on this information, which project should the selection committee recommend?

    A. First project as it has a smaller payback period

    B. Second project as it has a smaller payback period

    C. None of them since both of them have the same payback period

    D. Either of the two projects since the payback period is not important

16. You are the project manager for a cable service provider that is providing Internet, TV, and phone service throughout the United States. Your company recently introduced its service in Canada and made you the project manager for a critical project, which is two years long. You are reporting on project elements such as deliverable status, schedule progress, resource utilization, costs incurred, and others. Which of the following inputs of the Monitor and Control Project Work does this describe?

    A. Deliverables

    B. Work performance information

    C. Change requests

    D. Project management plan

17. While managing a large construction project, you are ready to assign resources to the project using a work authorization system. All of the following statements are true about a work authorization system EXCEPT:

    A. It is a formal, documented procedure to describe how to authorize and initiate work in the correct sequence at the appropriate time.

    B. It is a tool & technique of the Monitor and Control Project Work process.

    C. It is a component of the enterprise environmental factors, which are inputs in the Monitor and Control Project Work process.

    D. It is used throughout the project executing process.

18. You are the project manager for ITPro Consultancy. You have a project in mind that will be able to meet the strategic objective of your organization. While evaluating the project, your team found out that the project would cost $600,000. Since you are introducing a new potential product in the market, you are very hopeful that your expected inflows will be $30,000 per quarter for the first two years and then $90,000 per quarter thereafter. What is the payback period of this project?

    A. Thirty-six months

    B. Thirty-eight months

    C. Forty-eight months

    D. Fifty-two months

19. While managing a data recovery project, you are performing the following activities: comparing actual project performance against the project management plan, analyzing, tracking, monitoring project risks, assessing performance to determine whether any corrective or preventive actions are required, providing information to support status reporting, monitoring implementation of approved changes, providing forecasts to update current costs and schedule information, and other things. Which process are you in at this time?

    A. Manage Stakeholder Expectations

    B. Monitor and Control Risks

    C. Direct and Manage Project Work

    D. Monitor and Control Project Work

20. While managing an agile project, a customer has requested a new feature be added to the project. What should the project team do next with this added feature?

    A. Complete the feature right away

    B. Add the feature to the product backlog and prioritize the feature themselves

    C. Consult with the change control board to have the feature approved

    D. Have the customer pass the request to the product owner and let the product owner re-prioritize the product backlog

21. A project manager for a pharmaceutical project is reviewing the project contract and going through the narrative description of products and services to be supplied under the contract. He is meeting with subject matter experts, key stakeholders, and business analysts to evaluate whether or not the project is worth the required investment of $1 million. He also asked the team members to carry out a feasibility study on the project and report to him the findings as soon as possible. Which of the following documents would be created as an output in the process?

    A. Project management plan

    B. Project statement of work

    C. Project charter

    D. Project requirement document

22. All of the following statements regarding integration management are true EXCEPT:

    A. The need for integration management is one of the major driving forces for communication in a project.

    B. Project integration is a key responsibility of the project team.

    C. The project manager's role as an integrator is to put all the pieces of a project into a cohesive whole.

    D. Project integration management is the set of combined processes implemented by the project manager to ensure all the elements of the project are effectively coordinated.

23. The scope management plan, schedule management plan, cost management plan, change management plan, and others are which one of the following to the project plan?

    A. Subsidiaries

    B. Appendices

    C. Constraints

    D. Glossaries

24. You are working on a construction project and successfully completed all the work. Your stakeholders were very pleased and recently communicated their final acceptance of the project. You are now meeting with your team to update the organizational process assets with a record of knowledge gained about the project to help future project managers with their projects. Once the lessons learned is completed, what should you do next?

    A. Release the team.

    B. Close the contract.

    C. Get formal acceptance.

    D. Write lessons learned.

Project Integration Management Answers

1. **D:** Only the project management plan contains the details about how to process, monitor, and control changes in a project.

2. **D:** The project management plan is developed later in the Develop Project Management Plan process, not in the Develop Project Charter process.

3. **D:** The project manager should not implement any change request prior to evaluating the impact of the change and receiving approval from the change control board.

4. **D:** The project management plan, developed through a series of integrated processes, is a single-approved document that defines how the project is executed, how it is monitored and controlled, and how it is closed. Generally, the project plan is considered to be a guide that is expected to change throughout the project life cycle, and any such change should be controlled and approved through the Perform Integrated Change Control process.

5. **B:** It may seem like there is no visible impact on time and cost for a minor change, but it can result in significant scope creep and may impact other project constraints such as risk, customer satisfaction, quality, and other things. The change control process should be followed by everyone on the project team. A team member should consult with the project manager prior to making a design change to evaluate the possible impact on all the different constraints.

6. **A:** You should not release the team until the lessons learned are documented and added to the organizational process assets, as you need the team's help with the lessons learned. Most contracts have payment terms that allow for some period of time before full payment is required; thus, the last thing you do on the project is close the contract.

7. **C:** The most appropriate action is to ensure that the stakeholder fully understands the project scope of work and the change control process. It is also very important to identify the root causes of his changes. You should have a meeting with the stakeholder first and get all the details prior to meeting with the sponsor about your concern.

8. **D:** The project management plan defines how the project is executed, monitored and controlled, and closed (not the project management information system). The project management information system, which can be electronic or manual, is used to track project information and performance. Such information kept by these systems can include the tracking of time worked, project costs, and other factors that would be communicated to project stakeholders.

9. **B:** There is no indication that there is anything wrong with the quality plan, test plan, or communication plan. The change control process was not properly followed in this case. Failure to follow the agreed-upon change control processes may create adverse risk situations and jeopardize the entire project.

10. **A:** Any kind of organizational policy, process, or guideline must be followed, and the project manager should discuss the change request with the project office. The project manager should not simply approve or deny a change request as the Change Control Board (CCB) is responsible for approving or denying a change request after evaluating it. The customer should not do the project manager's job and take the change request to the project office.

11. **A:** Stakeholder identification is a continuous, complex, and manual process carried on by the project manager and the team members throughout the project. The Project Management Information System (PMIS) can be used for collecting and distributing information; describing the different versions and characteristics of the product, service, or result (Configuration Management System); and scheduling.

12. **C:** The project manager should be focusing on all of these options, but he/she should be very proactive and always try to prevent unnecessary changes as much as possible.

13. **A:** This output describes a deliverable. Note that deliverables can be intangibles, such as the completion of a training program.

14. **C:** Assumptions are not based on factual information, and failure to validate may result in significant risk events. Assumptions are documented mostly during the project initiating and planning processes. These assumptions are not absolute and can be negotiable.

15. **A:** The first project will have a cash inflow of $75,000 in the first twelve months ($250,000 – $75,000 = $175,000), and for the rest of the investment, it will take seven quarters to recapture it; thus, for the first project, the total payback period is 12 + 21 (each quarter has three months; thus, seven quarters have 7 * 3 = 21 months) = 33 months. The first project has a smaller payback period than that of the second project; thus, we should select the first project.

16. **B:** Work performance information describes how far a deliverable is from completion and how it is progressing compared to the planned progress. It can include several work performance data of interest, such as deliverable status, schedule progress, resource utilization, costs incurred, and quality standards.

17. **B:** A work authorization system is not a tool & technique of the project monitoring & controlling process. It is a subset of the Project Management Information System (PMIS). It is a formal, documented procedure to describe how to authorize and initiate work in the correct sequence at the appropriate time and is used throughout the executing process group.

18. **A:** The cash inflow is $30,000 per quarter, so in the first year, the project will get back $120,000 in four quarters. In the first two years, the project will have a return of $240,000. The remaining investment will be $600,000–$240,000=$360,000. It will take four quarters or twelve months to have it back at a rate of $90,000 per quarter in the third year. The total amount of time it will take to get the entire investment back will be 24 months + 12 months = 36 months, or three years.

19. **D:** All these activities are performed in the Monitor and Control Project Work process.

20. **D:** On an agile project, when someone requests a change, the change is usually added to the product backlog by the product owner, and then the product backlog is re-prioritized based on the value of the new change.

21. **C:** The project manager is in the Develop Project Charter process in project integration management. The output of this process is a project charter, which is used to formally initiate a project. In this case, the project manager is using a Statement of Work (SOW) to understand the product requirements and descriptions. The project will be initiated under the contract, and the SOW was given to the project manager by the client.

22. **B:** Project integration is a key responsibility of the project manager.

23. **A:** The subsidiary plans are usually included to support the overall project management plan and are developed for the purpose of providing more detailed information, guidelines, and control processes for specifically defined project elements or planning components. These are the outputs of some of the other planning processes associated with scope, time, cost, quality, human resources, communications, risk, procurement, and stakeholder management. Additional plans, such as change management, process improvement, and configuration management plans, can also be added to the project management plan.

24. **A:** You should release the team once the lessons learned are documented and added to the organizational process assets. Most contracts have payment terms that allow for some period of time before full payment is required; thus, the last thing you do on the project is close the contract. When closing the project, the order should be: get formal acceptance, write lessons learned, release the team, and close the contract.

Chapter 6

Project Scope Management

This knowledge area is very important, not just for your exam but also in actual real-life project management. The scope is what the project will actually accomplish. The scope should include the work required and only the work required to complete the project. As a project manager, you should avoid doing extra work that is not in the scope baseline. This is called 'gold plating', and is not allowed in project management because it could increase risk, cost, schedule problems, and quality problems.

Here are two terms that sound very similar but are very different:

Product scope: Features and functions that characterize a product, service, or result. The product scope is the requirements for the product. An example of a product scope would be a Microsoft exchange server that allows you to send e-mails, receive e-mails, and synchronize contacts and calendars. This does not tell you what the project is about; it just tells you what this product can actually do.

Project scope: The work that is needed to deliver a product, service, or result with specified features and functions. The project scope will actually tell you what the project is about. An example would be installing a Microsoft exchange server and updating all user accounts and all user workstations. In this particular example, what you're looking at is the project scope, which will tell you what the project is trying to accomplish versus what the product is trying to accomplish. That's the main difference between the two.

Here are the 6 processes and their main outputs that we will cover in this section:

Process Name	Process Group	Main Output
Plan Scope Management	Planning	Scope Management Plan, Requirement Management Plan
Collect Requirements	Planning	Requirement Documentation, Requirement Traceability Matrix
Define Scope	Planning	Project Scope Statement
Create WBS	Planning	Scope Baseline
Validate Scope	Monitoring and Controlling	Accepted Deliverables, Work Performance Information
Control Scope	Monitoring and Controlling	Change Request, Work Performance Information

If you're working on an agile or hybrid project, expect the scope to change as the project evolves. Agile tries to get work done as quickly as possible, and it plans and gathers requirements throughout the project. This all leads to the scope frequently changing as more of the product is understood.

When it comes to the scope of an agile project, the team will need to determine the number of iterations or sprints it will take to complete the project. There will be two main types of planning when it comes to the scope of an agile project. Sprint planning and release planning.

Sprint planning is when the agile team determines what features will get done in what sprint. For example, the team may determine that in the first sprint, they will only be able to create 60% of the user interface. In the next sprint, they will be able to create the remaining 40% of the user interface.

Release planning will determine what features will be released to the customers. Release planning generally includes multiple sprints. For example, a team that completed one sprint with just half of the user interface may not be able to push that to the customers. It's only after two or three sprints that they will be able to release that particular feature to the customer.

Another important concept to know about an agile project is something called the product roadmap. The product roadmap is more of a high-level document that outlines what would be expected of the actual product itself. The product roadmap will generally outline all of the different releases of the project.

Plan Scope Management

This process is about creating scope and requirement management plans. These plans will document how the project will collect the requirements, as well as define, validate, and control the scope. The project manager will document the steps needed to do the next 5 processes in this knowledge area.

This process involves outputs that are inputs to the project management plan. If you look at the inputs, you will notice that the project management plan is an input to this process, but the output is an input to the project management plan. You have to remember these processes are iterations. The project management plan is here as input even though it is not finished. It could still be used to help create the scope and requirement management plans.

On agile or hybrid projects, this process could be done to help build the product backlog and to help determine the methods by which the product backlog could be populated by the product owner. It can also outline that the product owner would prioritize the product backlog. Keep in mind, on a hybrid project, there is no right or wrong way to conduct the management of the product backlog since they incorporate both traditional and agile methods.

Inputs

Project Charter

This is the document that officially authorizes the project or phase to start. It will have high-level requirements that may help to create the scope and requirement management plans.

Project Management Plan

The project management plan is an input, although it is not completed. The plan may have other parts that will be helpful in creating the scope and requirements management plan.

Enterprise Environmental Factors – Covered in Chapter3

Organizational Process Assets – Covered in Chapter 3

Tools and Techniques

Expert Judgment – Covered in Chapter 3

Data Analysis – Covered in Chapter 3

Meetings – Covered in Chapter 3

Outputs

Scope Management Plan

The scope management plan will document how you are going to write the scope statement, how you are going to baseline the scope, how you are going to control the scope, and how you will get the scope accepted (validated). This plan is part of the project management plan.

Requirements Management Plan

The requirements management plan document shows the requirements to be collected, analyzed, documented, and managed. This plan is part of the project management plan.

Exam Tip: *All management plans are "how tos." They all basically give the steps needed to manage that section of the project. For example, the scope management plan states how to manage the scope; the cost management plan states how to manage the budget; the quality management plan states how to manage the quality processes, etc.*

Exam Tip: *An easy way to memorize a few of the outputs for the planning process is by looking at the process name to get the outputs. Look at all the processes like "plan knowledge area management"; its output is the "knowledge area" management plan. For example, "Plan Scope Management": the output is the Scope management plan, "Plan Schedule Management Plan": the output is the schedule management plan. In other words, put the word "Plan" at the start of the process and put the word "Plan" at the end for the output.*

Collect Requirements

This is the process of defining and documenting stakeholders' needs to meet the project objectives. This process is very important at the beginning of the planning section of the project. It's in this process that you go out and interact with the stakeholders to gather the requirements that they would like to see in the project.

Collecting requirements from stakeholders is vitally important to ensure the project is successful and actually meets the needs of the stakeholders. If you do not gather the correct requirements from your stakeholders, you can end up making a product, service, or result that does not conform to the customer's requirements.

For example, if you plan to paint a room, you should gather what color paint the stakeholders would like to have and whether it should be semi-gloss, glossy, or flat. The more detailed requirements, the more successful the project.

When collecting requirements, you want to make sure you collect requirements from the most important stakeholders: the customers that will actually use the project. Often, project managers gather requirements from the boss of the customers, who do not actually use the product themselves. Therefore, to ensure greater success, you want to gather requirements from all stakeholders, not just a certain few. This will ensure that the project is successful.

On a traditional project, the project manager will try to conduct this process as thoroughly as possible the first time around and then build a large plan around all these requirements to get them done. Then the project will be executed, and hopefully, there will be no more requirements together when the project is executed.

On an agile project, this is vastly different. Agile project customers will continue to give requirements to the project as they become more visible and known. Since agile projects are mostly done with products that are undefined, we can expect requirements to be given to the project throughout the entire duration of the project.

Inputs

Project Charter – Covered in Chapter 5

Project Management Plan – Covered in Chapter 3

Project Documents – Covered in Chapter 3

Business Documents

Business documents usually include the business case and the benefits management plan. The business case gives the cost-benefit of doing the project, and the benefits management plan shows you what benefits the organization will get from the project. Refer to the integration management chapter for more information on these two documents.

Agreements

An agreement is a contract between a buyer and a seller for work to be performed or for the sale of products. If the project has an agreement with a vendor, then it will have the cost included in it.

Enterprise Environmental Factors – Covered in Chapter 3

Organizational Process Assets – Covered in Chapter 3

Tools and Techniques

Expert Judgment – Covered in Chapter 3
Data Gathering

One of the main things you will be doing in this process is to collect information from the stakeholders. You can use any of the following methods to gather their requirements:

- **Brainstorming:** A technique where stakeholders generate and gather many ideas. It usually allows all stakeholders to document their ideas.

- **Interviews:** Interviews are formal or informal discussions to discover information from stakeholders. This is probably one of the easiest ways to gather requirements. If you're looking to gather requirements from particular stakeholders, you should just speak to them and ask what their requirements are for this project.

- **Focus groups:** Focus groups are where subject matter experts and stakeholders gather to discuss their project expectations. A focus group is very similar to an interview done with subject matter experts.

- **Questionnaires and surveys:** A set of questions that will allow the project manager to collect requirements from the stakeholders. They might change depending on who the stakeholders are. For example, the customer questionnaires might be very detail-oriented, while the senior management survey might not be.

- **Benchmarking:** Benchmarking is looking outside the project to provide a measurement of performance. You can observe work within your organization or in other organizations. An example would be looking at industry best practices for how fast a website should load once a user visits it.

Data Analysis

As you gather the requirements from the stakeholders, you would then have to use a method to analyze the data. This can include analyzing documents, agreements, policies, proposals, or business plans.

Decision Making – Covered in Chapter 3
Data Representations

After you gather the data, you then need a method to present the data to the stakeholders. Two methods include:

- **Idea/mind mapping:** A technique where ideas are drawn instead of written. This may help to generate new ideas.

- **Affinity diagram:** This allows many ideas to be put into groups.

Interpersonal and Team Skills

- **Nominal group technique:** This is how you rank and prioritize the ideas in brainstorming.

- **Delphi technique:** This is where requirements are collected anonymously from SME's. This way, stakeholders cannot influence each other.

- **Observations/Conversation:** Observation, also known as job shadowing, involves viewing the stakeholders in their work environment. Observation works very well because you can watch your stakeholders show you the problem that they have with the current system and what may need to be done to fix it. Conversations simply involve talking directly with people to understand what the requirements would be on a project.

- **Facilitation:** Facilitation is when you bring together stakeholders to gather requirements. One method could be a workshop. Facilitated workshops are interactive discussions designed to quickly define requirements, solve differences, and build trust. Having a workshop with different stakeholders allows participants to see what differences they may have regarding the project requirements and how to solve them. One example is a joint application development (JAD) session. This is where subject matter experts and developers meet to improve the software development processes.

- **User Stories:** One common tool that is used on an agile project to help facilitate and get users involved in the project is the creation of user stories. User stories are descriptions of required functionality and are generally developed during the requirements workshop. User stories are generally short and simple and follow this outline:

  · *As a <role/user type>, I want <goal> so that <motivation/reason>.*

- An example of user stories would be: As an accounts payable clerk, I want to be able to enter bills so that I can pay all my bills on time. In this story, the user-type is a person in the accounts payable department, their goal is to enter the bills into an accounting software, so they can get paid on time.

- User stories should be non-technical and easily understandable by users. This will allow the team to understand the true value from a user's perspective. These stories are generally the smallest unit of work on an agile project. Once the stories are clearly defined, you have to ensure that it is visible to the entire team, and the team has an understanding of what users are actually looking for in the agile project.

Prototypes

Prototypes are working models of a product that stakeholders can interact with. This gives the stakeholders a great view of what the final product will be when the project is finished. Stakeholders will give feedback on the product and how they might want to change it to better meet their requirements. Many software development projects use prototypes to collect stakeholder requirements as the software is being programmed. Agile development uses prototypes extensively.

One prototyping technique that is used on agile projects is called storyboarding. Storyboarding is generally a series of images or illustrations that are used to show a mockup of what the program would look like once a user is using it. For example, on an accounting software, the first image shows what the screen would look like when they first login, then the next image shows what it would look like when they click on the accounts receivable button, then the next image shows what the screen would look like when they click on enter invoice. Storyboarding helps the users to visually see what the program will look like when it's finished. This is a great way to gather requirements from the users and set their expectations for when the software is finished developing.

Context Diagrams

Context diagrams are used to visually show how a business process, other systems, and people interact. They use drawings to show the inputs and outputs of a system.

Outputs

Requirements Documentation

Requirements documentation is the documentation of the actual requirements that are needed on the project. Requirements documentation should be very detailed. The more detailed the documentation, the more likely the project will meet the customer's requirements. It could be very high-level at the beginning, but it must become very detailed before the project can be executed. Before the project plan is approved, the requirements should be measurable, testable, and acceptable to the stakeholders of the project.

In addition to the scope requirements for the project, other components may include:

- Business requirements
- Stakeholder requirements
- Organizational impacts
- Quality requirements
- Requirements, assumptions and constraints
- Legal or ethical compliance

Requirements Traceability Matrix

The requirement traceability matrix is a table that is created to link the requirements back to their origin. The traceability matrix basically tracks where the requirement suggestion came from, which stakeholder gave the requirement, and why it was added to the actual project. It will help to keep track of the requirement as the project is carried out.

Define Scope

This is the process where you will create the project scope statement. All the requirements from the requirements documentation will need to be analyzed and understood. The scope statement will select the final requirements to become the final product, service, or results of the project or phase.

The scope of the project is iterative. In the early planning of the project, the scope may be high-level and later may become more detailed. You may discuss the scope with the main stakeholders, such as the sponsors or customers, to ensure the scope includes all their requirements.

Once a project scope has been baselined (in the next process, "create WBS"), you will need an approved change request to change it. External events such as adding to scope because of a competitor offering a better product would require an approved change request.

On a traditional project, this process would be done multiple times to ensure the scope is well-defined before the work actually starts. This may take many iterations of this process to actually define what the project will include and what it will not include. Generally, on a traditional project, the execution of the work should not start until the scope has been well defined and agreed upon.

On agile and hybrid projects where much of the work is unknown and uncertain, this process may only be done once or twice before the work actually starts. Once the work starts and customers are more involved and actually start to see the creation of the product, then the scope would become more refined. The initial product backlog in an agile project may only contain a few items as the customers may not know what it is that they're looking for on this particular product. But once the work starts and the customer starts to actually use increments of the product, they will then refine the scope and come up with more detailed scope requirements.

> **EXAM TIP:** *On a traditional project, the scope of the project is stored in the project scope statement, while on an agile project, the scope or requirements are stored in the product backlog.*

Input

Project Charter

The charter officially authorizes the project. It will be needed to ensure the project scope statement meets the requirements in the charter.

Project Management Plan

At this point, the project management plan will not be finished, but it should contain the scope management plan that will guide the project manager through this process of developing the project scope statement.

Project Documents

Although many of the 33 documents can be used in this process, the main ones should be the requirements documentation, which contains the requirements for the project, and the risk register to show what risks can affect the scope.

Enterprise Environmental Factors – Covered in Chapter3

Organizational Process Assets – Covered in Chapter 3

Tools and Techniques

Expert Judgment – Covered in Chapter 3

Data Analysis – Covered In Chapter 3

Decision Making – Covered In Chapter 3

Interpersonal and Team Skills – Covered In Chapter 3

Product Analysis

If a project has a product as the deliverable, you will need to analyze the product to ensure it matches the requirements of the stakeholders.

Output

Project Scope Statement

The project scope statement is one of the most important documents to be created in the planning processes. The scope statement should include the project and the product scope. Its main purpose is to describe in detail the project deliverables and the work that will be required to produce those deliverables. The greater the detail of the scope, the better the team will understand how to reach a successful project end state. The less detail in the scope statement, the greater the chance of project risks, as well as the possibility of greater scope creep.

Details should include, but not be limited to:

- Description of the product scope.

- Detailed list of the deliverables.

- Acceptance criteria: That which must be done in order to have the deliverable accepted.

- Exclusions: These should state what the project will not get done or accomplished. If you are installing a phone system that will not include voice-to-email, this should be listed under exclusions.

- Constraints: If the project is limited by time or cost, it should be stated. If a project has a preset budget, this may be listed as a constraint since the scope will be impacted by it.

- Assumptions: If the project team has any assumptions, these should also be stated. In an operating system upgrade project, the team may assume there is no need for hardware upgrades since all the hardware is one year old.

Keep in mind that the project scope statement is a very detailed document. The more detailed it is, the more likely you are to reach the successful completion of the project. The project charter is a high-level document that was just used to authorize the project to get started. So, in essence, the scope statement is really a more specific and detailed project charter that will be used by the project team to execute the project.

> **EXAM TIP:** *The scope statement tells you what the project will not be doing, not just what it will be doing. At a minimum, all scope statements should have a detailed list of deliverables.*

Project Documents Updates – Covered in Chapter 3

Create WBS (Work Breakdown Structure)

This is the process of breaking down the deliverables into smaller, more manageable components (decomposition). The main output of this process is the scope baseline, which includes the scope statement, WBS, and the WBS dictionary.

This is a very important process for the creation of the project management plan. It is where the work listed in the scope statement is broken down. It will detail the work needed to complete the project deliverables. The scope baseline is the main output.

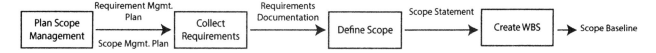

Input

Project Management Plan

At this point, the project management plan will not be finished, but it should contain the scope management plan that will guide the project manager throughout this process of developing the scope baseline.

Project Documents

Although many of the 33 documents can be used in this process, the main ones should be the requirements documentation, which contains the requirements for the project, and the scope statement, which will have the deliverables of the project.

Enterprise Environmental Factors – Covered in Chapter 3

Organizational Process Assets – Covered in Chapter 3

Tools and Techniques

Decomposition

Decomposition is a technique in which you take the project deliverables from the scope statement and divide them into smaller parts, known as work packages. The work packages are the lowest level on the WBS that will be used for estimating time and cost. Since all projects are unique, the level of detail that needs to be broken down will depend on the project and the project team. The project manager will need to decide how much detail will be needed to accurately estimate the cost, time, and resource assignments. If the WBS is too high-level, the estimates may not be accurate.

Expert Judgment – Covered in Chapter 3

Outputs

Scope Baseline

This is the main output of this process. One of the three baselines, the scope baseline is one of the main components in the project management plan. The scope baseline is made up of three components: the project scope statement, WBS, and the WBS dictionary.

Let's look at each of these components in detail:

- **WBS:** The WBS is the subdivided work that needs to get done to produce the project deliverables listed in the scope statement. It provides a structure for the summation of cost, schedule, and resource information. The WBS is hierarchical in design. The top-level is very general, and the lower level is very detailed. The WBS will have control accounts that are broken down into the work packages. All control accounts have one or more work packages associated with them. Complex projects may not be able to decompose all the deliverables at the start of the project. The team might wait until the work is better understood, then decompose them. This is known as rolling wave planning.

See the diagrams below for examples of a WBS.

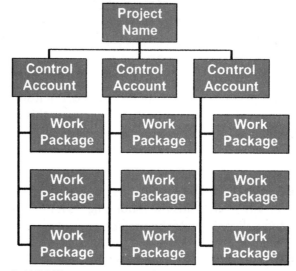

Sample WBS illustrating control accounts and work packages

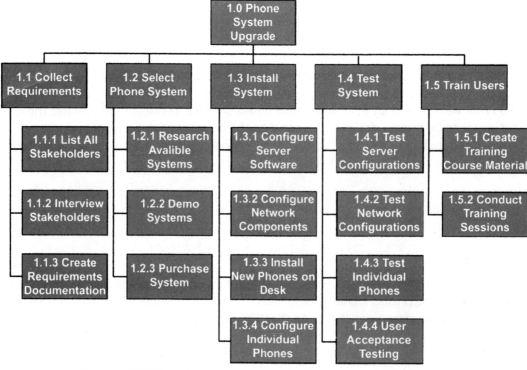

Sample WBS by phases upgrading a phone system for a company

- **WBS Dictionary:** The WBS Dictionary is a document that has more details about each work package in the WBS, as shown in the example below. It supports the WBS. Information in the WBS dictionary includes a more detailed description of the work, scheduling, cost estimates, assumptions, constraints, and acceptance criteria.

Project Name: Phone System Upgrade		Work Package ID: 1.3.1	
Work Package Name: Configure Server Software			
Work Package Description: Install a new virtual server. Install the phone server software. Configure the software to support 100 phones and voice mail to email. Ensure all updates are applied to the operating system before installing the phone system software.			
Assigned to:	Bob Peterson	**Duration:**	5 Days
Date Assigned:	12/30/2017	**Due Date:**	1/30/2018
Estimated Cost:	$5,000	**Account Code:**	PSU-882.3

- **Project Scope Statement:** The scope is a detailed list of the project deliverables.

    EXAM TIP: *The scope baseline includes the scope statement, WBS, and WBS dictionary. After the project plan is approved and the project is executed, any changes to the scope baseline will need a change request. Work that was not within the scope of the project charter should not be approved.*

Project Documents Updates – Covered in Chapter 3

On an agile project, it is important to understand how work is decomposed. Agile projects use the concepts of epics, features, and stories. In the diagram below, you can see the epic is decomposed into features, and features are decomposing to user stories.

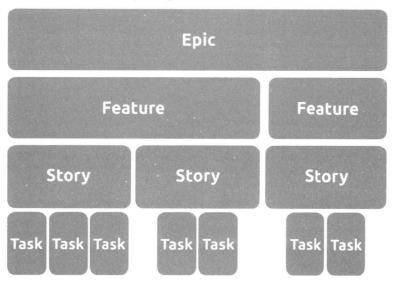

Epics on an agile project are generally large initiatives to deliver new products or solutions to the customer. They are generally made up of a large collection of different features and a span of multiple releases. For example, an epic may be to create an entire accounting system for an organization. The different features of this epic will be in the Accounts Payable section, accounts receivable section, and payroll. The user stories will be a decomposition of the features. For example, in the accounts receivable feature, they would have a story that would be as follows: as an accounts receivable personnel, I would like to input invoices, so we can receive payments on time. Tasks are the decomposition of these user stories. For example, a few tasks would be to enter the customer's name into the accounting system, create an invoice, and send the invoice. See the diagram below for a sample of what this would look like.

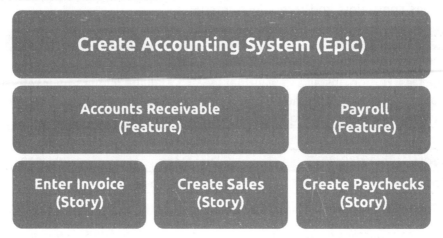

Definition of done

The definition of done is a shared understanding of what it means when work is considered finished between the customers and the project team. The team agrees on and displays a list of criteria that must be met before a product increment is considered done. Failure to meet these criteria at the end of a sprint normally implies that the work should not be counted toward that sprint's velocity.

Breaking down the work from an epic to a task will allow both the team and product owner to define what done means. Generally, this will be tested once the iteration is over, and the customer reviews it.

Validate Scope

This is the process where the project deliverables are formally inspected and accepted by the customer or sponsor. It's in this process that the customer or sponsor actually inspects the deliverable to see if it meets their requirements. If it does, then you will get the main output of the accepted deliverable. If the customer finds that it doesn't meet their requirements, then you will need to repair it (change request). This process is done at the very end of all the executing and monitoring and controlling processes.

After you have completed the executing and monitoring and controlling processes, you will have a deliverable. After the customer or sponsor has accepted the deliverables, then the project can be formally closed in the "close project or phase" process. The output of this process, the accepted deliverable, is the input to the "close project or phase" process.

This process is done immediately after "control quality," or sometimes they can be done together. "Control quality" is the process where the deliverable is inspected to see if it meets the quality requirements. Before you take a deliverable to a customer or sponsor for formal acceptance, the project manager should have inspected the deliverable to ensure it meets the quality requirements. Quality requirements ensure the deliverable is correct and need to be checked before they can be formally accepted. For example, you should ensure that the painted room has been painted correctly before calling in the sponsor to formally accept the job. The output of "control quality," a verified deliverable, is the input to this process. You will generally perform the "control quality" process, then the "validate scope" process. In some projects, both processes can be done at the same time.

Input

Project Management Plan

The project management plan consists of the scope baseline and the scope management plan. These documents will tell the project manager and the team the steps needed to get the scope validated.

Project Documents

Although the project manager can use any of the 33 project documents to get the deliverable accepted, they're most likely to use the requirements traceability matrix, requirements documentation, lessons learned register, and the quality reports.

Verified Deliverables

The verified deliverable is the output of the control quality process. A verified deliverable is a deliverable that has been inspected to ensure that quality requirements have been met.

Work Performance Data

This is the raw information of the work that was done to create the project deliverables.

Tools and Techniques

Inspection

This is the main tool of this process. The customer or sponsor will need to measure, examine, and validate that the deliverable meets his/her requirements. This can include walk-throughs, audits, or visual inspection, as in the case of inspecting a painted room.

Decision Making – Covered in Chapter 3

Outputs

Accepted Deliverables

Accepted deliverables are deliverables that have met the acceptance criteria and have been formally signed off by the customer or sponsor. Once you have the accepted deliverable, you are ready to formally close the project or phase. This output of accepted deliverable will become the input to the integration process of "close project or phase."

Change Requests

If the deliverable does not meet the acceptance criteria and cannot be accepted, you may need to spend more time and money to fix it. This will lead to a change request where the defect will need to be repaired. An example: If you painted the room with the wrong shade of green paint, you would need additional time and money to repaint it correctly.

Work Performance Information

This will give the status of the deliverables. This will state its progress, such as if it was accepted or needs to be fixed.

Project Documents Updates – Covered in Chapter 3

Control Scope

The goal of "control scope" is to ensure that the project stays on the scope as it is executed. You are basically "controlling" the scope. You will need to ensure that the work the project team is doing is actually within the scope of the project. The project manager will need to monitor the scope to ensure that unapproved changes are not added to the scope. Unapproved expansion of the scope is known as scope creep.

This is a process where you're looking at the actual work getting done in comparison to the project plan. The project manager determines if there are any changes to the scope made during the work progress. If the project manager does detect a modified scope, he/she will need to get a change request to bring the project back on plan.

Do not get this process confused with the previous process, "validate scope." Validate scope is where you get the project deliverables formally accepted. Validate scope is done at the end of the project, after the deliverable has been made. This process (control scope) will be done on a daily basis to ensure the project stays within the scope. In other words, "validate scope" will be done at the end when the deliverable is finished, whereas "control scope" is done every single day the project is being executed to ensure the project stays within the scope.

On a traditional project, it is important to control the scope to ensure there are no unauthorized changes or modifications to the scope as the work is getting done. It's not uncommon for the project manager on a traditional project to discover team members doing work that is outside of the project scope. When this happens, the project manager would either need to submit a change request to the change control Board in order to add that additional work in or tell the team members not to do it and stop that particular unauthorized change.

On agile and hybrid projects, changes are welcome and are less controlled by the scope. Any time a customer wants to add a feature or make a scope change to the project, it is welcomed and added to the product backlog, where it will be prioritized by the product owner.

> **EXAM TIP:** On a traditional project, any changes to the scope must go through the perform integrated change control process, where this change must be reviewed and authorized. On an agile or hybrid project, any changes to the features of the product would just be added to the product backlog and be prioritized by the product owner.

Input

Project Management Plan

The project management plan will include the scope baseline and the scope management plan. The plan will tell us how to control the scope as the project progresses, and the scope baseline will outline what to look for as the work is getting done. Other plans that may be needed to control the scope may include the change, configuration, and requirements management plan.

Project Documents

Although the project manager can use any of the 33 project documents to control the scope, they're most likely to use the requirements traceability matrix, requirements documentation, lessons learned register, and the quality reports.

Work Performance Data

This is a very important input to this process since this will document the actual work that is getting done. This is the raw information of the work that was done on the deliverable. This will be compared with the scope baseline in the project management plan to see if the project is within the scope.

Organizational Process Assets – Covered in Chapter 3

Tools and Techniques

Data Analysis

As the project is progressing and the project manager is monitoring the scope, he/she will need a method to analyze the data. Two methods are variance analysis and trend analysis.

- **Variance Analysis:** Variance analysis will determine if there is a variance between the planned work (project management plan) and the actual work (work performance data). The project manager will need to ensure that there is no variance on the project that is related to scope. If there is a variance between planned and actual work, the project manager might need a change request to fix the project scope.

- **Trend analysis:** Trend analysis will be used to determine if a trend is emerging as the project progresses. For example, is the project regularly staying within the scope, or is it frequently going beyond the scope. The project manager will need to analyze the trend in order to assess what is happening in terms of scope.

Outputs

Work Performance Information

Work performance information will state the difference between the planned work of scope and the actual work on the project. This is the status of the scope of the project. Basically, it will state if the project is on scope or not.

Change Requests

If the project is off the scope, the project manager may need to get a change request. The change request can include the corrective or preventive actions needed to bring the project back on scope.

Project Management Plan Updates – Covered in Chapter 3

Project Documents Updates – Covered in Chapter 3

Organizational Process Assets Updates – Covered in Chapter3

EXAM TIP: All of the monitoring and controlling processes (starting with "validate scope") on the process table have the project management plan and work performance data as inputs. They then have an output of work performance information and change requests.

Think about it: how do you control a project? You need to look at the planned work (project management plan) and the actual work (work performance data), then compare them to see if they match up, which would create the work performance information.

The output of all these processes will be the work performance information (status of the work) and change requests. Change requests are needed in case there's something wrong with that section of the project. These would address it by implementing corrective or preventive actions, if necessary, to bring the project back on track.

Project Scope Management Questions

1. You have been assigned as the project manager for a web-based application project to automate the sales and marketing processes for one of your clients. You have decided to utilize a group creativity technique to identify the project and product requirements during the Collect Requirements process. All of the following are valid group creativity techniques EXCEPT:

   A. Nominal group technique

   B. The Delphi technique

   C. Affinity diagram

   D. Tornado diagram

2. The project scope statement that describes project deliverables and the work required to create them in detail, enables the project team to perform more detailed planning, guides the project team's work during execution, and provides the baseline for evaluating changes, includes all of the following EXCEPT:

   A. Detailed Work Breakdown Structure(WBS)

   B. Project constraints

   C. Project deliverables

   D. Product acceptance criteria

3. Which one of the following refers to unapproved and undocumented changes, and what occurs when changes to the scope are not detected early enough or are not managed?

   A. Scope baseline

   B. Residual risks

   C. Scope creep

   D. Variances

4. You are the project manager for a cashier system project to produce cashier applications and software for the retail industry. You have recently discovered that one of your key competitors is also working on a similar project, but their new applications will include a computer-aided program and a web-based interface that your project does not offer. You have implemented a change request to update your project in order to include these exciting missing features. This is an example of which of the following?

   A. A change due to an error and omission in the business case

   B. A change due to a legal requirement and constraint

   C. A change due to an error or omission in the planning phase

   D. A change due to an external event

5. While trying to obtain the formal acceptance of the completed project scope and associated deliverables, with whom should the project manager validate the product?

   A. The sponsor, key stakeholders, and customers

   B. The project team

   C. The quality control team members

   D. The change control board members

6. Determining if the project scope has been completed by describing project deliverables and the work required to create them in detail, enabling the project team to perform more detailed planning, guiding the project team's work during execution, providing the baseline for evaluating changes, and other factors, relies mostly upon the use of:

    A. Statement of work

    B. Project plan

    C. Project charter

    D. Project scope statement

7. You are working as a project manager for an Enterprise Resource Planning (ERP) application to automate the accounting and financial processes for one of your key customers. Due to a mismatch with the customer's requirement, you have been forced to redesign one of the major components. This is a significant setback since a substantial amount of code that has already been developed will have to be recoded to match

the updated design. This rework has caused huge expenses, and you noticed a sign of extremely low morale among team members. Which of the following is TRUE in this situation?

    A. The team discovered this issue as a result of the Identify Risks process.

    B. The team did a poor job while creating the WBS.

    C. This problem was a result of poor collect requirements.

    D. The team carried on a rigorous Control Quality process and discovered the issue.

8. While overseeing a construction project, you discovered that one of the team members, on her own initiative, added extra windows to increase air circulation and light in the basement. The original plan did not include the cost of these extra windows, but the team member thought they were absolutely required due to poor air circulation and low light in the basement. This is an example of which of the following?

    A. Value-added change

    B. Self-motivated team member

    C. Team member exceeding expectations

    D. Inefficient change control

9. After a major milestone release, some of the key stakeholders are not happy and complain that their requirements are not met. The project manager should have involved them in which of the following processes to ensure their approval for the release?

    A. Project Management Plan Development

    B. Identifying Constraints

    C. Validate Scope

    D. Schedule Management

10. Which one of the following mostly includes the product acceptance criteria that outline requirements a project must meet before stakeholders accept the final product or service?

    A. Quality management plan

    B. Project scope statement

    C. Scope management plan

    D. Requirements management plan

11. ITPro Consultancy, LLC has been offering cable TV, Internet, and phone services to its East Coast customers for almost five years now. Recently, they have initiated a project to introduce their service to the West Coast and have assigned a project manager. The project manager left the company, and you took over the project, as per the instruction of the CEO, when the project was almost ready to enter execution. While reviewing the existing documents, you discovered that the team had done a great job in developing the requirements document and the project scope statement, but there was no WBS. What should you do FIRST in this situation?

    A. Immediately inform management and provide them with relevant oversight.

    B. Politely request to be excused from the project.

    C. You should not enter execution until the WBS is created for the project.

    D. You should refer to the WBS dictionary for the required detail needed to continue to execution.

12. While discussing the scope of your project with the stakeholders and team members, you realized that all of the following statements are TRUE about scope EXCEPT:

    A. Product scope describes the features and functions that characterize a product, service, or result.

    B. Project scope management includes the processes concerned with "all the work" and "only the work" required to successfully deliver to the stakeholders' expectations, manage changes, minimize surprises, and gain acceptance of the product in order to complete the project.

    C. Project scope describes the work needed to deliver a product, service, or result with the specified features and functions.

    D. The project team should go above and beyond the defined scope and impress the customers by implementing extra features that will be beneficial for them.

13. Which one of the following is NOT true about the Define Scope process?

    A. It is the process of developing a comprehensive, detailed description of the project and product.

    B. Expert judgment is used as a tool & technique in this process.

    C. The requirements document is the key output in this process.

    D. A detailed project scope statement that is created in this process is critical to project success and builds upon the additional analysis of requirements, major deliverables, assumptions, constraints, and other factors that are documented earlier in the project.

14. You have been assigned as the project manager for a web-based application project to automate the recruiting process for one of your clients. You have decided to utilize a group decision-making technique to generate, classify, prioritize, and drive decisions forward. All of the following are valid group decision-making techniques EXCEPT:

    A. The decision is based on the most influential block in a group, even if a majority is not achieved.

    B. The decision is based on a single course of action decided by everyone in the group.

    C. The decision is based on the support from more than 50 percent of the members of the group.

    D. The decision is made for the group by one individual, mostly the project manager.

15. Product scope describes the features, functions, and physical characteristics that characterize a product, service, or result. Completion of the product scope is measured against which one of the following?

    A. Scope statement

    B. Project requirements

    C. Project objectives

    D. Product requirements

16. As per the project manager's instruction, the team has decomposed project deliverables and project work into smaller, more manageable components to develop a WBS and WBS dictionary. The team finalized the WBS by establishing control or cost accounts and unique identifiers for the lower-level components of the WBS called work packages. Normally presented in chart form, this WBS provides a structure for hierarchical summation of:

    A. Cost and schedule information

    B. Cost and requirements information

    C. Cost, resource, and schedule information

    D. Schedule and requirements information

17. A project manager managing a data center project had the opportunity to attend several meetings about the project prior to the creation of the project charter. In one of the meetings, the sponsor specifically denied funding for two very specific items. Two months into the project, a couple of stakeholders requested the project manager add work for one of the items that were strongly denied by the sponsor. What will be the best thing the project manager can do in this situation?

    A. Add the work if it does not have much impact on the schedule.

    B. Inform the stakeholders that the work cannot be added.

    C. Evaluate the impact of adding the work on time, cost, quality, risk, human resource, and other elements.

    D. Immediately inform the sponsor about the request that was denied by him.

18. Verified deliverables are inputs in which of the following scope management processes?

    A. Define Scope

    B. Create WBS

    C. Validate Scope

    D. Control Scope

19. All of the following are true regarding the Control Scope process EXCEPT:

    A. It assures that the underlying causes of all requested changes and recommended corrective actions are understood and processed through the Integrated Change Control process.

    B. One of the key focuses in the process may be dispute resolution related to project scope.

    C. It monitors the status of the project and product scope, maintains control over the project by preventing overwhelming scope change requests, and manages changes to the scope baseline.

    D. It verifies the correctness of work results.

20. Your project is approaching completion, and you were able to release some of the team members from the team to be assigned to other projects. Your team has successfully resolved all the issues in the issue log except for one, which will be fixed in the next version of the application as per the agreement with the client. You are ahead of schedule, but $3,500 over budget due to an unexpected price increase for one of the major pieces of equipment. Your team also successfully performed quality control inspections and met quality requirements for all of the items except one. You called a meeting and requested the client for product verification, and surprisingly the client mentioned that they wanted to make a major change to the scope. In this situation, the project manager should:

    A. Immediately inform management about this surprising new change

    B. Have an urgent meeting with the team members to explore the feasibility of making the change

    C. Inform the client that it is too late now to make a major change

    D. Ask the client for a description of the change

21. Your company, ITPro Consultancy, has assigned you as the project manager to upgrade the call center in your organization. The number of calls the customer support agents have to answer each month has increased drastically in the last five months, and the phone system is approaching the maximum load limit. Your team has worked on the requirements document and the project scope statement, and you are now ready to create the WBS with the help of your team members. All of the following are true regarding the WBS EXCEPT:

    A. The WBS represents all the work required to be completed in the project.

    B. Each level of the WBS represents a verifiable product or results.

    C. Activities in the WBS should be arranged in the proper sequence they will be performed.

    D. The WBS should be decomposed to a level called the work package level, where cost and schedule can easily be calculated.

22. The sponsor has recently assigned you as a project manager to design and develop a custom video conferencing tool. As per the sponsor, the project must be completed in four months and should integrate with the existing infrastructure and applications in the organization. This is an example of which of the following?

    A. Constraints

    B. Assumptions

    C. Expert judgment

    D. High-level planning

23. All of the following are TRUE about the Validate Scope process EXCEPT:

    A. Customer acceptance of the project deliverables is a key output of this process.

    B. It is an input to the Develop Project Management Plan process and an output of the Control Quality process.

    C. It should be performed at the end of each phase of the project.

    D. This process is closely related to the Control Quality process.

24. A large international organization is currently developing a new accounting software that will be used by the entire accounting department. They have decided to use a hybrid approach where the beginning of the project, such as gathering the requirements and building the software, will be done using agile in a traditional method to deploy the software. Halfway through the software development, three customers have requested major scope changes to the project. How should the agile project manager proceed with the scope changes?

    A. Have the customers fill out a change request form and submitted to the change control board.

    B. Assess the changes and determine their impact.

    C. Facilitate a meeting with the product owner to alert him of the new features.

    D. Inform them changes cannot be done during the middle of a project.

25. A project manager is in the Control Scope process of monitoring the status of the project and product scope, maintaining control over the project by preventing overwhelming scope change requests and managing changes to the scope baseline. Which one of the following is NOT true about this process?

    A. The Control Scope process must be integrated with other control processes.

    B. It should be performed prior to scope planning.

    C. Variance analysis is used as a tool & technique in this process.

    D. Work performance information and change requests are the key outputs in this process.

26. Your project to build a new substation to supply power to a newly developed industrial park is not going too well. You are overwhelmed with numerous issues in the project and got really frustrated when the city conducted an inspection and reported a building code violation. You were asked by management to ensure full compliance with the mandatory city and construction industry standards. At this time, you are also approaching the final deadline of the project in two weeks. You have identified a couple of changes that will drastically enhance performance and make your clients very happy. While trying to sort out all these messes, you received a call from the senior engineer informing you that he would be leaving the company soon. Which is the MOST critical issue you should address first?

    A. Notify the customers about the possible delay in the project.

    B. Initiate the change control process to implement new changes.

    C. Find a replacement for the senior engineer.

    D. Ensure compliance with the city and construction industry standards.

27. Sarah, a project manager, is in the Define Scope process of developing a comprehensive, detailed description of the project and product. Which of the following is NOT a tool & technique used in this Define Scope process?

    A. Product Analysis

    B. Expert Judgment

    C. Data Analysis

    D. Data Representation

28. You have been selected as the project manager for a major data center upgrade at your company headquarters. The sponsor has handed you a project charter and wished you the best of luck. What should you do next as the first step?

    A. Instruct the team to work on a project scope statement.

    B. Instruct the team to work on the WBS.

    C. Review the charter and make sure that all key stakeholders have inputs into the scope.

    D. Start working on planning the project.

29. Walkthroughs, reviews, product reviews, and audits are examples of which one of the following methods of examining work or a product to determine whether it conforms to documented standards or not?

    A. Observation

    B. Verification

    C. Inspection

    D. Group decision-making techniques

30. A project manager is in the Collect Requirements process of collecting and documenting quantifiable needs and expectations of the sponsor, customer, and other stakeholders. Which of the following is NOT true regarding this process?

    A. It describes project deliverables and the work required to create them in detail, as well as deliverables description, product acceptance criteria, requirements assumptions and constraints, and exclusions from requirements.

    B. Requirements documentation and requirements traceability matrix are the key outputs in this process.

    C. Interpersonal and team skills and data representations are used as tools & techniques in this process.

    D. The scope management plan and requirements management plan are inputs in this process.

31. The team members are analyzing the objectives and description of the product stated by the customer or sponsor and turning them into tangible deliverables, and finally creating the project scope statement. Which of the following BEST describes what the team members are doing?

    A. Performing the product analysis

    B. Performing the plan quality management

    C. Conducting a multi-criteria decision analysis

    D. Determining the product description

Project Scope Management Answers

1. **D:** A Tornado diagram is not a component of the Group Creativity techniques. It is mostly used during the Perform Quantitative Risk Analysis process to display the sensitivity analysis data in order to determine which risks have the most potential impact on a project. This diagram can be used to determine sensitivity in cost, time, and quality objectives and will be helpful to determine a detailed response plan for the elements with greater impacts.

2. **A:** The detailed Work Breakdown Structure (WBS) is developed after the project scope statement has been defined and accepted. The scope baseline consists of the project scope statement, WBS, and WBS dictionary.

3. **C:** Scope creep refers to the unapproved and undocumented changes, and it occurs when changes to the scope are not detected early enough or managed. All these minor changes slowly add up and may have a drastic impact on budget, schedule, and quality.

4. **D:** This is a change due to an external event, mainly to remain competitive. The features that the competitors are offering were not included in the scope of the project; thus, they were never discussed during the initiation or planning phases. Due to the risk of losing a potential market, the project manager decided to include them in the project. Also, there was no legal requirement or constraint to include the missing features in this case.

5. A: The project manager should get approval from the sponsor, key stakeholders, and the customers.

6. **D:** The statement of work generally precedes a contract and provides a narrative description of work to be completed. The project plan is derived from the project scope statement. Once a project is selected, or a contract is signed to perform a project, a project charter is created to formally authorize a project or a phase, but is not a detailed plan. The scope statement answers the questions of what, why, who, where, and how and, in combination with the work break down structure, provides a detailed description of what must be accomplished.

7. **C:** This problem was a direct result of scope misunderstanding due to poor collect requirements. Obviously, the team did not utilize all the tools & techniques to collect requirements from the customers and also did not spend quality time defining and developing a detailed description of the project and product.

8. **D:** This is an example of inefficient change control as the team should be focused on "all the work" and "only the work" needed to complete the project, not extra. The key objective should be to complete the project with the agreed-upon deliverables on time, within quality requirements, and within budget. This kind of "gold plating" increases risk and uncertainties and introduces problems into the project, and should be monitored and controlled by the project manager.

9. **C:** Validate Scope is the process of formal acceptance of completed project scope and deliverables by stakeholders through a signature on paper or via an e-mail that specifically states project approval. Prior scope validation would have avoided the dissatisfaction of stakeholders after the milestone release.

10. **B:** The project scope statement documents the characteristics and boundaries of the project and its associated products, results, and services in addition to the acceptance criteria.

11. **C:** You should inform management and provide relevant oversight, but doing so will not resolve the issue immediately. You can refuse to manage a project in a case where there is a conflict of interest or ethical concern, but not in this kind of situation. A WBS dictionary is the detail of the work packages, so a WBS should be created first. You should always have a WBS since it is the foundational block to the initiating, planning, executing, monitoring & controlling, and closing phases. Creating the WBS should not be a lengthy process that will require a long time; thus, you should take the time to create it prior to entering the execution.

12. **D:** The project team should be concerned with "all the work" and "only the work" required to successfully complete the project, and try to avoid extra work or gold plating in every way possible.

13. **C:** The requirements document is the output in the Collect Requirements process, not the Define Scope process.

14. **A:** The decision may be based on the largest block, not the most influential block in a group, even if a majority is not achieved.

15. **D:** Completion of the product scope is measured against the product requirements to determine successful fulfillment. The project requirements, project objectives, and the project scope statement are associated with the project scope.

16. **C:** A Work Breakdown Structure (WBS) is the foundational block to the initiating, planning, executing, monitoring & controlling, and closing phases. Normally presented in chart form, it is a deliverable-oriented hierarchical decomposition of the work to be executed by the project team to accomplish the project objectives and create the required deliverables. It provides a structure for the hierarchal summation of cost, schedule, and resource information.

17. **B:** The most appropriate thing to do in this kind of situation is to find out the root cause of the problem, but the option is not presented here. Based on the information provided, there is no reason to find out the details and try to convince the sponsor to add the work (C & D). The project manager should inform the sponsor, but the best course of action will be to inform the stakeholders that the work could not be added. There is no need to do any evaluations because this kind of change has already been denied.

    Even though there is no impact on the schedule, there may be an impact on other areas. A project manager should not implement a change request without performing an impact analysis and must get approval for the change from the change control board.

18. **C:** Verified deliverables are the deliverables that have been completed as per the documented scope and checked for defects by the project team members in the Control Quality process. These deliverables are inputs in the Validate Scope process and are given to the customers and stakeholders for their acceptance.

19. **D:** Verifying the correctness of work is associated with the Control Quality process.

20. **D:** Note that in this kind of situation, you should always try to gather as much information as possible if the time allows. You should not simply say no without knowing the details of the change and its possible impact on the project (C). The client only mentioned that they wanted a change, but did not provide you with any description of it. You may inform management (A) and also have a meeting with the team if their inputs are needed (B), but not before understanding what the change is all about.

21. **C:** Note that we do not usually include the activities in the WBS, especially for large projects, even though we decompose the WBS work packages to get our activities during the Define Activities process in schedule management. Once the activities are defined, sequencing is done in the Sequence Activities process. Note that WBS has no particular sequence to it.

22. **A:** Constraints specify the limitations and restrictions, such as constraints on time, budget, scope, quality, schedule, resources, and technology that a project faces. By specifying a time limit and technology compliance, the sponsor is limiting the options for the project.

23. **B:** The output of the Validate Scope process is customer acceptance of the project deliverables. This process is performed during the monitoring & controlling process group. To get the approval of the phase deliverables, it is done at the end of each project phase in addition to other points to get approval for the interim deliverables. Both the Control Quality and Validate Scope processes can be performed simultaneously, but Control Quality is usually performed prior to Validate Scope. Control Quality verifies the correctness of the work, whereas Validate Scope confirms completeness. Control Quality is focused on measuring specific project results against quality specifications and standards, whereas Validate Scope is mainly focused on obtaining acceptance of the product from the sponsor, customers, and other stakeholders. It is not an input to the Develop Project Management Plan or an output of the Control Quality process.

24. **C:** On an agile project, any additional features that need to be added to the project are generally added to the product backlog by the product owner and are prioritized by the product owner. The best course of action here would've been for the project manager to facilitate that meeting with the product owner to alert him about the new features. All other choices are applied more towards a traditional project and not an agile project.

25. **B:** Scope planning should be performed prior to the Control Scope process. A change in one control process impacts the others; thus, the Control Scope process is integrated with other control processes.

26. **D:** A project manager is responsible for prioritizing the most critical issue to concentrate on. The situation here does not really specify whether the senior engineer is playing a vital role in the project or not. "Gold Plating," or giving customers extra, is not actually required in the project. The project manager should evaluate the current situation and then determine if the project will require additional time or not to complete. The most critical item for the project manager is to ensure full compliance with the city and construction industry standards.

27. **D:** Data representation is not in the Define Scope process.

28. **C:** You should review the project charter and make sure that you have inputs from all key stakeholders in order to avoid confusion and unnecessary change requests in the future. You should then concentrate on creating the project scope statement, the WBS, and the project plan.

29. **C:** Inspection includes activities such as measuring, examining, and verifying to determine whether work and deliverables meet requirements and product acceptance criteria. Inspections are sometimes called walkthroughs, reviews, product reviews, and audits.

30. **A:** Option A describes the scope statement, not the requirements documentation. The project scope statement describes project deliverables and the work required to create them in detail, as well as the deliverables description, product acceptance criteria, requirements assumptions and constraints, and exclusions from requirements.

31.   **A:** The team members are gaining a better understanding of the product of the project to create the project scope statement by performing the product analysis. The team must have a product description before they can perform product analysis. The level of quality desired is analyzed in the plan quality management, not in product analysis. The multi-criteria decision analysis is a technique to evaluate and rank ideas. This technique uses a decision matrix based on factors such as uncertainty, expected risk levels, cost and benefit estimates, and time estimates to quantify requirements.

Chapter 7

Project Schedule Management

Schedule management includes the processes required to manage the timely completion of the project. This knowledge area is about creating the schedule baseline, project schedule, and ensuring the project stays on schedule. This section is one of the largest knowledge areas with 6 processes. We will review all 6 processes and go over the critical path method at the end of the section.

Creating a project schedule can be a very hard and long task. Having to document all the activities needed to create a schedule can take not just time, but lots of critical thinking by the project manager and team. Most projects will have automated software that can be used to help generate the schedule quickly and easily. Creating network diagrams and

Gantt charts without the help of software could become very difficult. On this exam, you will not have software to help you calculate the critical path or find float on an activity. As a PMP exam candidate, you will need to know how to do the calculations manually.

If you are working on an agile project, the schedule will be shorter than most traditional projects. Agile creates the deliverables in increments, with iteration durations between one to four weeks. This would mean that the project team would constantly be doing these processes throughout the entire life cycle of the project for each iteration.

In this knowledge area, we will be creating the schedule management plan, developing the schedule, and controlling the project to ensure we stay on schedule. Here are the 6 processes, their process groups, and main outputs.

Process	Process Group	Main Output
Plan Schedule Management	Planning	Schedule Management Plan
Define Activities	Planning	Activity List, Activity Attributes, Milestone List
Sequence Activities	Planning	Project Schedule Network Diagram
Estimate Activity Durations	Planning	Activity Duration Estimates
Develop Schedule	Planning	Schedule Baseline, Project Schedule, Schedule Data, Project Calendars
Control Schedule	Monitoring and Controlling	Work Performance Information, Change Request

The processes listed above are from the PMBOK Guide and are mostly used on traditional projects. Although they could be used on certain types of hybrid projects if the hybrid project utilizes more traditional methods than it does agile methods. On a pure agile project, scheduling is done differently than you would on a traditional project. For this reason, we will be covering agile scheduling as the last process in the section.

Plan Schedule Management

This is the process where you will document how to do the next 5 schedule processes. The output of the schedule management plan is very important, as it will describe the steps of how to accomplish the other 5 processes.

Inputs

Project Management Plan – Covered in Chapter 3

Project Charter – Covered in Chapter 4

Enterprise Environmental Factors – Covered in Chapter 3

Organizational Process Assets – Covered in Chapter 3

Tools & Techniques

Expert Judgment – Covered in Chapter 3

Data Analysis – Covered in Chapter 3

Meetings – Covered in Chapter 3

Outputs

Schedule Management Plan

The schedule management plan will document the steps needed to conduct the other 5 processes in time management: how the project defines the activities, sequences the activities, estimates the resources, develops the schedule, and controls the schedule to ensure the project stays on schedule. You will document all the steps and procedures in your schedule management plan. The plan will also state how to measure the schedule, and how to fix it if there are variances from the schedule baseline. This plan is part of the project management plan.

Define Activities

This is the process of taking the work packages on the WBS and breaking them down (decomposition) into activities. Activities are the specific work that will need to get done by the project team to create the project deliverables. Activities are more detailed than work packages. Each work package usually contains many activities.

Once you have decomposed the work packages into activities, you will then store them in the activities list (main output). The activities list will then be used to estimate the duration and cost of the project.

Inputs

Project Management Plan

The project management plan will contain the schedule management plan, which will list the steps to define the activities. It will say how to decompose each work package into activities. It will also contain the scope baseline, which is made up of the project scope statement, WBS, and WBS dictionary. This is a very important input. The WBS has the work packages that need to be decomposed. The WBS dictionary and scope statement may have additional details needed to do the decomposition, such as constraints or assumptions.

Enterprise Environmental Factors – Covered in Chapter 3

Organizational Process Assets – Covered in Chapter 3

Tools & Techniques

Decomposition

Decomposition means breaking down work; that is, taking the work packages in the WBS and breaking them down into specific activities. Activities represent the work efforts needed to accomplish the work packages.

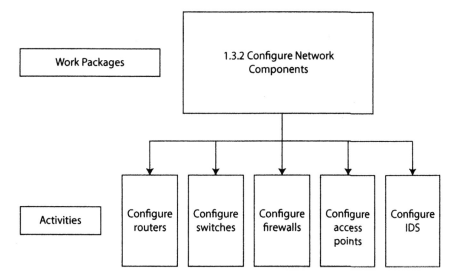

Rolling Wave Planning

Rolling wave planning is a form of progressive elaboration. This means work packages happening soon can be decomposed now. Work packages happening later in the project will be decomposed at a later date when more details of the work are known.

Expert Judgment

Expert judgment is when one uses subject matter experts (SME) to help decompose the work packages. SME can be team members, consultants, or anyone with expert knowledge of the work.

Outputs

Activity List

The activity list is a list of all the scheduled activities on the project. This is a detailed list of the work needed to complete each work package. Each activity should map back to only one work package, since each work package has many activities. Activities should also include an identifier, which is a number that uniquely identifies each activity.

Activity Attributes

Activity attributes are more detailed information about each individual activity. This can include the resources needed to complete the activity, location of the activity, cost, assumptions, constraints, leads and lags, and relationships to other activities.

Milestone List

A milestone list consists of all the project or phase milestones. A milestone is an activity that has no duration and is used to represent a major accomplishment or event. An example

of a milestone would be getting a permit or finishing a major work package or phase of a project.

Change Request

Not all work packages may be decomposed into activities before the project plan is approved. If the work packages are decomposed later in the project, it may result in additional work, time, and cost to get done. This might result in a change request.

Project Management Plan Updates – Covered in Chapter 3

Sequence Activities

Sequence activity is a process where you take the list of activities and put them in the order that you will perform them. The main output of this process is the project schedule network diagram, which is a diagram that shows the order in which you will do each individual activity.

This process will also show the relationships between each activity. Activities will have relationships and dependencies between them. One process may need to be done after you have the activity list and activity attributes from the previous process ("define activities").

Inputs

Project Management Plan

The project management plan will contain the schedule management plan, which will list the steps to sequencing the activities. It will also include the scope baseline, which is made up of the project scope statement, WBS, and WBS dictionary.

Project Documents

Of the 33 project documents, the ones you are most likely to use in this process will include:

- Activity list: The activity list has to be an input because it has the activities that need to be sequenced.

- Activity attributes: This provides more information about each individual activity that may affect the order in which the activities are done.

- Milestone list: This is a list of all the milestones on a project. It is added to the sequence of activities. The milestone of getting a permit can affect how the work of building a house is done.

- Assumption log: This will keep track of any assumptions that are made during the project. Assumptions and constraints could affect how the schedule is built and may impact the lead and lag between activities.

Enterprise Environmental Factors – Covered in Chapter 3

Organizational Process Assets – Covered in Chapter 3

Tools & Techniques

Precedence Diagramming Method (PDM)

PDM is a technique that is used to build a sequence using the activities. This technique is what is used to create the network diagram. One method of doing PDM is to use an activity-on-node (AON) precedence diagram. In this method, the boxes are the activities, and the numbers above them represent the durations. The following diagram shows the sequence of the activities.

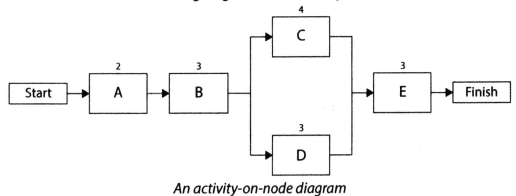

An activity-on-node diagram

Activities are related to each other using four different relationships. Activities are either predecessors or successors. A predecessor comes before the successor. Here are the four different relationships:

- **Finish-to-Start (FS):** This is the most frequently used relationship between the four. First, you finish activity A, then you can start Activity B. Activity A is the predecessor, and Activity B is the successor. You have to install the memory, then the operating system on a computer

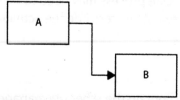

Finish-to-Start (FS) Relationship

- **Finish-to-Finish (FF):** This is when activities need to finish simultaneously but not necessarily start at the same time. Activity A and B must be done simultaneously but may not start at the same time.

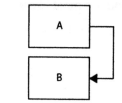

Finish-to-Finish (FF) Relationship

- **Start-to-Start (SS):** This is when Activity A must start before Activity B can start. The starting of B depends on the starting of A.

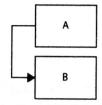

Start-to-Start (SS) Relationship

- **Start-to-Finish (SF):** This is when Activity B cannot finish until Activity A has started. This is rarely used in project management.

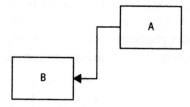

Start-to-Finish (SF) Relationship

Dependency Determination

To determine the dependency of activities, you will need to know what the activities are and in what sequence they may get done. Here are the four dependencies:

- **Mandatory Dependencies:** Also known as hard logic or hard dependency. This means you have to finish one activity to start the next activity. For example, you must finish installing memory in a computer before you install the operating system. Without memory, the operating system cannot be installed.

- **Discretionary Dependencies:** Also known as soft logic, this is when activities do not need to get done in a specific order. For example, you do not need to install the operating system updates to install the office software.

- **External Dependencies:** These are when activities are dependent on activities outside the control of the project team. For example, one may have to wait on a permit to start construction.

- **Internal Dependencies:** These are when activities are dependent on activities within the control of the project team. For example, you might test a computer after installing all the software. The project team controls how to install the software and how fast it gets done.

Leads and Lags

Leads and lags are used to show an overlap or delay in a schedule. A lead is an overlap between activities. For example, in painting a room, you can start taping up the fixtures after half of the furniture has been removed. This would be a 50% lead time. In other words, Activity B will start when Activity A is 50% done.

Lags are delays between activities. For example, when you finish painting a room, you give it a lag of 1 day before putting the furniture back so that the paint can dry. This would be a 1-day lag between Activities A and B.

Project Management Information System – Covered in Chapter 3

Outputs

Project Schedule Network Diagrams

The diagram directly below will show all the activities, and the order in which they are performed. The AON diagram explained above is what will be covered on the exam. We will cover more of these diagrams and the critical path method at the end of this chapter.

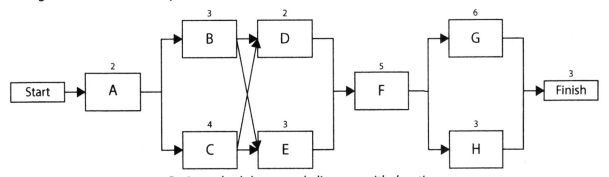

Project schedule network diagram with durations

Project Documents Updates – Covered in Chapter 3

Estimate Activity Durations

In this process, you will analyze each activity to determine how long each will take to accomplish. Activities are assigned some kind of duration measurements such as hours, days, weeks, or years. The activity duration estimates will then be used to create the overall project schedule in our next process, "develop schedule."

Many things can affect a project schedule, including risk, resources needed and their availability, and the scope of work. These are all listed as inputs to this process. The tools will be very important for the PMP exam, as we will cover three formulas you will need to know for your exam.

Inputs

Project Management Plan

The project management plan will contain the schedule management plan, which will list the steps to estimate the activity durations. It will also contain the scope baseline, which is made up of the project scope statement, WBS, and WBS dictionary.

Project Documents – Covered in Chapter 3

Of the 33 project documents, the ones you are most likely to use in this process include:

- **Activity list:** This is the list of all the activities on the project. This list will be needed to estimate the duration of each activity.

- **Activity attributes:** Activity attributes provide more information about each activity. This can include information that could affect the duration, such as location, leads, lags, and cost.

- **Assumption log:** This will keep track of any assumptions that are made during the project. Assumptions and constraints could affect how the schedule is built and may impact the lead and lag between activities.

- **Milestone list:** This is added to the sequence of activities. The milestone of getting a permit can affect how the work of building a house is done.

- **Resource calendars:** Resource calendars show the availability of resources. Resources significantly affect the duration of each activity. If resources are not available, this will negatively affect the duration.

- **Risk register:** The risk register will list all the identified project risks, as well as their impact and response. Risk response can lead to adding reserve time to activities.

- **Resource break down structure:** The resource break down structure is the hierarchical breakdown of resources by their categories and types.

- **Lessons learned register:** This is a listing of all of the lessons learned so far on the project. Previous lessons learned on the project can help to increase the accuracy of the duration estimates.

- **Project team assignment:** This is the listing of the project team that will be assigned to complete the work. The project manager will need to know who is doing the work, which will affect the duration of the activity.

- **Resource requirements:** The resources needed to complete each activity will affect the duration of each activity. Equipment and HR resources can have a significant effect on the activity. For example, hiring a professional painter with a paint gun will ensure painting a room goes much faster than if a novice paints it with just a paintbrush.

Enterprise Environmental Factors – Covered in Chapter 3

Organizational Process Assets – Covered in Chapter 3

Tools & Techniques

Expert Judgment

Expert judgment is most favorably used in this process. It is getting subject matter experts to help estimate the duration of each activity. It might be difficult for you to estimate how long it will take to paint a 400 Sq. Ft. room; it is better to get a painter. He/she can give a better estimate than you can if you have never painted a room.

Analogous Estimating

Analogous estimation is also known as top-down estimation. Analogous estimation relies on historical information to assign the current duration to the activities. It is based on a limited amount of information. Analogous estimation is quick to do; however, it is considered less accurate than other estimation types. Because all projects are unique, this approach can lead to less precise estimates.

Parametric Estimating

Parametric estimating uses a mathematical algorithm to calculate cost or duration. The calculation is based on historical data and variables. For example, if it takes one hour to write one line of code, it would take 1,000 hours to write 1,000 lines of code. Another example: if it takes three days to remodel a room, it will then take 12 days to remodel four rooms. This type of estimation can be very accurate if the assumptions are correct. If one hour for one line of code is accurate, then the estimate will be correct.

Three-Point Estimating

Three-point estimation is also known as PERT (program evaluation and review technique). PERT uses 3 different values to calculate the duration or cost of an activity. The 3 values are:

- **Optimistic:** This would be the best case for the activity or the least amount of time needed to complete the activity. It is the smallest of the 3 values.

- **Most likely (realistic):** This would be the most likely or realistic case for the activity to be completed. It is usually a value between the optimistic and pessimistic.

- **Pessimistic:** This is the worst case for the activity. This is the longest time it would take to complete the activity. It is the biggest of the 3 numbers.

PERT has 3 basic formulas you will need to understand and memorize for the exam: beta distribution, triangular distribution, and standard deviation. Let's look at each formula in detail:

Beta Distribution: This is the normal PERT formula. It places more weight on the realistic estimate:

$$\frac{(\text{Optimistic} + 4 * \text{Realistic} + \text{Pessimistic})}{6}$$

If a team member tells you the earliest he can finish installing the server is 2 days, most likely 4 days, and at the worst case 6 days, how long would you estimate the server's installation to take?

Use PERT as follows: **(2 + 4 * 4 + 6)/6 = 4 days.** Don't forget order of operations; do the multiplication first.

Standard Deviation: This formula is used to give a range of an estimate.

$$(Pessimistic - Optimistic)/6$$

In our example, the range would be **(6 - 2)/6 = 2/3**. The range would be 2/3 of a day on the project.

Triangular Distribution: This is the average of the 3 numbers.

$$\underline{(Optimistic + Realistic + Pessimistic)\ 3}$$

Using triangle distribution as follows: **(2 + 4 + 6)/3 = 4 days**.

Here is a table of some values to practice finding the beta, standard deviation, and triangle distribution:

Activity	Optimistic	Realistic (Most likely)	Pessimistic	PERT (Beta)	SD	Triangular
A	5	10	20	10.83	2.5	11.67
B	20	30	50	31.67	5	33.33
D	50	55	80	58.33	5	61.67
E	30	50	150	63.33	20	76.67

EXAM TIP: *If the exam asks to calculate PERT and doesn't specify what formula to use, always use the beta. Only use standard deviation when asking for range or variance.*

Bottom-Up Estimating

Bottom-up estimation is known as one of the most accurate methods to estimate cost or time. The work has to be very detailed for this type of estimation to take place. Bottom-up estimating takes a very long time to complete, but will be very accurate. It is done by breaking down the work to the lowest levels and then aggregating the work back up to find an overall duration. For example, when painting a room, you can estimate how long it would take to paint the entire room, or you could use bottom-up estimating, in which case you would estimate how long it will take to paint each wall and aggregate the four walls to find the total duration. As you can see, bottom-up estimating requires more work and time to complete.

Data Analysis

You will be acquiring a lot of data in this process related to the duration of the activities. This tool will allow you to analyze that data to estimate the duration of each activity correctly. In particular, there is one technique that you should be using:

- **Reserve analysis:** This is adding extra time to an activity because of risk. Reserves are just extra time added in case a risk arises. For example, when coding complex functions, you might want to add extra time in case a function doesn't work initially and needs more testing.

Decision Making – Covered in Chapter3

Meetings – Covered in Chapter 3

Outputs

Duration Estimates

The main output will be the duration estimates for each individual activity. This is done as a numerical estimation, such as how many hours, days, or weeks are required. It is also a good idea to include ranges in the estimate, if known, such as ± 3 days, when assigning durations to activities.

Basis of Estimates

The basis of the estimates is how the estimates were developed and their ranges. It can also include all assumptions and constraints made to create the estimate. For example, if an assumption was made that the project doesn't need to upgrade the network wiring for the phone system installation project, this will need to be listed.

Project Documents Updates – Covered in Chapter 3

Develop Schedule

This is the process of creating the schedule baseline and the project schedule. By reviewing all that you have done in the previous schedule processes of defining the activities, sequencing, and assigning their durations, you will be able to create the overall project schedule.

Keep in mind that this is an iterative process and will be done throughout the planning process. Many aspects of the project can affect the schedule, such as cost, quality, scope, resources, risk, and agreements. Expect as the project manager to keep coming back to this process and updating the schedule as you complete the other planning processes.

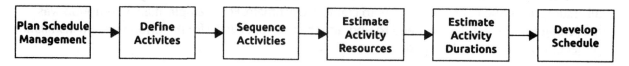

Inputs

Project Management Plan

The project management plan will contain the schedule management plan, which will list the steps to developing the schedule. It will also contain the scope baseline, which is made up of the project scope statement, WBS, and WBS dictionary.

Project Documents – Covered in Chapter 3
Of the 33 project documents, the ones you are most likely to use in this process include:

- **Activity list:** This is the list of all the activities on the project. This list will be needed to estimate the duration of each activity.

- **Activity attributes:** Activity attributes provide more information about each activity. This can include information that could affect the duration, such as location, leads, lags, and cost.

- **Assumption log:** This will keep track of any assumptions that are made during the project. Assumptions and constraints could affect how a schedule is built and may impact the lead and lag between activities.

- **Milestone list:** This is added to the sequence of activities. The milestone of getting a permit can affect how the work of building a house is done.

- **Duration estimates:** This will be the estimated duration of each activity.

- **Basis of estimates:** This will list what information was used when the estimate was created. Information may include the range of the estimate, assumptions, and constraints.

- **Resource calendars:** Resource calendars show the availability of resources. Resources can greatly affect the duration of each activity. If resources are not available, this will negatively affect the duration.

- **Risk register:** The risk register will list all the identified project risks, as well as their impact and response. Risk response can lead to adding reserve time to activities.

- **Resource breakdown structure:** Resource breakdown structure is the hierarchical breakdown of resources by their categories and types.

- **Lessons learned register:** This is a listing of all of the lessons learned so far on the project. Previous lessons learned on this project or similar projects can help to increase the accuracy of the schedule.

- **Project team assignment:** This is the listing of the project team that will be assigned to complete the work. The project manager will need to know who is doing the work, as this will affect the duration of the activity.

- **Resource requirements:** The resources needed to complete each activity will affect the duration of each activity. Equipment and HR resources can have a big effect on the activity. For example, hiring a professional painter with a paint gun will ensure painting a room goes much faster than if a novice paints it with just a paintbrush.

- **Project schedule network diagrams:** This is a diagram of how the activities are related to each other and shows the sequence of activities in the project.

Agreements

If parts of the project are going to be given to contractors, they will have input on how the schedule is created. Sometimes, they are the ones that will create a schedule, and other times they will be working with the project manager to create the schedule.

Enterprise Environmental Factors – Covered in Chapter3

Organizational Process Assets – Covered in Chapter 3

Tools & Techniques

Schedule Network Analysis

This technique helps to generate the project schedule. It will use other tools, such as the critical path method or resource optimization, to create the schedule.

Critical Path Method

The critical path method is a very important tool for the exam. Expect a few questions on this topic. The critical path is defined as the longest path through a network diagram. When looking at a network diagram, it is important to know which activities, if delayed, will affect the project schedule. Any delays on the critical path will delay the project. Activities on the critical path have the highest risk within a project and are therefore considered high-risk activities. Activities on the critical path have no float, which is the amount of time you can delay the activities without delaying the project end date. We will be covering this topic in greater detail at the end of this chapter.

Resource Optimization Techniques

All project managers will need to know how to manage their resources correctly. Here are two methods that can be used to ensure resources are utilized correctly:

- **Resource Leveling:** This is a technique where resources are limited or over-allocated. An over-allocated resource is a resource that is working on two or more activities at the same time. When resources are limited or over-allocated, the project manager will need to adjust the schedule for that. In resource leveling, you will extend the activity dates or resequencing activities to accommodate the resource constraints. For example, if you are using resource leveling and have two activities that are happening in parallel of each other using the same resource (over-allocated), you would then move them to happen sequentially instead of in parallel. Doing this would most likely lengthen the critical path. Indeed, resource leveling generally increases the length of the critical path.

- **Resource Smoothing:** This technique is used to ensure the critical path does not change. It will allow activities to change if there is a float. This method doesn't affect the critical path as resource leveling does.

Data Analysis

Data analysis can include what-if scenarios and simulations. When building the final project schedule, you will go through a series of different what-if scenarios, sometimes referred to as a Monte Carlo Simulation. This might include projecting things such as what would happen if you run two parallel activities or what-if you add more resources to these activities. You might run different simulations on what would happen if activities are delayed or finished faster.

Leads and Lags

As the project manager develops the schedule, he/she will need to know the lags (delay) or leads (overlap) between activities. It is very important to build lags and leads into a schedule from the start. Giving time for the paint to dry before putting the furniture back should not be a surprise when a project is implemented.

Schedule Compression

Sometimes a project manager might need to compress a schedule that is too long. Here are two methods to accomplish that:

- **Crashing:** This is a method where you add more resources to activities to complete them faster. This can include adding more painters to finish painting more quickly or buying a paint gun instead of using a small brush. Crashing generally increases cost and sometimes causes risk.

- **Fast-tracking:** This is a method where you do activities in parallel instead of sequentially. For example, instead of installing the server and then the workstation, you would install the server and workstation at the same time. Fast-tracking would get the project done quicker, but it generally increases risk.

    ExamTip: Crashing increases cost, and fast-tracking increases risk. Try to compress the schedule before getting it approved.

Project Management Information System – Covered in Chapter 3

Agile Release Planning

If you work on a project that follows agile development, you will be releasing the products in increments. In this case, the schedule will be broken up into smaller iterations, as opposed to a traditional project where the schedule is for the entire product release. By releasing

The products in increments, it gives the customers an opportunity to give feedback on the product. This is usually done with a lease plan and an iteration plan. A release plan is a set of iterations that will help to create a product that would be given to the customers for feedback. An iteration plan is a plan that will be used to create a single iteration for part of the product.

Outputs

Schedule Baseline

The schedule baseline is part of the project management plan and can only change with an approved change request. This is the version of the schedule that the project manager and team will use to measure the progress of the project schedule. It will include the baseline start and end dates of the project.

Project Schedule

The project schedule will include the start and end dates for all the activities on the project. The project schedule can be very detailed, as in a project schedule network diagram or summary contained within a milestone chart. The project schedule can be displayed using one or more of the following formats:

- **Bar Chart (Gantt Charts):** The Gantt Chart is a time-phased graphical display of activity start dates, end dates, and durations. This bar chart will show all the activities and their durations. The longer the bars, the bigger the activity. This makes it easy to read.

ID	Task Name	Duration	Start
1	Gather requirements	1 day	Mon 2/5/18
2	Buy paint	1 day	Tue 2/6/18
3	Remove furniture	2 days	Wed 2/7/18
4	Paint room	4 days	Fri 2/9/18
5	Put furniture back	2 days	Thu 2/15/18
6	Get sponsor approval	1 day	Mon 2/19/18

Sample Gantt chart for paint room project

- **Milestone Charts:** These charts will only show the major deliverables on the projects. They will be a summary of the entire project. They will most likely be used when presenting the project updates to senior management. Milestones are points in time and have no duration.

ID	Task Name	Duration	Start
1	Complete project charter	0 days	Mon 1/8/18
2	Get project management plan	0 days	Fri 2/2/18
3	Start project work	0 days	Mon 2/5/18
4	Complete building inspection	0 days	Fri 2/23/18
5	Get customer approval	0 days	Fri 3/9/18
6	Clsoe project	0 days	Fri 3/16/18

Simple milestone chart

- **Project schedule network diagrams:** These diagrams will show the duration and the sequencing of every activity on the project. Network diagrams are covered in detail at the end of this chapter under the "critical path method."

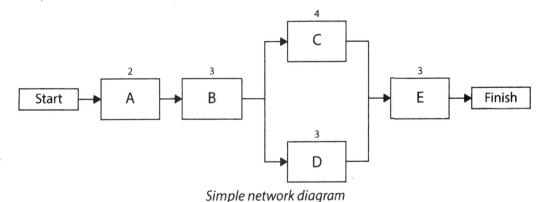

Simple network diagram

Schedule Data

The schedule data will list all the data that was used to create the project schedule. It will contain all the assumptions and constraints that were made while creating the schedule.

Project Calendars

The project calendar will display the working days and shifts for the activities. For example, some projects may have shifts on weekends while some may not. Some projects may have different calendars for different parts of the project, such as coding that can be done during the day, but installation that can only be done at night.

Change Requests

Once the project schedule has been created, it may modify other components of the project plan, such as the scope or budget. For example, if a stakeholder wants to shorten the schedule, you may have to add to the cost of the project in order to speed up the work. This would result in a change request.

Project Management Plan Updates – Covered in Chapter 3

Project Documents Updates – Covered in Chapter 3

Control Schedule

This is the process of controlling the project work to ensure it will finish on the schedule baseline. As the work is done, the project manager will ensure that activities are done according to the project schedule.

This is the daily process of keeping your project on schedule. It is about looking at the work getting done and asking, are we on schedule? You will look at the project management plan (plan work) and compare it to the work performance data (actual work) to see if there is any variance. If there is, you might need to get a change request in order to fix the schedule or any other part of the project that may be causing the project to go off schedule.

Inputs

Project Management Plan

The project management plan will include the schedule management plan and the schedule baseline. This plan will state how to control the project schedule. This plan will outline the steps the project manager will need to take to ensure the project stays on schedule.

Other important components in the project management plan include the scope and cost baselines, along with their respective management plans.

Project Documents

Of the 33 project documents, the ones you are most likely to use in this process include:

- **Project Schedule:** The project schedule will contain the network diagram and the Gantt chart. This will show the start and end dates of all the activities on the project.
- **Schedule Data:** The scheduled data are used to show what data were used to create the schedule. It will include all the constraints and assumptions made to create the project schedule.
- **Resource Calendars:** Resource calendars show the availability of resources.
- **Lessons Learned Register:** The listing of all of the lessons learned so far on the project.
- **Project Calendars:** The project calendar will display what is happening day-to-day on a project. It can display exactly what is happening on a project for a specific date in time.

Work Performance Data

This is the actual work that is being done on the project. It will state when activities are being done and how long it will take to do them.

Organizational Process Assets – Covered in Chapter 3

Tools & Techniques

Data Analysis

All projects will generate lots of different types of scheduling data. It would be up to the project manager to analyze this data in this process. Here are some techniques we can use to analyze the data:

- **Earned value analysis:** Earned value is a series of formulas that are used to numerically analyze the performance of a project's related costs and time. We will be reviewing all of the relevant earned value formulas for this exam at the end of the "cost management" chapter.

- **Iteration burndown chart:** A burndown chart, as shown below, is generally used on an agile project to keep track of the work that needs to be done. The Y-axis of the chart generally shows the amount of work that needs to get completed and the X-axis shows the duration. As the project progresses, the chart would show you how much work is left to be done on the project. A straight line that goes from the X to Y-axis is ideally how the project should progress. The wavy line maps the work that is getting done and will then illustrate how much work is left to be done. You can see this in the burndown chart below:

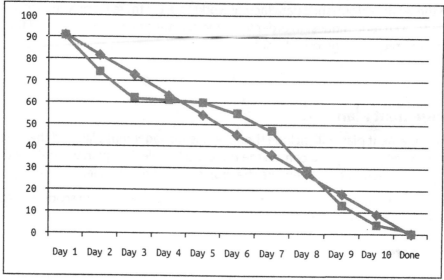

Simple burndown chart

- **Performance Reviews:** As the project is being completed, the project manager will need to track the progress of the planned work vs. the actual work completed. Performance reviews look at the planned work and actual work performed. The project might be on schedule, or 10% behind or ahead of schedule.

- **What-if Scenarios:** These can be used to help fix the schedule or reorganize it. Looking at different scenarios for the project schedule will help the project manager to optimize the best schedule and to determine what risks may affect it.

Critical Path Method

Finding and understanding the critical path on the project will be essential to the successful completion of the project on time. The critical path is defined as the longest path through a network diagram on a project. Knowing your critical path as you're executing the project will be vitally important to ensure success. See the end of this chapter for the section on the Critical Path Method.

Project Management Information System – Covered in Chapter 3

Resource Optimization Techniques

As the project work is being done, the project manager might need to analyze the schedule for any resource scheduling problems. These techniques include resource leveling and smoothing, as discussed in the develop schedule process earlier.

Leads and Lags

Leads and lags include any delay or overlapping of activities. As the project progresses, you might have to adjust the lags and leads on the activities.

Schedule Compression

As the work is done, the project manager might need to shorten the schedule by crashing or fast-tracking.

Outputs

Work Performance Information

This will show the performance of the work being done. It will show the difference between real work and planned work. It will use the SV (Schedule Variance) and SPI (Schedule Performance Index) earned value formulas covered in the cost chapter.

Schedule Forecasts

This is a forecast of when the work could be done. It will be based on the progress that you are making now. This can be calculated using the EAC (estimate at completion) earned value formula. We will look at this formula in the cost chapter.

Change Requests

If the project is falling behind schedule or is already behind schedule, the project manager will need to make a change request to implement necessary corrective or preventive actions. These can include adding more money or time to finish the project. All change requests will be sent through the "perform integrated change control" process for approval.

Project Management Plan Updates – Covered in Chapter 3

Project Documents Updates – Covered in Chapter 3

Agile and Hybrid Project Scheduling

On agile projects, the work that needs to get done is stored in the product backlog. The amount of time it takes to complete an agile project would be dependent on how large the product backlog is. Coming up with the number of iterations and releases can also be a complex task that will require the team to know how fast they can get the work done. This is done by estimating how long it will take to complete each of the user stories. Assigning times and durations can be a complex task, and agile would prefer to use a high-level method to just get a quick estimate of how long it will take to complete the user stories. Here are a few ways to estimate the duration of the user stories:

- **T-shirt sizing:** T-shirt sizing is a high-level relative estimation where you assign T-shirt size to the different stories on the project. You can also use this method to apply it to features also. To use this estimation, you would come up with different sizes of T-shirts such as extra small (ES), small(S), medium (M), large (L), and extra-large (XL). You then assign each of the user stories that represent features to these different categories. For example, if one of the user stories is just to edit customer information on a record, you can assign that to ES. If a feature or user story requires a lot of work, such as adding an accepting credit card payments feature into a software, you can assign that as XL. As you can see, T-shirt sizing is based on a relative scale where the size of the T-shirt corresponds back to the amount of work it would take to get that user story complete. T-shirt sizing allows for quick high-level estimation that both customers and team members can understand.

- **Planning poker:** Planning poker is when the team uses a series of "playing cards" with a set of numbers written on them. These numbers generally represent what is known as the Fibonacci sequence. The Fibonacci is a sequence of numbers that are relative based on the size. The Fibonacci sequence of numbers are: 1, 2, 3, 5, 8, 13, 21. To calculate the Fibonacci sequence you would start with numbers one and two and then just keep adding the numbers directly preceding it. For example, to get 3 you would compute 1+2, to get 8 you compute 2+3, to get 8 you would get 3+5, and to get 13 you would compute 5+8.

The way the planning poker session is done is that the product owner or customer will read a user story, and then the team will decide which one of these cards will be applied to it. The numbers on the card matters as its relative based on the amount of work needed to complete that user story. For example, if the team assigns a user story a card with three, that means it has as much work as a user story that would be assigned 1 and 2. If a story is assigned a size of 8 it means it would require as much work as a story of 3 and 5.

Agile Tools to help track the progress

On an agile project using things such as the Fibonacci sequence and planning poker, you will be able to assign a certain number of points to each user story. This would give a number of points to the overall project backlog. For example, if the project backlog had four features, and they were each worth five points, then the total number of points in the product backlog would be 20. This helps to put a relative number on the amount of work it will take to complete the project. On large projects, it's not uncommon to see the product backlog having 200 to 800 points of work.

Once the team is able to estimate the number of points on the product backlog, they will then be able to track the progress of the project using a variety of tools such as:

Cumulative Flow Diagram (CFD): One diagram that is able to track how much work is getting done on the project while seeing the number of points is a Cumulative Flow Diagram (CFD). You can see one in the image below.

CFD's diagrams are used to track the amount of work that is getting done on a project. In the diagram above, the project has about 600 points worth of work to get done. The diagram is displaying the amount of work the project has to get done and how much of the is getting done over time.

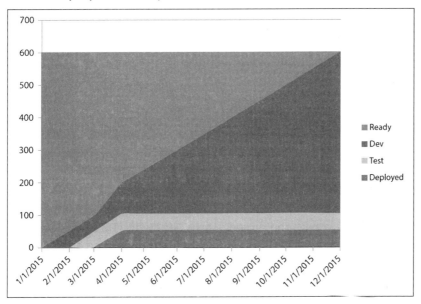

Keep in mind that the number of points is at 600 throughout the project, if more work is added to the project backlog, the number can eventually go up to 700 or even 1000.

Team Velocity: One other important concept to know would be how many points a team can get done in each iteration. This would be done by estimating how much they can do in the next sprint based on how fast they did the previous sprint. This is known as the velocity. It basically estimates how many points worth of work the team can get done during the sprint. Here is an example of a velocity chart

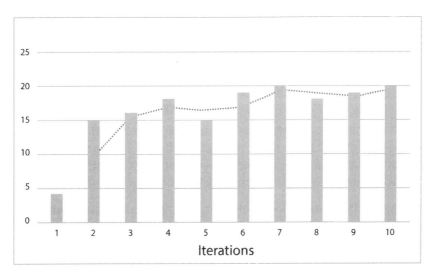

Based on this chart, the team velocity is about 16. This represents an estimated average and how much work they will likely get done in the next sprint or iteration.

Burn Charts: Another chart that agile teams used to manage the project's progress is known as a burn chart. They can either be a burnup or burndown chart.

A burnup chart will show you what work has been done on a project as follows:

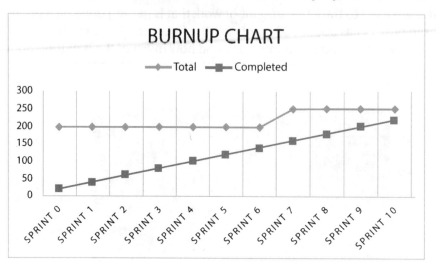

On this project in the Burnup chart, the project started out with 200 points worth of work and then increased to 250 points as the project progressed. The team is working at around 20 points per iteration. So, by Sprint 4, they will have done around 80 points worth of work.

The opposite of a Burnup chart is a burndown chart. A burndown chart will show you the amount of work that remains to be done.

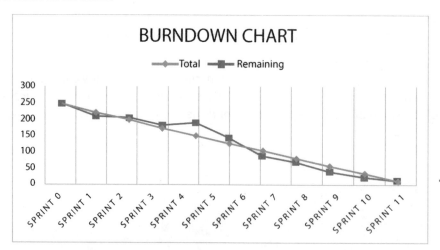

In this burndown chart, the project started with about 250 points worth of work to complete. In Sprint 1, there are 250 points left to be done. But by the time Sprint 2 has come around, the project team was able to complete some work, and now there is about 225 points worth of work. A burndown chart shows you at any point how much work is remaining to be done on the project.

Exam Tip: These two charts, Burnup and Burndown, are favorites for your exam. Note that they're generally used in tracking the overall progress of the project and can tell you how much work was done or how much work is remaining to be done on the project.

Lead and Cycle Time

Two terms that you should be familiar with for an agile project are cycle time and lead time. There's also a formula associated with these terms. The definitions are as follows:

- **Lead time:** How long something takes to go through the entire process

- **Cycle time:** How long something takes to go through a part of the process. This is part of lead time.

These two terms are commonly associated with the use of Kanban. Lead time to say how long it will take to go across the entire Kanban board, while cycle time will talk about how to go through a part of it as you can see from the diagram below:

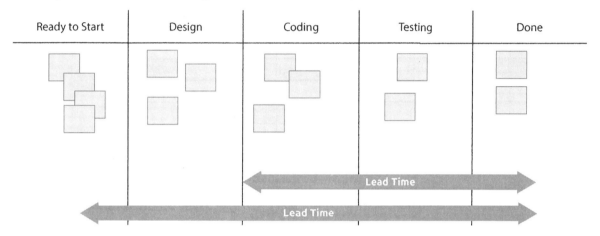

In this diagram, you can see that the lead time would be from when the user story is ready to start all the way to the completion. The cycle time would be from the start of coding to completion. Remember, your exam cycle time is part of lead time.

Cycle time is generally associated with what is known as work in progress. On an agile project, you try to reduce the work in progress. Having too much work in progress can create a bottleneck and leads to inefficient processes. It can also not be discovered until the product is in the hands of the customer. This means you have to reduce the cycle time. To do this, you would first have to calculate the cycle time with the following formula:

$$\text{Cycle Time} = \frac{(\text{Work in Progress})}{\text{Throughput}}$$

Throughput is the amount of work that can get done in a particular period of time. For example, if your work in progress is to read this entire book of 600 pages (WIP) and you're able to read 10 pages per hour (throughput), then your cycle time would be 60 hours.

Another example would be if there is 60 points worth of work to get done and the team completes 20 points a week. What would the cycle time to complete all 60 points be? The answer would be three weeks. 60/20 = 3 Weeks.

Know how to use this formula for your exam, as it's a pretty common formula on the current exam. It should not be too difficult.

Hot Topic: Critical Path Method (CPM)

The critical path method is a guaranteed exam topic. It includes using a network diagram and calculating the critical path and its start and finish dates. We will first look at a network diagram and some terminologies, then do a forward and backward pass on the diagram.

The activities on a network diagram represent the work that needs to get done to complete the project. In the first example below, Activity A would be to buy paint, B would be to remove the furniture, C would be to paint one side of the room while someone else is painting the other side in D, and E would be to put the furniture back. Going forward, don't worry about what the activities mean, just know that they represent work.

Here is a table of a network diagram that you will need to draw out:

Activity	Preceding Activity	Durations (in days)
Start		0
A	Start	2
B	A	3
C	B	4
D	B	3
E	C, D	3
Finish	E	0

When drawing out this diagram, start with the start Activity. Then do the following:

- Draw a box and label it Start with a duration of 0.

- Draw another box after Start and label it A with a duration of 2. Connect a line to Start.

- Draw another box after A and label it B with a duration of 3. Connect a line to A.

- Draw another box after B and label it C with a duration of 4. Connect a line back to B

- Draw another box after B and label it D with a duration of 3. Connect a line to B.

- Draw another box after C and D and label it E with a duration of 3. Connect a line to C and D.

- Draw another box after E and label it F with a duration of 0. Connect a line to E.

The diagram should look like the diagram below:

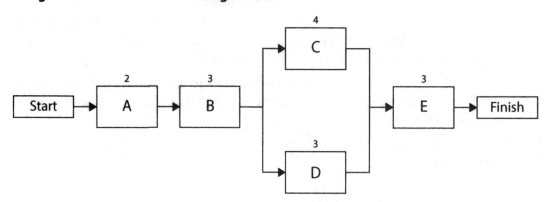

The first step you should take when looking at the network diagram is to find all the paths through it and their durations. A path is defined as a point from start to finish with no loops.

On this diagram, we have two paths as follows:

1. Start, A, B, C, E, Finish = 12
2. Start, A, B, D, E, Finish = 11

As you can tell, the longest path is path 1, with 12 days total. This path is known as the critical path. **The critical path is the longest path through a network diagram.** It will represent the longest amount of time to complete the project. The longest this project will take to complete is 12 days. Note that you cannot start E if you have not done C and D. That means that E will start when the longest of C and D is done. In other words, you cannot put back the furniture until both sides of the room have been painted.

Activities on the critical path have no slack (a.k.a float). Slack, or float, is defined as the amount of time you can delay an activity without delaying the project end date. Free float is defined as the amount of time you can delay the activity without delaying the next activity. If you notice that activities A, B, C, and E are on the critical path, this means that they have no slack. If you were to delay any of them by just one day, the entire project would be increased by one day. For example, if you delay B by one day, the entire project would become 13 days.

The only activity on the diagram that is not on the critical path is D. Activity D has a slack of one day. If you increase D by one day, the project end date of 12 will not change. However, this would make 2 critical paths, as path 2 would also become 12 days. This will add more risk to the project. There must always be a critical path that is the longest path on the diagram. If we increase D by two days to make it 5 days then path 2 will become the new critical path with a total of 13 days.

All activities have four dates associated with them, Early Start, Late Start, Early Finish, and Late Finish. Here is what they mean:

Early Start (ES): The earliest you can start the activity without delaying the project end date.

Late Start (LS): The latest you can start the activity without delaying the project end date.

Early Finish (EF): The earliest you can finish the activity without delaying the project end date.

Late Finish (LF): The latest you can finish the activity without delaying the project end date.

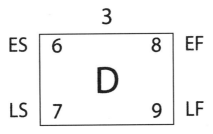

By looking at this diagram, you can tell the ES, LS, EF, and LF. We can say that if Activity D starts on day 6 and lasts 3 days, it will not delay the project. If it starts on day 7 and lasts 3 days it will not delay the project; however, if it starts on day 8 and lasts 3 days, it will delay the project by 1 day. If Activity D finishes on day 8 or 9 it will not delay the project. If it finishes on day 10, it will delay the project by 1 day.

These numbers allow you to calculate the slack of the activities by using the following formulas:

LS – ES = Slack

or

LF – EF = Slack

In this example, the slack would be 1 day. If you don't start on day 6, you can start on day 7 without delaying the project. If you don't finish on day 8, you can finish on day 9 without delaying the project. You can use either formula, and it should always give the same number.

You can calculate the EF by knowing the ES and the duration. Activity D starts on day 6 with a duration of 3 and will finish on day 8 because it will occur on days 6, 7, and 8. You can also use a simple formula, which is:

ES + Duration – 1 = EF

From the diagram above, this would be 6+3–1=8. **You need to subtract the 1 because you actually start on that day.** This formula is used on a forward pass to calculate slack.

You can also calculate the LS by knowing the LF and duration. If something finishes on day 9, and is 3 days in duration, it must have started on day 7. It occurred on days 9, 8, and 7. You can also use a simple formula for this:

LF – Duration + 1 = LS

For the diagram above, it would be 9-3+1=7. This formula is used on a backward pass to calculate slack. This formula is just the reverse of the one above.

On this exam, you will need to know how to calculate the slack for each activity on the diagram. To do this, you will need to do a forward pass and a backward pass. Let's do it for the diagram above.

Forward pass: The forward pass must be done first before the backward pass. The Forward pass will find the ES and EF. Here are the steps for a forward pass on this diagram and remember to use the formula of ES + Duration - 1 =EF

- Start with Activity A, and put a 1 on the ES of A. This means that it starts on day 1. It is 2 days in duration, so it will end on day 2, the EF. It occurs during all of day 1 and 2. You can also use the formula from above: 1 + 2 – 1 =2

- On Activity B, make the ES 3 because it will start the day after A. It is 3 days in duration and finishes on day 5, the EF. It will go all day, 3, 4, and 5. You can also use the formula from above:

- 3+3-1=5

- On Activity C, make the ES 6 because it starts one day after B. The EF would be 9. That you can get from the formula: 6+4–1=9

- On Activity D, make the ES 6 because it starts one day after B. The EF would be 8. That you can get from the formula: 6+3–1=8

- On Activity E make the ES 10 because it will start one day after C, the longest of the convergence of C and D to E. E cannot start until both C and D are done. The EF would then become 12. That you can get from the formula: 10+3–1=12.

It should look like this at the end of it:

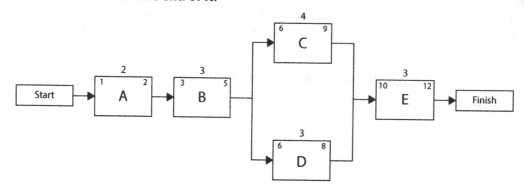

You can tell that this is correct because you will notice that the last activity before finishing E is ending on the critical path. Once you reach the end of the diagram, you have to make sure that at least one activity that links to the finish has the critical path number.

Next is the backward pass. The backward pass is difficult for lots of students. It is the complete opposite of the forward pass. It will calculate all the bottom numbers of LF and LS. Do this a few times to ensure you get it. Here are the steps for this diagram:

- Start with Activity E, and make the LF 12, since that is the latest the project can finish. Then use the backward pass formula, as follows: 12–3+1=10. That would make the LS 10.

- On D, make the LF 9, since E will late start on 10. The LS will be 7. That you can get using the formula: 9 – 3 + 1 =7.

- On C, make the LF 9, since E will late start on 10. The LS will be 6. That you can get using the formula: 9 – 4 + 1 =6.

- On B, make the LF 5, since C will late start on 6. The LS will be 3. That you can get using the formula: 5 – 3 + 1 =3.

- On A, make the LF 2, since B will late start on 3. The LS will be 1. That you can get using the formula: 2 – 2 + 1 =1.

ExamTip: When doing a backward pass and there is path convergence of C and D to B, use the lowest LS of the activities to get the LF of the next activity. Notice how the LF of C was 6, and D was 7. We used the 6 on C to get the LF 5 on B.

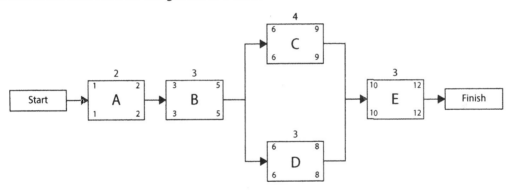

ExamTip: When going forward at a convergence of paths, use the highest number. When going backward, use the smallest number.

You can notice from this diagram that all the critical path activities have no slack. All the top numbers equal all the bottom numbers on the critical path activities. The only activity that has slack is D, with slack of 1.

Practice 1

Here is a table of the network diagram that you will need to be able to draw out and answer the following questions about:

Activity	Preceding Activity	Durations(in days)
Start		0
A	Start	2
B	A	3
C	A	4
D	B, C	2
E	B, C	3
F	D, E	5
G	F	6
H	F	3
Finish	G,H	0

1. What is the critical path?

2. What is the slack on Activity D?

3. What is the late start on Activity H?

4. What happens if Activity E is increased to 5 days?

Your first task would have been to draw the diagram as follows:

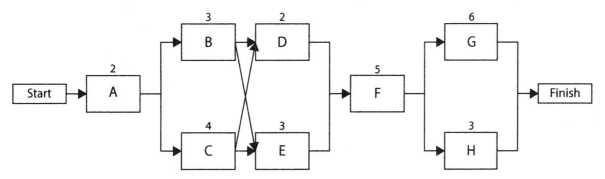

Make a box for Start and then follow the table to link the activities. Next, we will find all the paths:

1.   Start, A, B, D, F, G, Finish =18

2.   Start, A, B, D, F, H, Finish =15

3.   Start, A, B, E, F, G, Finish =19

4.   Start, A, B, E, F, H, Finish =16

5.   Start, A, C, E, F, H, Finish=17

6.   **Start, A, C, E, F, G, Finish=20**

7.   Start, A, C, D, F, G, Finish=19

8.   Start, A, C, D, F, H, Finish=16

The critical path is Start, A, C, E, F, G, Finish. That is the longest path on the diagram. Next, we will do the forward and backward passes as follows:

Forward Pass:

- On A, make the ES 1 because it starts on day one. The EF would be 2. That you can get from the formula: 1+2–1=2

- On B, make the ES 3 because it will start the day after A. The EF would be 5. That you can get from the formula: 3+3–1=5

- On C, make the ES 3 because it starts one day after A. The EF would be 6. That you can get from the formula: 3+4–1=6

- On D, make the ES 7 because it starts one day after C, which is the longest of B and C. The EF would be 8. That you can get from the formula: 7+2–1=8

- On E, make the ES 7 because it starts one day after C, which is the longest of B and C. The EF would be 9. That you can get from the formula: 7+3–1=9

- On F, make the ES 10 because it starts one day after E, which is the longest of D and E. The EF would be 14. That you can get from the formula: 10 + 5 – 1 =14

- On G, make the ES 15 because it starts one day after F. The EF would be 20. That you can get from the formula: 15+6–1=20

- On H, make the ES 15 because it starts one day after F. The EF would be 17. That you can get from the formula: 15+3–1=17

The diagram should look like the one below. We still cannot answer all the questions without doing a backward pass

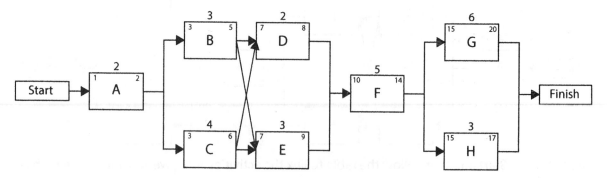

Backward Pass:

- On H, make the LF 20, since that is the latest the project can be done. The LS will be 18. That you can get using the formula: 20 – 3 + 1 =18.

- On G, make the LF 20, since that is the latest the project can be done. The LS will be 15. That you can get using the formula: 20 – 6 + 1 =15.

- On F, make the LF 14, since G will late start on 15. The LS will be 10. That you can get using the formula: 14 – 5 + 1 =10.

- On E, make the LF 9, since F will late start on 10. The LS will be 7. That you can get using the formula: 9 – 3 + 1 =7.

- On D, make the LF 9, since F will late start on 10. The LS will be 8. That you can get using the formula: 9 – 2 + 1 =8.

- On C, make the LF 6, since E will late start on 7. The LS will be 3. That you can get using the formula: 6 – 4 + 1 =3.

- On B, make the LF 6, since E will late start on 7. The LS will be 4. That you can get using the formula: 6 – 3 + 1 =4.

- On A, make the LF 2, since C will late start on 3. The LS will be 1. That you can get using the formula: 2 – 2 + 1 =1.

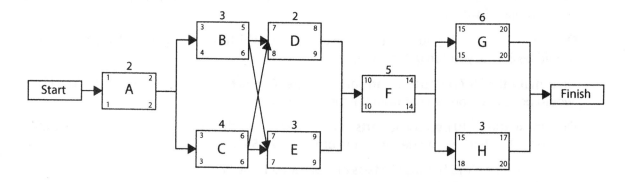

The answers to the questions are as follows now that we have the full diagram:

1. **What is the critical path:**

   Start, A, C, E, F, G, Finish = 20

2. **What is the slack on activity D?**

   The slack of D is one day, since LF-EF or 9 – 8 = 1 or LS-ES or 8 – 7 = 1. This means that you can delay activity D by one day and still not affected the project schedule.

3. **What is the latest you can start on activity H without delaying the project?**

   Day 18

4. **What happens if I increase E to 5 days?**

   Since E is on the critical path, it would increase the end date of the project to day 22 instead of day 20. It would extend the entire project schedule by 2 days.

Practice 2

Here is a table of the network diagram that you will need to be able to draw out and answer the following questions:

Activity	Preceding Activity	Durations(in days)
Start		0
A	Start	3
B	A	3
C	A	4
D	A	5
E	B, C	3
F	B, C, D	6
G	E, F	5
H	G	4
Finish	H	0

1. What is the critical path?

2. What is the slack on activity C?

3. What is the late start on activity F?

4. What happens if B is increased to 7days?

Your first task would have been to draw the diagram as follows:

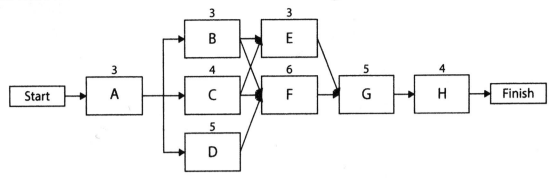

Make a box for Start and then follow the table to link the activities. Next, we will find all the paths:

1. Start, A, B, E, G, G, H Finish =18

2. Start, A, B, F, G, H, Finish =21

3. Start, A, C, E, F, G, H, Finish=19

4. Start, A, C, F, G, H, Finish=22

5. **Start, A, D, F, G, H, Finish=23**

The critical path is Start, A, D, F, G, H, Finish. That is the longest path on the diagram. Next, we will do the forward and backward passes as follows:

Forward Pass:

- On A, make the ES 1 because it starts day one. The EF would be 3. That you can get from the formula: 1+3–1=3

- On B, make the ES 4 because it will start the day after A. The EF would be 6. That you can get from the formula: 4+3–1=6

- On C, make the ES 4 because it starts one day after A. The EF would be 7. That you can get from the formula: 4+4–1=7

- On D, make the ES 4 because it starts one day after A. The EF would be 8. That you can get from the formula: 4+5–1=8

- On E, make the ES 8 because it starts one day after C, which is the longest of B and C. The EF would be 10. That you can get from the formula: 8+3–1=10

- On F, make the ES 9 because it starts one day after D, which is the longest of B, C, and D. The EF would be 14. That you can get from the formula: 9 + 6 – 1 =14

- On G, make the ES 15 because it starts one day after F. The EF would be 19. That you can get from the formula: 15+5–1=19

- On H, make the ES 20 because it starts one day after G. The EF would be 23. That you can get from the formula: 20+4–1=23

The diagram should like the one below. We still cannot answer all the questions without doing a backward pass

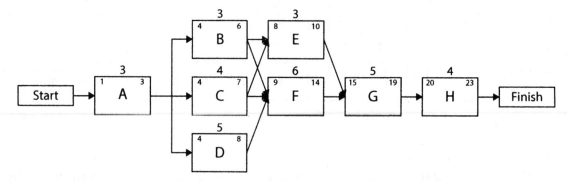

Backward Pass:

- On H, make the LF 23, since that is the latest the project can be done. The LS will be 20. That you can get using the formula: 23 – 4 + 1 =20.

- On G, make the LF 19, since H will late start on 20. The LS will be 15. That you can get using the formula: 19 – 5 + 1 =15.

- On F, make the LF 14, since G will late start on 15. The LS will be 9. That you can get using the formula: 14 – 6 + 1 =9.

- On E, make the LF 14, since G will late start on 15. The LS will be 12. That you can get using the formula: 14 – 3 + 1 =12.

- On D, make the LF 8, since F will late start on 9. The LS will be 4. That you can get using the formula: 8 – 5 + 1 =4.

- On C, make the LF 8, since E will late start on 9. The LS will be 5. That you can get using the formula: 8 – 4 + 1 =5.

- On B, make the LF 8, since E will late start on 9. The LS will be 6. That you can get using the formula: 8 – 3 + 1 =6.

- On A, make the LF 3, since D will late start on 4. The LS will be 1. That you can get using the formula: 3 – 3 + 1 =1.

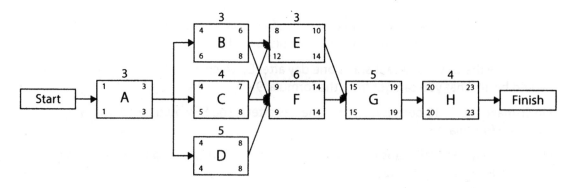

The answers to the questions are as follows now that we have the full diagram:

1. **What is the critical path?**

   The critical path is Start, A, D, F, G, H, Finish = 23

2. **What is the slack on activity C?**

The slack of C is one day, since LF-EF or 8 – 7 = 1 or LS-ES or 5 – 4 = 1. This means that you can delay activity C by one day and still have it not affect the project schedule.

3. What is the latest we can start activity F?

Day 9

4. What happens if B increased to 7 days?

Increasing B to 7 days would change the critical path to Start, A, B, F, G, H, Finish. The new end would be on day 25 instead of day 23.

Project Schedule Management Questions

1. One of your team members working on the project has informed you that a work package would most likely require ten weeks to complete. In the best-case scenario, if everything goes well and there are no surprises, it will take eight weeks. Since he is involved in more than two projects and has several pending deliverables, this specific work package may take eighteen weeks to complete. Based on this information, what would be the correct estimated time to complete the work package?

    A. Eleven weeks

    B. Ten weeks

    C. Nine weeks

    D. Eighteen weeks

2. Your project's sponsor is extremely disappointed with the project as it is over budgeted by

    $15,000 and also behind schedule by several weeks. The sponsor has asked you to take care of the situation immediately and do whatever it takes. While exploring different options to shorten the project duration, you decide to put some of the non-critical activities on hold so that some of the resources working on these activities can be assigned to the activities with the most schedule risk. You also asked for a couple of additional external resources to be added to the project. The sponsor agrees to pay the additional costs, time is now a critical factor. This is an example of which of the following?

    A. Crashing

    B. Fast-tracking

    C. Critical chain method

    D. Resource leveling

3. A project manager is in the Sequence Activities process of identifying and documenting relationships among defined activities and arranging them in the order they must be performed. While in this process, the project manager decided to utilize a software tool to create a Precedence Diagramming Method (PDM) network diagram. This network diagram creates a schematic display of the sequential and logical relationships, dependencies, and the order in which activities in a project must be performed. The project manager also added each activity's duration in the network diagram to calculate the critical path. Which one of the following is FALSE about the critical path?

    A. It is the longest duration path through a network diagram.

    B. It determines the shortest time to complete the project.

    C. The activities on the critical path represent the highest schedule risk in the project.

    D. The activities on the critical path represent critical functionality.

4. While reviewing your project resource histogram, you notice several peaks and valleys, as resources are not evenly distributed in your project. In order to evenly utilize resources as much as possible, you decide to move some activities from the week when you are using a lot of resources to the week when you are hardly using any. Which technique are you using in this case?

    A. Resource leveling

    B. Overtime

    C. Schedule compression

    D. Schedule control

5. Which one of the following takes the progressive elaboration approach and plans the near-term work in detail and future work at a higher level?

    A. Scope definition

    B. Rolling wave planning

    C. Decomposition

    D. SWOT analysis

6. Your team just finished the design activities for a software development project. You have ordered a server and a couple of PCs to set-up the development environment and are waiting for the vendor to deliver it to you, so that the team can start the development work. The vendor informs you that it will take twelve days for the equipment delivery, set up, and configuration. The twelve days waiting time can be defined as:

    A. Mandatory dependency

    B. Lag

    C. Lead

    D. Internal dependency

7. The product owner on an agile project would like to know how much work is remaining to be done on the project. What should the agile project manager use to provide this information?

    A. Burndown chart

    B. Burnup chart

    C. Velocity chart

    D. Kanban

8. One of your team members is always late completing his deliverables. In order to help him out with proper planning for his activities, you'd like to explore different options with him. You asked the team member to send you information about the total float and free float for all of his activities, if there is any. How does free float differ from a total float?

    A. Total float and free float are the same thing.

    B. Free float affects only the early start of the successor activities.

    C. Total float is the accumulated amount of free float.

    D. Subtracting the total float from the critical path duration will give the free float.

9. A project manager is managing a web-based application project to automate the accounting processes of his organization. The project has an estimated budget of $120,000 and a duration of nine months. While reviewing the project, the project manager notices that activities were scheduled in sequential order, but coding work was initiated twelve days earlier than planned. What type of relationship represents the start of the coding work to the completion of the design work?

   A. Finish-to-start relationship with a twelve-day lag

   B. Finish-to-start relationship with a twelve-day lead

   C. Start-to-finish with a twelve-day lag

   D. Start-to-finish with a twelve-day lead

10. While working with your team members on activity sequencing, a team member identifies that even though a series of activities are planned to be completed in a specific sequence, they can be performed in parallel. What type of activity sequencing method may be utilized in this situation?

   A. Critical path

   B. Resource leveling method

   C. Monte Carlo simulation

   D. Precedence Diagramming Method(PDM)

11. You are the project manager overseeing the implementation of a new computer infrastructure at a local hospital. Your sponsor has informed you that all the existing applications must work in the new infrastructure, and the project should be completed in three months. These are examples of:

   A. A lag

   B. A lead

   C. An estimation

   D. A constraint

12. One of your team members is always late completing his deliverables. You decided to keep an eye on this team member's activities to avoid any project delay. While reviewing one of the activities of this team member, you found out that the activity has an early start of day 5, an early finish of day 12, a late start of day 15, and a late finish of day 22. The team member tells you that he needs an additional four days to complete the activity due to various reasons he can think of. Which one of the following statements is TRUE?

   A. This activity will delay the project.

   B. This activity will most probably not delay the project.

   C. The activity has a lag.

   D. The successor activity will be delayed.

13. Which one of the following analysis methods usually uses Monte Carlo simulation to simulate the outcome of a project by making use of three-point estimates (Optimistic, Pessimistic, Most Likely) for each activity, a huge number of simulated scheduling possibilities, or a few selected scenarios that are most likely, and the network diagram?

    A. Precedence Diagramming Method(PDM)

    B. What-if scenario analysis

    C. Critical chain method

    D. Resource leveling

14. A project manager managing a recruitment automation application project just completed developing the schedule and requested approval from the stakeholders and the client. The sponsor has expressed her frustration about the unexpectedly long duration of the project, and has demanded the schedule be compressed as much as possible. While exploring different options, you find out that you cannot really change the network diagram due to various constraints, but the sponsor has agreed to pay for additional personnel resources if needed. What will be your BEST option in this situation?

    A. Apply the critical chain method

    B. Fast-track the project and also apply the resource leveling method

    C. Crash the project

    D. Crash and fast-track the project

15. Your project sponsor is extremely disappointed with the project as it is over budgeted by $20,000 and also behind schedule by several weeks. The sponsor has asked you to take care of the situation immediately. While exploring different options to shorten the project duration, you decide, with management's approval, to perform several activities in parallel rather than in sequential order as originally planned. You know your option will possibly result in rework, increase risks, and require more communication, but you decide to go for it anyway. This is an example of which of the following?

    A. Critical chain method

    B. Crashing

    C. Resource leveling

    D. Fast-tracking

16. You have recently been assigned as a program manager to implement an ERP solution in your organization. Initially, the team will only work on five key modules in the first phase of the project. The second phase of the project has not been approved yet. You have estimated that three of the modules will take ten days each, and the remaining two will be completed in fifteen days each. It is not possible to work on these modules in parallel. What would be the approximate duration for the first phase of your project?

    A. Fifty-five to sixty-five days

    B. Fifty days

    C. Ten days

    D. Ninety days

17. You are in the Control Schedule process of monitoring the status of the project by comparing the result to the plan, updating project progress, and managing changes to the project schedule baseline. You are mainly focused on the current status and changes to the project schedule, influential factors that create schedule changes, and management of actual changes as they occur. Which of the following is NOT a tool or technique in this time management process?

    A. Schedule compression

    B. Data Analysis

    C. Resource optimization techniques

    D. Schedule forecasts

18. Steve has just been assigned as a project manager for a newly approved software development project. The sponsor is interested in knowing a high-level estimation of the total duration of the project and asks Steve to send him the information by the end of the day. What kind of estimate should Steve use in this kind of situation?

    A. An analogous estimate

    B. A heuristic estimate

    C. A three-point estimate

    D. A bottom-up estimate

19. You are in the Estimate Activity Durations process. These estimates usually originate from project team members most familiar with the activity and then get progressively elaborated. Which one of the following is TRUE about this process?

    A. This process must be performed after the Develop Schedule process.

    B. Padding is a common practice, and the project manager should not be too worried about it.

    C. The activity duration estimates are outputs in this process.

    D. It is not important that all estimates in this process should use a common work unit/ period.

20. You just completed developing the schedule for your project and got the approval from stakeholders and the sponsor. One of the team members assigned to work on a critical component informs you that she needs additional time to complete her activities because several relevant pieces were missed during planning. Her updated estimate would have no impact on the critical path; thus, the project duration would be the same. The best approach the project manager may take in this situation will be:

    A. Find a replacement for the resource who can complete the task within the allocated time.

    B. Inform the resource that it is too late for any kind of change in the project schedule.

    C. Inform her that it is OK as you have sufficient schedule reserve to handle this kind of situation.

    D. Update the project schedule and other relevant plans to reflect the new estimate.

21. You are overseeing a data center project for one of your clients. The team members have finished creating the Work Breakdown Structure (WBS) and work breakdown structure dictionary. The team members also submitted their activity duration estimates to you. What should you focus on NEXT?

    A. Sequence the activities using the precedence diagramming method.

    B. Create the activity list.

    C. Determine high-level project assumptions and constraints.

    D. Develop the project schedule.

22. Your IT project is progressing well and is on schedule when a vendor sends you an e-mail stating that the equipment delivery will be delayed by a week due to a severe snowstorm on the East Coast. Which of the documents would best capture the impact of the delay on the project schedule?

    A. Risk register

    B. Issue log

    C. Network diagram

    D. Work breakdown structure

23. Your IT project has ten team members, and recently you have hired three more database developers. You are using a time-phased graphical display of activity start dates, end dates, and durations for tracking progress and reporting to the team. Which chart are you using?

    A. Milestone chart

    B. Work breakdown structure

    C. Network diagram

    D. Gantt chart

24. You are overseeing a project to implement a web-based traffic monitoring system. You have requested three programmers, three database developers, and two testers; senior management only approved five team members for your project. Which one of the following may you use to produce a resource-limited schedule by letting the schedule lengthen and the cost increase in order to deal with a limited amount of resources, resource availability, and other resource constraints?

    A. Resource leveling

    B. Fast-tracking

    C. Crashing

    D. Critical path method

25. Steve is the project manager for a construction project to convert an old nursing home into a new multi-story office complex. The architectural design and site surveys are completed, and Steve is now waiting for the clearance and permit from the city to start the construction. This is an example of which kind of dependency?

    A. Mandatory dependency

    B. Internal dependency

    C. External dependency

    D. Discretionary dependency

26. Your team has been working with the WBS for a while and has completed the decomposition of the work packages. After a week, the team finalized the estimates of all activities and completed the network diagram. Which of the following activities will they be expected to concentrate on next?

    A. Develop a preliminary schedule and get approval from the team members

    B. Finalize the project scope statement

    C. Use the precedence diagramming method for sequencing the activities

    D. Develop the risk management plan and add it to the total project management plan document

27. Which of the following is FALSE about analogous estimating?

    A. It measures the project parameters such as budget, duration, size, complexity, and duration based on the parameters of a previous similar project and historical information.

    B. It is usually done during the early phase of the project when not much information is available.

    C. It uses a bottom-up approach.

    D. It usually is the overall project estimate given to the project manager from the management or the sponsor.

28. You recently took over a project from another project manager. While reviewing the network diagram, you find that there are four critical paths and three near-critical paths. What can you conclude about the project?

    A. The project will likely be completed on time and within budget.

    B. The project is at high risk.

    C. The project will require more people and an additional budget.

    D. The project should be terminated.

Project Time Management Answers

1. **A:** PERT allows the estimator to include three estimates: optimistic, pessimistic, and most likely, given by the equation: $= (8 + 4*10 + 18) / 6 = 11$ weeks

2. **A:** The best option here is to add additional resources to the project activities on the critical path to complete them quickly. Fast-tracking is the technique of doing critical path activities in parallel when they were originally planned in series. Resource leveling is used to produce a resource-limited schedule by letting the schedule lengthen and cost increase in order to deal with a limited amount of resources, resource availability, and other resource constraints. The critical chain method is another way to develop an approved, realistic, and resource-limited formal schedule. It provides a way to view and manage uncertainty when building the project schedule.

3. **D:** The activities on the critical path do not necessarily represent the critical functionalities in the project. The critical path is the longest duration path in the network diagram, and this duration is the shortest time needed to complete the project. The activities on the critical path have no buffer, and any delay in the critical path activities will delay the project; thus, the critical path activities represent the highest schedule risk.

4. **A:** Resource leveling is used to produce a resource-limited schedule by letting the schedule lengthen and cost increase in order to deal with a limited amount of resources, resource availability, and other resource constraints. It can be used when shared, or critically required resources are only available at certain times, are in limited quantities, or when resources have been over-allocated. We may have several peaks and valleys in our resource histogram. In order to level the resources, evenly utilize them as much as possible, or to keep resource usage at a constant level, we can move some of our activities from the week when we are using a lot of resources to the week when we are using fewer.

5. **B:** Rolling wave planning takes the progressive elaboration approach and plans near-term work in detail and future work at a higher level. During the early strategic planning phase, work packages may be decomposed into less-defined milestone levels since all details are not available, and later they are decomposed into detailed activities. This kind of planning is usually used in IT and research projects, but is very unlikely in construction projects where any unknowns are extremely expensive and destructive.

6. **B:** A lag is an inserted waiting time between activities.

7. **A:** A burndown chart will show you the amount of work that remains to be done.

8. **B:** Total float is the amount of time an activity can be delayed without affecting the project completion date. Free float is the amount of time an activity can be delayed without affecting the early start of its successor.

9. **B:** A lead is an acceleration of the successor activity, or in other words, a successor activity getting a jump start. A lead may be added to start an activity before the predecessor activity is completed. There is a finish-to-start relationship between the design and coding, meaning that design work should be completed prior to starting coding. But in this case, coding work had a jump start as it was initiated twelve days before the design was completed. This can be described as a finish-to-start relationship with twelve days lead.

10. **D:** The precedence diagramming method creates a schematic that is part of the sequential and logical relationships of the project activities. Usually, it shows dependencies and the order in which activities in a project must be performed. Critical path is not a diagramming method.

11. **D:** These are examples of a constraint or limitation that limits options and eliminates alternatives in the project.

12. **B:** There is not much information to determine if the activity has a lag or not. The float of this activity is Late Finish – Early Finish = 10 days. The activity is not on the critical path because it has a float or buffer of ten days. Even if the team member takes four additional days to complete the activity, it probably will have no impact on the project schedule or on the successor activity.

13. **B:** "What if" scenario analysis usually uses Monte Carlo simulation to simulate the outcome of a project by making use of a few selected scenarios that are most likely, and the network diagram. The outcome of this analysis may be used to evaluate the project schedule under adverse conditions and to develop the preventive and contingency action plan to reduce the impact and probability of unexpected situations.

14. **C:** Fast-tracking is the technique of doing critical path activities in parallel when they were originally planned in series. Fast-tracking will not be an option in this case since you cannot change the network diagram, or in other words, you cannot perform activities in parallel that were originally planned to be completed in sequence. The best option here is to add additional resources to the project activities on the critical path to complete them quickly. Resource leveling is used to produce a resource-limited schedule by letting the schedule lengthen and cost increase in order to deal with a limited amount of resources, resource availability, and other resource constraints. The critical chain method is another way to develop an approved, realistic, resource-limited, and formal schedule. It provides a way to view and manage uncertainty when building the project schedule.

15. **D:** Fast-tracking is the technique of doing critical path activities in parallel when they were originally planned in series.

16. **A:** The duration of three modules is 10*3=30days, and the remaining two modules is 2*15=30days. The first phase of the project will take 30+30=60days, or approximately between fifty-five and sixty-five days.

17. **D:** The schedule forecasts are outputs of the Control Schedule process, not tools & techniques.

18. **A:** An analogous estimate is usually done during the early phase of the project when not much information is available about the project. It is less accurate even though it is less costly and less time consuming. In a bottom-up approach, one estimate per activity is received from the team members; it requires significant time to develop. A heuristic estimate is based on the rule of thumb. A PERT estimate, also known as a weighted average estimate, is usually associated with specific project activities and requires significant time to develop as well.

19. **C:** The activity duration estimates are outputs in the Estimate Activity Durations process. This process should be performed before the Develop Schedule process. Adding additional time or padding the estimate is a common practice in this process, so the project manager should make sure that the estimates from the team members are realistic. It is important that all estimates in this process should use a common work unit/period.

20. **D:** The best course of action will be to update the project schedule and other relevant plans to reflect the new estimate.

21. **A:** Your team has created the WBS, WBS dictionary, and activity list and has submitted the activity durations. The next step should be to sequence the activities by creating a network diagram using the precedence diagramming method. Determining high-level project assumptions and constraints is done as part of project initiation and is completed much earlier. The Develop Schedule process follows the Sequence Activities process. Note that sequencing activities can be done before or after the activity duration estimation is done.

22. **C:** The project network diagram represents activities and their logical relationships, dependencies, and sequence; thus, the network diagram will best capture the impact of the delay on the project schedule. The work breakdown structure is a deliverable-orient- ed hierarchical decomposition of the work to be executed by the project team to accomplish the project objectives and create the required deliverables, but it does not focus on the duration of the project activities. The risk register would show an increase in project risk but would not help to determine the impact of a delay on the project schedule. An issue log will also capture the root cause, the person assigned, due date, and other factors, but will not give out much information about the impact of the delay on the project schedule.

23. **D:** A bar chart or Gantt chart is a time-phased graphical display of activity start dates, end dates, and durations. It is useful for tracking progress and reporting to the team and can be easily modified to show the percentage of completed work. As the project progresses, bars are shaded to show which activities are now complete. The work breakdown structure is a deliverable-oriented hierarchical decomposition of the work to be executed by the project team to accomplish the project objectives and create the required deliverables, but it does not focus on the duration of the project activities. A milestone chart is similar to a bar chart, but only shows major events. It is a good tool for reporting to management and customers. This type of chart is reserved for brief, high-level presentations as too much detail may be undesirable and distracting to senior management. A network diagram is a schematic display of the sequential and logical relationships of the project activities. It shows dependencies and the order in which activities in a project must be performed.

24. **A:** Resource leveling is used to produce a resource-limited schedule by letting the schedule lengthen and cost increase in order to deal with a limited amount of resources, resource availability, and other resource constraints. It can be used when shared, or critically required resources are only available at certain times, are in limited quantities, or when resources have been over-allocated. Fast-tracking is the technique of doing critical path activities in parallel when they were originally planned in series. Crashing is the technique of adding additional resources to a project activity to complete it more quickly. The critical path is the longest path through a network diagram and determines the shortest time to complete the project as well as any scheduling flexibility. It is not the project schedule, but it indicates the time within which an activity could be scheduled considering activity duration, logical relationships, dependencies, leads, lags, assumptions, and constraints.

25. **C:** External dependencies are driven by circumstances or authority outside the project and must be considered during the process of sequencing the activities. Internal dependencies are based on the needs of the project and are mostly under the control of the project team. Mandatory dependencies are mandatory and unavoidable dependencies that are in the nature of the work or are contractually required. They are like laws of nature and are also called "hard logic." Discretionary dependencies are also called "preferred logic" or "soft logic" as they are the preferences of the project manager and the team members. These dependencies may be determined by best practices or by local methodology and may vary from project to project.

26. **A:** The project manager should now focus on developing the preliminary schedule and getting approval from the team members. Finalizing the project scope statement should have been completed prior to completing the WBS. The team members have completed the network diagram, which suggests that the activities sequencing is also completed. Since the project schedule is an input to risk management, developing the risk management plan should be done once the schedule is completed.

27. **C:** Analogous estimates take a top-down approach, and this overall project estimate is usually given to the project manager from upper management or the sponsor. It is usually done during the early phase of the project when not much information is available. It is less accurate, however it is also less costly and less time-consuming. In a bottom-up approach, one estimate per activity is received from the team members.

28. **B:** The project is definitely at high risk because if any of the activities on the critical path or near critical path are delayed, the entire project will be delayed. Having more than one critical path and several near-critical paths does not necessarily mean that more resources and additional budget will be required to complete the project. There is no valid reason to terminate the project just because it is at high risk of schedule delay.

Chapter 8

Project Cost Management

Cost management is about creating the cost baseline (project budget) and ensuring the project stays on budget. There are not as many processes to cover as there were in Schedule Management, but the processes are important to know. The Earned Value Management formulas at the end of the chapter will be important for the exam.

When looking at the cost of a project, you will have to consider the cost of all the resources needed to complete the project. These can include HR, materials, equipment, permits, and vendors. Almost all aspects of a project will affect the cost in one way or another. Here are a few different types of costs:

- **Variable Cost:** A variable cost will change as the project progresses. For example, gas prices or airline tickets for the project team.

- **Fixed Cost:** A fixed cost will stay the same as the project progresses. For example, location rentals, management wages, or utilities.

- **Direct Cost:** A direct cost will be included in the cost baseline. This is a cost that the project work will directly incur, such as for materials, equipment rentals, or project team wages.

- **Indirect Cost:** An indirect cost is a cost that is not included in the project budget. This can include the sponsor's time spent helping the project manager or paper for a printer.

- **Sunk Cost:** The amount of money that has already been spent on the project.

- **Value Engineering:** Aka, value analysis is finding a less costly way of doing work. It will look at how to achieve a goal/scope in a less costly way.

  ExamTip: Know the different types of costs on a project and how they will affect the budget.

Process	Process Group	Main Output
Plan Cost Management	Planning	Cost Management Plan
Estimate Costs	Planning	Cost Estimates, Basis of the Estimates
Determine Budget	Planning	Cost Baseline, Project Funding Requirements
Control Costs	Monitoring and Controlling	Work Performance Information, Change Requests, Cost Forecasts

When working on an agile project, budgeting is done differently than on a traditional project. On a traditional project, the entire budget is calculated during planning for all the project activities. Agile projects are funded incrementally as each of the iterations is getting done. In the last section of this chapter, we will be discussing how agile budgeting is done.

ExamTip: Traditional project funding is done upfront, while in an agile project, funding is done incrementally.

Plan Cost Management

This is the process where you will create the cost management plan. This plan will give you the steps required to complete the other three processes in cost. Creating this plan will be very important in ensuring that the other cost processes are done correctly.

Inputs

Project Management Plan – Covered in Chapter 3

Project Charter – Covered in Chapter 4

Enterprise Environmental Factors – Covered in Chapter 3

Organizational Process Assets – Covered in Chapter 3

Tools and Techniques

Expert Judgment – Covered in Chapter 3

Data Analysis – Covered In Chapter 3

Meetings – Covered in Chapter 3

Outputs

Cost Management Plan

The cost management plan is part of the project management plan. This plan will direct us on how to estimate the cost of each activity, create the project budget, and monitor and control the cost of the project. The cost management plan can include how to determine the level of accuracy on the estimates, and how the EVM will be used to control the cost.

Estimate Costs

In this process, you will analyze each individual activity and assign a cost to each activity. Almost all the other knowledge areas will affect cost in one way or another. You can see this from the inputs and tools. The scope, time, quality, risk, HR, and procurement will affect the cost of the activities.

The estimated cost of each activity should include labor, material, equipment, services, and facilities. If it is an extended project, you may have to include inflation. You should also include any reserves that are added for risk.

When determining the cost of the activities, it is important to know the different types of estimates on the project and their ranges as follows:

Rough Order of Magnitude (ROM): This estimate is the most inaccurate, as it can be between -25% to +75%. This is most likely used in the initiating part of the phase or project.

Budget Estimate: This is better than a ROM. It is usually expected to have about -10% to +25% variance.

Definitive Estimate: This is the best estimate you can get with a -5% to +10%. This is considered very accurate and will most likely be done during the later parts of planning the project.

> **EXAM TIP:** *Know the estimate types and their ranges.*

Inputs

Project Management Plan

Although the project management plan has many components, there are a few components in particular that you might be using here, including:

- **Cost Management Plan:** This is important because it will give us the steps needed to do this process. It will state what inputs and tools to use to create the estimated cost of each activity.

- **Quality Management Plan:** This plan will outline the steps the project team will take to ensure the project meets its quality requirements. Quality will affect the cost of the project, and it's important to understand what the steps are as you estimate the cost of each activity.

- **Scope Baseline:** The scope baseline includes the project scope statement, WBS, and the WBS dictionary. Knowing the work that needs to get done and how to get it done will affect the cost of the project activities.

Project Documents

Of the 33 project documents, the ones you are most likely to use in this process include:

- **Project schedule:** The project schedule includes the network diagram, the Gantt chart, and the milestone chart. Knowing how long it will take to complete each of the activities will affect the cost of the activity.

- **Risk register:** The risk register will list all the positives (opportunities) and negatives (threats) that could affect the project. This will be used to determine the amount of reserves needed for the activities.

- **Lessons learned register:** A listing of all of the lessons learned so far on the project.

- **Resource requirements:** The resources needed to complete each activity will affect the duration of each activity. Examples of resources can include people, equipment, and materials.

Enterprise Environmental Factors – Covered in Chapter 3

Organizational Process Assets – Covered in Chapter 3

Tools and Techniques

Expert Judgment

Expert judgment involves having an expert estimate of the cost of the activities. For example, a consumer has a painter estimate the cost of painting a room. This is one of the most common tools in the PMBOK® Guide. It can produce some of the more accurate estimates.

Analogous Estimating

Analogous estimating, also known as top-down estimating, is based on previous projects. This estimate is generally quick to perform but could be very inaccurate. If the previous project is not very similar, the estimate will be inaccurate. For example, if the last time we painted a 400-sq.ft room, it cost $2,000, would paint another 400-sq.ft room cost the same? The answer is maybe, depending on the layout and how fast it needs to get done.

Parametric Estimating

A parametric estimate is a type of mathematical estimation; it's generally something multiplied by something or something divided by something. For example, if one square foot cost $2 to paint, how much would 500 square feet cost to paint? Easy: $1,000. This estimate uses historical data and could be very accurate, depending on the complexity of the work.

Bottom-Up Estimating

Bottom-up estimation is known as one of the most accurate methods to estimate cost or time. The work has to be very detailed for this type of estimation to take place. Bottom-up estimate involves breaking down the work to identify its pieces and then aggregating it back up to form the overall cost estimates of each activity. For example, instead of estimating the cost of writing an entire module of the software, you can use bottom-up estimating to assign a cost to each individual line of code and then aggregate all costs per line of code to form the overall cost of the module. This method would, of course, be very accurate, but it can be very complex and time-consuming to do.

> *Exam Tip: Know the difference between analogous (top-down) and bottom-up. They are the opposite of each other. Analogous is quick but not accurate, and bottom-up is long, but very accurate.*

Three-Point Estimating

This tool was covered in the "Schedule Management" chapter within the "estimate activity duration" process. You will get questions on PERT formulas related to both time and cost on the exam.

Data Analysis

As you start to assign a cost to each activity, you will acquire a large amount of data related to the work on the project. Here are some techniques that we can use to help assign costs:

- **Reserve analysis:** Anytime you estimate work, you might want to add reserve time to cover work risks. The risk register will indicate how to respond to the risk, which could include adding more cost to the activity if a risk occurs. This can be a percentage of the cost or a fixed cost, depending on the work. All project work will contain some kind of unknown, and this will account for that risk.

There are two types of reserves on a project: contingency and management reserves. Contingency reserves (known unknowns) are included in the cost baseline and are within the control of the project manager. The project manager adds contingency reserves just in case he/she might need the money for project unknowns. Management reserves (unknown unknowns) are added to the project by the organization's management and are not included in the project cost baseline. This is just extra money management allocates in case the project needs more funds to complete. Management reserves are under the control of the organization's management, and the project will need an approved change request to access these funds.

Exam Tip: Know the difference between contingency and management reserves.

- **Cost of quality:** The cost of quality is the amount of money you spend to ensure quality requirements are met on the project. That could include the cost of better machinery, more trained workers, or better materials. If the quality requirements are not met on a project, you might have to scrap the work and start over or rework the product to fix any defects on it. We will be covering this in more detail in the next chapter quality management.

Project Management Information System – Covered in Chapter 3

Decision Making – Covered in Chapter 3

Outputs

Cost Estimates

This is the cost of each individual activity. It includes labor, materials, equipment, technology, exchange rate, reserve, and inflation.

Basis of Estimates

The basis of the estimates is how the estimates were developed and their ranges. It can also include all assumptions and constraints made to create the estimate. For example, if an assumption was made that the project doesn't need to upgrade the network wiring for the phone system installation project, it will need to be listed here.

Project Documents Updates

After coming up with the estimates for the activities, you might need to update other project documents, such as the risk register.

Determine Budget

This process is where you take all the activity cost estimates and aggregate the cost into the project cost baseline(budget). The project performance will be measured against the cost baseline when the project is executed.

Keep in mind that the cost baseline will include the contingency reserves, but will not include the management reserves.

Inputs

Project Management Plan

Although the project management plan has many components, there are a few components in particular that you might be using here, which include:

- **Cost management plan:** This is important because it will give you the steps to do this process. It will state what inputs and tools to use to create the estimated cost of each activity.

- **Resource management plan:** This plan will outline the steps the project team will take to ensure the project meets its quality requirements. Quality will affect the cost of the project, and it's important to understand what the steps are as you estimate the cost of each activity.

- **Scope baseline:** The scope baseline includes the project scope statement, WBS, and the WBS dictionary. Knowing the work that needs to get done and how to get it done will affect the cost of the project activity.

Project Documents

Of the 33 project documents, the ones you are most likely to use in this process include:

Activity cost estimates: Knowing the cost of each activity will be critical in determining the overall project budget.

Basis of estimates: The basis of the estimates is how the estimates were developed and their ranges. It can also include all assumptions and the constraints made to create the estimate.

- **Project schedule:** The project schedule includes the network diagram, the Gantt chart, and the milestone chart. Knowing how long it will take to complete each of these activities will affect the cost of the activities.

- **Risk register:** The risk register will list all the positives (opportunities) and negatives (threats) that could affect the project. The risk register will be used to determine the amount of reserves needed for the activities.

Business Documents

Business documents usually include the business case and the benefits management plan. The business case gives us the cost-benefit of doing the project, and the benefits management plan shows what benefits the organization will get from the project. Refer to the integration management chapter for more information on these two documents.

Agreements

An agreement is a contract between a buyer and a seller for work to be performed or for the sale of products. If the project has an agreement with a vendor, then it will have the cost included in it.

Enterprise Environmental Factors – Covered in Chapter3

Organizational Process Assets – Covered in Chapter 3

Tools and Techniques

Cost Aggregation

Cost aggregation is rolling up the activity costs into work packages and then the work packages into deliverables. Knowing the costs of all the deliverables will give the cost of the entire project.

Expert Judgment

Expert judgment involves having an expert help determine the cost of the project. Experts can be consultants, team members, and sometimes customers.

Historical Information Review

Historical information review is a form of parametric estimating. If you look at previous projects you've done that are similar to this project, you will be able to use some of the data to estimate the project cost. For example, the last time you painted a room, you spent $2 per square foot. This project has 3,000 square feet to paint. This project will cost roughly $6,000. This only works when the two projects are very similar.

Funding Limit Reconciliation

Funding limit reconciliation is when the organization limits the project funding because of year-end budgets or other expenses a company might have throughout the year. This might result in the rescheduling of the project work until the funds become available.

Financing

This tool is about acquiring money for the project, generally from an external source. External sources can include getting the required funds from the public, government, or external investors. This is common on big projects such as building a large skyscraper.

Data Analysis – Covered in Chapter 3

Outputs

Cost Baseline

The cost baseline is the cost of the project. It will include all the costs of all the deliverables on the project. The cost baseline is what will be included in the project management plan and will be used to measure the performance of the project once it is executed. This is also known as the budget at completion (BAC).

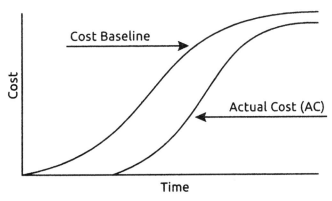

Cost can be displayed as an S-curve graph, which shows how the project is spending the budget. Generally, the project will spend less at the beginning, most in the middle, and less in the end, as shown below.

> ***EXAMTIP:*** *The cost baseline represents the project cost, which includes the contingency reserves. The total budget of the project is: cost baseline + management reserves.*

Project Funding Requirements

Project funding requirements will state how and when the project will be funded. It might state how much is needed every month or quarter to keep the project work going.

Project Documents Updates

Project documents that could be affected by the budget include the risk register, project schedule, and activity cost estimates.

Control Costs

This process is a monitoring and controlling process where you will try to keep the project on budget. It is very important for any project manager to ensure that the project stays on budget.

You will be comparing the planned work (project management plan) and the actual work (work performance data). If there are any variances, you will need to investigate them and determine the best course of action. That can include performing any type of corrective or preventive actions (via a change request).

This process will take place throughout the project. Almost all phases of a project will have cost control from planning to closing.

Inputs

Project Management Plan

The project management plan will have the cost baseline and the cost management plan. This will be needed to guide this process and to determine if the project is still on budget.

Project Documents – Covered in Chapter 3

Project Funding Requirements

Project funding requirements will state how and when the project is funded. It might state how much is needed every month or quarter to keep the project work going.

Work Performance Data

This is the actual work that is being done on the project. This will state the actual cost of the work that has been done so far on the project.

Organizational Process Assets – Covered in Chapter 3

Tools and Techniques

Expert Judgment – Covered in Chapter 3

Data Analysis

As the project manager is monitoring the execution of the project and watching the resources being used, he/she would have to analyze the data related cost to ensure the project stays on budget. Here are a few techniques that the project manager can use:

- **Earned value analysis:** Earned value analysis is a series of calculations that will give you important statistics about the performance of the project. This will be covered at the end of the chapter "Earned Value Management."

- **Reserve analysis:** As the project work is done, you will need to ensure that any risk that takes place is correctly responded to. You will have to use plan contingency and requested management reserves as required throughout the project. These services will cover any unknown risks that might arise as you execute the project.

- **Variance Analysis:** Variance analysis will determine if there is a variance between the planned work (Project Management Plan) and the actual work (work performance data). The project manager will need to ensure that there is no variance on the project that is related to costs. If there is a variance between planned and actual work, the project manager might need a change request to fix the project budget.

- **Trend analysis:** Trend analysis will be used to determine if a trend is emerging as the project is progressing. For example, is the project continuously staying on budget, or is it continuously going off-budget. The project manager will need to analyze the trend in order to assess what is happening and take appropriate corrective action if necessary.

To-Complete Performance Index (TCPI)

The to-complete performance index (TCPI) is how we will measure the level of the work that needs to be done to finish the project within the budget. This will be covered at the end of this chapter, under "Earned Value Management."

Project Management Information System – Covered in Chapter 3

Outputs

Work Performance Information

This will show the performance of the work being done. It will show the difference between real work and planned work. It will cover the CV (Cost Variance), and CPI (Cost Performance Index) earned value formulas.

Cost Forecasts

This is a forecast of how much the project could cost in the end. It will be based on the rate of spending now. This can be calculated using the EAC (Estimate at Completion) earned value formula.

Change Requests

If the project could be over-budget or is already over-budget, the project manager will need to get a change request to implement any necessary corrective or preventive actions. This can include adding more money or time to finish the project. All change requests will be sent through the "Perform Integrated Change Control" process for approval.

Project Management Plan Updates – Covered in Chapter 3

Project Documents Updates – Covered in Chapter 3

Organizational Process Assets Updates – Covered in Chapter 3

Agile and Hybrid Cost Management

Many agile and hybrid projects will follow several of the different processes we have covered in this chapter, but agile does have a few different ways to manage costs since the project is being funded incrementally.

Agile budgeting is linked to different iterations. The more iterations, the higher the budget of the project. For example, if an organization calculates that each iteration takes $10,000 of labor, then if the project contains six iterations, it would be $60,000. The way this would be calculated would be using something called the burn rate cost approach.

The burn rate cost can be calculated by:

- Average cost per hour per person. This is a very simple calculation where you look at the number of people working on the agile project and find out how much each of them is costing per hour and how many hours they're working. For example, if the agile team is made up of three people, each getting $60 an hour and each work 40 hours a week, that would mean your weekly expenditure would be 60×40×3 = $7,200 per week. If an iteration takes four weeks, then it would be $7200 times four per iteration, for a total of $28,800. If this project were only four iterations, the total cost would be $115,200.

Another way to do agile budgeting would be to come up with the cost per feature. This would be an estimated cost that would be assigned to each individual feature in the product backlog. For example, if one feature is very large, the project team might estimate it to take $50,000 worth of work to do, whereas another feature which is very small might only take $5,000 worth of work. By going through the entire product backlog and assigning a cost to each individual feature, you would then be able to come up with an overall cost for the project.

Hybrid projects will generally utilize both traditional methods of doing budgets all upfront and using the incrementally funded methods of agile. For example, on a hybrid project, if the development party is using an agile method, it can use the burn rate costs as a way to estimate the budget, and during a traditional project method of deploying the application, they can use the different processes we covered in this chapter to calculate the budget.

Hot Topic: Earned Value Management

EVM stands for Earned Value Management. It is a series of formulas that gives you a numerical

analysis of the project. EVM is guaranteed to be on your exam. Expect at least 10 questions that deal with the formulas and their meanings. There are two key aspects.

- Know the formulas and how to calculate them. This will take memorization and practice. These questions will be straightforward.

- Know what the numbers actually mean. A lot of questions will ask you to interpret the numbers. For example, if they say the CV of this project is this much, and the SPI is this much, then what's happening on the project? Expect more of these types of questions than simple calculation problems.

Here is a table with just the formulas you will need to know for the exam:

Term	Description	Formula
Budget at Completion (BAC)	Original budget of the project.	None, just the original budget.
Planned Value (PV)	Amount of money worth of work we that should have been done on the project.	PV= Planned % Complete x BAC
Earned Value (EV)	Amount of money worth of work you actually did on the project.	EV= Actual % Complete x BAC
Actual Cost (AC)	Amount of money you already spent on the project	None, just the amount already spent on the project.
Cost Variance (CV)	The difference between the work done and money spent. This value should be positive for under budget. **Negative values indicate over budget**	CV = EV - AC
Cost Performance Index (CPI)	The rate of how we are spending to actually earning on the project. **This value should be 1 and over for projects under budget.**	CPI = EV / AC
Schedule Variance (SV)	The difference between the amount of work we should have done vs. the amount actually done. This value should be positive for ahead of schedule. **Negative values indicate behind schedule**	SV = EV - PV
Schedule Performance Index (SPI)	The rate of how we are meeting the project schedule. **This value should be 1 and over for a project to be ahead of the schedule.**	SPI = EV / PV
Estimate at Completion (EAC)	Forecasting the total cost of the project at the end based on the current spending rate of the project.	EAC = BAC / CPI
Estimate to Completion (ETC)	Forecasting the amount that will be needed to complete the current project based on the current performance.	ETC = EAC - AC
Variance at Completion (VAC)	The difference between the original budget and new forecasted budget. This value should be positive for projects that may end at or under budget	VAC = BAC - EAC
To-Complete Performance Index (TCPI)	The performance that needs to be met to finish the project within the budget.	TCPI = (BAC – EV) / (BAC – AC)
Earned Valued Memorization Chart		

Scenario 1:

Project manager Bill is currently executing a project to install new fences for a building. The project has a budget of $100 and a duration of five days in total. Today is the end of the third day. The project team has completed 75% of the project and has spent $70.

Summary:

Budget: $100
Duration: 5days
Now . . . . 3rd day completed
Completed: 75%
Total Spent: $70

Here are the formulas we will need to find:

BAC:	**PV:**	**EV:**	**AC:**
CV:	**CPI:**	**SV:**	**SPI:**
EAC:	**ETC:**	**VAC:**	**TCPI:**

Where to use this scenario to figure out the 12 Numbers that we need:

- **BAC:** BAC stands for Budget at Completion, and it is just the budget of the project. It is either going to be a given number on the exam or a parametric calculated number. For our scenario, the BAC is $100.

- **PV:** PV stands for Planned Value; PV is equal to the BAC x Planned Percent Complete. In our scenario, the planned percent completed is 60%. We should have accomplished 60% of the work by the end of the third day. The formula here would be $100 x 60%. PV is $60. What this actually means is that the project should have completed $60 worth of work by the end of day 3.

   ExamTip: Sometimes, to calculate the planned percent complete, if it is not given, is to take the now(current time) and divide by the overall duration. In this example, it would be 3÷5=60%.

- **EV:** EV stands for earned value, and is equal to the BAC x the Actual Percent Complete. This project has completed 75% worth of work. The formula here would be $100 x 75%, which is equal to $75. What this means is that this project has done $75 worth of work.

- **AC:** AC stands for actual costs. AC is just the amount of money that was spent on the project. It is either a given number or sometimes a simple calculation. AC is equal to $70 on this project since that is all we spent so far on the project.

While looking at these four numbers, we can tell that this project is doing great. We were supposed to have done $60 worth of work, we did $75 worth of work, and we only spent $70 doing it. Let's see what the other 8 numbers will tell us.

   ExamTip: The first four numbers will be added to the remaining formulas.

- **CV:** CV stands for cost variance, the formula is EV minus AC. EV tells you how far you are off from your budget. In our scenario, we did $75 worth of work, and we spent $70 doing it. So the formula is, $75 - $70 = $5.

That means that we are $5 under the budget on this project as of right now.

CV should be zero or positive. If your CV is negative, you are over budget by that much. If your CV is positive, you are under budget by that much.

- **CPI:** CPI stands for Cost Performance Index. It is equal to EV / AC. In our scenario, it is equal to: $75 ÷ $70 = 1.07

- There are a few different ways to read the CPI. One way to read it is by saying for every dollar the project spends, we do $1.07 worth of work on this project. Another way to read it (and the way you should read it for your exam) is that we are 7% under budget at this point in the project.

  Your CPI should be one or greater. If your CPI is under one, that is not good. For example, if your CPI is .8, that means you're 20% over your budget. If your CPI is 1.2 that means you're 20% under the budget.

- **SV:** SV stands for schedule variance. It is equal to EV – PV. In our scenario, the formula is

  $75 - $60 = $15

  SV tells us how much money worth of work we are ahead or behind schedule. In our scenario, we are $15 worth of work ahead of schedule. We should have done $60 worth of work, but we did $75 worth of work. This is good.

- **SV should be zero or positive**. For example, if your SV is $100, that means you're $100 worth of work ahead of schedule. If your SV is -$200, this means you are $200 worth of work behind schedule.

- **SPI:** SPI stands for Schedule Performance Index. It is equal to EV / PV. In our scenario, this would be $75 ÷ $60 =1.25.

  This is read as a percentage. In this particular project we are 25% ahead of schedule.

  SPI should be one or greater. For example, if your SPI is 1.2, that means you are 20% ahead of your schedule. If your SPI is .8 that means you're 20% behind your schedule.

- **EAC:** EAC stands for Estimate at Completion. It is equal to BAC/CPI. In our scenario, that would be equal to $100/1.07=$93.45. EAC is the forecast. What this is telling us about this project is that if this project continues at its current pace, it will finish at $93.45.

  ExamTip: When they ask for the forecast, you calculate the EAC.

- **ETC:** stands for Estimate to Complete. This is equal to the EAC – AC. In our scenario, that would be equal to

  $93.45 - $70 = $23.45.

  This is read as the amount of money needed to finish the project. We have currently spent $70 and need $23.45 more to complete it.

- VAC: VAC stands for variance at completion. It is equal to the BAC - EAC. In our example, that would be

  $100 - $93.45 = $6.55.

  This number represents the amount of money you would have left over or need in order to finish a project.

  VAC should be positive. A positive VAC will tell you how much money you have left over at the end of the project. A negative VAC will tell you how much more money you will need to finish the project.

- **TCPI:** TCPI stands for To Complete Performance Index. It is equal to the (BAC – EV) / (BAC – AC). In our scenario, this would be ($100 – $75) ÷ ($100 – $70) = 83.

This formula tells you how much effort your project team needs to put in in order to finish this project within budget. Do we need to put in 100% effort to finish this project within its budget? No, if the project team only puts in 83% of the effort into finishing this project, it will be finished at $100. If the team puts in 100% of its effort, it will be finished at $93.45.

TCPI should be one or under. If your TCPI is 1.2, this means your project team must work 20% harder to finish the project within its budget. If your TCPI is .8 this means your team can work 20% less to finish the work within the budget.

BAC:	$100	PV:	$60	EV:	$75	AC:	$70
CV:	$5	CPI:	1.07	SV:	$15	SPI:	1.25
EAC:	$93.45	ETC:	$23.45	VAC:	$6.55	TCPI:	.83

Scenario 2:

Project manager Mary is currently executing a network upgrade project. The project has a budget of $4,000 and a duration of 4 years total. Mary just completed the 17th month of the project. The project team has completed 35% of the project work and has spent $1,500.

Summary:

Budget: $4,000
Duration: . . . . 4 Years
Now . . . . 17th month completed
Completed: 35%
Total Spent: $1,500

Find the following values:

BAC:	PV:	EV:	AC:
CV:	CPI:	SV:	SPI:
EAC:	ETC:	VAC:	TCPI:

When calculating the numbers, round to the tenths place, since we are working with currency. If your calculations are slightly off from what's in this book, don't worry, it might just be how you rounded the numbers. The main goal is to understand the formulas and how to calculate them.

- BAC is 4,000.

- PV is $4{,}000 \times (17/48) = 1{,}416.67$.

- EV is $4{,}000 \times 35\% = 1{,}400$.

- AC is a given at 1,500.

- CV=EV-AC is $1{,}400 - 1{,}500 = -100$. That means this project is over its budget by $100.

- CPI=EV/AC is $1{,}400 \div 1{,}500 = .93$. This project is 7% overbudget at the current time.

- SV = EV - PV is $1{,}400 - 1{,}416 = -16.67$. This project is currently $16 worth of work behind schedule.

- SPI=EV/PV is $1{,}400 \div 1{,}416.67 = .98$. That means this project is about 2% behind schedule. This number could be one or on schedule, depending on how you rounded the planned percentage complete in the PV.

- EAC=BAC/CPI is $4{,}000 \div .93 = 4{,}300$. That means we are forecasting that at the current rate of work, we will have spent $4,300 to complete the project by the end.

- ETC = EAC - AC is $4{,}300 - 1{,}500 = 2{,}800$. That means we currently need $2,800 more to finish the rest of the project.

- VAC=BAC-EAC is $4{,}000 - 4{,}300 = -300$. That means that when this project is over, we would need an additional $300 more to finish it off.

- TCPI=(BAC-EV)/(BAC-AC) is $(4{,}000-1{,}400) \div (4{,}000-1{,}500) = 1.04$. This means we need to work 4% harder to finish the project within the budget.

BAC:	4,000	**PV:**	1,416.67	**EV:**	1,400	**AC:**	1,500
CV:	-100	**CPI:**	.93	**SV:**	-16.67	**SPI:**	.98
EAC:	4,301	**ETC:**	2,801	**VAC:**	-301	**TCPI:**	1.04

All values are in currency except the indexes (CPI, SPI, TCPI).

Scenario 3:

Project manager Peter is currently executing a new phone system installation project. The project has a budget of $3,000 and a duration of 11 months total. Peter just completed the 8th month of the project. The project team has completed 90% of the project work and has spent $2,900.

Summary:
Budget: $3,000
Duration:............ 11months
Now................. 8th month completed
Completed: 90%
Total Spent: $2,900

Find the following values:

BAC:	PV:	EV:	AC:
CV:	CPI:	SV:	SPI:
EAC:	ETC:	VAC:	TCPI:

When calculating the number, round to the tenths place, since we are working with currency. If your calculations are slightly off from what's in this book, don't worry, it might just be how you rounded the numbers. The main goal is to understand the formulas and how to calculate them.

- BAC is 3,000.

- PV is 3,000×(8/11)=$2,181.

- EV is 3,000×90%=2,700.

- AC is a given at2,900.

- CV=EV-AC is 2,700–2,900=-200. That means this project is over its budget by $200.

- CPI=EV/AC is 2,700÷2,900=.93. This project is 7% overbudget at the current time.

- SV = EV - PV is 2,700 - 2,181 = 519. This project is currently $519 worth of work ahead of schedule.

- SPI = EV / PV is 2,700 ÷ 2,181 = 1.23. That means this project is about 23% percent ahead of schedule, which is great.

- EAC=BAC/CPI is 3,000÷.93=3,226. That means we are forecasting that at the current rate of work, we would have spent $3,226 to complete the project in the end.

- ETC = EAC - AC is 3,226 - 2,900 = 326. That means we currently need $326 more to finish the rest of the project.

- VAC=BAC–EAC is 3,000–3,226=-226. That means that when this project is over, we would need an additional $226 to finish it off.

- TCPI=(BAC–EV)/(BAC–AC) is (3,000-2,700)÷(3,000–2,900)=3.That means we need to work 300% harder to finish the project within the budget. That number may look high, but if you think about it, we did $2,700 worth of work and spent $2,900 to do it. The budget is telling us we need to do $3,000 worth of work. That means we have $100 to complete the additional $300 (difference between the EV and BAC) worth of work, so we will have to work 3x harder.

BAC:	3,000	**PV:**	2,181	**EV:**	2,700	**AC:**	2,900
CV:	-200	**CPI:**	.93	**SV:**	519	**SPI:**	1.23
EAC:	3,226	**ETC:**	326	**VAC:**	-226	**TCPI:**	3

Scenario 4:

Project manager Peter is currently executing a new server installation project. The project has a budget of $5,000 and a duration of 15 months in total. Peter just completed the 9th month of the project. The project team has completed 35% of the project work and has spent $2,900.

Summary:

Budget: .... $5,000 Duration: 15 months
Now: .... 9th month completed
Completed: 35%
Total Spent: $2,900

Find the following values:

BAC:	PV:	EV:	AC:
CV:	CPI:	SV:	SPI:
EAC:	ETC:	VAC:	TCPI:

When calculating the number, round to the tenths place, since we are working with currency. If your calculations are slightly off from what's in this book, don't worry, it might just be how you rounded the numbers. The main goal is to understand the formulas and how to calculate them.

- BAC is 5,000.

- PV is 5,000×(9/15)=3,000.

- EV is 5,000×35%=1,750.

- AC is a given at 2,900.

- CV=EV-AC is 1,750–2,900=-1,150. That means this project is over its budget by $1,150.

- CPI=EV/AC is 1,750÷2,900=.6. This project is 40% overbudget at the current time.

- SV = EV - PV is 1,750 - 3,000 = -1,250. This project is currently $1,250 worth of work behind schedule.

- SPI = EV / PV is 1,750 ÷ 3,000 = .58. That means this project is about 42% percent behind schedule, which is bad.

- EAC=BAC/CPI is 5,000÷.6=8,333.33. That means we are forecasting that at the current rate of work, we would have spent $8,333 to complete the project in the end.

- ETC = EAC - AC is 8,333 - 2,900 = 5,433. That means we need $5,433 more currently to finish the rest of the project.

- VAC=BAC–EAC is 5,000-8,3333=-3,333. That means that when this project is over, we would need an additional $3,333 more to finish it off.

- TCPI=(BAC–EV)/(BAC–AC) is (5,000–1,750)÷(5,000–2,900)=1.55. That means we need to work 55% harder to finish the project within the budget.

BAC:	5,000	**PV:**	3,000	**EV:**	1,750	**AC:**	2,900
CV:	-1,150	**CPI:**	6	**SV:**	-1,250	**SPI:**	.58
EAC:	8,333.33	**ETC:**	5,433.33	**VAC:**	-3,333.33	**TCPI:**	1.55

Cost Management Questions

1. For an IT project your EV = $130,500, PV = $125,500, and AC = $129,000. Which one of the following statements is TRUE?

   A. The project is behind schedule and overbudget.

   B. The project is ahead of schedule and under budget.

   C. The project is behind schedule and under budget.

   D. The project is ahead of schedule and over budget.

2. You recently took over a project from another project manager who left the organization. You find out that the project has a BAC = $45,000, PV = $30,000, cumulative AC = $25,000, and cumulative EV = $24,000. You decided to perform a forecasting analysis and calculated the values for EAC, ETC, TCPI, and VAC. Which of the following is NOT true?

   A. You will need $21,875 more to complete this project.

   B. The project will cost $46,875.

   C. The project performance is not good as TCPI is 1.05.

   D. The project will be under budget by $1,875.

3. You are in the Determine Budget process of developing a budget or cost baseline and project funding requirements. All of the following are inputs in this process EXCEPT:

   A. Work performance data

   B. Cost management plan

   C. Activity cost estimates

   D. Project schedule

4. To develop an online accounting application for your software development project, you are working on figuring out the total funding requirements, including all project reserves. Which of the following will help you the MOST in this case?

   A. Project budget and contingency reserves

   B. Funding limit reconciliation

   C. Cost baseline and management reserves

   D. Management reserves and contingency reserves

5. You are in the Determine Budget process of developing a budget or cost baseline and project funding requirements. All of the following are tools & techniques in this process EXCEPT:

   A. Cost aggregation

   B. Data analysis

   C. Funding limit reconciliation

   D. Performance review

6. You are the project manager of a construction project that will take six months to complete and will cost $75,000/month. At the end of the third month, you were asked to find out the cumulative SPI for the project and report it to management. While reviewing the project status, you found that you have spent $80,000 in the first month,

    $72,000 in the second month, and $75,000 in the third month. You also found that the project was 15 percent complete at the end of the first month, 35 percent complete at the end of the second month, and 45 percent complete at the end of the third month. If you planned to complete 50 percent of the work by this time, what is the cumulative SPI at the end of month three?

    A. 0.5

    B. 0.9

    C. 0.34

    D. 1.1

7. A project manager working on a construction project planned to install new carpets in all four rooms of the house. She measured the square footage of all the rooms and then multiplied that figure by a set cost factor to estimate the cost for installing the carpet. This is an example of:

    A. Bottom-up estimating

    B. Analogous estimating

    C. Parametric estimating

    D. Three-point estimating

8. With the help of your team members, you just finished the development of an approximation of the costs of all resources, such as labor, materials, equipment, services, facilities, and other special items associated with each scheduled activity. What should you do NEXT?

    A. Control costs

    B. Resource leveling

    C. Bottom-up estimating

    D. Determine budget

9. Steve, a project manager, is trying to figure out the performance that must be achieved in order to meet the financial and schedule goals in his project. He is using a measurement that will give him the status on the remaining work with respect to the funds remaining. Which of the following measures is Steve using?

    A. Cost aggregation

    B. Variance analysis

    C. Trend analysis

    D. To-Complete Performance Index (TCPI)

10. You are overseeing a mobile application development project. While reviewing an earned value report, you observe that the SPI is 1.2 and the CPI is 0.9. Which statement can you make about the project?

    A. On track, according to schedule and budget baselines.

    B. Behind the schedule and over budget.

    C. Ahead of the schedule and over budget.

    D. On schedule and under budget.

11. Your project has a budget of $900,000 and is running well. In the latest earned value report, the team reported that the CPI = 1.1, the SPI = 0.9, and the PV= $600,000. You want to know, from this point on, how much more the project will cost, but could not find it in the report. What will be the estimate to complete, or ETC, be in this case?

    A. $300,000

    B. $327,272

    C. $818,181

    D. $490,909

12. You asked one of your team members about the schedule variance (SV) for one of her key deliverables. She mentioned that she is behind schedule, but there would not be any cost variance. Which of the following is NOT true in this case?

    A. EV and PV were the same

    B. EV and AC were the same

    C. EV is less than PV

    D. CPI is 1

13. There were eight potential projects in your organization, and your senior management wanted to select the best project that would meet and exceed the organizational strategic goals and objectives. As your organization has limited resources and time constraints, it developed business cases for these projects and compared the benefits to select the best project. Out of eight projects, management has selected two projects and later on decided to go for Project X, which would yield $250,000 in benefits, instead of Project Y, which would yield $200,000. What is the opportunity cost for selecting Project X over Project Y?

    A. $250,000

    B. $200,000

    C. -$250,000

    D. -$200,000

14. You are overseeing a project to implement an accounting application for a dentist's office. In one of the performance meetings, you came up with the following measurement: AC=500, PV=600, and EV=650. What is going on with this project?

    A. Both CV and SV are positive numbers; thus, you are under budget and ahead of schedule.

    B. You do not have enough information to calculate SPI and CPI.

    C. The CV is a negative number, which means you have spent more than planned.

    D. The SV is a negative number, which means the project is behind schedule.

15. The project manager and the team members have just finished working on the WBS and have almost finalized the project schedule. The project manager is also planning to start working on the project budget. Which document will be used for planning, estimating, budgeting, and controlling costs so that the project can be completed within the approved budget?

    A. Earned value management

    B. Cost baseline

    C. Cost management plan

    D. Funding limit reconciliation

16. The Earned Value Management (EVM) will NOT be very beneficial in which situation?

    A. To measure a project's progress against the project scope, cost, and schedule baselines.

    B. To forecast future performance and the project's completion date and final cost.

    C. To provide schedule and budget variances during the project.

    D. To develop the project cost baseline.

17. A project manager is working on a project designed to create an internal website for ITPro Consultancy, LLC that will allow them to schedule the conference room online. While reviewing the status of the project, the project manager found out the EV, AC, and PV (listed in the table below). What are the SPI and CPI?

Project	PV	EV	AC
	242,200	224,000	140,500

    A. 0.925 and 1.59

    B. 1.59 and .925

    C. 0.919 and 1.77

    D. 1.77 and 0.919

18. You are preparing a cost management plan for the data center project you are managing for ITPro Consultancy, LLC. All of the following is true regarding this plan EXCEPT:

    A. Activity cost estimates will be rounded to a prescribed precision; for example, nearest $100, nearest $1,000, and so on.

    B. Units of measurement, such as hours, days, weeks, or a lump sum amount, will be used to estimate resources.

    C. The primary concern is determining the amount of resources needed to complete the project activities.

    D. The WBS provides a framework for the cost management plan, and a control account (CA) in the WBS is used to monitor and control the project cost.

19. You estimated your project cost to be $80,000 with a timeline of eight months. After four months in the project, you found out that 40 percent of the project is completed; the actual cost is $25,000. What does the SPI tell you in this case?

    A. There is not enough information to calculate the SPI.

    B. The project is behind schedule.

    C. The project is ahead of schedule.

    D. The project is progressing as per the plan.

20. You estimated your project cost to be $80,000 with a timeline of eight months. As of today, you found out that 40 percent of the project is completed; the actual cost is $30,000. What does the CPI tell you in this case?

    A. There is not enough information to calculate the CPI.

    B. The project is over budget.

    C. The project is under budget.

    D. The project is costing as per the plan.

21. Which one of the following is FALSE about TCPI?

    A. TCPI calculates the performance that must be achieved in order to meet financial or schedule goals.

    B. TCPI usually determines the status of the remaining work with respect to the funds remaining.

    C. If the cumulative CPI falls below the baseline plan, all future work must be performed at the TCPI to achieve the planned BAC.

    D. If the cumulative CPI falls below the baseline plan, all future work must be performed below the TCPI to achieve the planned BAC.

22. All of the following statements are true about the cost baseline EXCEPT:

    A. It is a time-phased budget used to monitor, measure, and control cost performance during the project.

    B. It is usually displayed in the form of an S-curve.

    C. It assigns cost estimates for expected future period operating costs.

    D. It aggregates the estimated costs of project activities to work packages, then to control accounts, and finally to the project.

23. While working on your project budget, you also calculated the contingency reserve. This contingency reserve is the estimated cost to be determined, managed, and controlled at your discretion to deal with which of the following?

    A. To compensate for inadequacies in your original cost planning.

    B. To address the cost impact of the risks remaining during the Plan Risk Responses process.

    C. To handle anticipated and certain events in your project.

    D. To handle unanticipated events or surprises in your project.

24. Lori is the project manager for a software development firm and has been assigned to create an accounting automation application for a dentist's office. While reviewing the cost estimate with Lori, the sponsor expressed her frustration with the higher cost and asked to reduce the estimate by at least ten percent. The sponsor is not too worried about the project duration estimate and suggested that Lori seek her help with the schedule if needed. What is the best course of action for Lori in this kind of situation?

    A. Replace a couple of expensive resources with lower-cost resources.

    B. Continue with the project and constantly find an opportunity to save money for a total savings of 10 percent.

    C. Have an urgent meeting with the team members and ask them to be innovative and squeeze their estimate.

    D. Inform the sponsor of the activities to be cut.

25. Selina is a project manager involved in the Estimate Costs process in the early phase of her project when a limited amount of detail was available to her. The range of her estimate was $75,000 to $200,000, and the actual cost came to be around $150,000. What would you call such an estimate?

    A. A variable estimate

    B. A definitive estimate

    C. A rough order of magnitude estimate

    D. A budget estimate

26. You have fifteen components to work on in a software development project. As per your estimation, the first six components would cost $1,500 each, and the remaining nine would cost $1,400 each. Your schedule projected that you would be done with 40 percent of the components today. While collecting the status updates from the team members, you found out that the first five components had a complete data cost of $8,000. What is the SPI?

    A. 1.20

    B. 0.132

    C. 0.833

    D. Cannot be determined

27. You are working on a project to convert an old nursing home to a new office complex. While reviewing the progress of your project, you found out that your EV = $26,000 and AC = $27,000. One of your site supervisors calls to inform you that there are several damages in the foundation that were not discovered earlier, and it will result in a significant cost overrun. What will you do FIRST?

    A. Make sure that the contingency reserves you have will be sufficient to cover the cost overrun.

    B. Call the sponsor immediately and inform her that additional funds will be needed.

    C. Ask the supervisor to figure out why these damages were not discovered earlier.

    D. Evaluate the cause and size of this cost overrun.

Project Cost Management Answers

1. **B:** The EV is greater than the PV, which indicates the project is ahead of schedule. The AC is smaller than the EV, which indicates the project is under budget.

2. **D:** We are given the following values: BAC=$45,000 PV =$30,000

    AC = $25,000

    EV = $24,000. We know:

    EAC = BAC/CPI ETC = EAC – AC

    VAC = BAC – EAC and

    TCPI = (BAC – EV) / (BAC – AC) CPI = EV/AC

    Thus CPI = $24,000/$25,000 = 0.96

    So EAC = BAC/CPI = $45,000/0.96 = $46,875 ETC = EAC – AC = $46,875 – $25,000 =

    $21,875

    TCPI = (BAC – EV) / (BAC – AC) = (45,000 – 24,000) / (45,000 – 25,000) = 21,000 / 20,000 = 1.05
    VAC= BAC – EAC = $45,000 – $46,875 = –$1,875

    The project will cost $46,875 since the EAC is $46,875. The ETC is $21,875, so you will need $21,875 to complete the project. The VAC is –$1,875; thus, the project will be over budget by $1,875. The project performance is not good as TCPI is 1.05. All of the statements are true except D. The project is over budget by $1,875, not under budget.

3. **A:** Work performance data is not an input in the Develop Budget process, but it is an input in the Control Costs process.

4. **C:** Total fund or cost budget = cost baseline + management reserves. Cost baseline = project cost + contingency reserves

    The cost baseline is the project cost plus the contingency reserves, and the cost budget, or how much money the company should have available for the project, is the cost baseline plus the management reserves. The project manager determines, manages, and controls the contingency reserves, which will address the cost impact of the risks remaining during the Plan Risk Responses process. On the other hand, management reserves are funds to cover unforeseen risks or changes to the project. In this case, the cost baseline and the management reserves will be most helpful to calculate the total funding and periodic funding requirements. Funding limit reconciliation is the technique of reconciling the expenditure of funds with the funding limits set for the project. As per the variance between the expenditure of funds and the planned limit, the activities can be rescheduled to level out the rate of expenditures.

5. **D:** Performance review is not a tool & technique in the Develop Budget process, but a tool & technique in the Control Costs process.

6. **B:** We have BAC = 6 * $75,000 = $450,000

    At the end of month three, we were supposed to finish 50 percent of the work. Thus, PV=BAC*Planned % Complete or PV=$450,000*50percent=$225,000. Also, project work is 45 percent completed at the end of three months.

    Thus, EV = BAC * Actual % Complete or EV = $450,000 * 45 percent = $202,500 We know SPI = EV/PV or SPI = $202,500/$225,000 = 0.9

7. **C:** Parametric estimate uses mathematical models based on historical records from other projects. It utilizes the statistical relationship that exists between a series of historical data and a particular delineated list of other variables. Depending upon the quality of the underlying data, this estimate can produce higher levels of accuracy and can be used in conjunction with other estimates to provide estimates for the entire project or specific segments of a project. Measures such as time per line of code, time per installation, and time per linear meter are considered in this type of estimate.

8. **D:** You just completed the Estimate Costs process and should be focusing on the Determine Budget process.

9. **D:** To-Complete Performance Index (TCPI) calculates the performance that must be achieved in order to meet financial or schedule goals.

10. **C:** A SPI of 1.2 means that the project is ahead of schedule, and a CPI of 0.9 or less than one means that the project is over budget.

11. **B:** We know ETC = EAC − AC, so we need to find out the values for Estimate at Completion (EAC) and Actual Cost (AC).

    We are given the following values: BAC=$900,000

    CPI =1.1

    SPI =0.9

    PV = $600,000

    We also know that EAC = BAC/CPI; thus EAC = $900,000/1.1 = $818,181 Now we have SPI

    = 0.9 or EV/PV = 0.9; thus EV = 0.9 * PV So EV = 0.9 * 600,000 = $540,000

    We also know that CPI=1.1 or EV/AC=1.1; thus, EV=1.1*AC So AC=EV/1.1 or AC= 540,000/1.1 =$490,909

    So ETC = EAC − AC or ETC = $818,181 − $490,909 = $327,272

12. **A:** We know SV=EV−PV. Since SV has a negative value, EV must be less than PV.

    Also CV = EV − AC. Since there will be no cost variance, EV and AC have the same value. CPI is also EV/AC = 1.

13. **B:** The opportunity cost is the value of the project that was not selected or the opportunity that was missed out on. In this case, the opportunity cost for Project X is the value of Project Y, or $200,000.

14. **A:** We know SV=EV−PV and CV=EV−AC. So SV=650−600=50 and CV=650−500= 150

A positive CV indicates that the project is under budget, and a positive SV indicates that the project is ahead of schedule.

15. **C:** The project cost management plan is a component of the overall project management plan, and it defines how the project cost will be planned, managed, expended, and controlled throughout the project lifecycle.

16. **D:** Earned value analysis provides a means to determine cost and schedule variances, not to develop the project cost baseline.

17. **A:** We know that SPI = EV/PV and CPI = EV/AC SPI = EV/PV = 224,000/242,000 =0.925

    CPI = EV/AC = 224,000/140,500 = 1.59

18. **C:** The primary concern for project cost management is to determine the cost of resources, not the amount to complete the project activities.

19. **B:** Here we have BAC = $80,000

    We know that EV = BAC * Actual % Complete

    So EV = BAC * 40 percent completion = $80,000 x 40 percent = $32,000 Also PV = BAC * (Time Passed/Total Scheduled Time)

    And PV = $80,000 * (4 months/8 months) = $40,000 So SPI = EV/PV = 32,000/40,000 = 0.8 SPI is less than one, which suggests that the project is behind schedule.

20. **C:** Here we have BAC=$80,000 and AC=$30,000

    We know that EV=BAC*Actual% Complete

    So EV = BAC * 40 percent completion

    = $80,000 * 40 percent = $32,000

    So CPI = EV/AC = 32,000/30,000 = 1.066

    CPI is more than one, which suggests that the project is under budget.

21. **D:** TCPI calculates the performance that must be achieved in order to meet financial or schedule goals and determines the status of the remaining work with respect to the funds remaining. If the cumulative CPI falls below the baseline plan, all future work must be performed at the TCPI to achieve the planned BAC.

22. **C:** Expected future period operation costs are considered to be ongoing costs and should not be part of the project costs.

23. **B:** The project manager determines, manages, and controls the contingency reserves, which will address the cost impact of the risks remaining (residual risks or known un- known risks).

24. **D:** The project manager is expected to come up with a realistic estimate that does not include padding. The project manager also should not simply reduce the estimate whenever asked by the sponsor or clients. If the project manager must reduce the estimate, she needs to explore other options such as cutting scope, reducing quality, or replacing expensive resources with low-er-cost resources. In this case, Lori should inform the sponsor of the activities to be cut in order to reduce the estimate by ten percent.

25. **C:** A rough order of magnitude (−25 percent to 75 percent) is an approximate estimate made without detailed data. This type of estimate is used during the formative stages for the initial evaluation of a project's feasibility. In this example,

    $75,000 and $200,000 are −25 percent to +75 percent of $150,000.

26. **C:** The budget for the first six components is 6*$1,500=$9,000, and the budget for the remaining nine components is 9*$1,400=$12,600. So BAC=$9,000+$12,600=$21,600

    We know PV = BAC * Planned % Complete So PV = 21,600 * 40 percent = $8,640

    We have a total of fifteen components and so far have completed five components. EV = BAC * (Work Completed/Total Work Required)

    So EV = $21,600 * 5/15 = $7,200

    So SPI = EV/PV = 7200/8640 = 0.833

27. **D:** The first step should be to get as much information as possible about the damages in the foundation by evaluating the cause and size of the damage and the amount needed for the fix. You can take other actions as appropriate once you have all the details.

Chapter 9

Project Quality Management

Quality management is going to be a very important knowledge area on your test. You will get quite a few questions about quality management. Most of the exam questions will come from knowing the processes and the tools that can be used in traditional, agile, and hybrid projects.

Any time people purchase a product or service, they worry if it is "good quality." Here are a few questions project managers should be asking themselves about quality on a project:

1. What are the quality requirements for the project?

2. How are we going to meet the quality requirements for the project?

3. What tools can we use to ensure our deliverables have met the quality requirements?

4. What are the quality policies of the company?

5. How do we know if our project has created a quality deliverable?

6. What can we do to ensure our deliverables have met the quality requirements?

7. How do we check our deliverables for quality?

8. How can we improve the processes we follow to create a quality deliverable?

Quality is defined as "the degree to which a set of inherent characteristics fulfill requirements." Having a good product or service will require that you have met the requirements for that product. One thing I always point out is that you have to collect the requirements before trying to meet them correctly. If your requirements are not detailed enough, you might not meet them.

Another term you might see on the exam is grade. The grade is defined as a design intent, a category assigned to deliverables having the same functional use, but different technical characteristics. Grade deals with technical characteristics. Things can be high or low grade. For example, buying a basic TV with no advanced characteristics such as web browsing, touch screen, or apps integration would be considered low-grade vs. a high-grade TV with many characteristics such as web browsing and many different apps.

You will need to understand the difference between grade and quality. Projects must always produce high-quality deliverables, and that means using high-grade or low-grade products as appropriate. For example, if your project was to set a kiosk at a building entrance and all you need is a TV that shows information about the building, then a low-grade TV would be just fine and meet all the project requirements. In this case, you have a high-quality deliverable with a low-grade product. It would not be acceptable to use a high-grade TV that breaks a lot or is very blurry. This would not meet the quality requirements. In this case, you would have a high-grade product, but low-quality.

Exam Tip: Quality must always be high, while the grade can be low or high.

Next, we will cover some quality theories and terms.

Just in Time: This is a practice in which a product-based company should have very low or no inventory. This way, companies always maintain the latest products. This will ensure a higher quality inventory and lower overall inventory cost.

Plan-Do-Check-Act: W. Edwards Deming popularized this. This theory advocates that business processes should be scrutinized and measured to detect sources of variations that cause products to deviate from customer requirements.

- **Plan:** Design or revise business process.

- **Do:** Implement the plan and measure its performance.

- **Check:** Access the measurements and report the results to decision-makers.

- **Act:** Decide on changes needed to improve the process.

Continuous Improvement: This is also known as Kaizen. This theory is about making small changes to improve a product or service. If a product or service does not continually improve, it will become obsolete and outdated. More updated products will offer better quality.

Total Quality Management (TQM): This another theory by W. Edwards Deming, that all employees of an organization are responsible for the quality of their products and services. Everyone in a company needs to be doing a quality job to ensure that they are providing a quality product or service. If you have the best product on the market and poor customer service, people will still consider your overall product of poor quality.

Customer Satisfaction: Customer satisfaction will be the ultimate test of quality. You will have to meet your customer's expectations by collecting, understanding, and managing their project requirements.

Prevention over Inspection: Quality is prevention-driven. Your job as a project manager is to ensure that quality is planned, designed, and built into the deliverables. Defects will cost more to fix after the deliverables have been made. It is generally more cost-effective to prevent defects than it is to fix them afterward. Prevention methods can include more quality materials, knowledgeable team members, or better equipment. More prevention will lead to fewer defects.

Six Sigma: Six Sigma is a quality theory that looks to improve the processes we follow to reduce defects. It is based on the standard deviation and the bell curve. You will not be required to know six sigma for the exam, but it is important to know what the theory is about.

Statistical Independence: This is a term used in probability that means one event cannot affect another event. For example, every time you roll a die, the probability of getting a six is independent.

Mutual Exclusivity: This means that two events cannot happen at the same time. For example, you cannot roll a die and get two and six at the same time.

Attribute Sampling: Attribute sampling is a measuring quality method that consists of observing the presence (or absence) of some characteristics (attributes). It is either good or bad, one or zero. There is no middle ground in attribute sampling.

Variable Sampling: Variable Sampling is a method of measuring quality that consists of how well something meets the requirements. It can be okay, good, very good, bad, or very bad. Unlike attribute sampling, variable sampling has a middle ground.

If you are working on an agile project, quality is and ought to be the most important asset, as in traditional project management. Because agile builds in increments, and the customer is giving continuous feedback, the quality of the project should remain high. Agile projects can and do lead to high-quality products, services, or results. In the last section of this chapter, we will be reviewing some specific agile tools and methods that can be used to ensure high quality.

The quality management knowledge area will be very important for your exam. Here are the processes we will cover:

Process	Process Group	Main Output
Plan Quality Management	Planning	Quality Management Plan, Quality Metrics
Manage Quality	Executing	Quality Reports, Test and Evaluation Documents
Control Quality	Monitoring and Controlling	Quality Control Measurements, Verified Deliverables, Work Performance Information

Plan Quality Management

This process is where you will identify the quality requirements and/or standards for the project and then document how the project will meet them. The project manager will have to know the quality requirements and how to meet them before the project is executed.

When this process is completed, you will have created a quality management plan and quality metrics. The plan will guide the rest of the quality processes, "Manage Quality" and "Control Quality." The quality metrics will be used to measure the deliverable against the quality standards.

On the exam, it's important to understand the tools in this process. Know what the tools are and how they can be used.

Inputs

Project Charter – Covered in Chapter 4

Project Management Plan

Components in the project management plan will help to develop the quality management plan; these include the scope, time, and cost baselines. Quality can affect the scope, time, and cost of the project.

Project Documents

Of the 33 project documents, the ones you are most likely to use in this process include:

- **Assumption log:** This will keep track of any assumptions and constraints that are made during the project.

- **Stakeholder register:** This is a list of all the stakeholders on the project. This might be needed to help identify which stakeholders might have an impact on project quality.

- **Risk register:** The risk register will contain all of the positive and negative risks that could affect the quality of the projects.

- **Requirements documentation:** The requirements documentation is created in the scope knowledge area process called "Collect Requirements." This document will have not only the scope requirements, but also the quality requirements.

- **Requirement traceability matrix:** This document will show where the requirements came from, such as which stakeholder originally requested them.

Enterprise Environmental Factors – Covered in Chapter 3

Organizational Process Assets – Covered in Chapter 3

Tools and Techniques

Expert Judgment – Covered in Chapter 3

Data Gathering

As you come up with the quality standards of the project, you will gather data from multiple sources, which can include doing brainstorming and interviewing stakeholders. Another technique that can be used is benchmarking. Benchmarking is comparing your quality requirements to other projects' quality requirements. For example, a project worker looks at how fast a web page loads on sites that are similar to your web design project's sites.

Data Analysis

Once you have acquired the data, you then need to analyze it. Here are two techniques for that:

- **Cost-benefit analysis:** The benefits of meeting quality requirements can include less rework, higher productivity, lower cost, increased stakeholder satisfaction, and increased profitability. However, the cost of meeting the quality requirements should never exceed its benefits.

- **Cost of quality:** The cost of quality is the amount we will spend to ensure we meet the quality requirements. Two costs that you will need to understand are the cost of conformance and the cost of nonconformance.

  The cost of conformance to quality includes all costs associated with meeting the quality requirements. This includes the prevention costs, such as training, materials, and equipment. It also includes the appraisal costs, such as inspection, laboratory measurements and analysis, machinery maintenance and calibration, field testing, and procedure checking.

  The cost of nonconformance includes the internal and external costs of defects and failures. Internal costs can include rework or scrap. If a deliverable fails to meet the quality requirements, then you will either have to fix it (rework) or scrap it and start over again. The external cost of the project can be a loss of business or liabilities.

Decision Making

Once the data has been acquired and analyzed, you then have to make a decision about what quality standards will be used on the project. One technique is to use multi-criteria decision analysis. This means making a table and listing different criteria that can be used to select the right quality standards.

Data Representation

- **Logical data model:** A logical data model is a method that's used to organize a company's data. It will give you a visual representation of the data, and you can then use it to identify the best methods to sort and organize it. This is mostly used on software projects when designing a database, to identify if there would be any integrity issues when it comes to the data.

- **Matrix diagram:** A matrix diagram will show the relationship between two or more groups. Matrix diagrams can show the relationship between the processes that we will follow.

- **Mind mapping:** Mind mapping is a great way to visually organize data. In general, you select one topic and then branch off into all the subtopics that are related to your main topic. For example, you can start by drawing a circle on a paper containing the words 'painting a room'. You would then branch out into all the things that are related to or dependent on painting a room, such as buying paint, removing furniture, selecting a color, and painting. This will help to tell you some of the quality requirements of the project.

- **Flowcharts:** Flowcharts show you a graphical representation of the process and any room for improvements. In terms of the exam, you will use a flowchart if you want to ensure that your team follows the process correctly. Flowcharts show all the relationships and links to the processes.

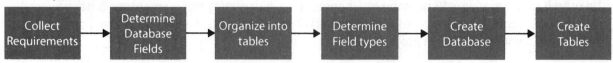

Flowchart showing how to create a database

Test and Inspection Planning

The project manager and team will need to come up with different ways to test the deliverable to ensure that it will meet the quality requirements. For example, on a software development project, the team may determine that the best way to ensure the software is meeting its quality requirements would be to do unit testing, regression testing, and user acceptance testing.

Meetings – Covered in Chapter 3

Outputs

Quality Management Plan

The quality management plan is part of the project management plan. It describes how the organization's quality policy and project quality requirements will be met. It will mainly include the activities that the project team will do to ensure the deliverables will meet all the quality requirements.

Quality Metrics

Quality metrics will be used to measure the project quality for either the deliverables or the processes. This can include how fast a program should load, the test coverage of software, or the improvements for processes. This will be used in both the quality assurance and control quality process.

Project Documents Updates – Covered in Chapter 3

Manage Quality

This is the process of executing the activities in the quality management plan. As the deliverables are getting made, the project manager and team will need to take certain steps to ensure that the deliverables have met their quality requirements.

Part of the "Manage Quality" process involves quality assurance. Quality assurance is what a project does to ensure that it follows the right processes correctly and to improve the processes that it follows. Most projects will have some form of quality assurance to check

whether the project team is following the correct processes while building the deliverables. Manage project quality includes quality assurance and also all the work that may be needed to design the product, such as looking at industry standard practices to ensure quality is met.

Keep in mind that the process of manage quality is something that everyone in the organization should be doing. This includes the customers, project manager, team members, sponsor, and even senior management. In order to achieve the right quality, everyone must be working together to ensure that the products and services that the organization creates meet its quality standards.

Inputs

Project Management Plan

The project management plan will contain the quality management plan, which will tell you how to conduct this process of manage quality and how to ensure quality is met for the deliverables and processes.

Project Documents

Of the 33 project documents, the ones you are most likely to use in this process include:

- Quality metrics: Quality metrics are used to measure the processes we will follow in order to improve them. Any time you try to improve something, you will need performance measurements.

- Quality control measurements: Quality control measurements are outputs of the "Control Quality" process. They are measurements of the activities done in the "Control Quality" processes to determine if the quality standards or policies were met.

- Risk register: The risk register will contain all of the positive and negative risks that could affect the quality of the projects.

- Lessons learned register: A listing of all of the lessons learned so far on the project.

Organizational Process Assets – Covered in Chapter 3

Tools and Techniques

Data Gathering

As the project team is creating the deliverables, the project manager would then have to gather data related to quality. One way to do that is by using a checklist and verifying that the deliverables are meeting the quality requirements.

Data Analysis

After the data has been gathered, you would then need to analyze it to see if there are any defects. One method would be to look for the root causes of defects, such as doing a root cause analysis, in which case you will look for the main reason why defects are happening.

Decision Making – Covered in Chapter 3

Data Representation

- **Affinity diagrams:** These are used to put large amounts of data into categories.

- **Matrix diagrams:** These will show the relationship between two or more groups. Matrix diagrams can show the relationship between the processes that we will follow.

- **Cause-and-effect diagrams:** Also known as an Ishikawa or Fishbone diagram, it will tell you the causes of defects. It also shows you the root causes of potential defects.

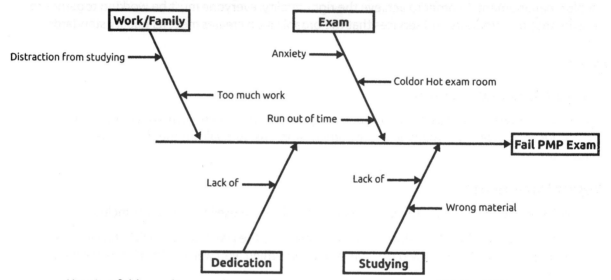

Here is a fishbone diagram showing the reasons why someone could fail a PMP exam.

- **Flowcharts:** Flowcharts show you a graphical representation of the process and any room for improvements.

- **Histograms:** Histograms are bar charts that show the distribution of numerical data. They are used to show frequency. This can be used to show the frequency of defects on a project.

Audits

Audits are done to ensure that the project is following the organization's quality policies, processes, and procedures. They can ensure that all the best practices are being done and indicate if there are any deficiencies that needs to be corrected. They are usually done by a team that's external to the project, such as the PMO or external and internal auditors. The audits can also verify if an approved change request was actually implemented. For example, if a stakeholder had requested to change the color of paint in a room through a change request, an audit can help to verify if that paint color was actually changed.

Design for X

Design for X (DfX) is generally used by engineers in order to design a particular aspect of a product. The X in Design for X is a variable. The X can be substituted for things such as assembly, costs, safety, quality, or deployment. For example, you can do a design for costs, which would be DfC. DfC would ensure that when you design a product, its design will bear the cost in mind to ensure that it's profitable when produced. DfX can lead to better quality products by bringing down costs and ensuring better performance.

Problem Solving

Almost all projects will encounter some kind of problems related to deliverables. Problems, in particular, would be defects. The project manager would need to come up with a system to solve the problems that are causing the defects. A simple system would include identifying the problem, determining what's causing it, looking at possible solutions, selecting a solution, implementing a solution, and verifying that it solves the problem.

Quality Improvement Methods

As the project is progressing, the project manager will have to find ways to improve the quality. Sometimes the project manager may measure a particular product and find that it is full of defects and will then need to implement solutions to improve their quality processes. This can be done by using theories such as Six Sigma.

Outputs

Quality Reports

Quality reports are one of the main outputs in this process. Such a report generally includes information about quality issues on the project and recommendations on how to improve the processes being used. This report will then be used by other departments in order to take corrective actions to fix the project processes and improve the overall project quality. These reports can then be given over to departments outside of the project, such as the PMO, in order for actions to be taken for project improvement.

Test and Evaluation Documents

The other main outputs are the test and evaluation documents. These documents generally take the form of a checklist that can be used when checking the quality of the deliverables. For example, on a software development project, a team may use a checklist when reviewing the code.

Change Requests

Since "Manage Quality" is about process analysis and improvement, you can expect that you might be changing some of the processes you follow on the project. Any changes to the processes in the project management plan will require a change request.

Project Management Plan Updates – Covered in Chapter 3

Project Documents Updates – Covered in Chapter 3

Control Quality

This is a monitoring and controlling process that looks at the work done (deliverables) in the executing part of the project and determines if it meets the quality requirements. It is in this process that you will look at the deliverable and determine if it has met the quality requirements.

You will be beginning this process once the project team has completed the deliverables. Once the deliverables are done, you should inspect them to see if they meet the quality requirements. For example, when the painters have finished painting the room, the project manager should inspect the room to ensure that it has met all the quality requirements, such as whether one side is darker than the other, missing a spot, or if the paint was dropped on the carpet.

> *ExamTip: The "Manage Quality" process looks at the processes that are used to produce the deliverables, while this process of "Control Quality" will inspect the deliverables to see if they meet the quality standards and/or requirements.*

Inputs

Project Management Plan

The project management plan includes the quality management plan and all the baselines of the project. The quality management plan will indicate how to do the quality control.

Project Documents

Of the 33 project documents, the ones you are most likely to use in this process include:

- **Quality metrics:** Metrics will be used to measure the work that has been done on the project to determine if it has met the quality requirements.

- **Test and evaluation documents:** These are documents that will be used to inspect the deliverable to see if it matches the quality requirements. Such documents generally take the form of checklists.

- **Lessons learned register:** A listing of all of the lessons learned on the project.

Work Performance Data

This is the actual work that has been done on the deliverable. This will be needed to compare to the planned work to determine if the quality requirements have been met.

Approved Change Requests

If a change request has been approved through the "Perform Integrated Change Control" process, that change will then need to be executed correctly.

Deliverables

The project deliverables will be inspected in this process to determine if they have met the quality requirements.

Enterprise Environmental Factors – Covered in Chapter 3

Organizational Process Assets – Covered in Chapter 3

Tools and Techniques

Data Gathering

- **Checklists:** Quality checklists will help the project manager determine what to check for when inspecting the deliverables.

- **Check sheets:** Check sheets are used to gather all defects and keep a running total. You can use check sheets to see how many defects you might be getting per week or day of a project.

    EXAM TIP: A checklist is used by the team to ensure that all components of the deliverables are checked correctly, and the check sheets are just used to keep a running total or tally.

- **Statistical sampling:** On all projects, you will need to inspect things, from lines of code to painted walls. You might not be able to inspect all of the code. You will then need to select a sample to inspect. You should get a statistical sample, which is a random sample of the code.

- **Questionnaires and surveys:** Questionnaires and surveys can be given to stakeholders to better understand what they may be looking for on a project and to better understand their needs.

Data Analysis – Covered in Chapter 3

Inspection

You will need to inspect the deliverable to ensure it meets the quality requirements. Inspections are often referred to as audits, walkthroughs, or peer reviews. Inspections can be done by the project manager, team, customer, or sponsor. They're usually done to find any type of defects and to verify the defects have been repaired.

Testing/Product Evaluations

Before the project team or manager can verify that a deliverable has met all its quality requirements, they would have to test these deliverables extensively. On a software development project, for example, they may do unit testing and integration tests. On an IT network installation project, they may transfer data across the network to see how

the routers and switches are responding. In any case, you will need to come up with certain tests that can be used to verify the amount and type of testing you will need to conduct, depending on the industry of the project.

Data Representation

- **Cause-and-effect diagrams:** Also known as Ishikawa or Fishbone diagram, it will tell you the causes of defects. This diagram also shows you the root causes of potential defects.

- **Control Charts:** Control charts will indicate if a process is in "control." The control chart will tell the project manager to either fix the process or inspect it. To create the chart, you will need to get a sample of products being made and then determine the desired results. For example, you might be cutting woodblocks and the height has to be 35 inches. The chart below shows that you were able to get 20 samples and measure them. The mean of the samples is represented by the line in the middle of the chart. The upper and lower control limits are three standard deviations from the mean. You will then plot each point on the graph.

When reading this graph for the exam, you will need to identify the rule of seven. It states that if you have seven consecutive points on one side of the mean, you will need to inspect the process. In our chart, it seems like the machine is leaning to the lower limit. This process will need to be inspected, as it is out of control. If you look at the chart and it has no rule of seven and everything is within limits, then you will do nothing, as the process is said to be in control. If you have a point or points above or below the control limits, you will need to fix the process.

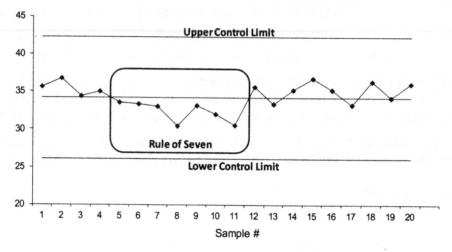

Control Chart showing the rule of seven

- **Scatter diagrams:** Scatter diagrams show trends in relation to different variables. This can show if a trend is forming or where the trend is going. A scatter diagram is made up of an X and Y-axis. In the example below, the X-axis is the number of weeks, and the Y-axis is the number of defects per week. You can see that in this project, it seems like the defects are growing as the project is progressing. Its main purpose is to show the relationship between two variables, such as time and the number of defects.

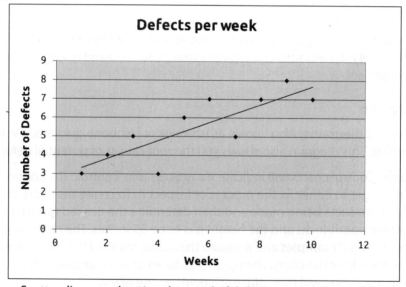

Scatter diagram showing the trend of defects increasing per week.

- **Histogram:** A histogram is a bar chart that can show the frequency of something. For example, how many defects are we having per week when writing the software code.

  One example of a histogram is a Pareto diagram. Pareto diagrams use the Pareto principle of 80/20. The 80/20 principle says 80% of problems are caused by 20% of the causes. Most things in life will follow Pareto. For example, 80% of your monthly expenses are caused by 20% of what you buy, or 80% of deaths are caused by 20% of diseases. The Pareto diagram shows this in a bar chart with a cumulative percentage.

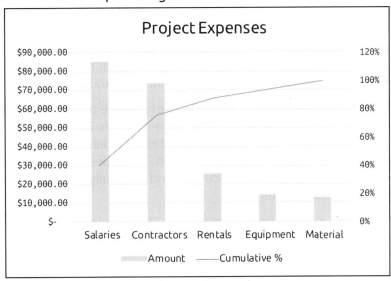

Pareto diagram showing project expenses. Salaries and contractors make up most of this project's expenses

Meeting – Covered in Chapter 3

Outputs

Quality Control Measurements

Quality control measurements inspect the results of the activities done in the "Control Quality" processes to determine if the quality standards or policies were met. This output would then be used in the "Manage Quality" process to identify if the quality standards that are used on the project are being met and, if not, whether they should be changed.

Verified Deliverables

As the main output of this process, a verified deliverable is one that has been inspected by the project manager or team and has met the quality requirements. The verified deliverables would then become an input to the process of "Validate Scope," where it will be formally accepted by a customer and/or sponsor.

Work Performance Information – Covered in Chapter 3

Change Requests

If the deliverable cannot be verified and does not meet the quality requirements, then the project manager will have to initiate a change request in order to fix it. This will usually include some kind of corrective action or defect repair.

Project Management Plan Updates – Covered in Chapter 3

Project Documents Updates – Covered in Chapter 3

Agile and Hybrid Quality Management

While many of the theories that we have covered in this chapter, along with many of the tools such as a Pareto chart or Fishbone diagram, can be used on agile projects, in this section, we will be covering some additional tools and methods agile teams can use.

During an agile project, there will be many interactions with the customer to check on the product as it's being built. Quality is about meeting the requirements, and if we can have the customer check on the product throughout its entire development, we should be better able to meet their requirements. That way, if there are any changes that are needed in order to fulfill the requirements, it can be detected early and fixed faster. This will lead to fewer quality defects. Customers are able to give their feedback on each increment of the product during the Sprint review meeting. This is where they're able to review the actual product and see what they like and what they don't like.

One way the team is able to improve their processes to ensure the quality of the deliverables getting made is when they do the retrospective at the end of the iteration. The retrospective is a time-boxed meeting that will last about two hours. During this meeting, the team will discuss what went well during the iteration and what they should improve upon. The issues that may have caused the defect during the previous iteration will be discussed, and hopefully, those issues will be solved and will not produce defects in the next iteration.

If an agile team is following extreme programming (XP). They would use the model for frequent verification and validation.

Planning/Feedback Loops [1]

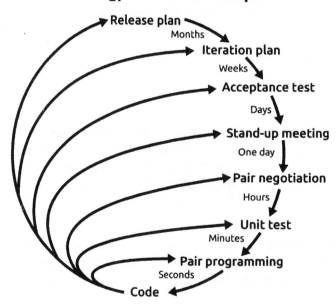

By using this model, the team would be able to check the code that is being written for the product more frequently and being able to validate it often. This would lead to fewer defects in the code and overall better quality software. Let's do a quick review of this model:

- As the code is being written, it's being checked by another programmer. This should be done with pair programming. This is almost an instant check of the codes as it's being done seconds after it's been written.

- Next up would be unit testing: real actual tests to determine if the code achieves the desired result and is able to function as needed.

- The next thing up would be speaking with the customers to see if the customers approve of the way the system is functioning, this would be in pair negotiation.

- On a daily basis, the team will do a stand-up meeting to verify what was done and if there are any issues that need to be solved.

- On a weekly basis, give an iteration plan to the customer to demonstrate the full functionality iteration.

- Every few months, you would conduct a release of the product to the customer, so they can use it in production.

As you can see from using this frequent validation and verification model, the work is being checked very frequently, leading to fewer defects and verifying that the product is meeting the requirements of the customer as the product is being built.

On hybrid projects, you may use many of the different methods that we have outlined in this chapter in order to ensure that you're meeting the project's quality. For example, on a hybrid project, you will combine some of the processes from the PMBOK Guide when managing the traditional section of your project and then utilize things like retrospectives and frequent validation and verification extreme programming on your agile sections.

Quality Management Questions

1. You have been asked to identify the primary reasons for the substantial amount of customer complaints your company is experiencing every day. Which of the following tools will most effectively assist you in further identifying the reasons for the failures?

   A. Cause and effect diagram

   B. Run chart

   C. Statistical sampling

   D. Design of experiments

2. While trying to isolate the root cause of a critical problem in the production process, your team has detected two variables—temperature and humidity—as

   possible contributors to the problem. There is a concern that these two variables are complicating the problem by affecting each other. Which of the following tools or techniques will assist in seeing if there is any interdependency between them?

   A. Cause and effect diagram

   B. Influence diagram

   C. Scatter diagram

   D. Pareto chart

3. Control Quality is the process of monitoring specific project results to determine if they comply with applicable quality standards and identifying ways to eradicate the causes of unsatisfactory results. All of the following are tools & techniques used in the Control Quality process EXCEPT:

   A. Inspection

   B. Testing/Product evaluations

   C. Quality metrics

   D. Control Charts

4. While using a control chart to monitor processes and to assure that they remain within acceptable limits or "in control," you noticed that seven data points are grouped together in a series on one side of the mean. All of the followings are false about this situation EXCEPT:

   A. This type of situation needs to be investigated, and a cause should be found.

   B. This trend is normal and expected within a process.

   C. This is a random cause of variation and can be ignored.

   D. The process is stable and in control as none of the data points are outside control limits.

5. Your team is using a particular method of measuring quality and approving only a tiny portion of the outputs as per an unyielding pass/fail standard. Which of the following techniques is your team using?

   A. Product analysis

   B. Process analysis

   C. Attribute sampling

   D. Statistical sampling

6. A project manager is working on a project to install a generator for a local power company. She is anxious that her project practices are not robust enough and asked for your expert opinion. You advised her to compare her actual or planned practices to those of other projects both in and beyond the performing organization to identify a basis for performance measurement, improvement ideas, and best practices. Which of the following tools & techniques have you asked her to utilize?

   A. Design of experiments

   B. Cost-benefit analysis

   C. Statistical sampling

   D. Benchmarking

7. You are the project manager of a project to implement a golf simulator for a local golf club. Quality is the first thing in your mind, and you hired a Subject Matter Expert (SME) to ascertain if the project activities comply with organizational and project policies and procedures. The SME is particularly interested in identifying ineffective and inefficient activities or processes used in the project as well as gaps and deficiencies in your processes. You have initiated which of the following?

   A. Design of experiments

   B. Develop quality control measurements

   C. Audit

   D. Prevention functions

8. You discovered a pattern of flaws in several projects you are working on as a senior project manager. You have the impression that some kind of deficiency in the process your organization is using may be contributing to these repetitive defects. You conducted a cause and effect analysis and formulated a few recommendations for process change to avoid this recurring problem in future projects. You are in which of the following processes?

   A. Perform Qualitative Risk Analysis

   B. Plan Quality

   C. Manage Project Quality

   D. Control Quality

9. You are the project manager supervising a project to develop a new wireless media streaming device. The client asked you to have vigorous quality as it is one of their major concerns. You are in the Plan Quality Management process of identifying all the pertinent quality requirements, specifications, and standards for the project and product and specifying how those specifications will be met. You will be using all of the following as inputs of the Plan Quality Management process EXCEPT:

   A. Scope baseline

   B. Stakeholder register

   C. Quality metrics

   D. Schedule baseline

10. Plan-Do-Check-Act is a cycle of activities designed to drive continuous improvement. This theory was popularized by which of the following quality theorists?

    A. W. Edwards Deming

    B. Ishikawa

    C. Joseph Juran

    D. Philip Crosby

11. You are the project manager for one of the top wood furniture producers in the world. You are currently overseeing a project to create and manufacture a large amount of custom furniture for several major local retailers. Your organization has decided to practice just-in-time management and asked you to explore the practice. You found out that all of the followings are FALSE about just-in-time EXCEPT:

    A. The project team will have no control over the inventory.

    B. It will allow less range of deviation than other inventory solutions.

    C. It will decrease the inventory investment.

    D. The organization will have lower quality of parts.

12. Monitoring specific project results to determine if they comply with relevant quality standards and identifying ways to eliminate causes of inadequate results is:

    A. Quality assurance

    B. Quality planning

    C. Quality control

    D. Quality management

13. You are planning to hire a third-party auditor to perform a scheduled or random structured review to determine whether your quality management activities comply with organizational and project processes, policies, and procedures. All of the following will be done in this quality audit EXCEPT:

    A. Identify ineffective and inefficient activities or processes used in the project.

    B. Identify the required improvements, gaps, and shortcomings in the processes.

    C. Create quality metrics.

    D. Recommend changes and corrective actions to Integrated Change Control.

14. You are overseeing a software application project to implement a custom accounting and financial system for medium to large-sized corporations. The quality assurance team submitted a defect report with relevant information on the description, severity, root causes, possible resolutions, owner, due date, and reporter of the defects. You intend to know which causes of defects are most serious so that you can prioritize the potential causes of the problems. Which of the following tools should you use to isolate the few critical causes of defects from the many uncritical causes?

    A. Control chart

    B. Pareto chart

    C. Scatter diagram

    D. Fishbone diagram

15. Control Quality is the process of monitoring specific project results to determine if they comply with relevant quality standards and identify ways to eliminate causes of unsatisfactory results. All of the following are tools & techniques used in Control Quality EXCEPT:

    A. Expert judgment

    B. Inspection

    C. Control chart

    D. Cause and effect diagram

16. A project manager was recently recognized for delivering a high-quality product with no noticeable defects. Some of the stakeholders were skeptical about the limited features offered by the product. This kind of product that has a high-level of quality but does not include many of the features of comparable products is referred to as:

    A. Low quality

    B. Low grade

    C. Inaccurate

    D. Sketchy

17. Plan Quality Management is the process of identifying all the relevant quality requirements, specifications, and standards for the project and product and detailing how the specifications will be met and how they should be performed:

    A. During the initial phase of the project.

    B. Prior to the approval of the project charter.

    C. After the work breakdown structure has been developed.

    D. In parallel with the other planning processes.

18. A project manager working on implementing WIMAX connectivity in a rural area has to deploy several network devices and set up POPs to house those devices. She performed a cost-benefit analysis and was apprehensive about the high cost of non-conformance, or cost that will incur if proper quality is not implemented in her project. In quality management, which one of the following is NOT an attribute of the cost of non-conformance?

    A. Processing customer complaints

    B. Machinery maintenance and calibration

    C. Bad word-of-mouth advertising

    D. Field repair work

19. As a project manager, you are trying to decide the trade-offs between quality and grade in your project. Which one of the following is correct with respect to a product developed or a service performed?

    A. There is no difference between quality and grade.

    B. Neither low grade nor low quality is acceptable.

    C. Low quality is acceptable, but low grade is not.

    D. Low quality is not acceptable, but low grade is.

20. A project manager for a business automation project works with the quality assurance department to improve stakeholders' confidence that quality management activities will comply with organizational and project processes, policies, and procedures. Which of the following MUST the project manager and assurance team have prior to initiating this Manage Project Quality process?

    A. Quality control measurements

    B. Change requests

    C. Validated changes

    D. Quality improvement

21. Proprietary quality management methodologies are used as tools & techniques in which of the following quality processes?

    A. Plan Quality Management

    B. Manage Project Quality

    C. Control Quality

    D. Perform Quality Management

22. Which one of the following statements is TRUE about verified deliverables? Verified deliverables are:

    A. Outputs of the Control Quality process and inputs to the Validate Scope process.

    B. Inputs to the Control Quality process and outputs of the Validate Scope process.

    C. Tools and techniques of the Control Quality and Validate Scope processes.

    D. Outputs of the Control Quality and Validate Scope processes.

Project Quality Management Answers

1. **A:** A cause and effect diagram or fishbone diagram is a root cause analysis tool. A run chart is a line graph that displays process performance over time. Upward and downward trends, cycles, and large aberrations may be spotted and investigated further using a run chart. Statistical sampling involves choosing part of a population of interest for inspection instead of measuring the entire population. Design of Experiments (DOE) is a statistical method, usually applied to the product of a project, and provides a "what-if" analysis of alternatives to identify which factors might improve quality.

2. **C:** The scatter diagram is used to determine the correlation between two variables.

3. **C:** Quality metrics are an output of the Plan Quality Management process and an input to both the Manage Project Quality and Control Quality processes.

4. **A:** The rule of seven refers to nonrandom data points grouped together in a series that total seven on one side of the mean. This type of situation needs to be investigated, and a cause should be found because even though none of the points are out of the control limit, they are not random, and the process may be out of control.

5. **C:** Attribute sampling is a method wherein the output is binary; either good or bad, pass or fail, on or off.

6. **D:** Benchmarking is comparing actual or planned practices to those of other projects, both in and beyond the performing organization, to provide a basis for performance measurement, to generate improvement ideas, and to identify best practices. Design of Experiments (DOE) is a statistical method usually applied to the product of a project

   and provides a '"what-if"' analysis of alternatives to identify which factors might improve quality. Statistical sampling involves choosing part of a population of interest for inspection instead of measuring the entire population. Cost-benefit analysis is a comparison of the cost of quality to the expected benefit. The benefit of quality must outweigh the cost of achieving it. The primary benefit of quality is increased stakeholders' satisfaction and less rework, which means higher productivity and lower cost.

7. **C:** An audit during the Manage Project Quality process is performed to determine if project activities comply with organizational policies and procedures.

8. **C:** You are in the Manage Project Quality process. This is the process to determine if the project activities comply with organizational and project policies, standards, processes, and procedures. This process is primarily concerned with overall process improvement and does not deal with inspecting the product for quality or measuring defects. The primary focus is on steadily improving the processes and activities undertaken to achieve quality.

9. **C:** Quality metrics is an operational definition that specifies how quality will be measured. It is an output of the Plan Quality Management process, not an input.

10.   **A:** Plan-Do-Check-Act is a cycle of iterative activities designed to drive continuous improvement. Initially implemented in manufacturing, it has broad applicability in business. This theory, popularized by Edwards Deming, advocates that business processes should be scrutinized and measured to detect sources of variations that cause products to deviate from customer requirements. The recommendation is to place the business processes in an unremitting feedback loop so that managers can isolate and change the parts of the process that need improvement. The four phases in the Plan-Do-Check-Act cycle involve the following:

- Plan: Design or revise business process components to improve results.

- Do: Implement the plan and measure its performance.

- Check: Assess the measurements and report the results to decision-makers.

- Act: Decide on changes needed to improve the process.

11.   **C:** Just-in-time (JIT) is an inventory management method whereby materials, goods, and labor are scheduled to arrive or to be replenished exactly when needed in the production process; this brings inventory down to zero or to a near-zero level. It decreases costs by keeping only enough inventory on hand to meet immediate production needs.

12.   **C:** Quality control is utilized to monitor and record results during the execution of quality activities.

13.   **C:** A quality audit is done in the Manage Project Quality process. Quality metrics, which are the outputs in the Plan Quality Management process, are used as inputs in the Manage Project Quality process.

14.   **B:** A Pareto chart illustrates which causes of error are most serious. It is displayed as a histogram and shows the frequency of error according to the cause. The concept is based on the 80/20 rule: "80 percent of the problems come from 20 percent of the causes;" thus, it is important to pay close attention to the 20 percent of critical causes in order to resolve 80 percent of the problems. A Pareto chart:

   –   Helps focus attention on the most critical issues

   –   Prioritizes potential causes of the most problems

   –   Is used to determine priorities for quality improvement activities

   –   Separates the critical few from the uncritical many

15.   **A:** Expert judgment is not listed as a tool & technique for any of the quality management processes.

16.   **B:** Products that are produced at an acceptable level of quality and meet the desired requirements of the customer but have limited functionality and features compared to similar products are referred to as low-grade.

17.   **D:** Quality management is integrated with many other project planning processes, especially cost and time management.

18.   **B:** Machinery maintenance and calibration is an appraisal function that is included in the cost of conformance. All other costs listed are costs of non-conformance.

19.   **D:** A product that is produced at a high level of quality, but does not include many of the features of comparable products is referred to as low-grade. A low-grade product with limited features may be acceptable, but a low-quality product or service is unacceptable.

20. **A:** Quality control measurements are relevant to quality level and compliance measurements. These measurements are inputs to the Manage Project Quality process. Change requests are outputs for both the Manage Project Quality and Control Quality processes, and validated changes are outputs for the Control Quality process. Quality improvement is the result of the Manage Project Quality process.

21. **A:** Proprietary quality management methodologies such as Six Sigma, Lean Six Sigma, Quality Function Deployment, and CMMI® are used as tools & techniques in the Plan Quality Management process.

22. **A:** Verified deliverables are outputs of the Control Quality process and inputs to the Validate Scope process.

Chapter 10

Project Resource Management

Resources are the backbone of any project. Resources are generally categorized into two main types: physical and human resources. Physical resources generally include materials, equipment, or facilities, whereas the project team would be human resources.

In this knowledge area, you will be organizing and leading the project team to complete the project. This is a very important knowledge area for your exam; you can expect quite a few questions on human resources. There will be a lot of questions on conflict management coming from these processes.

Project management deals a lot with managing people. All projects have people, and this may be one of the hardest aspects of project management. A dysfunctional project team is more likely to produce a failed deliverable. One of the project manager's main jobs on a project is to ensure the team functions well and that he/she manages conflicts that will occur as the project progresses.

On an agile project, the project team will play an important role because they're usually the main decision-makers and problem-solvers on the project. On agile projects, the project manager is more of a "servant-leader" and just provides the tools the team will need to complete the work.

Professional and ethical behaviors must be maintained within project development. The team should be aware of this and follow those behaviors. In addition, it is important to understand that the project manager should be influencing the project team, including managing the environment, communications, and cultural issues.

Process	Process Group	Main Output
Plan Resource Management	Planning	Resource Management Plan, Team Charter
Estimate Activity Resources	Planning	Resource Requirements, Resource Breakdown Structure, Basis Of Estimates
Acquire Resources	Executing	Physical Resource Assignments, Project Team Assignments, Resource Calendar
Develop Team	Executing	Team Performance Assessments, Change Requests
Manage Team	Executing	Change Requests
Control Resources	Monitoring and Controlling	Work Performance Information, Change Requests

Plan Resource Management

This is the process of identifying who will be doing which project role and their responsibilities, reporting, and creating the resources management plan. The resource management plan will express project roles and responsibilities, reporting relationships, and how we will hire, manage, and release the project team. This process will also document how to acquire, manage, and use physical resources as well.

Inputs

Project Charter – Covered in Chapter 4

Project Management Plan – Covered in Chapter 3

Project Documents

Of the 33 project documents, the ones you are most likely to use in this process include:

- **Project schedule:** The project schedule shows the activities and resources needed over the project timeline.

- **Requirements documentation:** This document will show what resources are needed for each activity.

- **Risk register:** The risk register is a listing of all the positive and negative risks on the project. The risk register may include the resources that may be needed in order to respond to some of the risks.

- **Stakeholder register:** This is a list of all the stakeholders on the project and how they may impact the project.

Enterprise Environmental Factors – Covered in Chapter3

Organizational Process Assets – Covered in Chapter 3

Tools and Techniques

Expert Judgment – Covered in Chapter 3

Data Representation

The methods used to present how the project is staffed will be very important. Here are a few techniques that can be used in order to show how the project will be staffed.

Hierarchical-type charts: A hierarchical-type chart shows the reporting relationships on a project. This is sometimes called an Organizational Breakdown Structure. It looks like a WBS, except it shows the positions and relationships between roles. This chart will break down the project's positions. It is the project organization chart when used on a project. It is arranged according to an organization's existing departments, units, or teams with their respective work packages.

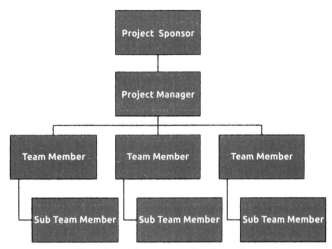

Simple project organization chart

- **Matrix-based charts:** The responsibility assignment matrix (RAM) will show the resources assigned to the work packages. An example of the RAM is a RACI chart as shown below. RACI means responsible, accountable, consulted, and informed. The people doing the work bear the responsibility. Accountable is the person who ensures the work is done. Consulted is a subject matter expert who can help you do the work. Informed is someone who needs to know the status of the work. It is important never to have more than one person held accountable. If two people are held accountable, they will blame each other for not getting the work done.

	Project Manager	Team Member	Sponsor	Customer
Develop Project Charter	A	I	R	I
Define Scope	A	R	C	I
Create WBS	R	A	C	I
Validate Scope	A	I	C	R

Simple RACI Chart

- **Text-oriented formats:** This document shows the roles and responsibilities in written format instead of a chart like the RACI.

Organizational Theory

Organizational theory is how the organization manages its resources. This will ensure your projects follow the organizational policies to manage the resources.

Meetings – Covered in Chapter 3

Outputs

Resource Management Plan

The resource management plan is part of the project management plan and is used to manage both physical and staff resources. It will guide the remaining five resource management processes and is made up of a few parts: the roles and responsibilities, the organization chart, and the staffing management plan.

The roles and responsibilities will define what everyone is doing on a project. You can use the RACI chart for this. The organization chart we illustrated above will be used to show who reports to whom.

The plan will describe how to acquire, develop, manage, control, and release the project team. The resource management plan should contain the following:

- **Staff acquisition:** How and where will you get the project staff? This could be from internal or external sources.

- **Staff release plan:** When and how are you going to release the project team after the project is over?

- **Training needs:** What training will be required to ensure the team has the right skills to complete the project work?

- **Recognition and rewards:** How will you recognize and reward team members for the work that was done? This will be addressed by the process "Develop Team."

- **Compliance:** How will we manage the project team to ensure we meet all regulations from the company and government?

- **Safety:** It is very important to address the safety of the team on the project, especially if the project includes work that could get people injured, such as building a house.

It is important to understand how the resources will be staffed on the project. When the project starts, it may not have many resources, but as it progresses, it may require more staff. A resource histogram can be used to show how many team members are on the project, how long they've been on the project, and when they should be released, as shown below.

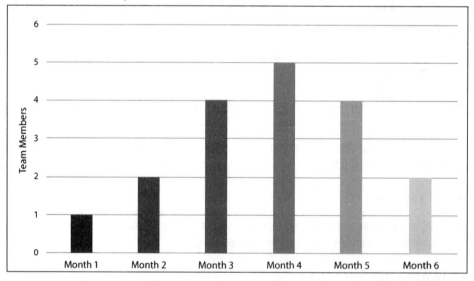

Team Charter

The team charter is a document that outlines what will be acceptable behavior within the project. This is an important document to ensure that the project team appropriately respects one another. It should include things like the general rules of conduct for meetings, decision-making, and one-on-one conversations. This team charter is best made by the project team for the project team. That way, everyone agrees with its content, and they are more likely to follow it if they made it.

Project Documents Updates – Covered in Chapter 3

Estimate Activity Resources

This is a process where you look at each individual activity and determine what and how many resources are needed to accomplish that activity. Resources are not just people, but also include equipment, machines, and different types of supplies needed to finish the activity. This process lists all the resources, both physical and staff, and how many of those resources are needed.

Inputs

Project Management Plan

The project management plan will contain the resource management plan, which will give guidance on how to perform this process. It will also contain the scope baseline, which is made up of the project scope statement, WBS, and WBS dictionary.

Project Documents – Covered in Chapter 3

Of the 33 project documents, the ones you are most likely to use in this process include:

- **Activity list:** This is the list of all the activities on the project. This list will be needed to estimate the duration of each activity.

- **Activity attributes:** Activity attributes provide more information about each activity. They can include information that could affect the duration, such as location, leads, lags, and cost.

- **Assumption log:** This will keep track of any assumptions that are made during the project. Assumptions and constraints could affect how the schedule is built and may impact the lead and lag between activities.

- **Resource calendars:** Resource calendars show the availability of resources. Resources can greatly affect the duration of each activity. If resources are not available, this will negatively affect the duration.

- **Risk register:** The risk register will list all the identified project risks, as well as their impact and response. Risk response can lead to adding reserve time to activities.

- **Cost estimates:** This will be the individual cost that is assigned to each activity. Knowing the cost of an activity will be critical to determining what resource should be used on the project.

Enterprise Environmental Factors – Covered in Chapter 3

Organizational Process Assets – Covered in Chapter 3

Tools & Techniques

Expert Judgment

Expert judgment is a very helpful tool when dealing with processes. If you are painting a room and need to estimate how much paint will be needed, then it would be best to ask a painter (subject matter expert).

Bottom-up Estimating

Bottom-up estimating is when you break down the activities in more detail until you can assign the resources. You can then aggregate them back up to the full activity. This form of estimation requires the work to be very detailed before it can be done. This is considered one of the best estimates to use because it is very accurate, but is also very time-consuming.

Analogous Estimating

Analogous estimating is also known as top-down estimation. Analogous estimation relies on historical information to assign the current duration to the activities. It is based on a limited amount of information. For example, the last time we painted a 400 Sq. Ft. room, we used 5 gallons of paint. We would then use that estimate to apply to any room that's about 400 Sq. Ft. without actually analyzing the physical room by itself. Notice, it's a quick estimate, but because you're not actually inspecting the work, it may not be very accurate.

Parametric Estimating

Parametric estimating uses a mathematical algorithm to calculate cost or duration. The calculation is based on historical data and variables. For example, if it takes one programmer to write one module, then it will take 10 programmers to write 10 modules. This form of estimation could be accurate depending on the accuracy of the data that's used to calculate it.

Data Analysis – Covered in Chapter 3

Project Management Information System – Covered in Chapter 3

Meetings – Covered in Chapter 3

Outputs

Resource Requirements

Activity resource requirements will document the number and types of resources needed to complete each activity. This should be very detailed. For example, if you are painting a room, this process would list the resource requirements as: 2 painters, 4 gallons of primer, 2 gallons of glossy white paint, 2 rollers, 1 roll of tape, 1 floor tarp, and 4 paint brushes.

Basis of Estimates

The basis of the estimate is a document that outlines what was used to create the estimates pertaining to the resources on the project and how the estimates were created. For example, what methods were used to develop the estimate, what assumptions and constraints were made, and the range of the estimates.

Resource Breakdown Structure (RBS)

This is a hierarchical breakdown of resources by their categories and types. On a phone system upgrade project, you can break down resources by software, hardware, and people. An RBS can help track project costs as it ties to the organization's accounting system.

Project Documents Updates – Covered in Chapter 3

Acquire Resources

Acquire resources is the process of getting the staff and physical resources needed to build the deliverables on the project. This is probably one of the first processes you will do in the execution of the project. Getting the right team and materials is very important to ensure the project is completed correctly. Teams can be dedicated to the project part-time, full-time, or virtually. You may also have teams that are contracted from outside of the organization, such as contractors and consultants.

Many different things can affect how the project team is acquired. This can include what type of organization you are working in, such as functional, matrix, or project-oriented. Your negotiation skills, the benefits of the project, and the timing of the project can also affect how you get the staff that you need.

This process is done continuously throughout the project or phase because the project manager will be releasing some teams and acquiring new teams as the execution of the project is progressing. For example, on a software development project, once the programming team is finished, the testing team will then come in to conduct the software tests.

Inputs

Project Management Plan

The project management plan will contain the resource management plan, which will give guidance on how to do this process. It will also contain the procurement management plan that will outline how to manage contractors working on the project and also the cost baseline to outline the budget.

Project Documents – Covered in Chapter 3

Of the 33 project documents, the ones you are most likely to use in this process include:

- **Resource calendars:** Resource calendars show the availability of resources. Resources greatly affect the duration of each activity. If resources are not available, this will negatively affect the duration.

- **Resource requirements:** The resources needed to complete each activity will affect the duration of each activity. Equipment and HR resources can have a big effect on the activity. For example, hiring a professional painter with a paint gun will ensure painting a room goes much faster than if a novice paints it with just a paintbrush.

- **Project schedule:** Project schedule shows the activities and resources needed over a timeline.

- **Stakeholder register:** This is a list of all the stakeholders on the project and how they may impact the project.

Enterprise Environmental Factors – Covered in Chapter 3

Organizational Process Assets – Covered in Chapter 3

Tools and Techniques

Decision Making

Multi-criteria decision analysis: You will need a method to select your team members to work on your project. This tool involves creating a table and then ranking its contents based on criteria such as communication capabilities, location, availability, cost, experience, and education. This will ensure that you get the right person for the right activity.

Interpersonal and Team Skills

Negotiation: Negotiation is a very important skill, as you will have to negotiate with functional managers, potential team members, and vendors.

Pre-assignment

Pre-assignment is when the project team has been selected by the functional managers before the project starts.

Virtual Teams

In today's technological world, virtual teams are becoming the norm. This includes having teams working through online meetings or one-on-one communication using the internet. This would allow you to have teams that span the globe. Although virtual teams may sound great, they do have some drawbacks such as difficulties with communication (language or cultural issues), technology cost, and feelings of isolation.

Outputs

Physical Resource Assignments

During this process, you have to document how you allocated the physical resources on the project. This usually includes assigning materials, supplies, equipment, or locations to the project work.

Project Team Assignments

You would also have to assign the project team to their roles and responsibilities. This usually includes adding team member's names to the corresponding activities.

Resource Calendars

As the staff is being assigned to the project, you will need to know their availability. This can include time spent working on the project, functional work, or vacations. This basically shows how the resources will be used on the project.

Change Requests – Covered in Chapter 3

Project Management Plan Updates – Covered in Chapter 3

Project Documents Updates – Covered in Chapter 3

Enterprise Environmental Factors Updates – Covered in Chapter 3

Organization Process Assets Updates – Covered in Chapter 3

Develop Team

This process is one of the most important processes because a dysfunctional project team ensures the project will fail. This could result in deliverables being late or full of defects. In this process, you take the team that you have just acquired and bring it together to ensure that the team members function as one.

The project manager should try to gain trust from the project team and show that he/she is a leader. Team members will try to get to know each other and understand each other's

strengths and weaknesses. It's during this process that everyone on the team learns to work with each other.

One model that may appear on your exam is called Tuckman's ladder. This theory includes five stages that a team will go through, from when the team is formed to when the project is completed. Here are the five stages that you should know for your exam:

- **Forming:** In this stage, the team comes together and starts to get to know each other. There is not much conflict or communication.

- **Storming:** In this stage, team members start to have conflicts with each other. They start to learn of each other's ideas and may not agree with them. Most conflicts take place in this stage.

- **Norming:** In this stage, the team members begin to agree with each other on the best methods to build the deliverables. Generally, everyone is coming to a consensus.

- **Performing:** In this stage, the team is performing well and is working without conflict. The project manager should only be overseeing the team.

- **Adjourning:** In this stage, the project is completed, and the team is reassigned.

Keep in mind that this process would be done multiple times on a project. Every time a new team comes on the project, the project manager will have to redo this process. Many projects will have multiple teams coming and going. For example, on a software development project, when the programming team is finished, the testing team will then join the project.

Inputs

Project Management Plan

The project management plan will contain the resource management plan, which will give guidance on how to do this process.

Project Documents – Covered in Chapter 3

Of the 33 project documents, the ones you are most likely to use in this process include:

- **Resource calendars:** Resource calendars show the availability of resources. Resources will greatly affect the duration of each activity. If resources are not available, this will negatively affect the duration.

- **Resource requirements:** The resources needed to complete each activity will affect the duration of each activity. Equipment and HR resources can have a big effect on the activity. For example, hiring a professional painter with a paint gun will ensure painting a room goes much faster than if a novice paints it with just a paintbrush.

- **Project schedule:** Project schedule shows the activities and resources needed over a timeline

- **Lessons learned register:** A listing of all of the lessons learned so far on the project.

- **Project team assignments:** This will list who is doing what work on the project.
- **Team charter:** This is a document that outlines what will be acceptable behavior by the project team.

Enterprise Environmental Factors – Covered in Chapter 3

Organizational Process Assets – Covered in Chapter 3

Tools and Techniques

Colocation

Colocation, also referred to as a "tight matrix" or "war room," is when you bring all of the team together to one physical space. This is sometimes known as face-to-face time. This will help team members to get to know each other better and to solve problems in a more formal space.

Virtual Teams – Covered in the previous process, "Acquire Resources".

Communications Technology

One very important aspect of developing a project team is the way the team communicates with each other. Communication technology looks at the different forms of technology that a team can use in order to enhance their communications. This can include e-mail, video-conferencing, virtual meeting technology, or a shared portal.

Interpersonal and Team Skills

The project manager's interpersonal and team skills will be mostly used to ensure the team stays motivated and focused. Here are a few techniques for that:

- **Conflict management:** Almost all projects will have some sort of conflict between team members. The project manager will have to use different methods in order to reduce or eliminate conflicts. We will cover more on conflict management in the next process, "Manage Team."
- **Influencing:** It's important to influence the project team in order to keep them motivated. This will ensure that the team can reach agreements on work that needs to get done.
- **Motivation:** One of the main jobs of a project manager is to keep their team motivated. This can be done by using various strategies and understanding the team members' needs.
- **Negotiations:** The project manager will need to negotiate with the team members to ensure that they can reach agreements with each other on complex issues.
- **Team building:** These are activities that will be done to ensure that the team functions well together. These activities could include face-to-face contact or group meetings. This will be an ongoing process as the project is progressing.

Recognition and Rewards

Recognition and rewards would allow you to have a system in place to reward team members who have done a good job on the project. Team members will be motivated to work if they know there is a reward to be gained at the end. Rewards could be tangible such as money, or intangible, such as personal recognition. Be very careful when giving special rewards (perks) to certain employees, such as more days off, as it might show favoritism.

Have a system that allows all team members to achieve the rewards.

Having a motivated team is critical to the success of a project. Here are a few motivational theories that may appear on your exam:

Maslow's hierarchy of needs: This theory was created by Abraham Maslow and shows the human needs required for motivation. They start at the bottom with physiological needs like food and rest, and work upward to self-actualization. From the graph below, you can tell that for someone to be motivated, he/she may need to be more toward the top of the triangle. We need to understand that if our more basic needs, such as safety, are not taken care of, then we may not be motivated to get the job done.

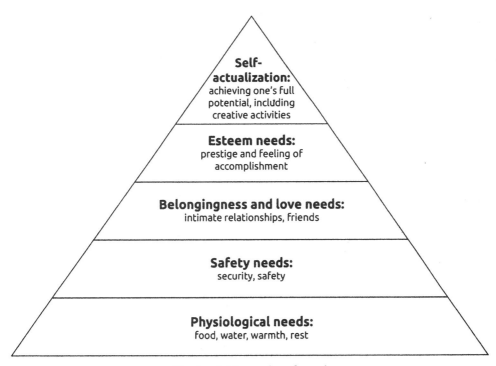

Maslow's Hierarchy of needs

McGregor's Theory X and Theory Y: Managers that use Theory X believe that people do not like to work and will try to avoid responsibilities. A Theory X manager is a micromanager. This is not a good theory to be following since it places a lot of pressure on individual workers. A Theory Y manager believes that people like to work and are willing to get the job done. They are less likely to be micro-managers and are better liked by their workers. For your exam, Theory Y is always the better theory to follow.

Theory Z: Theory Z was introduced by Dr. Willam Ouchi. This theory is concerned with increasing employee loyalty to an organization. This theory emphasizes the well-being of the employees, both at work and outside of work. It encourages steady employment, leads to high employee satisfaction and morale, and, overall, results in increased productivity and support for the organization.

David McClelland's theory of needs: This is also known as the achievement theory or three needs theory. It states that for workers to be motivated, they need to have three things in place: achievement, power, and affiliation. Without these three things, people will not be motivated. Achievement is when you have a strong need to set and accomplish challenging goals. Affiliation involves wanting to belong to a group and wanting to be liked. Power is wanting control to influence others, and wanting to win.

Herzberg's theory: Also known as the two-factor theory, it states that for people to be motivated, hygiene factors and motivation factors are important. If hygiene factors are not present, there will be no motivation factors. Failing to meet hygiene factors such as job security, salary, work conditions, good pay, paid insurance, or vacations would lead to dissatisfied employees. Motivating factors such as achievement, responsibility, opportunity to expand, and decision making can only be achieved if the hygiene factors are present.

Expectancy theory: This theory states people will perform according to the benefits they expect to receive. If people expect a large reward, they will work very hard to earn it.

Forms of Power: This deals with the power the project manager will have over the project team. Depending on the power the project manager uses, a more effective team may result. Here are the forms of power you should know for your exam:

- **Reward Power:** This is the power that allows a project manager to give rewards for the work that was done. This can include things like pay raises or time off.

- **Expert Power:** This power is when the project manager is an expert on the subject. This is one of the best powers to have, as the team is more likely to listen to you if the members think you are an expert in the subject. This can include having experience, certifications, or licenses.

- **Formal (legitimate) Power:** This power is when you use the position to control the project team. Saying things like, "I am the boss, that's why you should listen to me" is an example of this.

- **Referent Power:** This power is based on someone's personality and charisma. This is wanting people to like you based on who you are. It can also be used to appeal to someone in a higher position of power to convince the team to follow you.

- **Penalty (Coercive) Power:** This power involves using punishment in order to manage the team. This type of power generally leads to more conflicts. An example is threatening the team members if they do not do the job properly.

On this exam, the best forms of power to use will be expert and reward power. Expert and reward power can lead to the project team being more motivated and happy while working on the project. One of the worst powers to use is the penalty because it can drive fear into the team, which can lead to future conflicts.

Training

Ensuring that the team has the right skills to do the job becomes essential for the completion of a deliverable. Training includes the activities needed to ensure your team members possess the right skills necessary to complete the work. This can include online or classroom training done by external organizations, other team members, or coaching. The cost of training could be included in the project budget. Sometimes, the organization might pay for the training if the skills that team members acquire will be used after the project has been completed.

Individual and Team Assessments

The project manager will need to assess how the project team is progressing. Project managers should assess the team's and each individual's strengths and weaknesses. They should look at how the team makes decisions, resolves conflicts, communicates, and ensures trust between each other.

Meetings – Covered in Chapter 3

Outputs

Team Performance Assessments

This is the overall evaluation of the project team. These evaluations can include the strengths and weaknesses of the project team and how the project manager would improve them. Improvements should be implemented right away to reduce conflicts and staff turn- over.

The project manager will utilize things such as training, mentoring, and coaching to improve the performance of the team. This can include teaching them how to communicate more efficiently and how to understand each other.

Change Requests – Covered in Chapter 3

Project Management Plan Updates – Covered in Chapter 3

Project Documents Updates – Covered in Chapter 3

Enterprise Environmental Factors Updates – Covered in Chapter 3

Organization Process Assets Updates – Covered in Chapter 3

Manage Team

This is the process of managing the project team as the project is progressing. This process will be done throughout the execution process group of the project. This will mostly involve the day-to-day management of the project team, which can include solving conflicts and coaching the team.

Successful management of a project team will generally ensure a successful project. But this will not be an easy task, since managing people is one of the most complicated functions on a project. The project manager should expect conflicts among team members, and he/she will need to come up with solutions for those conflicts. Many conflicts may occur because of scheduling issues or inter-personal disagreements, and the project manager will have to use their interpersonal skills in order to make sure these problems are solved promptly and do not impact the output of the project or phase.

Managing a team of experts can be a very complicated task. Expect a lot of questions on the exam that come from this process. Most of the questions will come from the conflict management tool used in this process.

Inputs

Project Management Plan

The project management plan will contain the resource management plan, which will give guidance on how to do this process.

Project Documents – Covered in Chapter 3

Of the 33 project documents, the ones you are most likely to use in this process include:

- **Issue log:** This is a listing of all issues on the project. For this process, it's more related to the HR issues, such as a conflict between two team members.

- **Lessons learned register:** A listing of all of the lessons learned so far on the project.

- **Project team assignments:** This will list who is doing what work on the project.

- **Team charter:** This is a document that outlines what will be acceptable behavior on the project.

Team Performance Assessments

This is the overall evaluation of the project team. These evaluations can include the strengths and weaknesses of the project team and how the project manager would improve them.

Work Performance Reports

Work performance reports will give you the overall status of the project. The reports compare the planned work against the actual work.

Enterprise Environmental Factors – Covered in Chapter 3

Organizational Process Assets – Covered in Chapter 3

Tools and Techniques

Interpersonal and Team Skills

Although there are many different techniques to help you with interpersonal and team skills, the most important one will be conflict management. Expect to see a lot of exam questions on this single tool. Conflicts can arise during any part of the project. These could include conflicts between team members, sponsors, customers, and functional managers. All projects have some form of conflict amongst the stakeholders at some point in the project. It is an essential skill to be able to manage conflicts to ensure the project is successful.

Many, if not most, conflicts on a project occur between project managers and functional managers. This is usually because of scheduling problems. Both the project manager and the functional manager want resources in order to complete their work. Since most exam questions are based on balanced matrix organization, the project manager and the functional manager will have equal power. For example, the functional manager may need a resource to stay on and complete the day-to-day operations of the organization, while the project manager needs that same resource to work on the project. In this situation, who will get the resource: the functional manager or the project manager? This is the conflict.

Here are a few techniques to deal with conflicts on a project:

- **Problem-solving/collaborate:** In this technique, stakeholders come together and come up with a solution that makes both sides happy. The problem is solved and goes away. This is known as a win-win scenario, because both sides feel the problem has been solved. This is the best way to solve problems and is the method PMI favors the most.

- **Compromising/reconcile:** In this technique, both sides might have to give up a little bit to come to a consensus on how to solve the problem. This is known as a lose-lose scenario, since both sides did not get everything they wanted.

- **Force/direct:** In this technique, one side gets everything they want, and the other side gets nothing. This is known as a win-lose scenario; one side wins completely, and the other side loses completely. This is the worst way to solve a problem, since this will lead to more conflicts between the stakeholders.

- **Smooth/accommodate:** In this technique, the stakeholders downplay the conflict. They might say things like "don't worry, it is not much of a problem" or "please take care of it later." This is known as a lose-lose scenario because the problem is not solved and may still exist.

- **Withdrawal/avoid:** In this technique, one of the parties walks away from the problem. They may say something like, "find your own way, I am leaving." This is known as a yield- lose scenario because one person walks away from the other, but the problem may still exist.

On this exam, when reading the scenarios, you want to pick the answer that sounds most like problem solving or collaborating. Ask yourself if the problem is solved and if both sides are happy with the solution. The other techniques are not the best methods to solve the problem and can lead to more future problems.

Always keep in mind that a problem should be solved with the best interests of the project in mind. Try to do what is right for the customers at all times. Personality conflicts between team members should not affect the deliverables of the project.

Below is the problem-solving technique that you should know for your exam:

- Define the cause of the problem (not just the symptoms).
- Analyze the problem (cause-and-effect diagram).
- Identify solutions.
- Implement the selected solution.
- Review the solution.
- Confirm that the solution solved the problem.

Any time you are solving a problem, you have to make sure you identify it first, then look for solutions, implement the chosen solution, review the solution, and then confirm that the problem is solved. This is true for all problems on a project, not just HR problems.

Sometimes you might encounter a problem that exceeds the authority of the project manager, such as when functional managers have issues assigning resources to you. In this case, you might have to ask the project sponsor or senior management to intervene and resolve the conflict

Emotional intelligence (EI): Another technique is emotional intelligence, which is the ability to understand and manage your personal emotions and those of the individuals around you. People with a high degree of emotional intelligence know what they're feeling, what their emotions mean, and how these emotions can affect other people. For project managers, emotional intelligence is crucial for success. After all, the leader who's most likely to succeed would be the one who stays in control and calmly handles all situations.

An American psychologist named Daniel Goleman outlines five key elements of emotional intelligence:

1. **Self-awareness:** you constantly know how you feel, and you know how your emotions and your activities can affect the individuals around you.

2. **Self-regulation:** Ability to stay in control.

3. **Motivation:** Ability to be Self-motivated and consistently toward a goal. Also, have extremely high standards for the quality of your work.

4. **Empathy:** Ability to put yourself in someone else's circumstances. This will help you respond better to people's emotions, allowing you to give constructive feedback and listen to others.

5. **Social skills:** Good social skills allow you to interact and communicate with people. This will solve issues and get work done correctly.

All projects require good leadership skills. A great project manager will be able to lead their team and inspire them to go beyond their current skills. This is usually done by having good communication skills and communicating the vision of the project clearly and continually to the team members.

Project Management Information System – Covered in Chapter 3

Outputs

Change Requests

In this process, change requests will deal mostly with staffing changes. These staffing changes can occur because people may be leaving for different assignments or to address issues that may cause them to be replaced. This change request will be processed in the "Perform Integrated Change Control" process to see how it will affect the other parts of the project.

Project Management Plan Updates – Covered in Chapter 3

Project Documents Updates – Covered in Chapter 3

Enterprise Environmental Factors Updates – Covered in Chapter 3

Organizational Process Assets Updates – Covered in Chapter 3

Control Resources

Control resource is a process that looks at how to correctly manage the physical resources on the project as the project is progressing. This process does not look at the HR resources which were covered in the previous process, "Manage Team."

As the project progresses, the team will consume physical resources in order to complete the deliverable. Physical resources usually include materials, equipment, and supplies. The project manager will have to ensure that the resources are being used correctly and efficiently.

Failure in this process will generally lead to the physical resources being misused. This can include resources being used unnecessarily or inappropriately. For example, a painter might use too much paint to paint a small room. This will lead to unnecessary budget increases and potential defects in the deliverables.

Inputs

Project Management Plan

The project management plan will contain the resource management plan, which will give guidance on how to do this process.

Project Documents – Covered in Chapter 3

Of the 33 project documents, the ones you are most likely to use in this process include:

- **Issue log:** This is a listing of all issues on the project. For this process, it's more related to the issues dealing with physical resources, such as if we have enough paint to paint the room.

- **Lesson learned register:** A listing of all of the lessons learned so far on the project.

- **Physical resource assignments:** This will list what physical resources are being used on the project.

- **Resource requirements:** The physical and HR resources needed to complete each activity will be stated here.

- **Risk register:** The risk register will list all the identified project risks, as well as their impact and response.

- **Project schedule:** The project schedule will contain the network diagram and the Gantt chart. This will show the start and end dates of all the activities on the project.

Work Performance Data

The work performance data will contain information on how the physical resources are being used on the project. For example, it might specify how much paint was used to paint a room.

Agreements

If the project required any resource from outside the organization, such as from a contractor, they will need the agreement or contract to verify if they're getting an adequate number of physical resources from the contractor.

Organizational Process Assets – Covered in Chapter 3

Tools & Techniques

Data Analysis – Covered in Chapter 3

Problem Solving

All projects can expect to encounter some kind of problems, particularly resource problems. This can include resources getting misused or damaged. The project manager should look for ways to identify what may be causing the problems and then come up with methods they can use to solve the problems. This may include training the team members in the correct usage of physical resources.

Interpersonal and Team Skills – Covered in Chapter 3

Project Management Information System – Covered in Chapter 3

Outputs

Work Performance Information

Work performance information generally shows how the actual work is progressing against the planned work. In this particular process, it will show how the physical resources were supposed to be used versus how they are actually being used.

Change Requests

If the project manager needs more physical resources or ways to correct the resources' usage, he/she might need a change request.

Project Management Plan Updates – Covered in Chapter 3

Project Documents Updates – Covered in Chapter 3

Resource Management Questions

1. You are in the Plan Resource Management process of identifying and documenting project roles, responsibilities, required skills, competencies, reporting structure, and other items. The structure that you are using is arranged according to an organization's existing departments, units, or teams with their respective work packages. Which of the following are you using?

    A. Resource Breakdown Structure (RBS)

    B. Responsibility Assignment Matrix (RAM)

    C. Position descriptions

    D. Organizational Breakdown Structure (OBS)

2. Project success is heavily dependent on the leadership and management style of the project manager. Even though we do not usually distinguish between leading and managing, it is generally believed that there is a difference between these two. Which of the following is typically considered to be a responsibility associated with managing?

    A. Consistently producing key results expected by stakeholders

    B. Establishing direction, mission, and vision

    C. Aligning team members to the established direction

    D. Motivating and inspiring

3. You made sure that one of the junior team members on your team received the required training to perform his activities. While assessing the team member, you were concerned that the team member was still lacking competency and required further improvement. What will be the BEST course of action?

    A. Replace the team member with an experienced resource.

    B. Have an urgent discussion with the team member and inform him that he will be out of the project if there is no immediate improvement.

    C. Have a discussion with the functional manager about the lack of competency of the team member.

    D. Identify the team member's current lack and provide more focused training.

4. A project manager is overseeing a complex custom CSM solution that has rigorous quality standards and tight schedule constraints. The project manager just found out that one of the key deliverables in the project was not completed because the team member responsible for it was assigned to another higher-priority project by her functional manager. Who will be the person for the project manager to address the issue within this kind of situation?

    A. The sponsor

    B. The president of the company

    C. The customers

    D. The team

5. A project manager recently got her PMP certification and joined a professional project management group. The group members meet on a regular basis to discuss new opportunities, trends, and issues in project management. The satisfaction that the project manager gains from the association with this group is MOST closely aligned with:

   A. Expectancy theory

   B. The third level of Maslow's Hierarchy of Needs

   C. Herzberg's Hygiene theory

   D. Theory X

6. You are currently managing the team through observing, using issue logs, keeping in touch, providing feedback, completing performance appraisals, resolving issues and conflicts, and through other methods. You are in which of the following human resource management processes?

   A. Plan Resource Management

   B. Acquire Resources

   C. Develop Team

   D. Manage Team

7. You are the project manager overseeing a project to build a navigation system for an auto company. You are in the Develop Team process, and your key focus is to enhance the project performance by building a sense of team and improving the competencies, team interaction, and overall team environment. You will be using all of the following tools & techniques in the process EXCEPT:

   A. Acquisition

   B. Ground rules

   C. Training

   D. Recognition and rewards

8. You are overseeing the implementation of a library management system for a local library. While in the execution phase, the functional manager informs you that his team needs to work on a higher-priority project, and he will be pulling out two critical resources from your project. What should you do FIRST as a project manager?

   A. Evaluate the impact by referring to the resource histogram.

   B. Reassign activities of these two members to the other team members.

   C. Immediately inform higher management.

   D. Request the functional manager to assign two new resources first before pulling out the existing members.

9. You are a member of a management team overseeing a critical construction project. Your team, which is a subset of the project team, is responsible for project leadership and management activities. Which of the following statements is FALSE about your team?

    A. Your team is responsible for managing people, which has been defined as being able to produce key results.

    B. Your team is responsible for establishing mission and vision, aligning team members to the established direction, motivating individuals, and inspiring them.

    C. Your team is responsible for project funding.

    D. The management team should be aware of professional and ethical behaviors and ensure that team members are following them.

10. A project manager is in the Develop Team process, focusing on enhancing project performance by building a sense of team and improving competencies, team interaction, and overall team environment. While referring to Tuckman's model, she notices that the greatest level of conflict in the five different stages of team building is most likely to appear in which of the following stages:

    A. Forming

    B. Adjourning

    C. Storming

    D. Exploring

11. You just completed working on your resource management plan and identified how human resources should be defined, staffed, managed, and eventually released from your project. Which portion of the plan will help you the most to determine when to release resources from your project?

    A. Training needs and certification requirements

    B. Recognition and rewards

    C. Compliance considerations

    D. Resource histogram

12. Which motivational theory below is concerned with increasing employee loyalty and support for the organization by emphasizing the well-being of employees both at work and outside of work and encouraging steady employment?

    A. Expectancy theory

    B. Theory Z

    C. Theory Y

    D. Theory X

13. A project team member's abilities or competencies, communication capabilities, relevant knowledge, skills, experience, cost (for adding the team member), attitude or ability to work with others, availability, and other factors such as time zone and geographical location are some examples of selection criteria that can be used to rate and score that team member. Which one of the following looks at all of these selection criteria when acquiring a team member for a project?

    A. Multi-criteria decision analysis

    B. Monte Carlo analysis

    C. Team performance assessment

    D. Project performance appraisal

14. A project manager overseeing a data center deployment project just completed negotiation unsuccessfully for three additional resources and extra reserve money for her project. During the negotiation, two of the functional managers were very skeptical about the request for additional resources and were reluctant to assign their resources due to other priorities. In this case, the conflict will require the assistance of which of the following to reach a solution?

    A. Functional manager

    B. Contractor

    C. Project sponsor

    D. Key customer

15. You are in the Plan Resource Management process to create an overall staffing management plan by identifying the availability of resources and those resources' skill levels. Which of the following is NOT a tool & technique is this process?

    A. Organizational charts and position descriptions

    B. Networking

    C. Organizational theory

    D. Colocation

16. A project manager is in the Develop Team process, focusing on enhancing project performance by building a sense of team and improving the competencies, team interaction, and overall team environment. While referring to Tuckman's model, she notices that the team members begin to start trusting and working together as they adjust work habits and behaviors to work as a team. What stage of team development is the project manager referring to?

    A. Forming

    B. Adjourning

    C. Storming

    D. Norming

17. You are considering the idea of putting all team members in the same physical location for the first time. All of the following is true about collocation EXCEPT:

    A. The goal is to enhance team members' ability to perform as a team.

    B. It is also called a war room.

    C. It is meant to identify concerns and issues and to come up with mutually agreed-upon solutions.

    D. The goal is to identify the individual(s) or team responsible for project issues and inform them about it.

18. You are in the Plan Resource Management process of identifying and documenting project roles, responsibilities, required skills, and other items. Which one of the following will you NOT use as a tool & technique in this process?

    A. Hierarchical-type organizational charts

    B. Recognition and rewards

    C. A responsibility assignment matrix

    D. Organizational theory

19. You were informed by management that an external audit team would be auditing your project to make sure that the project complies with standard organizational project management policies and procedures. During the audit, the key auditor wants to review the training plan for the team members as well as their certification requirements. You should refer the auditor to which of the following?

    A. Resource management plan

    B. RACI chart

    C. Training and certification management plan

    D. Resource breakdown structure

20. While overseeing a data center project, you notice that one of the team members is extremely dedicated to the project and a consistent overachiever. In order to appreciate her spectacular work and great contribution, you made her the 'team member of the month' three times in a row. What kind of impact will this have on the project team?

    A. This will initiate a healthy competition among the team members.

    B. This will drastically improve team cohesiveness.

    C. This will negatively impact team morale.

    D. Team members hardly care about recognition and rewards; thus, there will be no impact.

21. You are a project manager who believes steady employment leads to high employee satisfaction and morale, increased loyalty to the organization, and increased productivity. Which theory do you subscribe to?

    A. Theory X and Theory Y

    B. Contingency theory

    C. Theory Z

    D. Expectancy theory

22. Mary, a project manager, is in the Develop Team process, focusing on enhancing project performance by building a sense of team and improving the competencies, team interaction, and overall team environment. While referring to Tuckman's model, she notices that the team is in a stage where her role is mostly overseeing and delegating. The team is in which stage of team development?

    A. Forming

    B. Adjourning

    C. Storming

    D. Performing

23. A project manager overseeing a construction project notices that her team members are having constant conflicts over issues. The situation was causing her a lot of concern, and she decides to identify the key causes of the conflicts. While exploring the causes, she finds that the most common causes of conflicts among team members are project priorities, resources, and:

    A. Personality

    B. Schedule

    C. Technical options

    D. Administration procedures

24. A project manager is overseeing a complex custom CSM solution that has rigorous quality standards and tight schedule constraints. Since the project manager is working in a weak matrix environment, none of the resources are reporting to her functionally. She also does not have either the power or the budget to reward the team members to encourage and motivate them for their performance and contribution to the project. What kind of power should the project manager try to use in this type of situation?

    A. Formal

    B. Punishment

    C. Referent

    D. Expert

25. You oversee a video conferencing application project and just completed negotiation for three additional resources from different functional areas and extra reserve money for your project. During the negotiation, two of the functional managers were very skeptical about the request for additional resources and were reluctant to assign their resources to your project. At last, a solution was reached in which you were allowed to obtain the resources you requested, but you had to agree to give up some other resources at an earlier date than you had originally planned. What type of conflict resolution technique was used in this situation?

    A. Smoothing

    B. Compromising

    C. Forcing

    D. Collaborating

Project Human Resource Management Answers

1. **D:** An OBS is similar to a company's standard organizational chart that looks like a WBS but only includes the positions and relationships in a top-down, graphic format. It is arranged according to an organization's existing departments, units, or teams with their respective work packages. Any operations department, such as manufacturing or engineering can identify all of its project responsibilities by looking at its portion of the OBS. An RBS also looks like a typical organizational chart, but this one is organized by types of resources. An RBS can help track project costs as it ties to the organization's accounting system. A RAM cross-references team members with the activities or work packages they are to accomplish. One example of a RAM is a Responsible, Accountable, Consult, and Inform (RACI) chart, which can be used to ensure clear divisions of roles and responsibilities. A text-oriented position description, or role-responsibility-authority form, is particularly important in recruiting. It is used to describe a team member's position, title, responsibilities, authority, competencies, and qualifications in detail.

2. **A:** Project management is heavily dependent on managing people, which has been defined as being able to produce key results. On the other hand, leadership is all about establishing a mission and vision, aligning team members to the established direction, and motivating and inspiring individuals.

3. **D:** The role of the project manager is to make sure that team members, especially the junior members with limited experience, get the required training and assistance to perform their activities.

4. **A:** It is one of the key roles of the sponsor to prevent unnecessary changes in the project in addition to providing funding for the project.

5. **B:** The third level of Maslow's Hierarchy of Needs is the need for social connections or belonging, such as love, affection, approval, friends, and association. The Expectancy theory, first proposed by Victor Vroom, demonstrates that employees who believe their efforts will lead to effective performance and who expect to be rewarded for their accomplishments remain productive as rewards meet their expectations. Herzberg's Motivator-Hygiene theory suggests that hygiene factors can destroy motivation, but improving them under most circumstances will not improve motivation. Motivating people is best done by rewarding people and letting them grow. Theory X managers believe that average workers are incapable, avoid responsibility, have an inherent dislike of work, and are only interested in their own selfish goals. The workers must be forced to do productive work as they dislike their work and are not devoted and motivated.

6. **D:** Manage Team is the process of managing the team through observing, using issue logs, keeping in touch, providing feedback, completing performance appraisals, resolving issues and conflicts, and other factors.

7. **A:** Acquisition is used as a tool & technique in the Acquire Resources process, where the main goal is to secure the best possible resources to build the project team so that they can carry on the project activities efficiently.

8. **A:** In this sort of situation, a project manager should always evaluate the impact of the changes and gather as much information as possible before taking any further steps.

9. **C:** The project sponsor usually assists with funding, not the project management team. The project management team is a subset of the project team responsible for project leadership and management activities. Project management is heavily dependent on managing people, which has been defined as being able to produce key results. On the other hand, leadership is all about establishing a mission and vision, aligning team members to the established direction, motivating individuals, and inspiring them. The management team should be aware of professional and ethical behaviors and should ensure that team members are following them.-

10. **C:** Storming follows the Forming stage, and it is where the team begins to address project work, technical decisions, areas of disagreement, and project management approaches. The team typically goes through some conflicts and difficulties in this stage more than any other.

11. **D:** A resource histogram is a graphical display that shows the amount of time that a resource is scheduled to work over a series of time periods.

12. **B:** Theory Z was introduced by Dr. Willam Ouchi. This theory is concerned with increasing employee loyalty to his/her organization. This theory emphasizes the well-being of the employees both at work and outside of work, it encourages steady employment, it leads to high employee satisfaction and morale, and overall, it results in increased productivity and support for the organization. Theory X managers believe that average workers are incapable, avoid responsibility, have an inherent dislike of work, and are only interested in their own selfish goals. The workers must be forced to do productive work as they dislike their work and are not devoted and motivated. Theory Y managers believe that workers are creative and committed to project objectives and goals. They are willing to work without supervision, need very little external motivation, can direct their own efforts, and want to achieve. The Expectancy theory demonstrates that employees who believe their efforts will lead to effective performance and who expect to be rewarded for their accomplishments remain productive as rewards meet their expectations.

13. **A:** Potential team members are often rated and scored by various selection criteria during the Acquire Resources process. These selection criteria are weighted according to their relevant importance and are developed using the multi-criteria decision analysis tool. A project team member's ability or competencies, communication capabilities, relevant knowledge, skills, experience, cost (for adding the team member), attitude or ability to work with others, availability, and other factors such as time zone and geographical location are some examples of selection criteria that can be used to rate and score team members.

14. **C:** Customers and contractors should not be allowed to be involved in internal re- source-related disputes in most cases. All efforts should be given to resolve the conflicts at the lowest levels of authority whenever possible. In some cases, conflict requires the involvement of the project sponsor or senior management, especially when there is a major concern regarding resource assignments.

15. **D:** Colocation is a tool & technique used in the Develop Team process, not in the Plan Resource Management process.

16. **D:** The team members are in the Norming stage as they are adjusting work habits and behaviors to work as a team. They begin to start trusting and working together.

17. **D:** The objective of collocation, or the war room, is to build a better relationship among the team members, enhance their ability to perform as a team, identify concerns and issues in the project, and figure out solutions for those issues. The idea is not to point fingers at other team members or get involved in any kind of argument.

18. **B:** Recognition and rewards are used as a tool & technique in the Develop Team process, not in the Plan Resource Management process. Hierarchical-type organizational charts, a responsibility assignment matrix (which is a matrix-type organizational chart), and organizational theory are all used as tools & techniques in the Plan Resource Management process.

19. **A:** The resource management plan identifies the training needs and certification requirements of the team members. One example of a responsibility assignment matrix is a RACI (Responsible, Accountable, Consult, and Inform) chart, which can be used to ensure clear divisions of roles and responsibilities. Training and certification management plan is a fake term. A resource breakdown structure (RBS) looks like a typical organizational chart, but this one is organized by types of resources. An RBS can help track project costs as it ties to the organization's accounting system.

20. **C:** A project manager can kill the team morale by consistently rewarding the same individual repeatedly as it can be perceived that the project manager is playing favorites. If the team members believe that the rewards are win-lose and that only certain team members will be rewarded, it may demoralize them. In this kind of situation, the project manager can consider team awards, which is a win-win as all the team members are recognized for their contributions.

21. **C:** Theory Z was introduced by Dr. Willam Ouchi. This theory is concerned with increasing employee loyalty to his/her organization: This theory emphasizes the well-being of employees both at work and outside of work, it encourages steady employment, it leads to high employee satisfaction and morale, and overall, it results in increased productivity.

22. **D:** As per Tuckman's model, in the Performing stage, the team functions as a well-organized unit. They are interdependent and work through issues smoothly and effectively. The role of the project manager is mainly overseeing and delegating.

23. **B:** There are several sources of conflict, including schedule priorities, scarce resources, personal work style, cost, and other elements, but it's important to note that personality differences are not the root cause of conflict; in fact, it's rarely the case. The three main causes of project conflicts are schedule, project priorities, and resources, as approximately 50 percent of all conflicts come from these three sources.

24. **D:** Reward and Expert are the most effective forms of power, and Punishment/Penalty/Coercive should be used as the last resort only after all other forms have been exhausted. Since the project manager has no power or budget to reward the team members, she should use her expert power in this situation.

25. **B:** Compromising is bargaining to some level of mutual (dis)satisfaction to both parties. Parties are asked to lose something to gain something. Smoothing is emphasizing areas of agreement and downplaying differences of opinion. Forcing is exerting one opinion over another while Collaborating focuses on working to combine multiple differing perspectives into one shared perspective and results in a win-win situation for all parties.

Chapter 11
Project Communication Management

This is one of the most important knowledge areas when it comes to real-life project management. Communication is the key to a successful project. The whole concept of management is about good communications. More than 90% of the daily tasks we do as project managers involve communicating internally or externally on the project.

The project manager's main job in this area will be to set the communication expectations for the project. This means letting people know what communications will be taking place on the project. The project manager should identify the communications needs of all the stakeholders on the project and ensure they are met. This will ensure that all stakeholders get the information that they need.

If you are working on an agile project, expect communications to be just as important as it is on a traditional project. On an agile project, you would be communicating more with the customers because of the iterations that are taking place on the project. This generally leads to the customers being more engaged throughout the life cycle of the project.

Most of the exam questions concerning communications will come from the communications formula and the communications management plan. They should not be very difficult to answer. Try to focus on why and how the plan and formula would be used. This knowledge area is very similar to the manage stakeholders knowledge area, so expect a few questions that test you on the difference between them. Most importantly will be the difference between the stakeholder and communication management plans. We will cover the difference in more detail in the "Stakeholder Management" chapter.

Process	Process Group	Main Output
Plan Communications Management	Planning	Communications Management Plan
Manage Communications	Executing	Project Communications
Monitor Communications	Monitoring and Controlling	Work Performance Information, Change Request

Plan Communications Management

Plan communications management is about creating the communications management plan. This process analyzes the communications requirements of the stakeholders and documents how the project will meet them.

This communications management plan will document how communication will be managed and controlled. It will define the following:

- Who needs what project information?
- When do they need it?
- How would they receive it?
- How will it be stored?

This process is done very early in the project to ensure that accurate communication is occurring throughout.

Inputs

Project Charter – Covered in Chapter 4

Project Management Plan – Covered in Chapter 3

Project Documents

Of the 33 project documents, you'll probably be using the following documents:

Requirements documentation: This document will show what resources are needed for each activity.

Stakeholder register: The stakeholder register is an output from the "Identify Stakeholder" process. It is a list of all stakeholders on the project and how they will be affected by the project. It will also document their communications requirements. This information will be needed to create the communication management plan.

Enterprise Environmental Factors – Covered in Chapter 3

Organizational Process Assets – Covered in Chapter 3

Tools and Techniques

Expert Judgment – Covered in Chapter 3

Communication Requirements Analysis

This involves analyzing the communications needs of the stakeholders. You will need to determine what information each stakeholder will need on the project. One way to analyze communication is by looking at the communication channels on the project. A channel is a link between stakeholders where communications might be needed. For example, the

channel between the sponsor and the project manager will need a weekly status report on the project. You will need to know how many communication channels are on the project and what the communication needs are for each.

The formula for calculating the communications channels of projects: $N(N-1)/2$=Number of channels on the project.

If a project has 4 stakeholders, how many channels will the project have? To answer this, just replace N with the number of stakeholders on the project as follows:

4(4-1)/2 = 6

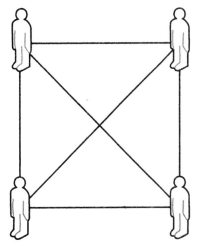

Project with four stakeholders and six channels.

If a project has 10 stakeholders, there would be 45 channels on the project. Here is the formula for that:

10(10-1)/2 = 45

Knowing that there are 45 channels on the project would allow the project manager to analyze each of them to determine the best communication need for that channel. For example, between stakeholder 1 and stakeholder 2 a monthly status report may be all that is necessary because stakeholder 1 is the CEO and stakeholder 2 is the project manager.

On agile projects, communications should always be done with the most low-tech high-touch options. While technology is great to communicate with, technology will never be able to replace the emotional expressions you can see in someone's face and experience their body language when communicating with someone. It's for these reasons that the richness of communication can increase when we actually face each other and discuss issues and plans. As you can see in the diagram below, the richness of the communication channel increases as people are more face-to-face and interactive.

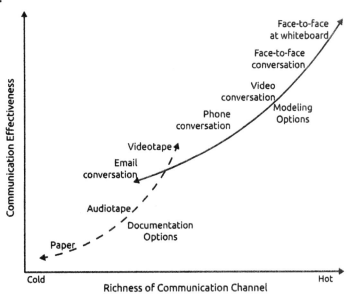

Exam Tip: When communicating on agile projects, always choose the lowest-tech and highest touch option. Always try to bring people together in the same room to have a face-to-face conversation.

Communication Technology

The way communication is done will differ between most projects. Some projects might use virtual meetings, while others may use in-person meetings. Here are a few things that can affect the technologies used on a project:

- **Urgency:** If information is needed right away, it might be best to call someone rather than sending that person an e-mail and waiting for a response.

- **Technology:** The different types of technology available to the project might change how communication is done. If virtual meeting software is not available, then people might choose to do a conference call or an in-person meeting.

- **Ease of use:** Some things are best done the easiest way. Look for technology that makes communicating easy.

- **Environment:** The overall environment of the business will affect the technology used in communicating. Some companies prefer personal meetings over virtual meetings.

- **Type of information:** Depending on the type of information being passed, the technology may change. For example, if you are sending confidential information to a receiver, you should be using an encrypted method.

Communication Models

A communication model is the overall exchange of information. All models have a sender and a receiver. It is the sender who is responsible for ensuring that the receiver understands the information. The way communication is performed can affect whether or not the receiver actually understands it.

Here are a few terms that you should know:

- **Sender:** The person or group sending the information.

- **Encoder:** The technology that encodes the information the sender is sending. For instance, this can be the e-mail server sending the e-mail from the sender.

- **Decoder:** The technology that decodes the information for the receiver. For instance, this can be the receiver's e-mail server getting the e-mail from the sender.

- **Receiver:** The person or group getting the information.

- **Para lingual:** This is the way you sound when talking, such as the pitch and tone of your voice.

- **Feedback:** The sender will have to confirm that the information was received and understood or whether they need more clarification.

- **Active listening:** This is when the listener is engaged in communications, such as asking questions.

- **Effective listening:** This is when the sender has the full attention of the receiver.

- **Nonverbal:** This is body language, such as the way you walk, hand motions, or expressions. About 55% of communication is done this way.

- **Communication Blocker:** This is anything that negatively affects the sender sending or the receiver receiving the information. This can include noise, which can affect the receiver receiving the information.

Communication Methods

Communication methods can be described as the following:

- **Interactive:** This is a two-way (or more) method of direct communication. This is when all parties are sending and receiving information. Examples: meetings or instant messaging.

- **Push:** This is to give out information. Examples: e-mails or memos.

- **Pull:** This is to get information from somewhere. The sender leaves the information in a central place where the receiver can access it. This is generally used for a large audience. Examples include e-learning, intranet sites, or postings on SharePoint.

You must also know the following communication types for the exam:

Type	Examples
Informal Written	E-mail, text messages, notes
Informal Verbal	Meetings, conversations, phone calls
Formal Written	Agreements, project management plans, charters
Formal Verbal	Presentations, speeches

It is very important to know when to use formal or informal communication. Formal communication is usually predefined and more structured than informal, which is generally less defined by the company and can happen more freely. For example, when updating the customers on the status of the project, you may do a formal verbal presentation about the project status (formal verbal). Day-to-day communication with the project team may not need to be scheduled and can be done using an e-mail (informal written). Informal is also used to solve problems on a project. Verbal can be faster, while written can take longer. It is faster to call and speak to someone than write an e-mail. Written communications allow you to track the communications and may be used to solve a complex problem as opposed to a small problem that needs a fast solution (verbal).

Interpersonal and Team Skills – Covered in Chapter 3

Data Representation – Covered in Chapter 3

Meetings – Covered in Chapter 3

Outputs

Communications Management Plan

The communications management plan will document how communication will be done on the project. It is part of the project management plan. It will describe how to conduct the other two communication processes, "Manage Communications" and "Monitor Communications."

Here are things the plan should include:

- Who needs what type of information?

- Why do they need it?

- When do they need it?

- How do they want it?
- How would they get it?
- Who would give it to them?

The communications should be tailored to the stakeholders receiving them. Senior management will only need a brief presentation overview of the project status, using less technical language, once a month. Project team members may require weekly or daily meetings to resolve project issues. Sponsors and customers might only need a quick presentation of the project status once a week. Always ensure that the receiver understands the information that is given to him/her. You might have to include definitions of technical terminology, charts, and diagrams.

Project Management Plan Updates – Covered in Chapter 3

Project Documents Updates – Covered in Chapter 3

Manage Communications

Manage Communications is a process that executes the communications management plan. If the plan states that you should hold a meeting with the sponsor on Friday, then hold that meeting on Friday. You are doing what it states in the plan.

Here are a couple of things to keep in mind when communicating:

- Choice of media, such as written vs. verbal or paper vs. electronics.
- Meeting management, which should include having an agenda and meeting minutes.
- Good presentation techniques, such as body language and a properly formatted presentation.
- Facilitation techniques that will allow groups to work better with less conflict.

Inputs

Project Management Plan

The communications and resource management plan will document how the communication and resource utilization will take place. The stakeholder management plan can also be used to identify how engagements with stakeholders will take place.

Project Documents

Of the 33 project documents, you are most likely to use:

- **Stakeholder register:** This is a list of all the stakeholders on the project and how they may impact the project.
- **Risk report:** This document will give an overall status of how the project is managing risks. This information should be communicated to the project stakeholders.
- **Quality report:** This report will describe any defects that have been discovered in the project and how the team is working to improve the processes and deliverables.
- **Issue Log:** This log will list all issues on the project. Stakeholders may want to be updated on the status of issues on the project.
- **Change log:** The change log will keep track of the status of all change requests on the project. The status generally indicates if the changes are being reviewed, approved, or denied.

Work Performance Reports

Work performance reports will tell you the overall status of the project. This will consist of the combination of all the work performance information, which is the comparison of the work performance data (actual work) to the project management plan (plan work).

Enterprise Environmental Factors – Covered in Chapter 3

Organizational Process Assets – Covered in Chapter 3

Tools and Techniques

Communication Technology – Covered in the Plan Communication Management process.

Communication Models – Covered in the Plan Communication Management process.

Communication Methods – Covered in the Plan Communication Management process.

Communication Skills

Good communication skills are essential for all managers, whether you're on a project or business operations. The project manager will be communicating with all stakeholders on the project. Being able to provide clear and effective communications is the key to great leadership. Some of the communication skills that will be used here would include feedback, nonverbal communication, and presentation skills. Feedback usually involves communications between the project stakeholders to inform them of their performance and what may need to be improved. Nonverbal communications generally account for more than 55% of communications. This generally includes facial expressions and movements, tone of voice, and eye contact. Presentation skills would include knowing how to present certain information to certain stakeholders. Project managers should have an idea of the audience that they are presenting to and present in a clear and concise way that the audience can understand. For example, a presentation to team members should be very detailed, whereas a presentation to senior management should be summarized and to the point.

Project Management Information System

When giving out project information, there are different ways to distribute it. The information system can use hard paper, such as letters or memos, or electronic communication such as e-mail or websites. The way you distribute the information will depend on the project's stakeholders.

Project Reporting

This tool creates reports about the project. It collects the project information and then creates a report that will satisfy the needs of the stakeholders. Performance reports generally include the actual work vs. planned work and how the work is progressing. This would include the performance of the scope, time, and quality. Different reports contain information about Earned Value Management, risk, communications issues, and completion status.

Interpersonal and Team Skills – Covered in Chapter 3

Meetings – Covered in Chapter 3

Outputs

Project Communications

The main output of this process is the project communications. Project communications involve communicating according to the communication management plan. This can include giving out the performance reports, holding meetings, making conference calls, or sending emails. The project communications will depend on the actual project and its stakeholders.

Project Management Plan Updates – Covered in Chapter 3

Project Documents Updates – Covered in Chapter 3

Organizational Process Assets Updates – Covered in Chapter 3

Monitor Communications

Monitor communication is the process of comparing the actual communications of the project to the communications management plan. If the plan is to hold a weekly meeting with the project's sponsors, did you hold that meeting, and what was the outcome?

If you find that the plan is not working and conflicts are increasing because of communication problems, then you might need to change the plan (change request). This can be the result of a customer being unhappy about the type and frequency of the reports you are sending him/her.

> ***Exam Tip:*** *Do not get confused with the process of "manage communications" and "monitor communications." They may sound alike but are, in fact, very different. In "manage communications," you are actually communicating and following the plan to communicate. In "monitor communications," you are checking to ensure you are actually following the communication plan and whether or not it needs changes.*

Inputs

Project Management Plan

The project management plan will contain the communications management plan. It describes how communications should take place on the project.

Project Documents

Of the 33 project documents, you will most likely use:

- **Project communications:** This is the output from the previous process, "manage communications." These are the documents and meetings held during the project.

- **Issue log:** The issue log is where all the issues are stored from the project. Issues are generally negative things that could affect the project, such as a supplier being late or a team member being out for an extended period.

- **Lessons learned register:** A listing of all of the lessons learned so far on the project.

Work Performance Data – Covered in Chapter 3

Organizational Process Assets – Covered in Chapter3

Tools and Techniques

Expert Judgment – Covered in Chapter 3

Project Management Information System – Covered in Chapter 3

Data Representation – Covered in Chapter 3

Interpersonal and Team Skills – Covered in Chapter 3

Meetings – Covered in Chapter 3

Outputs

Work Performance Information

Work performance information is the comparison of the actual communications to the planned communications to check whether we are following the plan or not.

Change Requests

If the project stakeholders feel that the communications for the project are not working and leading to more conflicts, then they should change the communications management plan by getting a change request.

Project Management Plan Updates – Covered in Chapter 3

Project Documents Updates – Covered in Chapter 3

Agile and hybrid Meetings

When working on an agile or hybrid project, many different meetings will be conducted. All of these meetings will be used on agile projects, while some may be used on a hybrid project. For your exam, ensure you understand the purpose of the meeting and its outputs. Although we did cover these meetings in our agile section at the beginning of this book, let's do a quick review of them since they are about communicating on a project.

Agile projects generally will have 4 meetings as follows:

- **Daily stand-up meeting:** the daily stand-up meeting is done by the agile project team on a daily basis and should last 15 minutes where each team member will answer the following three questions:

  1. What have you done since the last stand-up meeting?

  2. What will you be doing today?

  3. Do you have any impediments or issues that need to be solved?

  The main objective of the daily stand-up meeting is to ensure that all team members are aware of what other team members are doing and to determine if team members are facing any issues. This will allow the team to help each other resolve issues as quickly as possible.

- **Iteration (sprint) planning meeting:** This meeting is done by the project team to determine what work from the product backlog will get done in the next iteration. This meeting happens right before each iteration.

- **Iteration (sprint) review meeting:** This meeting takes place at the end of each iteration, and it is where the customers are able to review the increment of the product that is created during that iteration. Customers will then give their feedback on what they like and what they didn't like and if there are any improvements needed.

- **Retrospective:** This meeting takes place at the end of each iteration, and it is where the project team will reflect on what happened during that iteration. They will determine what they did correctly and should do more of and what was done incorrectly and to do less of.

Communications Management Questions

1. In your network infrastructure project XYZ, you have determined the type, format, value, and information needs of the stakeholders through communication requirements analysis. Project resources should be expended only on communicating information that:

   A. Originates from the sponsor or the project management office.

   B. Has been generated by the project team members only.

   C. Is relevant to the most influential and powerful stakeholders.

   D. Contributes to project success or where a lack of communication can lead to a failure.

2. A project manager is in the process of ensuring that the information needs of the project stakeholders are met by monitoring and controlling communication throughout the project lifecycle. The project manager is involved in which process?

   A. Direct and Manage Project Work

   B. Monitor and Control Project Work

   C. Monitor Communications

   D. Manage Communications

3. You are in the Plan Communications Management process to identify the information and communication needs of the people involved in your project by determining what needs to be communicated, when, to whom, with what method, in which format, and how frequently. Which of the following is MOST closely linked to this process?

   A. Communication requirements analysis

   B. Information management system

   C. Interpersonal skills

   D. Performance reporting

4. A project manager is leading a team of fifteen team members. One of the team members is not dedicated to the project and is having a performance issue. What form of communication can the project manager use to address this kind of situation?

   A. Informal written

   B. Informal verbal

   C. Formal written

   D. Formal verbal

5. You recently successfully completed a data center project that has been in production for more than a month. All the stakeholders have formally approved the project, and no issues have been reported since it has been in production. While reviewing one of your project deliverables with a project manager who is preparing for a similar project, you discover a problem in your project that may cause a minor safety issue in the future. What should you do under this circumstance?

    A. Communicate with your management about your findings, both verbally and in writing.

    B. There is no need to bring this minor safety issue to the attention of the customers since no complaints have been filed.

    C. Call the customers immediately and inform them about the safety issue.

    D. Since it is a minor safety concern, it can be fixed without letting the customers know about it.

6. As a project manager, you know you will be spending 90 percent of your time communicating with all the players involved in your project. You need to make sure that you have the proper physical manner, facial expressions, hand gestures, and body language while conveying a message. You also need to be particularly observant of the pitch and the tone of your voice, and you should try to receive comments and feedback from the receiver while communicating. Your communication skills will be utilized MOST during which of the following processes?

    A. Communication Change Control

    B. Manage Communications

    C. Report Performances

    D. Plan Communications Management

7. You are successfully managing a software project to automate the business processes for one of your clients. A key stakeholder articulates her concern to you about the lack of relevant information on her team's deliverables in the project status reports that you have been sending out. She is worried that her team has no visibility in this project and has requested you to look into the matter as soon as possible. What should you do FIRST in this situation?

    A. Revisit the information distribution process in your project.

    B. Have an urgent meeting with the stakeholders to understand what her team is working on.

    C. Ask the stakeholder to send her team's status so that you can incorporate them in your report.

    D. Revisit your communications management plan.

8. A project manager overseeing an ERP implementation project planned to distribute large volumes of information about the project to a large audience. He decided to post the information in an online knowledge repository for access at the discretion of the stakeholders. This type of communication method is known as:

    A. Interactive communication

    B. Push communication

    C. Pull communication

    D. Expert judgment

9. As a project manager, you are required to report project performance to all your stakeholders on a regular basis. Which one of the following can utilize Earned Value Management (EVM) in its preparation for management?

   A. Status reports

   B. Trend reports

   C. Progress reports

   D. All of the above

10. Which communication method is used essentially for prominent documents that go into project records?

    A. Informal verbal

    B. Informal written

    C. Formal verbal

    D. Formal written

11. In your project, you are facing many multifaceted problems that need to be discussed and resolved. You have explored different communication methods to use in solving complex problems. Extensive use of which of the following methods will most likely help solve complex problems in your project?

    A. Nonverbal

    B. Verbal

    C. Written

    D. Para lingual

12. A project manager supervising a video conferencing implementation project has several internal and external stakeholders to whom she needs to send project progress, status, and forecast reports on a regular basis. The project manager is making sure she is sending information to the specific recipients who need to know it. Even though she ensures that the information is distributed, she is not concerned with whether it was reached or was understood by the intended audience. This type of communication method is known as:

    A. Interactive communication

    B. Push communication

    C. Expert judgment

    D. Pull communication

13. A project manager is in the process of making relevant information available to project stakeholders in a timely manner as planned. The project manager is involved in which of the following processes?

    A. Plan Communications Management process

    B. Manage Communications process

    C. Monitor Communications process

    D. Distribute Information process

14. A project manager is in the Manage Communications process of collecting and distributing performance information and is especially focused on reporting against the performance baseline. Which one of the following is an output in this process?

    A. Performance reporting

    B. Information management system

    C. Communication methods

    D. Project communications

15. Your project currently has ten more people assigned to the team besides you. As your project is getting delayed, management wants you to add four additional team members to your project at the end of the month. How many more communication channels will you have added once the additional team members are added?

    A. 55

    B. 50

    C. 105

    D. 160

16. Which one of the following is not a noteworthy factor in the determination of the method that may be used to transfer information to, from, and among project stakeholders?

    A. Availability of technology: Appropriate systems may already be in place, or you may need to procure a new system or technology.

    B. Urgency of the need for information: There may be a need to have frequently updated information available at a moment's notice, or regularly issued written reports may be sufficient.

    C. Stakeholder identification: It will provide a list of stakeholders affected by the project and who have an interest in the project.

    D. Duration of the project: Technology will not likely change prior to the project's completion, or it may need to be upgraded at some point.

17. You set up a project status meeting with key stakeholders and customers, but it is not going too well. Participants are discussing various topics at random, talking at the same time and interrupting each other, a few of the attendees are not participating in the discussion at all, and two of the customers are busy over the phone. To avoid this kind of situation and have an effective meeting, what meeting rules should you apply?

    A. You should have a real purpose for the meeting and invite the right people.

    B. You should always schedule your meeting in advance so that people have plenty of time to be prepared for the meeting.

    C. You should create and publish an agenda with specific topics to discuss and set-up ground rules.

    D. You should control who is allowed to speak and who is not and ask everyone to demonstrate courtesy and consideration to each other.

18. You have several internal and external stakeholders involved in your construction project. As a project manager, you need to identify the information type, format, value, and needs of all these stakeholders. Which of the following tools & techniques is used to identify this type of information?

    A. Stakeholder management strategy

    B. Communications requirements analysis

    C. Trend analysis

    D. Value analysis

19. You have fifteen identified internal and external stakeholders in the network infrastructure project you are supervising. You are sending out progress and status reports to all your stakeholders on a regular basis as per your communications management plan. One of the stakeholders needs a very specific progress report on her team's deliverables and sends you an urgent e-mail requesting you to send the report as soon as possible. Your bandwidth is almost fully occupied in various project-related activities, but you have to find some spare time to fulfill this unexpected request from the stakeholder. What will be your BEST course of action?

    A. Consider it to be part of the Manage Communications process and send out the requested report.

    B. Consider it to be gold plating and ignore the request from the customer.

    C. Inform the stakeholder that you are unable to send out ad-hoc reports as it is not included in the project communications management plan.

    D. Complain to the sponsor about this unreasonable request from the stakeholder.

20. You are the project manager of a very important software development project in your organization. As you are closely monitoring and managing your project, you are happy that the project is progressing as per your plan. You reviewed the status of all the deliverables with your team members prior to having a project status update meeting with the stakeholders. Your team has developed a prototype or a working model of the proposed end product, and it will be presented to the stakeholders for interaction and feedback. This will be an iterative process, and the prototype may be modified numerous times to incorporate the feedback until the requirements have been finalized for the product. Which one of the following will you do in your status meeting?

    A. Do not mention anything about the prototype.

    B. Demo the prototype to the stakeholders and obtain their formal approval.

    C. Report on the progress of the prototype and point out that it's a completed task.

    D. Review the technical documentation of the prototype and obtain formal approval.

21. While planning communication for the network infrastructure project to which you have been assigned as the project manager, you know you have to pay particular attention to your body's mannerisms, facial expressions, and the tone and pitch of your voice to communicate effectively. All of the followings are FALSE about communication EXCEPT:

    A. Acknowledge means the receiver has received and agreed with the message.

    B. Encode means to translate ideas or thoughts so that others can understand them.

    C. Noise has nothing to do with sending and receiving messages.

    D. Verbal communication is more important than nonverbal communication.

22. While working on your communications plan, you have considered several communication technologies to transfer information among project stakeholders. Communication technology will take into account all of the following factors that can affect the project EXCEPT which one?

    A. Urgency of the need for information: Are regularly issued written reports enough for the project, or is frequently updated information needed at a moment's notice?

    B. Expected project staffing: Are the proposed communication systems compatible with the experience and expertise of the project participants, or is extensive training and learning required?

    C. Duration of the project: Is the available technology likely to change before the project is over?

    D. Reason for the distribution of information: What are the reasons for distributing information?

23. You are managing a software development project and have worked on the stakeholder register and communications management plan. Now you are about to execute your communications management plan. Which one of the following iş TRUE regarding Manage Communications?

    A. Manage Communications will end when the product has been accepted.

    B. Communication methods such as individual and group meetings, video and audio conferences, computer chats, and other remote communication methods are used to manage communications.

    C. Manage Communications is a monitoring & controlling process.

    D. Manage Communications only carries out predetermined communication and does not respond to unplanned requests from stakeholders.

24. The project manager who has been managing a large, multi-year network infrastructure project recently left the company, and you were assigned as a project manager to continue with the project. There are more than five different vendors, fifteen team members, and several key stakeholders involved in this very important project. While trying to identify stakeholder communication requirements, format, method, time frame, and frequency for the distribution of required information, which of the following will you be referring to?

    A. Communications management plan

    B. The information distribution plan

    C. Project management plan

    D. Stakeholder management strategy

25. A Project Management Information System (PMIS) is used as a tool & technique in many of the 49 processes. Which statement describes a PMIS BEST?

    A. A PMI certification for project management focused on information systems.

    B. A necessary log for timekeeping.

    C. A repository for project information used for future reference.

    D. An automated system to support the project by optimizing the schedule and helping to collect and distribute information.

Project Communications Management Answers

1. **D:** Communications requirements analysis determines the information type, format, value, and needs of the stakeholders and identifies information that is most critical to success or where a lack of communication can lead to failure.

2. **C:** Monitor Communications is the process of ensuring that the information needs of the project stakeholders are met by monitoring and controlling communication throughout the project life-cycle. The focus of this process is to ensure efficient Information flow to all stakeholders, at any moment in time, within the project.

3. **A:** Communication Requirements Analysis is a tool & technique in the Plan Communications Management process. Performance reporting and information management systems are tools & techniques within the Manage Communications process. Interpersonal skills are associated with the Manage Stakeholder Engagement process (stakeholder management).

4. **B:** The project manager should have an informal verbal discussion with the team member about the lack of dedication and poor performance. The goal is to address the concern of the project manager and to identify areas for improvement as well as any training needs for the team member. If this method is not effective, then the project manager should consider a formal written approach as the next step.

5. **A:** Even though no complaints have been filed and the issue is relatively minor, the project manager should report this sort of finding to management and take action as per management's recommendation.

6. **B:** Communication Change Control and Report Performances are not valid processes. Communications planning involves identifying the information and communication needs of the people involved in a project by determining what needs to be communicated, when, to whom, with what method, in which format, and how frequently. Manage Communications is the execution of your communications management plan, which covers a broad range of topics such as what, how, when, and how frequently information will be communicated and requires strong communication ability and skills.

7. **D:** Since the stakeholder is receiving the status reports, there is no issue with the information distribution process. You should revisit your communications management plan first to understand the information need, communications requirements, format, method, timeframe, and frequency for the distribution of required information for this specific stakeholder. You may want to have an urgent meeting with the stakeholder once you have the details.

8. **C:** Pull communication utilizes intranet sites, e-learning, knowledge repositories, and other types of accessible databases for a large volume of information or for a large audience who will be accessing the contents at their own discretion. Expert judgment generally refers to the input from subject matter experts. Interactive communication is between two or more parties performing a multidirectional exchange of information; in push communication, information is distributed, but it is not certified that the information reached its intended audience or was understood.

9. **D:** Earned Value Management (EVM) terms such as Actual Cost (AC), Earned Value (EV), Planned Value (PV), Estimate at Completion (EAC), Estimate to Complete (ETC), Variance at Completion (VAC), and Budget at Completion (BAC) can be used for all kinds of performance reports such as status, trend, and progress reports.

10. **D:** Prominent records such as complex problems, the project management plan, the project charter, important project communications, contracts, legal notices, and other items use the formal written method.

11. **C:** Both verbal and written communications should be used in solving complex problems. But in written communication, your words will be documented and presented in the same form to everyone. In the case of the other methods listed, the same message will not be received by everyone; thus, they will not be as helpful as a written method.

12. **B:** Push communication is a way of sending information to specific recipients who need to know it. This ensures that the information is distributed, but it is not concerned with whether it reached and was understood by the intended audience.

13. **B:** Manage Communications is the process of making relevant information available to the project stakeholders in a timely manner by creating, collecting, storing, retrieving, and distributing project information. It is performed throughout the entire project lifecycle and in all management processes.

14. **D:** Performance reporting, information management system, and communications methods are tools & techniques in the Manage Communications process; only project communications are the outputs.

15. **B:** Your team currently has eleven team members, including you; thus, the number of communication channels is calculated by using the formula: # of Channels=n*(n−1)/2

    11 (11 − 1)/2 = 55

    If you add four more resources, then you will have 11 + 4 = 15, team members. So the number of channels will be 15 (15 − 1)/2 = 105

    So you will have 105 − 55 = 50 more channels after adding the new resources.

16. **C:** The methods used to transfer information to, from, and among project stakeholders can vary significantly. Factors such as availability of technology, expected project staffing, urgency of the need for information, project environment, duration of the project, and other things may play a significant role in determining the method that may be used to transfer information among project stakeholders. Stakeholder identification will provide a list of stakeholders affected by the project and does not play much of a role in this situation.

17. **C:** 'A' and 'B' will not help too much in this kind of situation as there is no indication here that the right people were not invited to the meeting or the meeting was not scheduled in advance. 'D' is not a rule for a meeting. People discussing topics at random suggest that there was no set agenda for the attendees to follow. Imposing ground rules will restrict people from talking at the same time and interrupting each other or remaining busy over the phone.

18. **B:** Stakeholder communications requirements are determined during communications requirements analysis. The intention is to identify information that is most valuable to stakeholders. The stakeholder management strategy is an output to identify the stakeholder communication process, and it defines an approach to manage stakeholders and to increase support for and minimize negative impacts on stakeholders throughout the entire project lifecycle. A trend analysis examines project results over time to see if performance is improving or deteriorating. Value analysis or value engineering is associated with product analysis, and it helps to find a less costly way to do the same work without a loss of performance.

19. **A:** Accommodating planned and ad-hoc information requests is part of the Manage Communications process.

20. **C:** Usually, the project manager reports on the project's progress in a status meeting rather than demoing any prototype or reviewing any technical documentation.

21. **B:** Acknowledge means the receiver has received the message, but it does not mean that the receiver necessarily agrees with the message. Noise or communication blockers play a vital role in effective communication. 55 percent of all communication is nonverbal, and verbal communication is not more important than nonverbal communication. Encoding is translating ideas and thoughts.

22. **D:** Communication technology will take into account urgency of the need for information, expected project staffing, and duration of the project, but not the reason for the distribution of information.

23. **B:** Some stakeholders will need information distributed even after the product has been accepted as they want to get information about the closure of the project and the contract. Manage Communications is an executing process. Manage Communications carries out not only predetermined communication but also handles responses to unplanned requests from stakeholders. The listed communication methods are used in Manage Communications; thus, the letter 'B' is the correct answer.

24. **A:** Even though the communications management plan is a part of the project management plan, the best option here will be the communications management plan, where the purpose for communication, communication requirements, method, timeframe and frequency for distribution, the person responsible for communication, methods for updating the communications management plan, and other communication-related items can be found.

25. **D:** PMIS is an automated tool used to gather, integrate, and disseminate project information.

Chapter 12
Project Risk Management

This knowledge area has quite a few processes and is generally a hot topic on the exam. Risk is defined as an uncertain event that can affect one or more project objectives. Risk is uncertain by definition; we do not know if a risk will take place or not. Everything we do in life has a risk. All projects will have risk, and we will need to document the risk, rank it, plan a response, and then monitor it.

Risk can be either positive or negative. Most people think of risk as just being negative, but it can be positive. Negative risks are known as threats, and positive risks are known as opportunities. Negative risk, such as a delivery from a supplier getting delayed for a few weeks, can increase the project budget or schedule. A positive risk, such as a permit being approved in one week vs. the normal two weeks, can decrease the project schedule, allowing it to start sooner. On this exam, you are expected to know that risk can be both positive and negative. Remember that all the risk processes are talking about both. For example, identifying risk is about identifying both positive and negative risks.

When managing risk on a project, it is important to know how much risk a company or person is willing to take. Risk appetite is the amount of risk someone is usually ready to take for a reward. For example, I am willing to drive my car because the reward is getting home faster than if I walked. Risk tolerance is how much risk someone is willing to take. For example, I am only willing to bet $100 on a slot machine when going to a casino. Your tolerance is the amount or volume of risk you are willing to take. Risk threshold is the point at which you will not accept the risk. For example, a risk that could raise the project budget by 40% is not acceptable and needs attention. These terms are important because they can affect how we respond to risk and the methods we will use. While some of us might find it acceptable to do nothing about possible floods, some might purchase flood insurance.

Risk, in general, falls into two levels on a project: individual project risks and overall project risks. Individual project risks generally have a negative or positive impact on the project objectives. This generally includes specific risks that may impact the project scope, time, or costs.

Overall, project risk is about whether the outcome of the project is positive or negative for the stakeholders. Overall, project risk is the sum of all the individual risks, and it gives you the uncertainty of the entire project. Instead of looking at the specific risks that can impact any of the baselines as you would in individual project risks, overall project risk looks at how risks, in general, will affect the objectives of the project.

The project manager is generally concerned with the individual risks on the project and creates the risk register to manage them. The project sponsor is most concerned with the overall project risks. The sponsor is not concerned with the specific day-to-day risk of the project but is more concerned with the bigger-picture risks that can affect the project. The overall project risk is generally stored in the project report. Keep these two levels of risk in mind as you read this chapter.

If you are working on an agile project, expect this process to be done continuously, usually during the sprint planning meeting. This is where you can identify some of the risks that can affect your project during the sprint and come up with strategies and responses to ensure that it does not affect the sprint once it is executed.

Here are the risk processes that we will be covering in this chapter and their main outputs

Process	Process Group	Main Outputs
Plan Risk Management	Planning	Risk Management Plan
Identify Risks	Planning	Risk Register, Risk Report
Perform Qualitative Risk Analysis	Planning	Project Documents Updates
Perform Quantitative Risk Analysis	Planning	Project Documents Updates
Plan Risk Responses	Planning	Change Request, Project Documents Updates, Project Management Plan, Updates
Implement Risk Responses	Executing	Change Requests
Monitor Risks	Monitoring and Controlling	Work Performance Information, Change Requests

Plan Risk Management

Plan risk management is about creating a risk management plan. This is identifying the steps we will take to complete the other five risk processes. This plan will become an input for the next five risk processes.

Inputs

Project Charter – Covered in Chapter 4

Project Management Plan – Covered in Chapter 3

Project Documents

Of the 33 project documents, the ones you are most likely to use in this process include:

- **Stakeholder register:** This was created in the "Identify Stakeholder" process. It will list the stakeholders on the project, their needs, impact, contact info, their roles, and how they feel about risk.

Enterprise Environmental Factors – Covered in Chapter 3

Organizational Process Assets – Covered in Chapter 3
Tools and Techniques

Expert Judgment – Covered in Chapter 3

Data Analysis – Covered in Chapter 3

Meetings – Covered in Chapter 3

Output

Risk Management Plan

The risk management plan is a plan that specifies how you will conduct the next five risk processes. It will define the methodology, roles and responsibilities, and timing of the processes. It includes the following:

- How will you identify risk?
- How will you do a qualitative risk assessment?
- How will you do a quantitative risk assessment?
- How will you respond to risk?
- How will you implement the risk responses?
- How will you monitor and control the risks once the project is executed?
- What is your risk breakdown structure (RBS), which is used to categorize risks?

This plan is very important and will become an input to the other risk processes in planning.

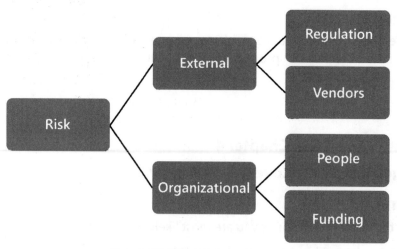

Simple RBS that categorizes risk

EXAM TIP: *The risk management plan does not list risks. The risk management plan states how you plan to execute the risk management processes. The risk register lists risks on the project. Also, keep in mind that the risk register is not part of the PM plan but the risk management plan is.*

Identify Risks

This process is where you will identify the risks that could affect the project. The project manager and the team will have to continually identify the risks that could affect the project.

Risk can affect all aspects of a project and because of that, you should do these processes throughout the initiating, planning, executing, and monitoring and controlling process groups of the project. The project manager should analyze each of the process groups to see how risk can affect them.

Risk changes and new risks arise every day. That means you will never stop identifying risk during a project. For example, once a software development project is executed and the

Programmers start programming the software, they may identify new risks that could affect the programming, such as a function not working or team members not having enough programming knowledge. In this case, the project manager will then add that risk to the risk register, assess it, and come up with a response plan.

Keep in mind that we are not just identifying the negative risks, but also the positive risks. The risk register will become the input to all the other risk processes going forward.

Inputs

Project Management Plan

Almost all aspects of the project management plan will be needed in order to identify risks. Here are a few of them:

- **Risk management plan:** The risk management plan will describe the steps to conduct the risk processes including: identifying the risk, performing a qualitative and quantitative assessment, risk response, and how to control the risk.

- **Cost management plan:** The cost management plan will describe how to manage the budget on the project, including creating the cost baseline and how to control cost on the project.

- **Schedule management plan:** The schedule management plan will describe how to create and control the project schedule.

- **Quality management plan:** The quality management plan will describe how to ensure the project meets the quality requirements, and how to perform quality assurance and control.

- **Resource management plan:** The resource management plan will describe how to acquire, develop, and manage the project team as well as physical resources.

- **Scope baseline:** The scope baseline is the scope of what the project will accomplish. It includes the scope statement, WBS, and WBS dictionary.

- **Schedule baseline:** The schedule baseline includes the start and finish dates for the project.

- **Cost baseline:** The cost baseline includes the overall cost of the project.

Project Documents

Of the 33 project documents, the ones you are most likely to use in this process include:

- **Cost estimates:** The cost estimates are the estimated cost of each activity on the project.

- **Duration estimates:** The duration estimates note how long each activity will take on the project.

- **Stakeholder register:** The stakeholder register is a list of stakeholders on the project, their needs, impact, contact info, and role.

- **Issue Log:** This log will list all issues on the project. Stakeholders may want to be updated on the status of issues on the project.

- **Stakeholder register:** This is a list of all the stakeholders on the project and how they may impact the project.

- **Assumption log:** This will keep track of any assumptions that are made during the project. Assumptions and constraints could affect how the schedule is built and may impact the lead and lag between activities.

- **Lessons learned register:** A listing of all of the lessons learned so far on the project.

Agreements

An agreement is generally a contract between a buyer and a seller for work. In this process, the agreement will be analyzed to identify any risks in the agreement that might affect the project.

Enterprise Environmental Factors – Covered in Chapter 3

Organizational Process Assets – Covered in Chapter 3

Tools and Techniques

Expert Judgment – Covered in Chapter 3

Data Gathering

Identifying risks to the project can be done by doing brainstorming, using a checklist, or interviewing the right people. Checklists might have been provided by suppliers, or you can use your RBS. The more detailed lower levels of the RBS are great checklists to use on your project. Keep in mind that risk affects all aspects of a project and a project manager should look at all components to help identify risks. You can also use the Delphi technique to gather risk from stakeholders anonymously. This can help to reduce conflicts and influencing between stakeholders.

Data Analysis

Once the data has been gathered, it must be analyzed to help identify risks. Here are a few techniques for that:

- **Document analysis:** Documentation analysis includes reviewing all the project documentation to look for risk. This can include all the baselines and plans that were created.

- **Assumptions and constraints analysis:** A constraint can be a major risk that could limit the project in certain ways, such as time or cost. Every assumption carries the risk that your assumption might be wrong. For example, I am assuming that all the computers in the network can handle the latest version of Microsoft Windows, so this project does not include any time and cost for hardware upgrades. But there is the possibility that we could be wrong. A few machines may not have enough RAM to install the latest version of Microsoft Windows.

- **Root cause analysis:** Root cause analysis will look at the underlying causes of potential problems. This includes looking at some of the main reasons why risk occurs. A Fishbone diagram can be used for this purpose; this was covered in the quality management chapter. For example, this analysis can identify that a project was underfunded, leading to many other risks such as poor quality or the project running behind schedule.

Strengths	Weaknesses
-Expert team -Management support	-Little free time -High cost
Opportunities	Threats
-New Market -New IT Systems	-Regulations -Staff Shortage

SWOT diagram

- **SWOT analysis:** SWOT stands for strengths, weaknesses, opportunities, and threats. The strengths and opportunities will identify the positive risks. Weaknesses and threats will identify the negative risk. This is a great way to identify both positive and negative risk.

Interpersonal and Team Skills – Covered in Chapter 3

Prompt Lists

A prompt list is a list of categories the project team can use to help identify risks. The risk breakdown structure is a great example of a prompt list.

Meetings – Covered in Chapter 3

Outputs

Risk Register

The risk register is a list of all of the identified individual project risks. It could be a spreadsheet that lists the positive and negative risks. This register will be updated when we do the next risk processes. The responses are just possibilities for now until we complete the "Plan Risk Response" process.

Risk ID	Risk	Response	Cause	Project Area
S1	Bad weather	Add 3 more days to schedule	Environment	Schedule
C1	Cost overrun	Add 10% more to budget	Supplier might increase cost	Cost

Simple Risk Register

Risk Report

The risk report will cover the overall project risks. They generally include things such as the source of the overall project risks, categories, and identified threats and opportunities.

> **EXAM TIP:** *The risk report describes overall project risks and the risk register describes individual project risks.*

Project documents updates – Covered in Chapter 3

Perform Qualitative Risk Analysis

Qualitative risk analysis is the process of prioritizing the risks listed in the risk register. After you have identified the risks, you will need to determine which risks have the most significance to the project. Risk is prioritized based on its impact and its probability of occurrence.

When ranking risk on a project, you have to think about how likely the risk is to occur and what its impact might be. Some risks may have a high impact on the project, but rank very low because of their probability. For example, an earthquake has a high impact, but low probability of occurrence (depending on where you are). Some risks have moderate impact and moderate probability, such as bad weather in the summer, and can rank higher than the earthquake. The organizational risk tolerance and appetite will play a big part in the ranking of the risk. Some companies are more willing to accept risk than others.

This process should be done after you identify the risks and will be helpful when you go to complete the next process of quantitative risk analysis. Qualitative risk analysis is done very quickly and is cost-effective.

Inputs

Project Management Plan

The project management plan will include the risk management plan, which will describe the steps of how to conduct this process of prioritizing the risks on the project.

Project Documents

Of the 33 project documents, the ones you are most likely to use in this process include:

- **Stakeholder register:** This is a list of all the stakeholders on the project and how they may impact the project.

- **Assumption log:** This will keep track of any assumptions that are made during the project. Assumptions and constraints could affect how the schedule is built and may impact the lead and lag between activities.

- **Risk register:** The risk register will list all the positive (opportunities) and negative (threats) risks that could affect the project. This will help rank the risks.

Enterprise Environmental Factors – Covered in Chapter 3

Organizational Process Assets – Covered in Chapter 3

Tools and Techniques

Expert Judgment – Covered in Chapter 3

Data Gathering

While determining how to prioritize risk, a project manager may be interviewing different stakeholders on the project to get their perspectives on the risks. Interviewing is the main technique used for data gathering in this process.

Data Analysis

- **Risk probability and impact assessment:** Risk probability and impact assessment is what you are doing in this process. You will look at the probability and impact of all the risks on the project. This can be done by interviewing or meeting with the project team. Values of high, medium, or low can be used to rank the risk.

- **Risk data quality assessment:** Risk data quality assessment refers to the accuracy of the data you are using to rank the risk. If we rank the bad weather as having a low probability of occurrence, would that be correct? It might be, if the data is coming from a good source. Inaccurate data can lead to a false ranking of risk.

Interpersonal and Team Skills – Covered in Chapter 3

Data Representation

- **Probability and impact matrix:** The risk probability and impact matrix is a table that contains all of the risks. Then you will assign a rating to each risk, such as high, medium, or low to create a ranking based on its probability and impact.

- **Hierarchical charts:** If a project team wishes to prioritize risks based on more parameters than probability and impact, then they should use other techniques such as a bubble chart to accomplish this. A bubble chart uses three different parameters instead of two. It is usually used in place of a scatter diagram. The parameters on a bubble chart are usually the x-axis, y-axis and the size of the bubble. For example, on the bubble chart below, the impact is on the x-axis, the probability is on the y-axis, and the size of the bubble represents the urgency of the risks. The bigger the bubble, the more urgent the risk is.

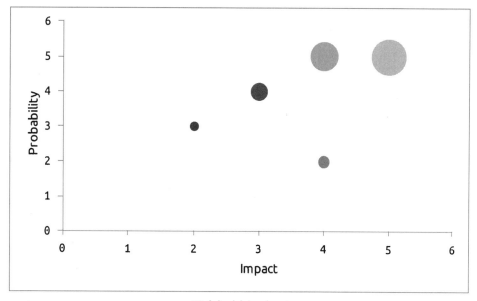

Risk bubble chart

Risk Categorization

If you categorize the risk on the project, you will be able to rank it more easily. Use the RBS to help categorize it. Risk can be categorized by its root cause or its section of the project.

Risk Urgency Assessment

Risk that has a high impact and probability will need to be addressed right away. For example, getting a bad contractor for a renovation project may have a high impact and high probability. This tool will display all the risks that need a near-term response.

Meetings – Covered in Chapter 3

Outputs

Project Documents Updates

Project documents updates will involve the risk register. You should go back to the risk register and then prioritize from the greatest to the least risk on the project. Other documents that you may need to update include the risk report, issue log, and assumption log.

Perform Quantitative Risk Analysis

Perform quantitative risk analysis is the process of numerically analyzing the risk on the project. This process can be difficult to do in real-life project management because it requires

a significant amount of time and skills to do. The PMBOK® Guide covers this process in a general way. Different industries have their own methods to numerically analyze risk. Do not worry too much about the specifics of this process, but understand what it is and why you need to do it.

A quantitative analysis will not produce a rank like the qualitative analysis, but it will produce a numerical analysis, such as bad weather costing the project a four-week delay. Another impact could be the price of supplies increasing by 10%, costing the project an additional $40,000. This is the kind of numerical analysis that should be produced in this process. Notice how it is not about ranking the risks, rather it's about producing numerical values.

Numerical analysis of a risk should be done after you have identified the risk. This way, you would know what the risk is for the project and how important it is to the project. Low ranking risks such as an earthquake might not need to be quantified.

Inputs

Project Management Plan

Although many components of the project management plan can be of use in this process, the main sections used will be the risk management plan, which will outline how to do this process, and the three main baselines, scope, schedule, and cost.

Project Documents

Of the 33 project documents, the ones you are most likely to use in this process include:

- **Assumption log:** This will keep track of any assumptions that are made during the project. Assumptions and constraints could affect how the schedule is built and may impact the lead and lag between activities.

- **Basis of estimates:** The basis of the estimates is how the estimates were developed and their ranges. It can also include all assumptions and the constraints made to create the estimate.

- **Risk register:** The risk register will list all the positive (opportunities) and negative (threats) risks that could affect the project. This will help rank the risk.

- **Risk report:** The risk report will give you the status of the overall project risks.

- **Milestone list:** This is added to the sequence of activities. For example, the milestone of getting a permit can affect how the work of building a house is done.

- **Resource requirements:** The resources needed to complete each activity will affect the duration of each activity. Equipment and HR resources can have a big effect on the activity. For example, hiring a professional painter with a paint gun will ensure painting a room goes much faster than if a novice paints it with just a paintbrush.

- **Duration estimates:** This will be the estimated duration of each activity.

- **Cost estimates:** Cost estimates are the cost of each individual activity.

- **Cost forecasts:** The cost forecasts can be calculated using the EAC earned value formula from the cost management chapter. The cost forecasts are usually an indication of how much the project will cost when is completed.

- **Schedule forecasts:** Schedule forecasting is looking at what the end date of the project may be, based on the current work.

Enterprise Environmental Factors – Covered in Chapter 3

Organizational Process Assets – Covered in Chapter 3

Tools and Techniques

Expert Judgment – Covered in Chapter 3

Data Gathering

Data gathering is an important part of this process. Techniques used in gathering the data include the following:

- **Interviewing:** Interviewing techniques will be very important for gathering information needed to complete the risk analysis.

- **Probability distributions:** Probability distribution would look at the probability of risks actually taking place. It is a numerical analysis of probability. Although this can be a very complex tool, it will be used on certain projects.

Interpersonal and Team Skills – Covered in Chapter 3

Representations of Uncertainty

The nature of risk is uncertainty. Trying to analyze risks numerically is a very difficult process, and that's why the project manager needs to have a way to represent this uncertainty through numerical analysis. One way of doing this is with probability distribution, which is a way of looking at the probability of risks actually taking place. It is a numerical analysis of probability.

Data Analysis

Once the data has been gathered, the project team will need to analyze it. Here are a few methods for data analysis:

- **Simulation:** Although there are different types of simulations to determine the numerical impact of a risk on a project, one useful example is Monte Carlo analysis. Monte Carlo analysis is done by a computer and looks at many different scenarios that can affect the project. For example, you might look at all the different scenarios that can affect scheduling, such as weather, suppliers, or people. We can then determine how the project will be impacted because of this risk.

- **Sensitivity analysis:** Sensitivity analysis looks at the risks that have the most impact on a project. It looks at how one risk affects multiple sections or parts of the project. One way of displaying this is by using a tornado diagram, as shown below. This diagram shows the results if our supplier were to raise or lower the price of materials we used on the project by 15%. On the left side, you have a negative risk, which shows what that price rise would cost the project. On the right side, you have the positive risk of what money could be saved in project, if the price lowered. The diagram typically shows the risks with the largest range at the top. This forms the tornado funnel shape.

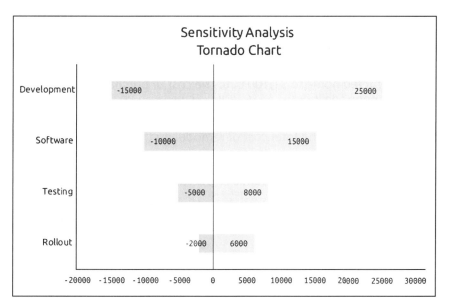

- **Expected monetary value analysis (EMV):** Monetary value analysis assigns a certain dollar amount to the risk. This can be done using decision tree analysis, aka make-or-buy analysis. Decision tree analysis uses the cost and the probability to determine the overall impact of that risk on the project shown below:

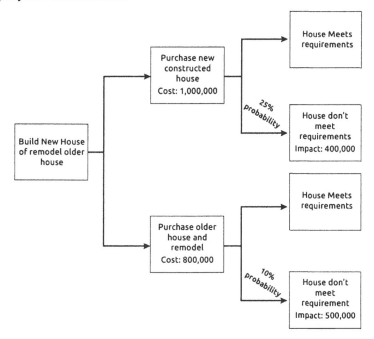

	Initial Cost	Risk Cost	Probability	EMV	Total
New Constructed House	1,000,000	400,000	25%	100,000	1,100,000
Remodel Older House	800,000	500,000	10%	50,000	850,000

To calculate the EMV, multiply the probability by the risk costs. To get the total, add the EMV to the initial cost.

In this decision tree, we are trying to decide if we should purchase a newly constructed house or purchase an older one and then remodel it. You can see that the cost of the newly constructed house would be $1,000,000. The probability of it not meeting our requirements and requiring a remodel is 25%. The cost to remodel the house to meet our needs would be $400,000. That brings the total cost of this newly constructed home to $1,100,000. The cost of purchasing an older house and then remodeling it would be $800,000, but the probability of it not meeting the requirements will only be 10%, because we would be choosing most of the house construction as opposed to buying something that is already constructed. The total cost of remodeling the older house would be $850,000. In this case,

it would make sense from a financial perspective to purchase the older house and then remodel it.

Outputs

Project Documents Updates

The main document to update is the risk register. In the "Identify Risk" process, we created the risk register. We put the risks in order during the "Perform Qualitative Risk" process, and now we have assigned a numerical value to the risks. Now, we can come up with a response to the risk in the next process.

Other documents that could be updated include the activity cost estimates, duration estimates, and the quality management plan. Since risk affects almost all parts of the project, many other documents could require updates.

Plan Risk Responses

Plan risk response is the last process done in risk planning. Do not respond to a risk if you have not assessed how that risk will impact the project. From the process chart below, you can see that "Plan Risk Response" comes at the end.

On this exam, there will be many questions where they want you to respond to a risk without assessing the risk. Never do this, because your response may not be adequate for the risk. When you get a question that deals with risk response and you are asked to identify the first thing you should do, always select the choice that talks about analyzing the risk first.

Inputs

Project Management Plan

The project management plan is used in this process to describe how this process will be done and to identify the methods that will be used to respond to the risks. The documents you will use include the risk and resource management plans along with the cost baseline.

Project Documents

Of the 33 project documents, the ones you are most likely to use in this process include:

- **Lessons learned register:** A listing of all of the lessons learned so far on the project.
- **Resource calendars:** Resource calendars show the availability of resources. Resources have greatly affected the duration of each activity.
- **Risk register:** The risk register will list all the positive (opportunities) and negative (threats) risks that could affect the project. This will help rank the risk.
- **Risk report:** The risk report will give you a status for the overall project risks.
- **Project team assignments:** This will list who is doing what work on the project.
- **Project schedule:** Project schedule shows the start and completion dates of the project.
- **Stakeholder register:** The stakeholder register is an output from the "Identify Stakeholder" process. It is a list of all stakeholders on the project and how they will be affected by the project.

Enterprise Environmental Factors – Covered in Chapter 3

Organizational Process Assets – Covered in Chapter 3

Tools and Techniques

Expert Judgment – Covered in Chapter 3

Data Gathering – Covered in Chapter 3

Interpersonal and Team Skills – Covered in Chapter 3

Strategies for Threats

Negative risks always negatively impact the project. Here are ways to respond to negative risks:

- **Escalate:** If the risk is determined to be outside the scope of the project and may be affecting multiple projects in the organization, the risk may be escalated up the ladder. This can include escalating the risks to the program or portfolio level of the organization. Once a risk is escalated, the project team will not be monitoring and controlling this risk anymore.

- **Avoid:** Avoidance is a method that's used to eliminate the risk entirely. This can include choosing a different software or hardware solution to complete your project. This can have a dramatic effect on the project, such as removing parts of the scope or a change in cost and schedule. For example, removing a work package that may have a lot of risk to your WBS would avoid those risks, but might reduce the scope.

- **Transfer:** Transfer is to give away the risk to another company. Most popular options include purchasing insurance or using a warranty. Anytime an exam question mentions outsourcing, it means transfer of risk.

- **Mitigate:** Mitigation is the process of reducing the risk probability and/or impact. Basically, the risks are decreased. For example, installing antivirus software on your computer would reduce a virus's impact on your computer. Keep in mind that mitigation does not remove the risk completely as avoidance would; it just reduces the risks. You can still get a virus even with antivirus software installed. The risk that is left over after the mitigation is called residual risk. Residual risk is a small amount of risk that the project is willing to keep.

- **Accept:** Accepting the risk means doing nothing about the risk and accepting the impact if it does occur. For example, an earthquake might be a risk to accept. In that case, you have decided not to purchase any insurance or build earthquake-proof buildings. You have decided that the earthquake probability is so low, you will just accept the consequences if it happens. Acceptance can be either active, where you setup a contingency plan, or passive where you will just monitor the risk and take no action.

Strategies for Opportunities

Positive risk generally impacts the project positively. Since most positive risk is the opposite of negative risk, these responses are opposites of the negative responses.

- **Escalate:** This works similarly to how escalate works for negative risks. If an opportunity is outside the scope of the project, then it may be escalated to higher levels within the organization, such as the program or portfolio that the project is under.

- **Exploit:** Exploit is the opposite of avoidance. Instead of eliminating the risks, you would try to ensure that they happen. For example, you realize that the project team is very knowledgeable and will exploit this to finish the project faster.

- **Share:** Sharing is the opposite of transfer. Instead of giving away the risks, you would share them with other projects, or other parts of the project. For example, if you found a great contractor, you would then use that contractor on other parts of the project or recommend that contractor for other projects in the company.

- **Enhance:** Enhance is the opposite of mitigate. Instead of reducing the risk, you will try to increase its probability or impact on the project. For example, you might try to get a lower price on the supplies from the vendor.

- **Accept:** Acceptance is the same for both positive and negative risks. If it happens, we will deal with it whether it is good or bad.

  ExamTip: Expect to see many questions about these responses. Questions will generally ask you what response a project manager should use in a scenario.

Contingent Response Strategies

Contingent response strategies mean responding to a risk if something else happens. For example, you might decide to transfer the risk to an outside consultant company after you have tried to install the product yourself.

Strategies for Overall Project Risks

Keep in mind that overall project risks relate to the sum of all the individual risks, and is generally looked at by the project sponsor or management. While the strategies listed above were for the individual project risks, you also need to have strategies in place for the overall project risks. Here are a few strategies you can use:

- **Avoid:** Avoidance is a method that's used to eliminate the risk entirely. When a risk is deemed unacceptable and will have a serious negative consequence on the project, it should be avoided.

- **Exploit:** If an opportunity is presented on a project and it can help enhance the project schedule, cost, or scope, it should be exploited to ensure that it happens.

- **Transfer/Share:** Sometimes, on a project, overall risk can best be given to a third party or vendors. In that case, you would be transferring the risks. If the risk can have a positive impact on not just the current project but other projects, then it's best to share the risks.

- **Mitigate/Enhance:** Mitigation is used for negative overall risk and enhance is used for positive overall risk on a project. Mitigation is to reduce the probability and/or impact, while enhance would increase the probability and/or impact on the project. When it comes to overall risks, examples of this include changing the scope or modifying the schedule.

- **Accept:** When a risk is deemed to be low on impact and/or probability, the company may choose to just accept the risk and manage the consequences if it materializes. Acceptance generally means to take no action against the risks, be it positive or negative.

Data Analysis – Covered in Chapter 3

Decision Making – Covered in Chapter 3

Outputs

Change Requests – Covered in Chapter 3

Project Management Plan Updates

Now that we have the responses to the risks, you might go back and update scope, time, and cost baselines. You may decide to add more time or cost to the project. Also, some management plans may change to accommodate the risk responses.

Project Documents Updates

The document that needs to get updated at the end of this process is the risk register. If a risk occurred, you will now go into the risk register and document the responses.

Implement Risk Responses

Once a project executes, the project manager should be monitoring the work during its execution to identify if any of the risks that are listed in the risk register are materializing.

If a risk materializes, the project manager should then follow the risk responses that were created during the planning processes, in order to respond to that risk. For example, if there was bad weather and the project was delayed, then the project manager should respond by hiring more resources in order to bring the project back on schedule.

Every project is unique, and so are most of their risk responses. The project manager should follow the risk management plan and risk register in order to ensure that the risks are responded to in a timely and efficient manner.

Inputs

Project Management Plan

The project management plan will include the risk management plan, which will describe the steps of how to conduct this process of implementing the responses.

Project Documents

Of the 33 project documents, the ones you are most likely to use in this process include:

- **Lessons learned register:** A listing of all of the lessons learned so far on the project.
- **Risk register:** The risk register will list all the positive (opportunities) and negative (threats) risks that could affect the project. This will help rank the risks.
- **Risk report:** The risk report will give you the status of the overall project risks.

Organizational Process Assets – Covered in Chapter 3

Tools & Techniques

Expert Judgment – Covered in Chapter 3

Interpersonal and Team Skills – Covered in Chapter 3

Project Management Information System – Covered in Chapter 3

Outputs

Change Requests

If a particular risk response results in changes to any of the 18 components of the project management plan, then the project manager will have to get a change request approved. For example, if a particular response results in an increase to the project budget, then the project manager should put in a change request for an increase on the cost baseline.

Project Documents Updates – Covered in Chapter 3

Monitor Risks

In this process, you will be looking at how the risk implementation methods have been working and whether they are being done according to the plan. This is essentially ensuring that the responses that have been implemented are done according to the plan and the risk register. Keep in mind that the executing and monitoring and controlling processes are performed in parallel.

This process also includes analyzing the work to see if there any new risks and whether any of the current risks in the risk register are changing. Every day that a project is moving along, new risks can arise, and old risks can change. For example, in different parts of the year, the weather may cause certain risks to increase or decrease, as in the case of a blizzard. Another example would be that a new risk may arise from recent regulations that were just passed by the local government.

Every day that project work is getting done, you will have to analyze the work to see if the risk we had planned for in the risk register is taking place and if it requires a response. You will look for the risk triggers. Risk triggers are symptoms or warning signs that a potential risk is about to occur within the project. For example, the weather forecast says a hurricane is approaching, so you will implement the response for bad weather.

Inputs

Project Management Plan – Covered in Chapter 3

Project Documents

Of the 33 project documents, the ones you are most likely to use in this process include:

- **Lessons learned register:** A listing of all of the lessons learned on the project.

- **Risk register:** The risk register will list all the positive (opportunities) and negative (threats) risks that could affect the project. This will help rank the risks.

- **Risk report:** The risk report will give you the status of the overall project risks.

- **Issue log:** This log will list all issues on the project. It generally contains open issues and may help to update the risk register.

Work Performance Data – Covered in Chapter 3

Work Performance Reports – Covered in Chapter 3

Tools and Techniques

Data Gathering

The project manager must gather data surrounding the overall management of risks. Here are a few techniques to accomplish this:

- **Technical performance analysis:** This will look at the technical aspects of the project, such as how fast an application should respond, and then determine if it's going according to the plan.

- **Reserve analysis:** Reserve analysis is about reviewing the cost and time reserves on a project to ensure that you still have sufficient reserves in case a risk occurs.

Audits

Risk audits are about looking at the risk management plan and how we are responding to the risks. You have to determine if the overall risk management strategy is working for the project. You audit in the process of monitoring risks to ensure risk does not affect the project.

Meetings – Covered in Chapter 3

Outputs

Work Performance Information – Covered in Chapter 3

Change Requests

If a risk arises and you need more time or money, you may require a change request. Sometimes, risk affects different parts of the project management plan that will almost certainly result in the need for change requests. Change requests may include both corrective and preventive actions. Corrective actions include contingency plans and workarounds. Workarounds are unplanned responses developed to deal with the occurrence of unanticipated risk events.

Project Management Plan Updates – Covered in Chapter 3

Project Documents Updates – Covered in Chapter 3

Organizational Process Assets Updates – Covered in Chapter3

Agile and Hybrid Risk Management

Agile and hybrid projects, by definition, generally have more uncertainty and risks. It is for these reasons that their frequent reviews are done at the end of each iteration and why the team members should be generalizing specialists that can help each other. In this section, a few things are regularly discussed that are unique to an agile project that you should be familiar with for your exam.

Risk-adjusted backlog: The risk-adjusted backlog is not new, it is the same product backlog that has been re-prioritized for risk. What this means is that certain high-risk activities may cause highly valuable items to be moved down and activities that are of less value but of less risk and move up the product backlog. The product owner generally does this with help from the team.

Risk-based spikes: A risk-based spike is a short proof of concept to investigate whether a particular solution would solve a particular risk. For example, an agile project team can use a risk-based spike to determine if a planned risk response would be adequate for these risks. This would show the project team if the response would actually work. This often leads to what is known as "fast failure." While this may seem like an issue at first, this will allow the team to discover that certain responses are not adequate and fix them before they turn into larger problems.

Risk burndown chart: A risk burndown chart will show you how the risk severity changes over the duration of the agile project. As you can see from the graph below, some risks are getting more severe while other risks are becoming less severe.

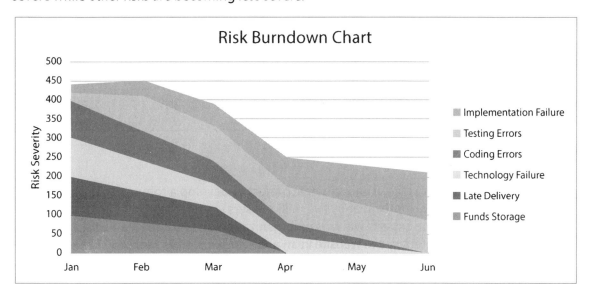

Risk Management Questions

1. You are working on the Plan Risk Management process to decide how to approach, plan, and execute risk management activities. All of the following are inputs to the Plan Risk Management process EXCEPT:

   A. Stakeholder register

   B. Project charter

   C. Risk register

   D. Project management plan

2. You are delivering specialized medical equipment, which is worth $600,000. You have been delivering equipment for a while without much hassle or accidents in the past. This time you estimate that there is a 5 percent probability that the equipment could be damaged or lost. While exploring the possibility of transferring this risk to an insurance company, you found out the insurance premium is $15,000. What will be your BEST course of action?

   A. You do not have enough information to make a decision.

   B. Do not buy the insurance premium.

   C. Develop a contingency plan.

   D. Buy the insurance premium.

3. Which one of the following is contained in the risk management plan and describes a risk category?

   A. Risk response plan

   B. Risk Breakdown Structure (RBS)

   C. Risk register

   D. Watchlist

4. You are working on a very critical and strategic project to develop a robust dynamic website, which will be available to approximately five million users your company has around the globe. You decided to survey the experts within your organization on any foreseeable risks with the design, structure, and intent of the website in an anonymous, simple form. You later sent out subsequent anonymous surveys to a group of experts with the collected information. This is an example of:

   A. A Delphi technique

   B. Identify Risks process

   C. Nominal group technique

   D. SWOT analysis

5. You are the project manager of a data center project. You have just completed an analysis of project risks and have prioritized them using a probability and impact matrix. The approach you used to prioritize the risks is:

   A. Qualitative analysis

   B. Quantitative analysis

   C. Sensitivity analysis

   D. Earned value analysis

6. Which one of the following is a comprehensive way of ordering risks according to their source?

    A. Product description

    B. Risk categories

    C. Assumptions

    D. Constraints

7. You oversee a project to implement an accounting application and are currently in the Identify Risks process of identifying and documenting the project risks. All of the following are tools & techniques for the Identify Risks process EXCEPT:

    A. Information gathering techniques

    B. Assumptions analysis

    C. Diagramming techniques

    D. Monte Carlo simulation

8. Your team is performing quantitative risk analysis using the Monte Carlo simulator. Which one of the following statements is FALSE about this Monte Carlo analysis?

    A. It translates the uncertainties specified at a detailed level into their potential impact on project objectives at the whole project level.

    B. It is a modeling technique that computes project costs one time.

    C. It involves determining the impact of the identified risks by running simulations to identify the range of possible outcomes for a number of scenarios.

    D. It usually expresses its results as probability distributions of possible costs.

9. One of your hardware vendors sends you an e-mail stating that due to severe weather, she may not be able to deliver the networking equipment on time. Which of the following statements is TRUE?

    A. This is a residual risk.

    B. This is a risk trigger.

    C. This is a risk event.

    D. This is a secondary risk.

10. You have identified several problems along with their causes in your web-based application-development project. Which one of the following have you probably used to show the problem and its causes and effects?

    A. Ishikawa diagram

    B. System flow diagram

    C. Process diagram

    D. Histogram

11. Your team performs a risk probability and impact assessment for each risk to investigate the likelihood and potential effect on the project objectives, such as time, cost, scope, and quality. What process are you in?

    A. Plan Risk Management

    B. Identify Risks

    C. Perform Qualitative Risk Analysis

    D. Monitor Risks

12. Expected Monetary Value (or simply expected value) is a statistical concept that calculates the average outcome of a decision. The two dimensions of risk used to determine this expected value are:

    A. Probability and threshold

    B. Probability and tolerance

    C. Consequence and contingencies

    D. Probability and impact

13. While overseeing a complex software project to develop a sophisticated golf simulator for a local golf club, you realize that the team is lacking the required technical expertise and experience. You also do not have the required tools and development environment for this kind of complicated software development. After discussing with the sponsor, you decide to give the design and development work to a vendor who specializes in the specific technical area. This is an example of:

    A. Passive acceptance

    B. Active acceptance

    C. Risk avoidance

    D. Risk transfer

14. Steve, a project manager, has a robust risk response plan for his ERP implementation project. The team has utilized all of the appropriate tools & techniques and has executed the predefined preventive and contingency actions to respond to identified project risks. He finds out that some of the risks have been reduced in impact but still remain as potential threats. Steve decides to develop additional contingency and fallback plans for these risks as soon as possible. These risks are called:

    A. Secondary risks

    B. Residual risks

    C. Primary risks

    D. Workarounds

15. You are in the Monitor Risks process of identifying, analyzing, and planning for newly arising risks, keeping track of identified risks, reanalyzing existing risks, monitoring trigger conditions, monitoring residual risks, and reviewing the execution and effectiveness of risk responses. Outputs from the Monitor Risks process include all of the following EXCEPT:

    A. Variance and trend analysis

    B. Work performance information

    C. Change requests

    D. Project management plan updates

16. Designing redundancy in the system, taking early action, adopting less complex processes, conducting more tests, and developing prototypes are all examples of:

    A. Risk avoidance

    B. Risk transfer

    C. Risk mitigation

    D. Risk acceptance

17. You are the project manager assigned to a critical project that requires you to handle project risk intentionally and methodically, so you have assembled only the project team. The team has identified thirty-two potential project risks, determined what would trigger the risks, and have rated and ranked each risk using a risk rating matrix. You have also reviewed and verified all documented assumptions from the project team and verified the data sources used to identify and rate the risks. You are continuing to move through the risk management process. Which one of the following important steps have you missed?

    A. Engage other stakeholders.

    B. Conduct a Monte Carlo simulation.

    C. Determine which risks are transferable.

    D. Determine the overall riskiness of the project.

18. You are managing the construction of a disaster center for a financial institute. After the preliminary survey, you found out that the location that was selected for the disaster center was highly prone to earthquakes. You raised your concern to management, but due to a specific strategic reason, you were told that changing the location would not be an option. In order to deal with this situation, you have selected a specific architectural design that is technologically advanced and earthquake resistant. This is an example of which of the following?

    A. Accept risk

    B. Transfer risk

    C. Avoid risk

    D. Mitigate risk

19. During the initial stage of project planning, you assumed that all the construction materials such as sand, cement, concrete, rods, and other items would be available at a reasonable price during building construction. While identifying the risk in your project, you found out that the cement price significantly increased due to heavy demand and low supply. You decided to add this as a new risk in your project. This is an example of:

    A. Assumptions analysis

    B. Diagramming techniques

    C. SWOT analysis

    D. Expert judgment

20. Steve, an IT project manager, is overseeing a project to develop a new wireless media streaming device. He is using a fishbone diagram to figure out what could cause potential risks to his project. Which one of the following risk management processes is he in now?

    A. Plan Risk Management

    B. Identify Risks

    C. Perform Qualitative Risk Analysis

    D. Monitor Risks

21. You have been working on the Plan Risk Management process of establishing the basis to approach, plan, and execute risk management activities and have developed a risk management plan. Which one of the following will NOT be included in your risk management plan?

    A. Methodology: Defines approaches, tools, and data sources for risk management.

    B. Roles and Responsibilities: Defines the roles and responsibilities and sometimes includes non-team members who may have certain roles in risk management.

    C. Identified Risks: A list of identified risks in the project.

    D. Risk Categories: A group of potential causes for risk that can be grouped into categories, such as technical, political, external, project, environmental, and others.

22. Which one of the following will NOT be considered a valid way of reducing risks in your project?

    A. Plan to mitigate the risk.

    B. Develop a workaround.

    C. Select a specific contract type to distribute risk between the buyer and the seller.

    D. Hire expert team members.

23. You are in the Plan Risk Responses process of developing options and actions to reduce threats and enhance opportunities to your project objectives. The tools & techniques of the Plan Risk Responses process include:

    A. Risk audits

    B. Avoid, transfer, mitigate, and accept

    C. Technical performance measurement

    D. Variance and trend analysis

24. You planned a trip to a destination four-hundred miles away from home. You found out that there is a long stretch of construction on one of the major highways that you are planning to use. You decide to use another highway for that stretch of driving, to avoid traffic. This is an example of:

    A. Avoiding risk

    B. Creating contingency reserves

    C. Creating a workaround

    D. Creating a fallback plan

25. Your team has identified several risks in the project as well as their probability, impact, and priorities. The team is now exploring the response strategies for these risks. The team identified that several of the programmers on the team might leave, which would significantly impact the project, but they decided to deal with it if and when it occurs. Which one of the following statements is true?

    A. This is acceptance.

    B. This is transfer.

    C. This is risk avoidance.

    D. This is risk mitigation.

26. You oversee a project to implement a smartphone application and are currently in the Identify Risks process of identifying and documenting the project risks. While exploring the elements of the enterprise environmental factors, your team will be exploring all of the following elements EXCEPT:

    A. Organizational risk attitudes

    B. Commercial databases

    C. Assumptions analysis

    D. Published checklist

27. You have been working on the Plan Risk Management process of establishing the basis to approach, plan, and execute risk management activities and have developed a risk management plan. Each of the following statements is true regarding the Plan Risk Management process EXCEPT:

    A. The risk management plan, which is a part of the overall project management plan, is an input to all other risk processes.

    B. The risk management plan includes a description of the responses to risks and triggers.

    C. The risk management plan is an output of the Plan Risk Management process.

    D. The risk management plan includes methodology, roles and responsibilities, budget, risk categories, the definition of risk probability and impact, revised stakeholder tolerances, reporting formats, and other items.

Project Risk Management Answers

1.   **C:** The risk register is an output of the Identify Risks process.

2.   **D:** The cost of probable loss or damage is $600,000 times 5 percent, which equals $30,000. The cost of the insurance premium is $15,000; therefore, you should purchase the insurance premium.

3.   **B:** Risk categories are a group of potential causes for risk and can be grouped into categories, such as technical, political, external, project, and environmental. In order to systematically identify risks to a consistent level of detail, we can use a simple list of categories or a Risk Breakdown Structure (RBS). It's a comprehensive way of ordering risks, according to their source.

4.   **A:** The Delphi technique is mainly focused on preventing group thinking and finding out the true opinions of the participants. This is done by sending a request for information to experts who are participating anonymously, compiling their responses, and sending the results back to them for further review until a consensus is reached.

5.   **A:** Perform Qualitative Risk Analysis is the process of prioritizing risks by assessing and combining their probability of occurrence and impact on the project if they occur. This fast, relatively easy to perform, and cost-effective process ensures that the right emphasis is on the right risk areas as per their ranking and priority and allocates adequate time and resources for them. This process utilizes the experience of subject matter experts, functional managers, best practices, and previous project records. Even though numbers are used for the rating to Perform Qualitative Risk Analysis, it is a subjective evaluation and should be performed throughout the project.

6.   **B:** Risk categories are a group of potential causes for risk that can be grouped into categories, such as technical, political, external, project, and environmental. In order to systematically identify risks to a consistent level of detail, we can use a simple list of categories or a Risk Breakdown Structure (RBS). Assumptions are information not based on factual data items and should be verified. Constraints are limitations that should be considered when developing project plans. The product description provides details about the complexity of the product to be delivered.

7.   **D:** The Monte Carlo simulation is associated with the Perform Quantitative Risk Analysis process and determines the impact of identified risks by running simulations to identify the range of possible outcomes for a number of scenarios.

8.   **B:** The Monte Carlo simulation generates information through iterations. Project information at the activity level is chosen at random during the process and produces data that illustrates the likelihood of achieving specific cost or schedule targets.

9.   **B:** Risk triggers are symptoms or warning signs that a potential risk is about to occur within the project. For instance, a key team member searching for a better job opportunity is a warning sign that the person may be leaving the team soon, causing schedule delay, increased cost, and other issues. Risk events are actual occurrences of an identified risk event. Residual risks are the remaining risks after the execution of risk response planning and for which contingency and fallback plans can be created. Secondary risks are new risks created by implementing the selected risk response strategies.

10. **A:** The Ishikawa diagram, also called a cause and effect flow chart or a fishbone diagram, shows the relationship between the causes and effects of problems.

11. **C:** Perform qualitative risk analysis is done by looking at the risk likelihood and effect to rank them.

12. **D:** Risk ratings are determined by the product of probability and impact or consequences when using qualitative analysis and determining Expected Monetary Value (EMV) when utilizing a decision tree (quantitative analysis). EMV is the product of the probability and consequences of an event or task.

13. **D:** Transferring is shifting the negative impact of a threat, along with the ownership of the response, to a third party to make it their responsibility. It only gives another party responsible for its management but does not eliminate the risk. It nearly always involves payment to the third party for taking on the risk. Risk mitigation simply means a reduction in the probability and/or impact of an adverse risk event to an acceptable threshold. Since it is seldom possible to eliminate all risks and also since the cost or impact of avoid, transfer, and mitigate can be too high, acceptance can be the preferred strategy. It indicates that the project team is simply accepting the risk and will continue with the project. Passive acceptance requires no action. The active acceptance strategy aims to establish contingency reserves to handle threats. Avoid indicates that you are eliminating the threat by eliminating the root cause of the threat.

14. **B:** Residual risks are the risks that remain after the execution of risk response planning and for which contingency and fallback plans can be created. Their probability and impact have been reduced through mitigation. These risks are included in the outputs of the Plan Risk Responses process and are expected to remain as threats. The primary risks included in the initial risk identification process are generally the most obvious. Secondary risks are new risks that are created due to the implementation of selected risk response strategies. Workarounds are unplanned responses developed to deal with the occurrence of unanticipated risk events.

15. **A:** Variance and trend analysis are the tools & techniques used in the Monitor Risks process.

16. **C:** These are all examples of risk mitigation. Risk mitigation simply means a reduction in the probability and/or impact of an negative risk event to an acceptable threshold. Transferring is shifting the adverse impact of a threat, along with the ownership of the response, to a third party to make it their responsibility. An example of this would be insurance bonds, warranties, guarantees, and contracts. Avoidance is eliminating the the threat by eliminating the cause or changing the project management plan. An example of this would be using as lower, but reliable technology instead of a cutting-edge one to avoid associated risk. Since it is seldom possible to eliminate all risks and also since the cost or impact of avoid, transfer, and mitigate can be too high, acceptance can be the preferred strategy. It indicates that the project team is simply accepting the risk and will continue with the project.

17. **A:** Stakeholders may be great contributors to identifying potential risks to the project. You should have involved other stakeholders instead of only working with the team members on risk management activities.

18. **D:** Since you are taking action to lower the probability and impact of the risk, you are mitigating the risk.

19. **A:** This is an example of assumptions analysis. This is an analysis of the validity of assumptions, hypotheses, and scenarios developed in project initiation to identify risks from inaccuracies, incompleteness, and inconsistency of assumptions. The assumptions that turn out to be invalid should be evaluated, qualitatively and quantitatively analyzed, and planned for, just like other risks.

20. **B:** The diagramming techniques, such as Ishikawa diagrams, and system or process flow charts, are used as tools & techniques in the Identify Risks process. An influence diagram shows how a set of influencers may influence others and affect outcomes. For instance, a delay in receiving equipment may influence other factors, such as triggering overtime work or a quality issue due to a lack of time to perform tasks.

21. **C:** A list of identified risks will be included in the risk register, not in your risk management plan.

22. **B:** Workarounds are unplanned responses developed to deal with the occurrence of unanticipated risk events, and are not valid ways of reducing risks in a project.

23. **B:** Risk audits, technical performance measurement, and variance and trend analysis are the tools & techniques used in the Monitor Risks process. Strategies for negative risks or threats such as avoid, transfer, mitigate, and avoid, are used as tools & techniques in the Plan Risk Responses process.

24. **A:** Risk avoidance is the elimination of the threat by eliminating the cause or changing the project management plan. This is an example of avoidance since you are changing your travel plan to eliminate the threat of traffic delay.

25. **A:** Since it is seldom possible to eliminate all risks and also since the cost or impact of avoid, transfer, and mitigate can be too high, acceptance can be the preferred strategy. It indicates that the project team is simply accepting the risk and will continue with the project. The team has decided to go for acceptance, which requires no action.

26. **C:** Assumptions analysis is a tool & technique in the Identify Risks process, not an input.

27. **B:** The Plan Risk Management process establishes the basis to approach, plan, and execute risk management activities throughout the project's life and develops the risk management plan. The risk management plan does not include a description of the responses to risks or triggers. Responses to risks are documented in the risk register as part of the Plan Risk Responses process.

Chapter 13

Project Procurement Management

The procurement management knowledge area is about getting products, services, or results from outside the project team. Although there are only three processes in this knowledge area, expect to see many questions about the types of contracts on the exam.

Although the organization can be a buyer or seller, the exam is generally tested from the perspective of a buyer. What that means is that when you are reading the exam questions, keep in mind that you are the buyer and you are looking to hire a seller for the project. The only time the question will come from a seller's perspective is if it specifically mentions that you are a seller. If the question does not identify whether you are a buyer or seller, always assume you are the buyer.

Exam Tip: Agreements and contracts are generally considered the same on the PMP exam.

A contract is a legally binding agreement between a buyer and a seller for products, services, or results. The only time a contract is not legal is when it is for illegal work (crime) to be performed. A contract can be terminated by both the buyer and seller for work not getting done or payments not being made.

Contracts generally include the following:

- Formal written document
- Scope of work to be performed
- Roles and responsibilities
- How to perform the work, including locations and times
- Terms and conditions
- Warranties and penalties
- Payment terms
- Termination clauses
- Change request process
- Incentives
- Insurance and performance bonds

There are three main types of contracts: fixed price, time and material, and cost-reimbursable. The subtypes of these contracts are as follows:

Fixed Price (Lump Sum): A fixed-price contract is when the buyer pays one flat price (lump sum) for all work in the contract. This would include all labor and materials. To use this contract, you would have to ensure the scope is well-defined and understood. For example, you might hire a seller (painter) to paint a room and specify that the seller buys all materials and does the labor of painting. In this type of contract, the seller takes all the risk of exceeding cost constraints for both labor and materials.

- **Firm Fixed Price (FFP):** This contract is when the price is fixed and cannot be changed.

- **Fixed Price Incentive Fee (FPIF):** This contract is when the fixed price includes an additional fee for meeting a target outlined in the contract. For example, finishing the work a week earlier can result in an additional $200.

- **Fixed Price Economic Price Adjustment (FP-EPA):** This contract is used to adjust the fixed cost over the contract's life because of economic conditions. These contracts usually cover longer periods. An example would be increasing the cost of the contract because of the rising cost of oil.

Cost Reimbursable: A cost-reimbursable contract is when the buyer pays for the work expenses and then pays the seller a fee for his profit. For example, you might get a seller to paint a room, but the buyer pays for all the paint, brushes, and rollers, then pays the seller a fee of $1,000. In this contract, the risk is with the buyer because the buyer covers the cost overrun of work expenses. You must keep an eye on the project's cost to ensure you are not being overcharged, such as auditing all invoices.

- **Cost Plus Fixed Fee (CPFF):** This contract is when the buyer pays the work expense and then a fixed fee to the seller for profit.

- **Cost Plus Incentive Fee (CPIF):** This contract is when the buyer pays the work expense and an additional fee, if a target is met, such as finishing two weeks earlier.

Time and Material: A time and material contract is when the buyer pays for both labor and material. For example, you might hire a seller (painter) to paint a room, but the buyer pays the painter by the hour and buys all the paint, brushes, and rollers. In this contract, the buyer takes all the risk of cost overrun for both the labor and materials. It should only be used when the scope is high-level.

Contract summary:

Contract Name	Who takes the risk	When to use it
Fixed Price	Seller	When the scope is defined
Cost reimbursable	Buyer	When the scope is not well defined
Time and material	Buyer	When the scope is high-level

EXAM TIP: When dealing with contract questions:

- *Always choose the best contract for the customer (buyer).*

- *Negotiate a price that is fair for both the buyer and seller.*

- *Incentive fees could keep the cost down.*

- *A contract can be legally voided if it breaks any local laws and regulations.*

If you're working in an agile environment, management contracts and procurement can be difficult. Since the work has no defined scope at the beginning, sellers would have to be willing to work with the project team in order to make the contract more customizable and be willing to accept the uncertainty of an agile project.

On a hybrid project that combines both agile and traditional project management, you may be using the different types of contracts as was discussed above on certain parts of the project that is following a traditional method, and may be using a more customized shared risk contract during the agile sections.

Plan Procurement Management

Plan procurement is the process where you will determine if the project should use outside services. This can include determining what to acquire, how to acquire it, how much is needed, and when it is needed.

The main objective here is to determine whether we really need to procure anything and how we plan to procure it. This can include looking at all of the project requirements' time and costs. Then you can determine your procurement requirements.

When we have decided what to procure, we would then create the procurement management plan to describe the steps needed to select a contractor, monitor the contractor's work, and close out the contract.

Inputs

Project Charter – Covered in Chapter 3

Business Documents

Business documents usually include the business case and the benefits management plan. The business case sets out the cost-benefit of doing the project, and the benefits management plan shows you what benefits the organization will get from the project. Refer to the integration management chapter for more information on these two documents.

Project Management Plan – Covered in Chapter 3

Project Documents

Of the 33 project documents, the ones you are most likely to use in this process include:

- **Requirements documentation:** Requirements documentation involves the requirements listed by the project stakeholders.

- **Risk register:** The register will list all the risks on the project and its appropriate responses. This may be important because if your response to a risk is to transfer it, then you will need to use a contractor.

- **Activity requirements:** Activity resource requirements will list all the resources for the activities. We might need a resource from outside the project.

- **Stakeholder register:** This was created in the "Identify Stakeholder" process. It will list the project stakeholders, their needs, impacts, contact info, and their roles.

Enterprise Environmental Factors – Covered in Chapter 3

Organizational Process Assets – Covered in Chapter 3

Tools and Techniques

Expert Judgment – Covered in Chapter 3

Data Gathering

Gathering data about how and what to procure can be a complicated process. One method to consider is market research. Market research is done to determine what the normal industry standards are for that work. For example, an industry normally hires outside consultants for the installation of complex ERP systems.

Data Analysis

When analyzing the data of whether or not to procure something, the project manager may want to consider doing a make-or-buy analysis. Make-or-buy analysis is done to determine if something on the project can be done by the team or by outside contractors instead. This can be a very complex technique because deciding whether to make something yourself or hire a contractor depends on many factors such as complexity, the time needed, cost, risk, or country laws (having insurance is mandatory for internal employees).

Source Selection Analysis

Before a contractor is selected, the project manager should analyze different selection criteria he/she might use to select a particular seller. While most people would like to choose the seller with the lowest costs, you might want to also consider other qualifications such as licenses, certifications, experience, or availability.

Meetings – Covered in Chapter 3

Outputs

Procurement Management Plan

The procurement management plan will describe the steps to conduct, manage, and close procurement. Here are some things it may contain:

- How to handle risk on the contract
- If independent estimates are needed
- How to handle constraints and assumptions
- Formats for different types of contracts or statement of work
- Metrics that will be used to evaluate the sellers.

Procurement Strategy

The procurement strategy outlines how the project manager would like to get the work done and the type of agreements he/she would like to use on the project. For instance, you might outline whether you want to use a fixed price or a time and material contract.

Bid Documents

The buyer writes procurement documents to inform sellers what will be needed to complete the contract. Some procurement documents are Request for Proposal (RFP) or Invitation for Bid (IFB). Invitation for Bid (IFB) or Request for Bid (RFB) is a request from a buyer for all potential sellers to submit a total price bid for work to be performed. A Request for Proposal (RFP) is a buyer's request to all potential sellers for the details of how work will be performed. A Request for Quotation (RFQ) is a buyer's request to all potential sellers for a price quote per item, hour, foot, or another unit of measure.

Procurement Statement of Work

The procurement statement of work defines what will be procured from outside the project. It is generally made from the scope baseline and outlines what work from the scope baseline will be done outside of the project. It should contain a clear and complete description of the work and the performance measures, reporting, and format of the work. For example, the scope may be to install a new phone system for the company, and the procurement statement of work will be about getting a consultant to set-up the voice to e-mail function of the new phone system.

Source Selection Criteria

Selecting a vendor can be a challenging task because many criteria could be used. When selecting a contractor, you may use criteria such as cost, location, license, certification, reference, warranty, or experience. Keep in mind that you will come up with the criteria before you select the seller.

Make-Or-Buy Decisions

The data analysis tool discussed a make-or-buy analysis; now the output is your make-or-buy decision. Once you've analyzed what you actually want to make internally or buy from an external source, you would then need to decide on which choice you'll implement. This will document the decision of whether to acquire outside support or not.

Independent Cost Estimates

Getting an independent estimate is important in evaluating proposals. An independent estimation would tell you whether or not a given seller is charging too much or too little for work. This can usually be done by inspectors or professional estimators.

Change Requests

Change requests may be needed because you may need to change the project plan in order to add to the seller's work. This can possibly be achieved by adding contractors later in the project. For example, while executing a project to install the new phone system, halfway into the project, you realize you will need consultants to help install some of it. This would lead to a change request to adjust the cost baseline for the new additional cost.

Project Documents Updates – Covered in Chapter 3

Organizational Process Assets Updates – Covered in Chapter 3

> *Exam Tip:* It's critical for success on the exam to understand the difference between the four different types of procurement documents. They are the procurement management plan, procurement strategy, procurement statement of work, and bid documents. The procurement management plan is part of the project management plan and describes how the project manager will conduct the other two procurement processes, "Conduct Procurements" and "Control Procurements." It would also have any type of constraints and assumptions about procurements. The procurement strategy will describe what type of agreement to use and how the project would like delivery to take place. The procurement statement of work describes what will be procured for the project. It basically outlines the specifications and quality requirements for a particular part of the project and if any warranties are needed. The bid documents are used in order to get a response from potential sellers, and generally include an RFP or RFQ.

Conduct Procurements

Conduct procurements is a process where you will select the seller and then award him/her the contract. Keep in mind that this is an executing process. This process uses seller proposals as an input. One of the key things you will be doing is evaluating those proposals. This will result in selecting a seller.

Exam Tip: You select the seller in the executing process group of the project, not in planning.

Inputs

Project Management Plan

The project management plan contains many components that can be used in this particular process, including the scope, requirements, communications, risk, and procurement management. Keep in mind that when selecting a vendor, it's important to understand how that vendor can affect multiple aspects of a project.

Project Documents

Of the 33 project documents, the ones you are most likely to use in this process include:

- **Requirements documentation:** Requirements documentation involves the requirements listed by the project stakeholders.

- **Risk register:** The risk register will list all the risks on the project and their appropriate responses. This may be important because if your response to a risk is to transfer it, then you will need to use a contractor.

- **Stakeholder register:** This was created in the "Identify Stakeholder" process. It will list the stakeholders on the project, their needs, impacts, contact info, and their roles.

- **Project schedule:** This document will describe the start and end date, so all activities on the project may also include when activities are supposed to be done by contractors.

Procurement Documents

The procurement documents that would be included in this input include the procurement statement of work, independent cost estimates, and source selection criteria. See the previous process, "Plan Procurement Management," for an explanation of these documents.

Seller Proposals

In the "Plan Procurement Management" process, we posted various documents such as the RFP. Now, we should get back the seller's proposal for the work. This will be evaluated, and a seller will be selected in this process.

Enterprise Environmental Factors – Covered in Chapter 3

Organizational Process Assets – Covered in Chapter 3

Tools and Techniques

Expert Judgment – Covered in Chapter 3

Advertising

Some contracts may require advertisement. For instance, certain government agency contracts may need to be advertised to the public in order for proposals to be sent in.

Bidder Conference

A bidder conference is when the buyer invites many sellers to a large gathering where the buyer explains what is needed on the project. These can sometimes be called contractor, vendor, or pre-bid conferences. Doing this would save time by allowing you to talk to many sellers at once, instead of doing it individually. It would also ensure that all sellers get an equal amount of information, and no one gets preferred treatment.

Data Analysis

The main data analysis in this process involves evaluating the proposals given to you by the potential vendors. Proposal evaluations are generally done to ensure the proposal matches the requirements for the project.

Interpersonal and Team Skills

The main interpersonal and team skill that can be used in this process is negotiations. This is one of the most important tools in this process, because when selecting a seller, you will need to negotiate the contract. Always negotiate a contract that is good for both the buyer and the seller and satisfies the contract requirements.

Outputs

Selected Sellers

Selecting a seller is one of the main outputs of this process. Depending on how you evaluate the proposal and the criteria that were used, you should now select a seller to award the contract.

Agreements

Procurement agreements or contracts are legally binding documents executed between the buyer and seller for work to be performed. See the beginning of this chapter for more of an explanation on what should be in agreement.

Change Requests – Covered in Chapter 3

Project Management Plan Updates – Covered in Chapter 3

Project Documents Updates – Covered in Chapter 3

Organizational Process Assets Updates – Covered in Chapter 3

Control Procurement

Control procurement manages the relationship between the buyer and seller. In this process, you're trying to make sure that the seller does what is in the contract. You will need to monitor the work to ensure it gets done appropriately. If a seller doesn't do the work in the contract, a default letter may be issued to inform them of the problem. Never take action against a seller without informing them of any defaults.

> **EXAM TIP:** *Do not get confused between "conduct procurement" and "control procurement." "Conduct procurement" is to select a seller and award the contract, while "control procurement" is to ensure the contractor is doing the work in the contract.*

Inputs

Project Management Plan – Covered in Chapter 3

Project Documents

Of the 33 project documents, the ones you are most likely to use in this process include:

- **Assumption log:** The assumption log will describe some of the assumptions and constraints that have been made earlier in the project. This would be related to the assumptions for procurement.

- **Lessons learned register:** A listing of all of the lessons learned so far on the project.

- **Requirements documentation:** Requirements documentation is the requirements listed by the project stakeholders.

- **Risk register:** The register will list all the risks on the project and its appropriate responses. This may be important because your response to a risk might include more inspections of a contractor's work.

- **Stakeholder register:** This was created in the "Identify Stakeholder" process. It will list the stakeholders on the project, their needs, impacts, contact info, and their roles.

- **Project schedule:** This document will describe the start and end dates of all activities on the project and may also include when activities are supposed to be done by contractors.

Agreements

Procurement agreements or contracts are legally binding documents between the buyer and seller for work to be performed.

Procurement Documents

The procurement documents that would be included in this input include the procurement statement of work, independent cost estimates, and source selection criteria. See the "Plan Procurement Management" process for an explanation of these documents.

Approved Change Requests

An approved change request is a change request that has gone through the "Perform Integrated Change Control" process and has been approved. This change will then need to be executed. The seller might have to perform that change.

Work Performance Data – Covered in Chapter 3

Tools and Techniques

Expert Judgment – Covered in Chapter 3

Claims Administration

A claim is a disagreement between the buyer and the seller concerning money specified by the contract. For example, a contractor who fixed a hole in the wall before painting may ask for an additional $200 that was not specified in the contract. The best method that can be used to resolve a claim is to negotiate a settlement of the claim that is good for both the buyer and seller.

Data Analysis – Covered in Chapter 3

Inspections

Anytime you hire a contractor to conduct work for you, you should make sure that you inspect the work that is getting done. There is nothing like going out and inspecting the actual work the contractor is doing. Methods include doing a walk-through of the work the contractor has done so far. Inspections should be done on a regular basis.

Audits

Audits review the procurement processes and determine how they were followed. This will lead to the project manager improving some of the procurement processes or adjusting them in order to match the project requirements.

Outputs

Closed Procurements

Once the seller has finished the work, they can then initiate closing out the contract. This usually involves the buyer giving the seller written notice that the work is done, and the seller giving a buyer notice of full payment. Moreover, all claims should be settled before a contract can close. The project manager should approve all of the deliverables before giving the seller notices that the work is done. If a contractor is not meeting the agreement's requirements, the project manager should inform them first before deciding if they want to close the agreement due to failure of work.

Work Performance Information

This work performance information will outline how the seller is performing on the project. It should include whether they are completing all of the work within the contract time and costs.

Procurement Documentation Updates – Covered in Chapter 3

Change Requests – Covered in Chapter 3

Project Management Plan Updates – Covered in Chapter 3

Project Documents Updates – Covered in Chapter 3

Organizational Process Assets Updates – Covered in Chapter 3

Procurement Management Questions

1. You are working on a construction project and successfully completed all the work. Your stakeholders were very pleased and recently communicated their final acceptance of the project. You are now meeting with your team to update the organizational process assets with a record of knowledge gained about the project to help future project managers with their projects. Once the lessons learned are completed, what should you do NEXT?

   A. Release the team

   B. Close the contract

   C. Get formal acceptance

   D. Write lessons learned

2. You are in charge of the bidding process for a government railway project. You are trying to come up with a set of minimum criteria sellers must meet to be considered. Which of the following are you working on?

   A. Source selection analysis

   B. Proposal evaluation technique

   C. A weighting system

   D. An independent or in-house estimate

3. You are working on a software development project to automate an accounting process. You, your team, and your senior manager all feel that the work is complete. However, one of your important clients disagrees and feels that one of the deliverables is not acceptable, as it does not meet the requirements specification. What is the BEST way to handle this conflict?

   A. Issue a change order.

   B. Renegotiate the contract.

   C. File a lawsuit to force the stakeholder to accept the deliverable.

   D. Meet with the responsible team member to review the WBS dictionary.

4. While in the Control Procurements process, you are meeting with your seller to check on the product itself and its adherance to specification. Which one of the following are you performing?

   A. Performance reporting

   B. Procurement performance reviews

   C. Inspections

   D. Claims administration

5. You requested that your experts prepare an independent estimate, or in-house estimate, for your contract to help judge whether the Statement of Work (SOW) was adequate in its description or that the seller understood and fully responded to it. You also want to check the reasonableness of the seller's response and proposed pricing. Which of the following BEST describes what you are doing?

   A. Plan procurement management

   B. Conduct Procurements

   C. Control Procurements

   D. Close Project

6. You are asked by management to select a contract type that will obligate the seller to accept all liability for poor workmanship, engineering errors, and consequential damages in the project. Which of the following contract types will you select?

    A. Fixed price

    B. Time &material

    C. Cost-plus incentive fee

    D. Purchase order

7. After reviewing your project schedule and resource calendars, you realize that your resources are 100 percent occupied and will have no time to work on a new component. So, you decide to outsource the component and start negotiating with a couple of potential vendors. While outsourcing, which of the following should you be MOST concerned about?

    A. The technical background of the vendor

    B. The financial capability of the vendor

    C. The relevant experience of the vendor

    D. Proprietary data of your organization

8. Sabrina, a project manager for ITPro Consultancy, LLC, is overseeing the design and development of a climate control device. While working on the procurement plan, she compared the cost of an off-the-shelf product to the cost of her programmers' design to develop the custom device. Sabrina is engaged in which of the following?

    A. Using expert judgment

    B. Coming up with source selection criteria

    C. Performing a Make-or-buy analysis

    D. Working on the procurement statement of work

9. While working on a data mining project, you realize that you need a data validation tool that was not thought of earlier. After reviewing your project schedule and resource calendars, you realize that your resources are 100 percent occupied and will have no time to work on this new component. So, you decide to outsource the component and start negotiating with a couple of potential vendors. You quickly realize that you do not have a clear definition of the scope, but the vendor agrees with you that the project will be relatively small, and you have an urgent need. Which contract type is MOST appropriate in this kind of situation?

    A. Cost Plus Fixed Fee(CPFF)

    B. Cost Plus Award Fee(CPAF)

    C. Fixed Price Economic Price Adjustment(FPEPA)

    D. Time and Materials (T &M)

10. You are in the Control Procurements process and are ensuring that the seller's performance meets contractual requirements by monitoring contract performance and making appropriate changes and corrections. Which of the following will you most likely NOT use as an input in this process?

    A. Procurement documents

    B. Work performance information

    C. Contract

    D. Seller proposals

11. You are the project manager of a data center construction project. Your company made it mandatory to solicit quotes from three separate vendors before submitting the purchase request to the finance department for buying switches, routers, firewalls, PCs, servers, etc., for the data center. What type of input is this policy to the procurement process?

    A. Make-or-buy decision

    B. Procurement document

    C. Source selection criteria

    D. Organizational process asset

12. Which of the following is the process of documenting project purchasing decisions, specifying the approach, defining selection criteria to identify potential sellers, and putting together a procurement management plan?

    A. Conduct Procurements process

    B. Plan Procurements process

    C. Close Project process

    D. Control Procurements process

13. Steve is a program manager overseeing an ERP implementation project where the team has already completed the finance, sales, and admin modules out of seven total modules. Steve was informed that the client had terminated the project as they found a cheaper and faster off-the-shelf solution for their need and no longer want the project to continue. Which of the following is TRUE?

    A. The team must keep working on the project to give senior management time to discuss with the client.

    B. Steve must stop all work and release the team immediately.

    C. Steve must work with the team to document the lessons learned.

    D. Steve must close the contract.

14. In which procurement management process will you ensure that the seller's performance meets contractual requirements, that both the buyer and seller meet their contractual obligations, and that the legal rights of both the buyer and seller are protected?

    A. Procurement performance reviews

    B. Inspections and audits

    C. Performance reporting

    D. Control Procurements

15. You are in charge of the bidding process for a government solar power plant project. You are trying to make sure that no seller receives preferential treatment and that all sellers have a clear, common understanding of the procurement (technical requirements, contractual requirements, etc.). Your key objective is to provide all potential contractors with the information they need to determine if they would like to continue with the contracting process. Which one of the following will assist you with your goal?

    A. Source selection criteria

    B. Bidder conference

    C. Independent estimate

    D. Procurement negotiation

16. During the Plan Procurement Management process, your team developed a procurement document to solicit proposals from prospective sellers and to compare their responses easily. All of the following statements are true about the procurement document EXCEPT:

    A. It may include the procurement statement of work and evaluation criteria.

    B. It should not be too rigorous to allow any flexibility for the sellers to be innovative.

    C. It contains clear, complete, and concise descriptions of performance, design, functionality, reporting, format, and support requirements.

    D. It may contain a Request For Proposal (RFP), an Invitation For Bid (IFB) or Request For Bid (RFB), and a Request For Quotation (RFQ).

17. While managing a nanotechnology project to build an elevator/tunnel from the ground to the space station, you need to procure a new carbon nanotube material, which is extremely strong and resistant to heavy air pressure. Due to patent constraints, there is only one supplier in a different state who can provide you with this material. You checked the supplier's website and realized that the price listed for the material on the site would be within your approved limit. What should you do in this situation?

    A. Consider purchasing the material from the source even though it is a sole source.

    B. Keep exploring the option to use some other material to build the tunnel.

    C. Notify management that there is only one source; thus, you cannot purchase the material from the single source.

    D. Ask the procurement department to take care of this situation.

18. As a buyer's project manager, you always try to bring the seller's objectives in line with those of yours. You also understand that for the sellers, the focus is on the profit. Your project has an emergency and needs contracted work to be completed as soon as possible. Which one of the following would be most helpful to add to the contract under this crucial situation?

    A. A Time is of the Essence clause

    B. A robust procurement statement of work

    C. A retain age clause

    D. Incentives

19. Lars is a project manager overseeing an online age verification application for a very important client of his organization. Three months into the project, Lars got a call from the client, who informed him that they would not be able to make the partial payment for the design work due to a financial crisis. The client also mentioned that they were very unsatisfied with the quality of the requirement document that the seller submitted. The client's organization thinks that the contract is no longer valid and needs to be terminated. Lars realizes that once signed, a contract is legally binding unless:

    A. The contract is in violation of applicable laws.

    B. The buyer's legal counsel considers the contract to be null and void.

    C. The seller fails to perform.

    D. The buyer fails to pay for the work.

20. As a buyer's project manager, what is the BEST way for you to ensure that the seller is not making extra profits in a Cost Plus Fixed Fee (CPFF) contract?

    A. You only pay the fee when the project is completed.

    B. You do not authorize any unexpected cost overrun.

    C. You audit all invoices and make sure that you are not charged for items not chargeable to the project.

    D. You ensure that the sellers are not cutting scope.

Project Procurement Management Answers

1. **A:** You should release the team once the lessons learned are documented and added to the organizational process assets. Most contracts have payment terms that allow for some period of time before full payment is required; thus, the last thing you do on the project is to close the contract.

   The order should be: get formal acceptance, write lessons learned, release the team, and close the contract.

2. **A:** A source selection analysis is a set of minimum criteria a seller must meet to be considered, such as proficiency with certain products or techniques, safety record, number of years of relevant experience, etc. Prior to reviewing the detailed proposals, a buyer may review the qualifications of sellers who have indicated an interest to bid. A weighting system is generally utilized to score qualified sellers after proposals have been submitted. The procuring organization can prepare its own independent estimate to judge whether the statement of work was adequate in its description or that the seller fully understood and responded to the statement of work. This estimate also helps the organization check the reasonableness of the seller's response and proposed pricing.

3. **D:** The very first thing we should do is to find out the details of the issue by reviewing the requirements and meeting with the responsible team member to review the WBS dictionary. We need to find out if there is something wrong with the details of the work package or with how the team member completed the work. If required, we can then issue a change order. When there's a dispute between a buyer and a seller, it's called a claim. Most contracts have some language that explains exactly how claims should be resolved, and since it's in the contract, it's legally binding, and both the buyer and seller need to follow it. Usually, it's not an option to renegotiate a contract, especially at the end of the project after the work is completed. Lawsuits should only be filed if there are absolutely no other options.

4. **C:** Inspections are activities mainly focused on the product itself and its adherance to specification. Performance reporting is an excellent tool that provides management

   with information about how effectively the seller is meeting contractual objectives. This report can produce earned values, schedule and cost performance index, trend analysis, etc. Procurement performance review is a structured review that consists of seller-prepared documentation, buyer inspection, and a quality audit of the seller's progress to deliver project scope and quality within cost and on schedule as per the contract. The objective is to identify performance progress or failures, non-compliances, and areas where performance is a problem. Claims handling is one of the most frequent activities in the Control Procurements process. Claims, disputes, or appeals are requested when the buyer and seller disagree on scope, the impact of changes, or the interpretation of some terms and conditions in the contract.

5. **B:** We use independent estimates as a tool & technique in the Conduct Procurements process.

6. **A:** The fixed price or lump sum contract, which usually pays a lump sum amount for all the work, places the risk on the seller. The seller may include a contingency in the contract to assist in minimizing the risk of reduced profits.

7. **D:** The technical background, financial capability, and relevant experience of the vendor are all very important factors while outsourcing, but we should be very concerned about the sensitive and confidential proprietary data of our organization that we may need to turn over to the vendor.

8.   **C:** Make-or-buy analysis is concerned with determining whether a product can be cost-effectively produced in-house or whether it should be purchased, leased, or rented. While performing this analysis, we must consider indirect as well as direct costs, availability in addition to related risk, schedule, etc. Source selection criteria is developed and used to select a contractor. Later on, it also helps to evaluate sellers by rating or scoring them. The procurement Statement of Work (SOW) describes the subject item in sufficient detail to allow prospective sellers to determine offerings (bids, proposals, etc.). It documents details of the work to be performed by the seller under a contract.

9.   **D:** This time-based fee, plus the cost of materials contract, is used for smaller amounts and shorter times and requires little or no defined scope of work. In a T & M contract, the seller pays a rate for each of the people working on the team plus their material costs. The "time" part means that the buyer pays a fixed rate for labor, usually a certain number of dollars per hour. And the "materials" part means that the buyer also pays for materials, equipment, office space, administrative overhead costs, and anything else that has to be paid for.

10. **D:** Seller proposals are inputs to the Conduct Procurements process for obtaining seller responses, selecting a seller, and awarding the procurement, usually in the form of a contract. This is an official response to the buyer's procurement document, including the details the buyer is looking for, how the work will be performed, and pricing. Procurement documents, work performance information, and contracts all are used as inputs for administering procurements in the monitoring & controlling process group.

11. **D:** Any type of corporate policy or formal and official procurement procedure is an organizational process asset.

12. **B:** Plan Procurement Management is the process of documenting project purchasing decisions, specifying the approach, defining selection criteria to identify potential sellers, and putting together a procurement management plan.

13. **C:** A project can be terminated at any time for a specific cause or simply for convenience of the buyer. If a project is terminated before the work is completed, you still need to document the lessons learned and add them to the organizational process assets. There are always important lessons that you can learn when a project goes seriously wrong, even when you did nothing to contribute to the disaster.14.   D: Control Procurements is the process of ensuring the seller's performance meets contractual requirements, ensuring that both seller and buyer meet their contractual obligations, and ensuring that the legal rights of both seller and buyer are protected. The focus here is to manage the relationship between buyer and seller, monitor contract performance, and make appropriate changes and corrections. Procurement performance reviews, inspections and audits, and performance reporting are tools & techniques used in the Control Procurements process.

15. **B:** A bidder conference is intended to assure that no seller receives preferential treatment and that all sellers have a clear, common understanding of the procurement (technical requirements, contractual requirements, etc.). The goal of the bidder conferences is to make sure that all questions are submitted in writing and issued to sellers as an addendum to the procurement document so that all sellers respond to the same scope of work, there is no collusion among sellers and/or buying agents, and sellers do not save questions for later private meetings in order to gain competitive advantage. The procuring organization often prepares independent estimates to judge whether the statement of work was adequate in its description and that the seller fully understood and responded to the statement of work. These estimates also help the organization check the reasonableness of the seller's response or cost proposal and proposed pricing. The goal of procurement negotiation is to achieve clarification and agreement on the structure and requirements of the contract prior to signing.

16. **C:** Usually a Statement of Work (SOW) document contains a clear, complete, and concise description of performance, design, functionality, reporting, format and support requirements, not a procurement document. Well designed procurement documents help in easier comparison of seller responses, more complete proposals, more accurate pricing, and a decrease in the amount of changes in the project. Procurement documents may contain all the work that is to be completed, as well as terms, conditions, and evaluation criteria. You want the seller to be as innovative as possible when they come up with the design and methods for completing your project. It may contain a Request for Proposal (RFP), Invitation for Bid (IFB), or Request for Bid (RFB), and Request for Quotation (RFQ).

17. **A:** In non-competitive forms of procurement, usually, a seller is selected from a list of qualified sellers interested in and capable of doing the job. Even though competition can result in the selection of a better seller and decreased price, there is no reason for going through the entire procurement process unless the law requires it. Two types of non-competitive forms of procurement are described below:

    Single-source (preferred seller): In this case, the buyer has worked with the seller before, and due to good experience and other convenience with the seller, the buyer does not want to look for another seller.

    Sole source (only seller): In this case, the seller may be the only one in the market or may have monopoly power to sell, thus limiting the ability to select other sellers.

18. **D:** Under normal circumstances, if you follow the proper project management processes, you should have a good definition of scope. In this situation, you should have a quality procurement statement of work. You need a good scope definition as well as incentives

    as you need the seller to share your need for speed. A quality procurement document alone will not ensure speed. Incentives will bring the seller's objectives in line with the buyer's and would be most useful in this case. The "Time is of the Essence" clause states that any delay will be considered as a material breach as delivery dates are extremely important. The "Retain age" clause states that in order to ensure full completion, an amount of money, usually 5 to 10 percent, is withheld from each payment and paid in full once the final work is completed. These two clauses may help, but would not be as effective as incentives.

19. **A:** It is important to understand that once signed, a contract is legally binding unless it is in violation of any applicable law. The failure to perform or make payment usually does not alter the fact that the contract is binding. The contract will remain binding even

if only one party considers that the contract is no longer valid. However, if both parties negotiate and agree to terminate the contract, the contract should move into the Close Procurements process.

20. **C:** In a Cost Plus Fixed Fee (CPFF) contract, the fee is usually paid on a continuous basis during the life of the project. It is unreasonable and unrealistic not to authorize any unexpected cost overrun. Cutting scope would not be a way for sellers to make additional profits as it decreases the profit for this type of contract. The best way is to audit all invoices and make sure that you are not charged for items not chargeable to the project.

Chapter 14

Project Stakeholder Management

This knowledge area is about documenting how you plan to keep your stakeholders engaged and actually engaging them on the project. Your main goal in this area is to keep the stakeholders engaged in the project and make sure their needs are met. You will first identify them and then create the plan to keep them engaged (stakeholder engagement plan).

When working on an agile project, this knowledge area is greatly expanded on because agile is more dependent on stakeholder engagement than traditional projects. The engagement of the stakeholders is a critical factor in agile projects because they are involved in giving requirements throughout the project and reviewing the iterations once they are completed. Stakeholders tend to be more involved in an agile project than a traditional project.

This chapter does not have too many new inputs, tools, or outputs. Most of the exam questions will be about the stakeholder register and stakeholder engagement plan.

Process	Process Group	Main Output
Identify Stakeholders	Initiating	Stakeholder Register
Plan Stakeholder Engagement	Planning	Stakeholder Engagement Plan
Manage Stakeholder Engagement	Executing	Change Request
Monitor Stakeholder Engagement	Monitoring and Controlling	Work Performance Information, Change Request

Identify Stakeholders

Identify stakeholders is an initiating process in which you create a register of all the stakeholders on the project. It is very important to know who your stakeholders are and how they will affect the project from the start. This is generally done right after the project charter is signed. It is also done throughout the entire project life cycle from start to finish.

A stakeholder is anyone who has a positive or negative interest in the project. When you are identifying the stakeholders, make sure to list not just the positive stakeholders, but also the negative ones.

The stakeholder register will be used in many planning processes. Expect a few questions on what the stakeholder register is and when it is used.

Inputs

Project Charter – Covered in Chapter 4

Business Documents

Business documents usually include the business case and the benefits management plan. The business case will outline the cost-benefit of doing the project, and the benefits management plan shows you what benefits the organization will get from the project. Refer to the integration management chapter for more information on these two documents.

Project Management Plan – Covered in Chapter 3

Project Documents – Covered in Chapter 3

Agreements

An agreement is a contract between a buyer and a seller for work to be performed or for the sale of products. This can be used in this process to identify potential contractors that may be stakeholders in the project.

Enterprise Environmental Factors – Covered in Chapter 3

Organizational Process Assets – Covered in Chapter 3

Tools and Techniques

Expert Judgment – Covered in Chapter 3

Data Gathering – Covered in Chapter 3

Data Analysis

The project manager must analyze current documents and data about the project in order to determine the stakeholders on the project. One way of doing this is stakeholder analysis. Stakeholder analysis analyzes who your stakeholders are and how they feel about the project. You will be looking at all the project documents that you currently have, such as the project charter or procurement documents, and thinking about who are the stakeholders on the project.

Here are some of the things you will need to analyze about the stakeholders on the project:

- What is the stakeholder's role, such as a team member, sponsor, or functional manager?

- How would the project affect them, either in a positive or negative way?

- Would they be active stakeholders, such as team members who work on the deliverable, or passive ones, such as customers who watch the project work get done?

- What is their power authority, such as sponsors who will be paying for the project?

Data Representation

Data representation will look at different techniques that can be used to visually see how the stakeholders will affect the project. Here are a few tools we can use:

- **Power/interest grid, power/influence grid, or impact/influence grid.** This is used to group stakeholders according to their level of authority, concern, ability to influence, and cause changes.

- **Stakeholder cube**

  - A three-dimensional methodology to support the mapping of a stakeholder's interest, power, and influence.

- **Salience model:** used on large complex projects to help describe stakeholders in terms of the following characteristics:

  - Power: Level of authority

  - Urgency: Immediate attention

  - Legitimacy: How appropriate is their involvement

- **Directions of Influence:** this will be used to classify stakeholders based on their level of influence on the project.

  - Upward: Senior management

  - Downward: Team members

  - Outward: Vendors, government, public, end-users

  - Sideward: peers such as other project managers

Meetings – Covered in Chapter 3

Outputs

Stakeholder Register

The stakeholder register is a document that lists all of the project stakeholders and their classifications. This register should be updated throughout the project, as stakeholders can change very frequently. The stakeholder register contains personal information regarding the project's stakeholders and should be kept in a secure location that can only be accessed by authorized individuals.

Here are a few other things the stakeholder register should contain:

- Stakeholders' contact information

- Role on the project, such as a sponsor or functional manager

- Communication requirements

- Expectations of the project

- How are they affected by the project

- Power influence level on the project

Change Requests

You may be asking yourself how you can have a change request in an initiating process, since the plan has not been created yet and the project is yet to be executed. Well, consider that this is a process you will be doing continuously throughout the project. The first time you do it, there will be no change request, but the next time, the project may have already been baselined and executed. It's during this time that the project manager may need to update or change the product, plan, or other documents because a new stakeholder has been identified.

Project Management Plan Updates – Covered in Chapter 3

Project Documents Updates – Covered in Chapter 3

Plan Stakeholder Engagement

In this process, the project manager determines what methods are needed to keep the stakeholders engaged in the project. When stakeholders are not engaged in the project, the project may not be able to meet its requirements as stakeholders feel alienated from the project.

The project manager will need to come up with methods to determine the best ways to keep the stakeholders engaged and then document these methods in the stakeholder management plan.

Inputs

Project Charter – Covered in Chapter 4

Project Management Plan – Covered in Chapter 3

Project Documents

Of the 33 project documents, the ones you are most likely to use in this process include:

- **Stakeholder register:** This was created in the "Identify Stakeholder" process. It will list the stakeholders on the project, their needs, impacts, contact info, and their roles.

- **Issue log:** This log will list all issues on the project. Stakeholders may want to be updated on the status of issues on the project.

- **Change log:** The change log will keep track of the status of all change requests on the project. The status generally indicates if the change is being reviewed, approved, or denied.

Agreements

An agreement is a contract between a buyer and a seller for work to be performed or for the sale of products. This can be used in this process to identify potential contractors that may be stakeholders on the project.

Enterprise Environmental Factors – Covered in Chapter 3

Organizational Process Assets – Covered in Chapter 3

Tools and Techniques

Expert judgment – Covered in Chapter 3

Data gathering – Covered in Chapter 3

Data analysis – Covered in Chapter 3

Decision making – Covered in Chapter 3

Data representation – CoveredinChapter3

One way to show how stakeholders can be engaged in the project is to use the stakeholder engagement matrix. A stakeholder engagement matrix classifies stakeholders based on five levels of engagement:

- **Unaware:** Unaware they are a stakeholder.

- **Resistant:** They're resistant to the project objectives, more likely considered negatively impacted stakeholders.

- **Neutral:** they know the project is happening but are neither supportive nor unsupportive.

- **Supportive:** They are aware of the project taking place, are very supportive, and welcome its outcome.

- **Leading:** They are aware the project is taking place and want to actively engage in the project.

Here is what an engagement matrix with looks like if you were to map out all your stakeholders. At first you would do the matrix and label certain stakeholders as being where there are currently and where you would like them to be in a desired state.

Stakeholder	Unaware	Resistant	Neutral	Supportive	Leading
Mary		Current		Desired	
Jane	Current				Desired
Bob			Desired		

Meetings – Covered in Chapter 3

Outputs

Stakeholder Engagement Plan

The stakeholder engagement plan will describe how the project team will keep the stakeholders engaged in the project. This will include what type of communication will be needed to engage them on the project. The stakeholder management plan is part of the project management plan.

Exam Tip: The difference between the stakeholder engagement plan and the communication management plan is how the communications and engagements would be done. The stakeholder engagement plan says why we need the engagements and the communication plan states how and when the engagements will be done. For example, the stakeholder engagement plan will state we need to engage the customers on a more personal level to get their feedback on the deliverables. The communication management plan will state we need to hold a weekly meeting with the customers.

Manage Stakeholder Engagement

In this process, you are using the stakeholder engagement plan and communication plan to actually engage the stakeholders. This will be done to keep stakeholders informed about the project performance and to address any issues the stakeholders might have with the project.

This process is very important for the success of the project. You will want to meet with the stakeholders and document their issues with the project, and then fix them. This will ensure that all stakeholders' concerns are heard and resolved.

Inputs

Project Management Plan

In order to keep the stakeholders engaged, the project manager will use the communications and risk management plans, along with the stakeholder engagement plan to ensure that stakeholders are participating at all levels of the project.

Project Documents

Of the 33 project documents, the ones you are most likely to use in this process include:

- **Stakeholder register:** This is a list of all the stakeholders on the project and how they may impact the project.
- **Issue log:** This log will list all issues on the project. Stakeholders may want to be updated on the status of issues on the project.
- **Change log:** The change log will keep track of the status of all change requests on the project. The status is general if the change is being reviewed, approved, or denied.
- **Lessons learned register:** A listing of all of the lessons learned so far on the project.

Enterprise Environmental Factors – Covered in Chapter 3

Organizational Process Assets – Covered in Chapter 3

Tools and Techniques

Expert Judgment – Covered in Chapter 3

Communication Skills

The project manager will be communicating with all the stakeholders on the project. Being able to provide clear and effective communications is the key to great leadership. Some of the communication skills that will be used here include feedback, nonverbal communications, and presentation skills.

Interpersonal and Team Skills – Covered in Chapter 3

Ground Rules

Ground rules are usually set within the team charter and are the general rules that the team will follow in order to effectively communicate with each other. Ground rules should be known from the start of the project and should be followed throughout the project. Keep in mind that ground rules will be similar from project to project, as they generally define acceptable behavior on a project.

Meetings – Covered in Chapter 3

Outputs

Change Requests

When people are actively involved in a project, you can expect them to ask for project changes. This can include scope, time, cost, or quality changes.

Project Management Plan Updates – Covered in Chapter 3

Project Documents Updates – Covered in Chapter 3

Organizational Process Assets Updates – Covered in Chapter 3

Monitor Stakeholder Engagement

This is the process of examining if the stakeholder engagement plan is being carried out and if it is working. This includes looking at the previous process of "Manage Stakeholder Engagement" and determining what was actually done. This will tell you whether the plan is working or needs to be changed.

All monitoring and controlling processes are concerned with comparing the plan to the actual work. In these processes, it is very important to ensure that we are engaging stakeholders and are following the plan.

Inputs

Project Management Plan – Covered in Chapter 3

Project Documents

Of the 33 project documents, the ones you are most likely to use in this process include:

- **Stakeholder register:** This was created in the "Identify Stakeholder" process. It will list the stakeholders on the project, their needs, impacts, contact info, and roles.
- **Issue log:** This log will list all issues on the project. Stakeholders may want to be updated on the status of issues on the project.
- **Change log:** The change log will keep track of the status of all change requests on the project. The status is generally, if the change is being reviewed, approved, or denied.
- **Project communications:** This document describes what communications have taken place on the project, such as memos, meetings, ore-mails.
- **Risk register:** This document will contain a listing of all the risks on the project and their potential responses.

Work Performance Data – Covered in Chapter 3

Project Documents – Covered in Chapter 3

Tools and Techniques

Data Analysis – Covered in Chapter 3

Decision Making – Covered in Chapter 3

Data Representation – Covered in Chapter 3

Communication Skills

Good communication skills are essential to ensure that the stakeholders understand the status of the project. Common techniques here include giving good feedback and using good presentation skills in order to update stakeholders on the project.

Interpersonal and Team Skills – Covered in Chapter 3

Meetings – Covered in Chapter 3

Outputs

Work Performance Information – Covered in Chapter 3

Change Requests

If you feel that the project management plan is not keeping the stakeholders engaged and conflicts are increasing, then you might want to change parts of the plan. Any change to the project management plan will require a change request.

Project Management Plan Updates – Covered in Chapter 3
Project Documents Updates – Covered in Chapter 3

Stakeholder Management Questions

1. You are efficaciously managing a business automation project, and most of the deliverables were delivered on time by the team members. This project is extremely critical as it will drastically cut down the time and cost of regular business activities for several departments. Stakeholders and customers have articulated their satisfaction with the project, but you were also criticized for the number of changes made in the project. Which of the following is the MOST likely cause of the project problem?

   A. You failed to identify some of the key stakeholders in your project.

   B. You should have more project management training and experience.

   C. Change Control Board (CCB) members approved almost all of the change requests.

   D. The project should have had a better change control system.

2. You are in the Monitor Stakeholder Engagement process of evaluating and monitoring overall stakeholder relationships and ensuring stakeholders' appropriate engagement in the project by adjusting plans and strategies as required. Which one of the following is an important input to the Monitor Stakeholder Engagement process?

   A. Customer register

   B. Project charter

   C. Change control log

   D. Issue log

3. You are in the Plan Stakeholder Management process of defining an approach to manage stakeholders throughout the entire project life cycle according to their interest, impact, importance, and influence over the project. Which of the following is an input to this Plan Stakeholder Management process?

   A. Impact/power grid

   B. Stakeholder register

   C. Stakeholder engagement assessment matrix

   D. Conflict log

4. You are in the Manage Stakeholder Engagement process and are focused on meeting and exceeding the stakeholders' expectations by continuously communicating with them, clarifying and resolving their issues, addressing their concerns, and improving project performance by implementing their change requests. Which of the following is a tool & technique used in this process?

   A. Interpersonal skills

   B. Change log

   C. Issue log

   D. Stakeholder management plan

5. You are assigned as a project manager for one of the most imperative and strategic projects in your organization. As the stakeholders will play a vital role in the success of your project, you are trying to identify all your internal and external stakeholders. In which project management process group will you identify stakeholders in your project?

A. Initiating

B. Initiating and planning

C. All process groups

D. Planning and monitoring & controlling

6. You have been managing a government railway project and dealing with several stakeholders. You have spent a considerable amount of time identifying all your internal and external stakeholders and their interest, influence level in your project, and their key expectations. Managing stakeholder expectations is the responsibility of which party?

A. Since the project manager alone cannot manage all the stakeholders on a complex, large project, the project manager and project team together are responsible for managing stakeholders' expectations.

B. Project sponsor, as this individual funds the project and has greater control over the stakeholders.

C. Stakeholders should make sure that their expectations are managed appropriately and receive the required information on the project as needed.

D. This is the responsibility of the project manager alone.

7. You have thirteen stakeholders in the construction project that you are overseeing. Your initial study about these stakeholders tells you that most of them will actively support your project to be successful, but you have a couple of stakeholders who may deleteriously impact your project. There is one specific stakeholder you are particularly concerned about as he is known to be exceptionally critical about the way the project managers in the organization manage projects. He also has a reputation for requesting many changes in projects and antagonistically pursuing his demands. You realized that you need to be meticulous in dealing with this stakeholder and plan to take which of the following approaches:

A. Carefully eradicate the need of this stakeholder and remove him from the stakeholder list.

B. Discuss with the stakeholder's boss and find a way to make the stakeholder support the project positively by not being too critical and aggressive.

C. Simply deal with the stakeholder and refuse his requests for changes.

D. Involve this stakeholder in the project as early as possible and work closely with him throughout the project.

8. A trustworthy, senior team member informs you that two of the stakeholders are very apprehensive about the ERP project you are overseeing. The first stakeholder is very panicky that once the ERP is implemented in his department a lot of people will lose their jobs. The second stakeholder is skeptical about the capability of the team to implement such a large, multifaceted project. As the project manager, what should you do in this kind of situation?

    A. Set-up a meeting with these two stakeholders and discuss their concerns.

    B. Report to the sponsor about these two stakeholders.

    C. Set-up a question and answer session about the project and invite all the stakeholders.

    D. You should send an official e-mail to the stakeholders, asking them to direct any queries about the project in writing to you.

9. While analyzing stakeholders in your project, you identified one stakeholder who is so formidable and influential that he forced the team to implement many of his last minutes change requests in one of the previous projects. There is also a common understanding that he used his influence to dismiss a very important project during executing in the past. What will be your BEST course of action with such a persuasive stakeholder?

    A. Involve this stakeholder as little as possible in the project.

    B. Involve this stakeholder from the very beginning and closely manage him.

    C. Give the highest priority to his expectations, concerns, and issues.

    D. Get approval from the sponsor to remove this stakeholder from the project.

10. You are assigned as a project manager to implement an ERP solution for one of your area retailers. Currently, you are working on identifying stakeholders and their level of involvement, roles, and responsibilities. Who will be able to help the team the MOST to identify what roles the stakeholders will play and how and what they will contribute to the project?

    A. The sponsor

    B. Senior management

    C. Functional managers

    D. Stakeholders

11. Due to time and budget constraints, senior management decided not to include the requirements of several stakeholders in a project. The project manager finalized the project management plan, but encountered significant challenges in receiving formal acceptance. The stakeholders were extremely upset and tried every possible way to include their requirements in the project as it would take several years for the organization to initiate another project to implement their desired functionalities. After several attempts, the project was finally approved and initiated a couple of months ago. Which of the following preventive actions should the project manager NOT consider in this case?

    A. Make sure that the stakeholders will not use the change control process as a means to add their requirements.

    B. Document what is out of scope and in scope in the project.

    C. Review and confirm the requirements that will be out of scope in the project with the stakeholders.

    D. Develop a stakeholder register and stakeholder management strategy.

12. Steve is trying to figure out whether a stakeholder is at an "unaware" state or not so that he can identify the required actions and communication needed to minimize the gap between the desired and actual level of engagement of this stakeholder. Which of the following is a tool to assess the current and desired state of engagement of a stakeholder on the project?

   A. Stakeholder analysis

   B. Issue log

   C. Stakeholder register

   D. Stakeholder management plan

13. You are reviewing the stakeholder management plan and communications management plan and focusing on meeting and exceeding the stakeholders' expectations by continuously communicating with them, elucidating and resolving their issues, addressing their apprehensions, and improving project performance by implementing their change requests. Which stakeholder management process are you in at this time?

   A. Monitor Stakeholder Engagement

   B. Manage Stakeholder Engagement

   C. Plan Stakeholder Management

   D. Identify Stakeholders

14. You are overseeing a web-based application project to automate the business process of one of your clients. You are working on identifying all the internal and external stakeholders who have interest in your project and can positively or negatively impact it. While identifying the stakeholders, you realize that stakeholder identification is:

   A. To be focused only on stakeholders who will contribute positively to your project:

   B. To be completed in the initial stage of the project lifecycle

   C. A responsibility of the project sponsor

   D. To be carried out throughout the project lifecycle

15. Stakeholder management necessitates all of the following EXCEPT:

   A. Giving stakeholder extras if needed to meet and exceed their expectations

   B. Identifying both internal and external stakeholders

   C. Assessing stakeholders' skills, knowledge, and expertise

   D. Identifying stakeholders' influence-controlling strategies

16. You are overseeing a project to build a plant for a semiconductor company. You have completed your internal and external stakeholder identification and have come up with a list of thirteen stakeholders for the project. You expect that most of the stakeholders will play an affirmative role in the project and will contribute significantly. While working on your project management plan, you were notified by one of the team members that a stakeholder from the automation department is missing in the published stakeholder list. What will be your best course of action in this situation?

    A. Add the stakeholder to your stakeholder list immediately and update everyone.

    B. It is too late to add any more stakeholders and consider their requirements, so ignore the stakeholder.

    C. Validate the information received from the team member.

    D. Set-up a meeting with the stakeholder and the team member.

17. You identified all people who would be impacted by the project and documented relevant information regarding their interests, expectations, involvement, and influence on the project success in a stakeholder register. The stakeholder register will NOT be used as an input to which of the following processes?

    A. Collect Requirements and Plan Scope Management

    B. Plan Risk Management and Identify Risks

    C. Plan Quality Management and Plan Communications Management

    D. Develop Project Charter and Perform Integrated Change Control

18. Your company, ITPro Consultancy, has assigned you as the project manager to upgrade the call center in your organization. The number of calls the customer support agents have to answer each month has increased drastically in the last five months, and the phone system is approaching the maximum load limit. While identifying the stakeholders, you realize that there are more than 180 potential stakeholders, 19 team members, and 6 different vendors that you will need to deal with. What will be your BEST course of action?

    A. Have an urgent meeting with the sponsor and request him not to include some of the stakeholders.

    B. Identify an effective approach to determine the needs of all stakeholders.

    C. Identify the key stakeholders and concentrate only on their needs.

    D. Report to the management that the project is too large to manage by one person.

19. Project stakeholder management consists of processes to identify the internal and external stakeholders, determine their expectations and influence over the project, develop strategies to manage them, and effectively engage them in project execution and decision. Which one of the following is the key objective of stakeholder management?

    A. Keeping the stakeholders happy and satisfied

    B. Maintaining a robust communication with all stakeholders

    C. Keeping a positive relationship with all stakeholders

    D. Establishing a good coordination among stakeholders

20. You are in the process of evaluating and monitoring overall stakeholder relationships and ensuring stakeholders' appropriate engagement in the project by adjusting plans and strategies as required. The work performance data that is an input to this Control Stakeholder Engagement process usually comes from:

    A. Validate Scope

    B. Perform Integrated Change Control

    C. Monitor and Control Project Work

    D. Direct and Manage Project Work

21. A stakeholder register includes all of the following items EXCEPT:

    A. Stakeholder classification: Internal/external, neutral/resistor/supporter, and others.

    B. Identification information: Name, title, location, organization, role in the project, position, and contact information.

    C. Assessment information: Key requirements and expectations, potential impact, importance, and influence on the project.

    D. Strategies: The strategies to interact with stakeholders.

Project Stakeholder Management Answers

1. **A:** The root cause of the significant number of changes in the project is that some of the key stakeholders were not identified, and their requirements were not captured. These missing stakeholders have submitted several change requests to accommodate their needs. Nothing in this scenario suggests that the project manager does not have the required project management training and experience. A vigorous change control board will be efficiently evaluating the change requests to approve or reject them, but they cannot really help with the number of changes a project will have.

2. **D:** The issue log is an important input to the Monitor Stakeholder Management process as a project document. An issue is an obstacle that threatens project progress and can block the team from achieving its goals. An issue log is a written log document to record issues that require solutions.

3. **B:** The stakeholder register is an input to the Plan Stakeholder Management process as a project document.

4. **A:** Interpersonal skills are a crucial tool & technique used in the Manage Stakeholder Engagement process.

5. **C:** Stakeholders can be identified throughout the project management process groups of initiating, planning, executing, monitoring & controlling, and closing. In order to determine the requirements and expectations of the stakeholders, they should be identified and should be involved at the beginning of the project as much as possible.

    If all the stakeholders' needs and requirements are not taken into consideration prior to plan finalization, the results may be very expensive changes or dissatisfaction later in the project.

6. **D:** The project manager is responsible for managing stakeholder expectations.

7. **D:** The project manager simply cannot remove the stakeholder from the stakeholder list since he has a stake in the project. It will be best to involve this stakeholder in the project as early as possible and work closely with him throughout the project to understand his requirements and expectations and gain his constructive support.

8. **A:** Informal verbal communication by setting up a meeting with these two stakeholders and discussing their concerns would be the best approach here. Reporting to the sponsor without much detail about these two stakeholders will not solve any real problem. Since not all stakeholders have concerns, setting up a question-and-answer session about the project with all the stakeholders will not be appropriate. Sending an official e-mail to the stakeholders asking them to submit any query on the project in writing to the project manager will most probably estrange them.

9. **B:** The project manager cannot simply remove the stakeholder from the stakeholder list since he has a stake in the project. It will be best to involve this stakeholder in the project as early as possible and work closely with him throughout the project to understand his requirements and gain his constructive support.

10. **D:** Stakeholders will be able to help the project manager and team members the most in identifying what roles they will play in the project. The project manager will decide how and what kind of contributions stakeholders will make to the project by discussing with team members, the sponsor, and stakeholders. The project manager should evaluate the knowledge and skill sets of stakeholders in order to identify stakeholders' roles and have a discussion with them to make sure that they approve the roles.

11. **C:** As the project was approved and work has begun, the issue should not be a concern anymore. Having further meetings with the stakeholders will be excessive and will not add any real value.

12. **A:** Stakeholder analysis is a tool used to identify and document any actions needed to manage stakeholders.

13. **B:** All these activities typically belong to the Manage Stakeholder Engagement process.

14. **D:** Stakeholder identification will persist throughout the project lifecycle. As the project proceeds through each phase, additional stakeholders may become involved while others will be released from the project. Some stakeholders will be identified during the initiating phase in the project charter, while other stakeholders may only be interested in the end product and will be involved only at the closing phase.

15. **A:** Giving stakeholders extras or gold plating should always be avoided. Gold plating is not the preferred way of meeting and exceeding stakeholder expectations.

16. **C:** Before you take any other step, you should validate the information received from the team member.

17. **D:** The stakeholder register will be used as an input to the Collect Requirements, Plan Scope Management, Plan Risk Management, Identify Risks, Plan Quality Management, and Plan Communications Management processes. It is not an input to the Develop Project Charter, and Perform Integrated Change Control processes.

18. **B:** In order to avoid numerous changes later in the project, you need to identify all stakeholders and their needs as early as possible. Stakeholder analysis will be a more complicated task if there are numerous stakeholders, and an effective way to determine their needs must be identified.

19. **A:** Keeping stakeholders happy and satisfied is the main objective of stakeholder management. Maintaining robust communication, keeping a positive relationship, and establishing good coordination will collectively contribute to achieving stakeholder satisfaction.

20. **D:** All work performance data comes from the executing process group. In this case, work performance data comes as an output of the Direct and Manage Project Work, an executing process.

21. **D:** The strategies to interact with the stakeholders are included in the stakeholder management plan, not in the stakeholder register.

Chapter 15
Examination Content Outline Review and the Mindset

This chapter will be reviewing the PMP examination content outline for exams starting in January 2021, and we will end off by looking at the mindset it takes to pass your PMP exam. The PMP examination content outline is the document made by the project management institute, and it outlines all of the different exam topics that the questions will come from. This study guide has covered all of the content from this outline already, so in this chapter, we will be reviewing each of them individually just to ensure you understand what they are and how to answer questions concerning them.

This chapter should not be read until you have read all the other chapters. As I review each of the bullet points, I will be mentioning terms and processes that you should be familiar with. I will also be providing examination tips throughout.

I recommend that all students download and review the following document from the PMI's website. The document is titled "project management professional examination content outline for January 2021 exam update." If you are having difficulty finding it on their website, just Google the above quotation and you will easily find it.

Examination Content Outline

The examination content outline is broken into three domains, as follows:

Domain	Percentage of Items on Test
I. People	42%
2. Process	50%
3. Business Environment	8%
Total	**100%**

As you will notice, the people domain is worth 42%, processes 50%, and the business environment is just 8%. Half of the examination will be about predictive traditional project management, and the other half will be about agile and hybrid approaches. So, it's important not just to review your PMBOK Guide but also to review all the agile processes, terms, and tools that I have covered in this study guide.

The domains are split into what is known as a task statement and enablers. A task is the responsibility of the project manager within that domain, and the enablers are examples of work that is associated with that particular task. While we are reviewing each of the enablers, keep in mind that there could be more examples that the exam could ask questions on.

Domain 1: People (14 Tasks)

Task 1: Manage Conflict

One of the most fundamental responsibilities of a project manager is managing conflicts between stakeholders on a project. Conflicts can occur between team members, between sponsors and team members, between suppliers and the project manager, and between any combination of stakeholders.

For any conflict, the first thing you want to do is to understand the source and stage of the conflict. Why did the conflict happen? What was the main underlining reason? How did it escalate to this? After you've understood the source of the conflict, the next thing to do would be to analyze the context of the conflict. You would then need to evaluate/recommend/reconcile the appropriate conflict resolution solution.

For example, if there is a conflict between two team members, your first step would be to interpret what was the main cause (source) of this conflict. This would include speaking to the team members and evaluating what exactly is the difference of opinion between them. Once you've evaluated and understood the main source of the conflict, look for solutions that would lead to a win for both sides.

When following the servant leadership role in managing conflicts, it is important to let the team select the appropriate solution while supporting their solution. As a servant leader, do not dictate to them a solution that you think is best as this may not actually be the best solution. Servant leaders are there to support the team, not dictate their every action.

Task 2: Lead a team

Part of being a project manager is about leading the team to complete the objectives of the project. This includes setting a clear vision and mission so the team can clearly understand what this project is about. This will provide direction and improve commitment. They will be better able to understand what this project is about and how it will benefit the organization.

Project Managers always support diversity and inclusion when managing a team. Use tools that are inclusive, not exclusive. Tools such as a whiteboard with markers would be more inclusive than using highly technical software, where everyone is just looking at a computer screen. Try to eliminate silo work where no one shares information, or communicate with each other, try to build an environment where everyone is sharing information and helping each other.

Be a servant leader and support the team. Remove obstacles and impediments that may cause delays or conflicts on your team. Do not micromanage or try to control the team like a dictator. Let the team decide what's best for the project and how to solve issues. This will lead to them feeling like their opinion matters.

Use the appropriate leadership style. Don't try to be autocratic where there is no regard for people's feelings, be more participative. Let all team members play a role, and you should be approachable and welcoming to them. Become more transformational by empowering the team, motivating, and inspiring them.

Set up a system where team members are rewarded for their work and coaching is available. At no point in the project should the team members feel that there is no help available for them. Create a safe environment where team members can have disagreements with no penalties. Disagreements often lead to some of the best solutions and the best work that mankind has ever created.

Understand team members' and stakeholders' influence on the project. The team has a direct impact on the project objectives since they are the one that are actually doing the project work. Their influence will more than likely determine the success of your project. The influence of the customers, sponsor, and functional management will also impact the success of the project. For example, the sponsor may fund the project, and the customers have to actually accept the deliverables. Know what role each of the individual stakeholders will play in your project and be ready to manage their expectations.

Task 3: Support team performance

As the project team starts to work on the project deliverables, it will be up to the project manager to assess how the team is performing. This can include appraising the team's performance against a particular key performance indicator (KPI). This KPI can help to know how much and how quickly work is getting done. By analyzing their performance, you will then be able to support their needs to grow and develop as a team. For example, if you notice that the team members are working very slowly because of a few members needing additional help, then you can coach them or provide the correct training so they could match the performance of the other members.

Always support and recognize team members' growth and development as a project is progressing. Give the correct feedback based on how they are growing. For example, if the team is performing well in completing a lot of work very quickly, then give them positive feedback with rewards. If the team is not performing well, have a discussion with them, and ask them what the reason is and what you can do to help increase their performance. Once you have implemented solutions to help increase their performance, such as more coaching or training, you will then need to verify whether the performance has improved or not.

Task 4: Empower team members and stakeholders

Projects are about people, not tools and materials. In fact, tools and materials don't actually produce deliverables; it's the people working on the project that will utilize these tools and materials in order to make a product or service. This is why it's so important to ensure that you empower your team members and stakeholders so that they can utilize these tools and materials in order to produce the correct products.

We must organize around the team's strengths. Analyze and assess the core strengths of your team, which can include communications skills or the usage of certain tools and processes. Then build and expand on those strengths as much as possible. We must also support the team task accountability. This will ensure that the team understands that they are accountable for the tasks that must get done to complete those particular deliverables.

Another aspect of empowering the team is the ability to bestow different levels of decision-making to the authority of the team. This will make the team feel empowered as they will have the power to make critical decisions about your project. This would follow the principles of a servant leader, as we allow the team to make decisions while supporting those decisions and removing impediments and obstacles from their decision-making process. Always remember, when a team makes a decision, it is usually more practical and implementable than when a manager does it.

Task 5: Ensure team members/stakeholders are adequately trained

A project team that is not adequately trained to complete their task will produce a project that will fail immediately. It's the responsibility of the project manager to ensure that the team members and stakeholders have been provided the correct training in order to build the deliverables correctly and defect-free. Adequate training will also boost the morale of the team members as they will have more confidence in the work that they're doing. This will lead to a reduction of conflict and being able to complete the work on time.

We would first need to determine the required competencies and elements of training the team would need. For example, if the team could be utilizing a certain programming language or set of tools, we would need to ensure that they receive the corresponding training for those programming languages and tools. Then we would look at different training options based on those needs. Training options can range from things such as a self-paced online training to a live instructor-led class. You would need to assess the team to see which one of these would be a better option. You will also need to approach management or the project sponsor to ensure that there are correctly allocated resources (funds) to finance this training. Once the training is done, you should measure the training outcomes. This would include assessing their ability to utilize new tools or processes, taking quizzes or certification exams, or having discussions with them about how the training has helped them on the project.

Task 6: Build a team

All project managers will be responsible for building a team that will fit the needs of the project. One thing I have learned over the many years of doing project management and authoring books on this topic is that the success of the project is directly tied to the project team. Not everyone is suitable for every team, and not every team is suitable for every project.

We need to ensure that when we build a team, we evaluate the stakeholder skills that will be joining the team. This will be done to determine whether their skills are adequate for this particular team. For example, you can't add a network administrator to a team of programmers to help them code applications. We would also need to consistently assess and refresh the team skills to meet the ever-changing needs of the project. One aspect of an agile project is to maintain the same team and not change team members, especially during iteration. Once the project or phase is done, there must be knowledge transfer between different teams, such as the coding team transferring the knowledge to the testing team and the testing team transferring the knowledge to operations. Generally, teams must work together in order to effectively create a product and deliver it to the customer. This will be the responsibility of a project manager.

Task 7: Address and remove impediments, obstacles, and blockers for the team

I have always said project management should be renamed to problem management. As a project manager, one of the main tasks is removing impediments, obstacles, and things that may block the team from functioning at their peak level. You first need to identify the critical impediments, obstacles, and blockers. These things can be caused by a negative stakeholder, delays in getting approval, lack of participation from product owner or customer, missing team members, unwillingness of certain team members to share knowledge, or conflicts between team members.

These impediments can lead to a delay of work and the reduction of quality in the project deliverables. We have to use a network of different resources, including different processes and skills, negotiation tactics, and emotional intelligence, to resolve or remove these impediments. We then have to consistently reassess to ensure that these impediments, obstacles, or blockers have been addressed and removed.

Impediments, obstacles, and blockers will always be presented on a project. When you remove one, another one will show up; it is just the nature of the work. So consistently reassessing and ensuring that these things are solved will be a key responsibility of your job as a project manager.

Task 8: Negotiate project agreements

Negotiating on a project will be one of your key skills. You will negotiate things such as (this is a short list):

- Work listed in the project charter
- Requirements on the project
- Project schedule
- Project budget
- Quality requirements
- Why team members should join your project
- Getting supplies from outside sellers
- Resolving conflicts

As you can see, you will be negotiating many different components of the project, and you will probably be doing this on a daily basis. You must first analyze the bounds of the negotiations for different types of agreements. On many projects, you may not have the power needed in order to complete the negotiations, especially if you're working in a functional organization. On agile projects, maybe the team members will be more involved, and you will be negotiating with outside sellers. You will also need to assess the different priorities and objectives when negotiating to ensure that the project gets what's best for that project. Project agreements are generally the contract between the project management and team and the customers. You have to ensure that the objectives of this project agreement are suitable for the needs of the project and would lead to the best outcome. This will include things such as reviewing the agreement terms and conditions to ensure the team is adequate for the project, and confirming that the customers are willing to participate if it's an agile project. You should be sure to participate in these agreement negotiations to ensure that the terms of these agreements match the objectives of the project and the team.

Task 9: Collaborate with stakeholders

On any project, collaboration will be one of its key indicators of success. Collaboration is going to be about the engagement of the different types of stakeholders on the project. You need to ensure that stakeholders are actively engaged in the project. For example, have the product owner prioritize the product backlog or have the customers assess the product increment on an agile project. Collaboration makes people feel that they are included in the project, and that their opinions actually matter.

Aligning the stakeholders' needs with their expectations and the project objectives will also be a key responsibility in this task. Stakeholders should have a clear expectation of what this project will deliver and how it will be done. For example, the customers should have a clear understanding of what the graphical interface would look like when the application is complete. This can be done with prototypes and also screen mockups so that everyone's expectations are the same.

This will help to build trust between the stakeholders on the project because now everyone that is impacted by this project will have a clear understanding of what this project will deliver once complete.

Task 10: Build shared understanding

As with the previous tasks of collaborating with stakeholders, this task will look to build a shared understanding between stakeholders. Whenever there are conflicts or issues on a project, you have to break down the situation and help to identify the main root causes of the problem. It could be something as simple as the customers expecting an application to have a particular report and the end product did not. It could also be something major such as the project team not understanding certain regulatory guidelines and implementing the wrong requirements leading the project to fail its regulatory requirements.

When building understanding, you should survey all necessary parties to ensure consensus is met, and that everyone understands what this project will deliver and how it will deliver. This is especially important during conflict management; this way, all parties in a conflict can understand what the resolution methods are, and they can all agree on it. Always investigate potential misunderstandings, even if it may be something small. While managing a project, if you feel that there may be a misunderstanding between stakeholders, investigate right away to ensure that it is cleared up and resolved. Fixing problems earlier will always lead to a better result than if the problem is left to escalate.

Task 11: Engage and support virtual teams

In today's digitally connected world, it is not uncommon for teams to be completely virtual. Now more than ever, you may find yourself working on a virtual team. Many team members can be working at home or in specific locations scattered across the world. This would make the use of technology vital to the success of the team. Technology can act as one of the biggest obstacles to communication but can also be one of your greatest assets when it comes to communication. A virtual team can lead to a project that runs on a 24-hour schedule with a widely diversified set of skills and cultures.

The first thing you need to do is examine the needs of your virtual team members. This can include the environment, geography, or culture. For example, in certain cultures, they will celebrate holidays and take specific days off on a project. Understanding the needs of language skills and scheduling on virtual teams and global projects will be critical. For example, team members may have to wake up at 2 AM in the morning to have conference calls with teams that are in other parts of the world.

You should investigate alternative communication tools such as a virtual co-location for virtual team engagement. This can include the use of online digital meetings such as using Zoom live meetings throughout the day on a project, the usage of digital whiteboards and VOIP communications. Also, the use of camera sharing tools and utilities and instant messaging software.

In short, you need to continuously evaluate the effectiveness of these different virtual tools to ensure that it is effective for your team. If you find your team is not collaborating efficiently, you may need to change the tools or conduct training on how best to use these tools to simulate a face-to-face, nonvirtual team.

Task 12: Ground rules

A project team should always have ground rules. Ground rules are defined in the team charter we created in the "project resource management" chapter. Ground rules should be set up early in the project to communicate the organization principles with the team and external stakeholders. Ground rules can be how we conduct meetings, for example, no use of cell phones during meetings, no talking over each other, respecting each other's opinions, no foul language, and no personal insults. You need to establish an environment that fosters adherence to these ground rules. This can include having the team and stakeholders sign an agreement that outlines these rules. You will also have to manage and rectify ground rules violations. Ground rules violation penalties can be things such as having a discussion with that particular stakeholder or even removal from the project team if the violation is serious enough, such as personal or racial insults to other members.

Task 13: Mentor relevant stakeholders

Mentorship is the process in which you will help to guide a less experienced or less knowledgeable person to a particular situation. On a project, you will have to mentor different stakeholders on how certain processes should be followed or the use of certain tools. You will have to ensure that you allocate the right time to mentoring. This can include clearing up your schedule to allocate time to the stakeholder that needs your mentoring.

When you find team members are not performing well, this may be an opportunity for you to act as a mentor. For example, if you see a team member incorrectly utilizing a communication tool such as a digital whiteboard, you should engage that team member and guide them through the process of how to efficiently use it to communicate with the other team members. Mentoring your team and keeping them engaged will not only enable them to work more effectively but also to have more trust and faith in you as the project manager.

Task 14: Promote team performance through the application of emotional intelligence

Emotional intelligence, as we covered in the chapter "project resource management," is a skill that all project managers must have in order to understand the needs and feelings of not just yourself but others around you. This will help you to assess the behavior of not just yourself but also the different team members and stakeholders on your project. You can look for personality indicators such as their tone of voice or facial expression to understand their feeling towards a particular requirement or solution to a problem. As the project manager, you will also be using these personality indicators to adjust your own emotional response to stakeholders. For example, if you notice a stakeholder is becoming irritated and hostile, you will then need to adjust your demeanor and responses to de-escalate the situation and respond in a positive manner to calm them down and come up with a solution that benefits the project. Expect to see quite a few questions on your exam about emotional intelligence and review this section in the "project resource management" chapter.

Domain 2: Process (17 Tasks)

Task 1: Execute project with the urgency required to deliver business value

Once planning has been completed on a project, the next step is to execute the project work in order to produce the deliverables for the customers. On a traditional project, execution will be done to build the entire deliverable in that phase or project all at once. On an agile project, execution is done multiple times as the product is getting delivered incrementally. A project manager should always assess if there are opportunities to deliver the product incrementally to maximize the value for your stakeholders.

As the team is building the deliverables, you should examine the business value throughout the project. Always ask yourself, is this project still delivering the value that the customers were expecting? This can be done by getting feedback from the customers through the use of iteration review meetings or prototyping. Also consider the use of a minimum viable product. While this is an agile concept, it could be used in traditional or hybrid projects to give the customer a product that may have minimal functionality but that allows them to start using the product faster than sooner. Minimum viable products allow the customer to give instant feedback and start realizing value immediately.

Task 2: Manage communications

All project managers should analyze the communication needs of all stakeholders. We covered this when we did the process of "plan communications management." You would need to analyze what your stakeholders' desired communication methods are, how often they would like to be receive communications, and what level of detail they would like in your communications. For example, upon the completion of your stakeholder communication analysis, you have determined that the project sponsor Bob would like to have a detailed status report about the project every Friday afternoon by 2 PM.

When asked how the project is progressing, you will need to effectively update and inform stakeholders about the overall progress of the project. This can mean distributing the work performance reports to the correct stakeholders. You will also need to confirm that the communication you send to the stakeholders is understood by them, and feedback is received from them. Communications should always be customized to the stakeholders' level of understanding and the level of detail they are requesting. For example, don't give out a detailed technical report to a senior manager on a software development project as they may not be able to understand the technical detail, and it would be a waste of time for them to review it. Customize the communication to the individual stakeholders so that communications are effective and efficient.

Task 3: Assess and manage risks

In the chapter "project risk management," we went through all of the different processes of identifying, assessing, and responding to risk. It will be very important for a project manager to assess risk early and often and come up with responses that adequately suppress or remove the risks.

It is important to understand that risk changes on a daily basis, and iteratively assessing and prioritizing risks will need to be done on a regular schedule. The assessment of and responding to risks should not be a one-time thing; instead, it should be an ongoing process and will not be done until the project is actually complete. Every day we wake up, there is a new risk in this world that can affect our personal lives and project, and as a project manager, we must be aware of these risks and respond accordingly.

Task 4: Engage Stakeholders

In the chapter "project stakeholder management," we went through the processes of identifying, analyzing, and engaging stakeholders. As early as possible in a project, we should identify who the stakeholders are and what their influence and impact on this project is. We can create things such as a power interest grid to help us determine these requirements. We should also categorize stakeholders based on their potential influence or impact on the project. Then we should engage them in these categories. For example, your project sponsor category should include engagements, such as meetings on a periodic basis to keep them up-to-date on the status of the project. You should also develop, execute, and validate the different engagement methods that you're doing on the project.

No project will ever be successful if stakeholders are not actively engaged in participating in the project. As the project manager, it is your responsibility to ensure that this is done. Analyzing their needs and creating methods to actively engage them is a key task here. Stakeholders should always feel welcomed and excited about the project. This can be done with the correct engagement strategies. These strategies can include periodic meetings, phone calls, one-on-one discussions, and product reviews.

Task 5: Plan and manage budget and resources

In the chapter "project cost management," we covered all the necessary activities you will need to create a project, get it approved, and manage the project budget. One fundamental aspect of the role of the project managers is to manage the project budget. Keeping a project within a budget will be a key indicator of how successful that project was.

One key aspect of this is ensuring that the budget is estimated correctly and is based on the scope of the work in previous lessons learned from past projects. This will ensure the estimates are actually accurate and will reflect the work that is about to get done. You should also anticipate any other future budget challenges by including additional reserves within the project for unanticipated risks. You will need to also monitor the budget as the work is getting done to ensure that the project is still within budget, and if not, to adjust the budget as needed. For example, if you notice that your CPI is .9 (10% over budget), you will need to plan accordingly or get more funds in order to complete your project within budget.

Task 6: Plan and manage schedule

In the chapter "project schedule management," we covered all the necessary activities for you to create, get approved, and manage a project schedule. All project managers will have to take certain steps in order to ensure that the project is completed on time. Project schedule management will be a key indicator of the success of the project, just like budgeting and scope.

You will need to ensure that the estimate for the project task is done correctly and accurately. On a traditional project, that would mean estimating the activities accurately, and on an agile project, it is assigning the correct story points. Estimating time will utilize benchmarks from previous projects and historical data. This will lead to more accurate estimates. Different projects may also have different schedule methodology that they would follow. For example, a construction project to build a new skyscraper would utilize a different scheduling method and tools than a software development project. As a project manager, you need to know what schedule method to use to best suit the project needs. You also modify the schedule needed in order to meet this methodology. While the project is getting done, the project manager will also need to coordinate with other projects and operations to ensure that adequate resources are available to complete the project within its schedule.

Task 7: Plan and manage quality of products/deliverables

In the chapter "project quality management," we reviewed all the necessary processes you should know for your exam in terms of quality standards, processes, and terms. Any project that is completed with low-quality deliverables will fail in its overall objectives. It is important for the project manager to determine what quality standards will be required for the project deliverables and how they should be met. The project manager should also recommend options for improvement in the overall quality of the deliverables as it's being built. This can include looking for quality gaps while utilizing tools such as an Ishikawa diagram or Pareto chart to help understand things that can cause defects that lead to a reduction in quality.

It is also vital to continuously survey the project deliverables for the quality requirements. This is usually done when the deliverables are built and quality is inspected. These inspections occur in the process of control quality on a traditional project, and it is done in the iteration review meeting on an agile project. If the customers find any type of quality defects, they will alert the project manager and team to correct them. This will lead to quality defects being detected early and fixed.

Task 8: Plan and manage scope

In the chapter "project scope management," we covered all the necessary processes you will need to know for your exam when it comes to gathering requirements, defining the scope, creating the WBS, and monitoring and controlling the project scope. Scope management is something that a project manager will do on a daily basis. The project is about completing the work listed in the scope. On a traditional project, the scope will generally be listed in the work breakdown structure and the scope statement, while an agile project will have the requirements listed in the product backlog.

Whether it is an agile or traditional project, the project manager will have to ensure that the work completed on a daily basis is being validated as part of the project scope. Work that is getting done outside of the scope would be referred to as scope creep and should be prevented as much as possible. If scope creep is detected, the project manager may need to implement a change request in order to incorporate that new work or remove it. Keep in mind, on an agile project, any new changes will be added to the product backlog without a strenuous change management process, but it will need to be prioritized by the product owner before getting developed.

Task 9: Integrate project planning activities

In the chapter "project integration management," we covered all the necessary activities the project manager will need to do to integrate and consolidate the various project phases and plans. The role of the project manager is to be an integrator. A project will have many different components, such as schedule, budget, scope, quality requirements, people, processes, and many plans. The project manager can be required to integrate all of these different components across many different phases in the project to ensure it is completed successfully.

This can include the consolidation of different projects/phases and plans. Assessing how the different project plans form dependencies upon each other and continuously assessing whether the project is delivering value to the customer. The project will produce a lot of data, such as timely completion of individual activities or cost factors that will need to be collected and consolidated into reports. It's based on these reports that the project decisions can be made. If the data is gathered incorrectly, decisions could be made incorrectly.

Task 10: Manage project changes

Changes to the project requirements are inevitable. Over my 20+ years of project management, I have never worked on a project that didn't have changes after the plan was approved. As a project manager, you should expect changes and have a procedure to handle them. A good project manager will anticipate and embrace the need for changes in the project. Keep in mind that when customers are asking for changes, it shows that they care about the end product and they want to be involved. I would be seriously concerned about the success of a project if my customers were not asking for changes, since it may show they are no longer interested. Keep in mind that the way changes are handled in a traditional project is different than it is in an agile project. The project manager must come up with a strategy to handle changes according to the methodology that is being used on the project.

On a traditional project, you must have a change management procedure where customers are able to submit a change request, and where change requests are assessed by the change control board before they're approved or denied. Any changes to any of the documents in the project management plan will need to have approved change requests.

On an agile project, you can anticipate and embrace changes more easily than you would on a traditional project. Any time someone wants to add a requirement, it is generally just added to the product backlog and prioritized by the product owner.

Every project will have to have some kind of change management methodology and processes. Both traditional and agile projects utilize a methodology that should be followed by all stakeholders. Project managers should also determine the right responses to these changes as they are being made on the project. This can include submitting it to the change control board or reviewing it with the product owner.

Task 11: Plan and manage procurement

In the chapter "project procurement management," we reviewed all different types of contracts and processes you will need to know to pass your exam on the status. Almost all projects will utilize some kind of outside supplier in order to finish the project work. This can be something large as buying steel in order to construct a building or purchasing software to help program an application. The project managers should anticipate this and be ready to manage it.

The project manager should define what resources are needed from outside of the project and then communicate these resource requirements to potential suppliers. After this, a contract will be required in order to purchase these outside products and services. Once the outside products and services have arrived, the project manager will need to create a procurement strategy in order to correctly utilize these additional resources in a method that can create value for the project.

Task 12: Manage project artifacts

Project artifacts are usually documents related to the project. Examples of this can include the project charter, business case, requirements, and stakeholder analysis. Artifacts are generally living documents that are formally updated when changes to the scope are made.

You will need to determine the requirements such as what, when, where, and who, for managing these different artifacts. For example, what is the need for a project charter, and when would it be done. The project manager will also have to validate that the information in these project artifacts is kept up-to-date and is accessible to all stakeholders. This can be done by utilizing a project information management system (PMIS) that would allow stakeholders continuous access to these artifacts. Continuously assessing the effectiveness of these project artifacts will also be a key task here. As the project is changing, these artifacts may become outdated and not truly reflect the current environment of the project.

Task 13: Determine appropriate project methodology/methods and practices

In today's environment, with so many different project management methodologies, such as predictive, agile, or hybrid, choosing one over the other is becoming increasingly complex. As a project manager, you will need to select which one of these methods worked in what parts of the project. There are certain projects where traditional will be applied throughout, and other projects where a hybrid or agile approach may be applied throughout. You will have to assess the project needs and complexity in order to determine what methodology will work. For example, in a highly regulated project such as constructing a skyscraper, a traditional method may be more applicable, while a software development project with intangible results and with fewer regulations could use an agile method.

The project manager will also have to recommend an execution strategy, i.e., how the project will be financed or contracted. On your exam, it is also important to understand that PMI prefers the use of iterative, incremental practices throughout your project lifecycle. This can include conducting lessons learned throughout the project, engaging your stakeholders, and conducting a risk assessment as the project is progressing.

Task 14: Establish project governance structure

Project governance is a structure that shows how the project is to be managed. They include the rules and responsibilities people will need to follow throughout the entire project. Governance changes by organization, and it will never be the same between two companies. Every company has a different reporting structure and methods of management. It will be important for the project manager to understand how the organization conducts governance and then to determine the appropriate governance for the project.

Project governance should also help to determine and define escalation paths and thresholds. Escalation paths are how issues can be escalated up the project management ladder and how they can be resolved. Thresholds are specific points that, if met, can indicate a potential issue on the project or success. These escalation paths and thresholds should be defined as all stakeholders having a clear understanding of how to manage this project.

Task 15: Manage project issues

A project issue is something that may have a negative impact on a project. A quick reminder; a risk is something that has not happened yet; if it does occur and impacts the project negatively, it becomes an issue, so an issue is a materialized negative risk. The project manager must recognize when risks become issues so the responses can be implemented quickly to minimize their impact. As part of risk management, the project manager should have already come up with responses to these particular issues. Attacking the issue with optimal action will help to achieve the project's success. This includes involving the project team in the decision-making on how to fix issues, and gaining consensus among stakeholders. Collaboration with all relevant stakeholders will be a key task in resolving any issue quickly and efficiently.

Task 16: Ensure knowledge transfer for project continuity

When the phases and the entire project is done, there will need to be a procedure to conduct knowledge transfer between teams. For example, when the programming team has finished developing the application, they would have to transfer the knowledge that they learned about the application to the testing team. This will help ensure that the tests are done correctly. The project manager should discuss these responsibilities with the teams on the project. This will help them to document any type of user defects that the other teams may experience while deploying or testing a deliverable. This will also help to outline the expectations in the working environment for the supporting teams. As a project manager, you have to ensure and confirm that knowledge transfer is done between the different teams within the organization.

Task 17: Plan and manage project/phase closure or transitions

At the end of every project, there must be some kind of formal closure of that project and the transition of that deliverable to operations. This would occur in both traditional and agile projects. The project manager would have to determine the criteria needed to successfully close the project or phase. This would include meeting certain requirements in certain inspections. The project manager should also validate the readiness for the transition between phases of the project. One question the project manager will ask is: is this deliverable ready for operations? The project manager will work with the project team and the customers to ensure that the deliverables are ready for transition.

Once a project or phase is finished, the project manager will have to ensure that a final lesson learned is completed, all procurement contracts are closed, all project expenses are paid, and that all resources tied to the project are released. These procedures will help future projects within the organization. For example, knowledge transfers can occur between one project and future projects within the business.

Domain 3: Business Environment— (4 Tasks)

In the business environment domain, the project manager should be knowledgeable about the organization where the project will be taking place. This would include understanding how that business is governed, government regulations it follows, the technology it utilizes, custom processes that it has created, and its mission. These things will have a drastic impact on how a project is initiated and when it closes. These four tasks will examine how compliance should be monitored, how value should be understood, and how to manage external business changes and organizational changes.

Task 1: Plan and manage project compliance

Most projects in large and small companies have to follow some kind of regulatory compliance that will need to be implemented in the project. For example, health and safety requirements will need to be implemented when building a large skyscraper. Another example would be financial regulatory requirements that need to be implemented in systems that produce financial reports for publicly traded companies.

When it comes to regulatory compliance, these requirements are not optional and must be understood from the very start of the project so that they can be implemented as part of the project's requirements. The project manager may work with the organization's legal department or regulatory departments in order to understand what these requirements are for a particular project. Compliance may be classified into different categories. These categories could be things such as regulatory compliance, security, or health and safety. Once again, they would need to be identified early in the project.

During planning, the project manager should determine potential threats to these compliances and implement responses to ensure that if these threats do materialize, they respond to it quickly and effectively. Threats such as scope creep can lead to not meeting financial regulatory controls due to work added that was not authorized. The project manager should add these threats to the risk register and have a valid risk response for them.

The project manager will also look at the consequences of not meeting these compliances. Consequences can be financial penalties or termination of a project. Having responses in place will cause actions to be taken early in case there is noncompliance and hopefully reduces the consequences.

When the project is executed, it will be the project manager's task to ensure that the project is in compliance with regulations such as safety regulations. For example, when construction workers are building a 50 story-skyscraper, they will need to wear a safety harness and follow certain procedures to be safe. The health and safety of the team should be something on the minds of all project managers, especially on construction projects where human life may be at risk. Also, if the safety regulations are not met, random inspection by the local county officials can lead to fines against the project.

As someone who has worked on many projects in the education and IT industry, I have always tried to research the different laws and regulations that apply to the project that I'm working on. There were times projects had to be terminated early or put on pause due to regulations not being met or waiting for approval from regulators. This is just the nature of how projects are conducted today in the US. A project manager needs to be familiar with these types of project compliance.

Task 2: Evaluate and deliver project benefits and value

Projects are about delivering value to their stakeholders. Value can come in terms of customer satisfaction, increased revenue, decreased expenses, or everything in combination. Project managers must investigate and ensure that the values are identified early in the project, such as during initiating, so all stakeholders have a thorough understanding of what benefits this project will deliver when it's completed. For example, it is critical on a software development project for the main value to be identified early before the work on the project actually starts. For example, perhaps this particular software being developed will lower the project's logistic costs by 30% over a 12-month period.

It will be important for the project manager to document and review the benefits realization managed in the benefits management plan with the project sponsor to ensure benefits are documented. This will ensure that when the project is completed, the output of the project can be measured against what was originally documented. The project manager will also need to create assistance to help verify these benefits. For example, if one of the benefits was to increase revenue by 10% because the new website allows a faster checkout, then the project manager should verify that the checkout function is faster than what they currently have.

The project manager will also evaluate different delivery options to demonstrate value to the stakeholder. For stakeholders to realize the benefit, they should be able to visually see it and experience it. This can be done through the use of prototyping or actual product use. Generally, user acceptance testing in software development will do this. Stakeholders should be informed of the value gained during the execution of the project. This can be done by using shorter iterations and building products in increments to get more feedback.

Task 3: Evaluate and address external business environment changes for impact on scope

In today's technology world, things change very quickly. New technology can cause disruptions in markets almost overnight. For example, the release of a new type of virtual conferencing software can change the way teams communicate. Sometimes these external changes can lead to projects being more efficient, but sometimes, these changes can also have a drastic impact on the project.

External business changes can be classified as regulations, technology, geopolitical, or changes in the organization of the market they do business in. For example, without much notice, a new regulation could get passed by the local government that could cause delays or lead to an unexpected expense. This would cause the project to be behind schedule or over budget. It can also cause the project to be completely terminated if it's not in compliance with new government regulations.

As a project manager, you need to survey all the different changes and stay updated with the external environment around which a project operates. This can be done by following local news bulletin boards or government websites to assess and validate any new kind of regulations. You can also use social media or technology message boards to learn the different technologies that can impact your project positively and negatively.

Once these changes are identified, you may need to assess and prioritize the impact on the project scope and recommend options on how to get these changes implemented. Keep in mind these changes on a traditional project would need to follow the change management procedures and be assessed and approved by the change control board. On agile projects, these new changes may just be added to the product backlog to be prioritized by the product owner.

Task 4: Support organizational change

A famous quote about change:

"It is not the strongest or the most intelligent who will survive but those who can best manage change."

-Charles Darwin

People always ask me what is the single most predictive factor for an organization to survive the test of time. My answer has always been the same, its ability to change. For an organization to change and meet its ever-changing customer requirements, it will have to build a culture that supports, embraces, and drives changes. Organizations should not look to change their products and services, rather, they should look to change the people within the organization who will change the products and services for the better. I'm not saying to change people by releasing them; I'm saying changing their skill set through education and training.

The organization's management will have to build a culture that supports changes within its staff. As a project manager, you should be aware of what different organizational changes can affect the project and how you should respond. You will have to determine the correct actions to meet those changes. For example, an organization in one industry may decide to completely change its focus and move to another industry, such as a yogurt producing company deciding to only sell cheese. This can cause projects to be terminated or refocused. A good project manager will be able to evaluate the impact of organizational changes and determine the right actions. This should be done from the start, middle, or even towards the end of a project.

The Project Management Mindset

In this section, I am going to be reviewing a few different things the project manager should always keep in mind when managing traditional, agile, or hybrid projects. This mindset will help you to answer your exam questions. Always keep these things in the back of your mind, and no matter what situation is presented to you on the exam, and be sure to remember the principles I'm about to outline. Also, many of these principles will be shared between agile and traditional projects.

On a traditional project, the mindset will include these principles:

- Identification and analysis of stakeholders is something that is done throughout the project, not just at the beginning.

- Always follow a plan and never allow changes to the plan without an approved change request.

- Any stakeholder that wants to change any component of the project management plan will need to submit a change request.

- All change requests will need to be reviewed and assessed.

- Never take action without first creating a plan.

- Consult with the project team before making decisions, as they will have a more practical approach.

- Your final decision should always benefit the objectives of the project. For example, if there are conflicting methods on how to complete a particular task, then choose the method that would deliver the most value to the project outcome.

- Try to use tools that are inclusive such as a whiteboard with a marker versus complex software.

- All scope changes should be assessed on how it will impact all other parts of the project, including schedule, cost, quality, resources, communications, risk, procurement, and stakeholders' engagement.

- When conducting estimation, use a bottom-up approach and not a top-down. This will lead to more correct estimates but will require more work.

- Your main job is to be an integrator of the many different components within a project. Do not concentrate your time and efforts on one particular thing while ignoring others.

- Update the lesson learned register throughout the entire project. This way, it can be transferred to future projects in the organization.

- When closing the project, ensure all bills are paid off and resources are released.

- Projects that are terminated early still need to be closed formally through the close project or phase process.

- The best people to create a work breakdown structure are the project team.

- The best people to determine what a particular activity may cause are also the project team since they will have the most knowledge about the work.

- Quality requirements should be defined early in the project and be checked often to ensure they're getting done.

- The customers are the best people to check a deliverable for scope and quality requirements being met as they are the ones that will actually use the product.

- Before resolving a conflict between team members, be sure to understand the source of the conflict.

- Conflicts between team members should always be resolved for the benefit of the project objectives, not to satisfy one member over another.

- Before communications are sent out to stakeholders, be sure to analyze their needs and determine what they're looking for, how often, what method they would like it to be delivered, and who will deliver it to them.

- Utilize the skills of emotional intelligence to analyze your own feelings and those around you to respond to stakeholders' needs and requirements. Emotional intelligence allows you to solve problems more quickly and effectively.

- Identify as much risk as possible as early as possible on a project. All identified risks should be documented in the risk register, along with their corresponding risk responses.

- A negative risk is known as a threat, while a positive risk is known as an opportunity. Be sure to identify and document responses to both.

- When selecting a contract to use on a project with potential sellers, always use a contract that is mutually beneficial to both the seller and the buyer.

- Engage stakeholders often and regularly. Use things such as meetings, one-on-one conversations, phone calls, and presentations to engage them.

- When engaging your stakeholders, ensure they understand the communications that they are receiving. Tailor your communications to individual stakeholder needs.

On an agile project, the mindset will include these principles:

- Be a servant leader to the team at all times. This includes empowering them and removing any impediments. Give them the tools they need to succeed while staying out of their way.

- The product owner will document features and prioritize them in the product backlog.

- Only the product owner can prioritize the features in the product backlog. If the product owner refuses to do so because they feel all of them are valuable, then you must train them on the benefits of doing so. DO NOT prioritize the features yourself; this is the job of the product owner.

- Engage the customers as much as possible. This is usually done in the iteration review meeting with the customers. The customers will have an opportunity to analyze the completed increment while providing feedback.

- Ensure a retrospective is done at the end of each iteration, so lessons learned during that iteration can be applied to the next one.

- Utilize tools that are low-tech, high-touch throughout the project.

- Always opt for a colocation over any other type of environment.

- Face-to-face communication with a whiteboard and markers is the best form of communication.

- Provide agile teams with lots of wall space so they can write on them and use sticky notes.

- Information should always be radiated through the use of large charts and graphs, such as the use of a burnup or burndown chart.

- Any problem that occurs on a project should be resolved by the project team. Always let the project team choose a solution while coaching and supporting their solutions.

- Provide a safe environment for disagreements. Do not punish anyone for having a difference of opinion. Understand that conflict is a positive step and an opportunity to learn.

- Try to limit the work in progress through the use of the Kanban. Kanban boards should be displayed either on a large whiteboard or, less ideally, on a large monitor.

- Consistently communicate and re-communicate the project vision to the team.

- Understand the needs of your team members and find out what may motivate them and what de-motivates them.

- Balance the needs of the project stakeholders and the team.

- Make sure people understand what failure and success will look like on the project. This will lead to functional accountability. People should be proud when accomplishments are made, but they should also be able to face failure. This would allow them to examine why something fails and learn from it.

- Be a central figure to the team, not a dictator.

- Have good ethical values, do not lie to the team, or create false hopes. This will lead to mistrust and disagreements between you and the team.

- Always ensure that the work was completed by doing a retrospective at the end.

- Utilize feedback loops. Feedback loops occur when you take what you've learned from one task and apply it to your next task to improve the results.

As you will notice, a few of these principles overlap between traditional and agile projects. For example, the engagement of stakeholders should be done on any project you're working on. If you notice, I do not have a list for hybrid projects since a hybrid project can utilize both of these lists. If a hybrid project utilizes traditional project management for one part and agile for another part, then you would use principles from both lists to complete that project.

Reread these lessons a few times and think about each of these bullet points and make sure that you understand them, not just memorize them. If you do not understand some of these, review this study guide again to ensure that everything makes sense to you. This will be key to passing your exam on the first try.

Professional Responsibility

On this exam, you might encounter questions about ethics and professional responsibility. PMI Code of Ethics and Professional Conduct is generally easy to understand. It is about doing the right thing. This section will give you some tips in case you encounter any questions about this topic. I have also included some questions about this topic at the end of the section.

Our responsibility as project managers will force us to take ownership of our decisions, admit our mistakes, and be responsible for our decisions and actions. As a project manager, you must make decisions based on the best interests of society, public safety, and the environment. It is not advisable to undertake a project that will work against the interests of the public.

Always tell the truth no matter the outcome. Although this may sound obvious, it could become complex when we dig deep. Sometimes telling the truth can be a very hard thing to do, because it could cause you to lose your job. For example, the project team tells you it will take 10 days to complete the project, but the sponsor asks you to tell the customer 6 days. What do you tell the customer? The truth: 10 days. That answer might get you fired, but you know that it is the right thing to do. Also, you should always report the project's status honestly, even if it makes the stakeholders upset.

Follow the laws of the country you are in. Never do anything that is against a country's law. National law can be tough on a project, but must be followed diligently. Always be respectful of another country's culture or customs. For example, if you have to wait for an inspection in order to proceed on the project, then wait, even if it means extending the project by a few months. If you also feel that a project might be against the laws of the country, don't do it. If you feel that a project could harm society, public safety, or the environment, don't do it.

Gifts and donations are not to be accepted unless it is a custom or a law of the country. While getting a gift at the start or end of a project may sound good, it can cause you to lose your integrity if you decide to receive the gift. For example, you know that if you finish the project more quickly, you will get a bonus of $10,000. Therefore you skip the quality inspections, which is a bad idea! The only time a gift might be acceptable is if it is a custom in that country.

Conflicts of interest must be reported to higher management. This is very important to understand. If you feel a conflict of interest might be present, you must report this to either senior management or the sponsor. For example, you are bidding for a project at a company where your best friend works; what do you do? The correct answer would be to alert your management about this and maybe ask to be released from the project because it would be unethical for you to be biased in favor of one of the vendors.

If you feel you might need to get permission to use something, get it, or don't use it. This can include copyrighted works or licenses. For example, you would like to use a song in your presentation for the customer's project, but you are not sure if you can. The best thing to do would be to contact the song's publisher and obtain permission to use it. If you cannot do that in time, then avoid using the song.

Any misrepresentation of PMI must be reported to PMI. Being PMP certified means, you agree to the code of ethics and that you will work with PMI. Any time you observe something that could harm PMI, you need to report it to PMI. For example, what would you do if you find out that someone is claiming to be PMP certified when you know for sure he/she is not? You must report this person to PMI.

Some tips on answering these questions correctly:

- Be honest at all times.

- Follow the local laws.

- Do not worry about losing your job. Just do the right thing.

- Do not accept gifts.

- Ensure you get permission to use other people's works.

- Always report the actual status of the project.

Things to Memorize

Now that you finished reading the entire book, this chapter will give you a few tips about what to memorize and how to approach the exam questions. These tips have helped the thousands of students that I have taught over the last 10 years to pass the PMP exam.

Formulas for the exam:

Term	Formula
Budget at Completion (BAC)	None, just the original budget.
Planned Value (PV)	PV= Planned % Complete x BAC
Earned Value (EV)	EV= Actual % Complete X BAC
Actual Cost (AC)	None, total amount already spent
Cost Variance (CV)	CV = EV - AC
Cost Performance Index (CPI)	CPI = EV / AC
Schedule Variance (SV)	SV = EV - PV
Schedule Performance Index (SPI)	SPI = EV / PV
Estimate at Completion (EAC)	EAC = BAC / CPI
Estimate to Completion (ETC)	ETC = EAC - AC
Variance at Completion (VAC)	VAC = BAC - EAC
To-Complete Performance Index (TCPI)	TCPI = (BAC – EV) / (BAC – AC)
PERT – Beta	$\dfrac{(Optimistic + 4*Realistic + Pessimistic)}{6}$
PERT - Standard Deviation	(Pessimistic – Optimistic)/6
PERT - Triangular Distribution:	$\dfrac{(Optimistic + Realistic + Pessimistic)}{3}$
Communications Channels	N(N-1)/2

49 Project Management Processes[1]				
Knowledge Areas	Process Groups				
	Initiating (2)	Planning (24)	Executing (10)	Monitoring & Controlling (12)	Closing (1)
Integration Management (7)	Develop Project Charter	Develop Project Management Plan	Direct & Manage Project Work Manage Project Knowledge	Monitor and Control Project Work Perform Integrated Change Control	Close Project or Phase
Scope Management (6)		Plan Scope Management Collect Requirements Define Scope Create WBS		Validate Scope Control Scope	
Schedule Management (6)		Plan Schedule Management Define Activities Sequence Activities Estimate Activity Durations Develop Schedule		Control Schedule	
Cost Management (4)		Plan Cost Management Estimate Costs Determine Budget		Control Costs	
Quality Management (3)		Plan Quality Management	Manage Quality	Control Quality	
Resource Management (6)		Plan Resource Management Estimate Activity Resources	Acquire Resources Develop Team Manage Team	Control Resources	
Communication Management (3)		Plan Communications Management	Manage Communications	Monitor Communications	
Risk Management (7)		Plan Risk Management Identify Risks Perform Qualitative Risk Analysis Perform Quantitative Risk Analysis Plan Risk Responses	Implement Risk Responses	Monitor Risks	
Procurement Management (3)		Plan Procurement Management	Conduct Procurements	Control Procurements	
Stakeholder Management (4)	Identify Stakeholders	Plan Stakeholder Engagement	Manage Stakeholder Engagement	Monitor Stakeholder Engagement	

EXAM TIP: *You will need to memorize this page. You should be able to write this entire page in about 5 minutes.*

1   Project Management Institute, A Guide to the Project Management Body of Knowledge, (PMBOK® Guide) – Sixth Edition, Project Management Institute Inc., 2017, Page 25

Description of Project Documents and Processes Created

1. Activity attributes	Detailed information about each individual activity.	Define activities
2. Activity list	List of all the activities on the project.	Define activities
3. Assumption log	List of all project assumptions and constraints.	Develop project charter
4. Basis of estimates	Describes how schedule, cost, and resource estimates were developed. Also includes their confidence level and ranges.	Estimate activity duration, estimate costs, estimate activity resources
5. Change log	Lists and describes the status of the change requests that are being processed or have been processed through the perform integrated change control process.	Perform integrated change control
6. Cost estimates	Cost of each individual activity.	Estimate costs
7. Cost forecasts	A prediction of how much the project will cost when it completes based on the current work.	Control costs
8. Duration estimates	Amount of time needed to complete each activity on the project.	Estimate activity durations
9. Issue log	List of all issues on the project. Could include history type, description, priority, status, and resolution.	Direct and manage project work
10. Lessons learned register	List of all lessons learned throughout the project.	Manage project knowledge
11. Milestone list	Description of milestones on a project.	Define activities
12. Physical resource assignments	Assignments of the physical resources to the activities or work packages.	Acquire resources
13. Project calendars	A calendar view of what takes place on a day-to-day basis on the project.	Develop schedule
14. Project communications	Communicate on the project by following the communications management plan.	Manage communications
15. Project schedule	A detailed breakdown of the work that needs to be done in order to complete the project. Will include a bar chart, milestone chart, and the project schedule network diagram.	Develop schedule
16. Project schedule network diagram	A sequencing diagram that shows the relationships amongst the activities and the sequence they will be performed. But it also shows the critical path.	Sequence activities
17. Project scope statement	A detailed description of the project or phase deliverables.	Define scope
18. Project team assignments	Assignment of the project team members to the work packages or activities.	Acquire resources

19. Quality control measurements	Results of the activities done in the "Control Quality" process to determine if the quality standards or policies were met.	Control quality
20. Quality metrics	An attribute that will be used to measure the project or deliverable to verify that it has met the quality requirements and/or standards.	Plan quality management
21. Quality report	A report which generally includes information about quality issues on the project and recommendations on how to improve the processes on the project.	Manage quality
22. Requirements documentation	Description of all requirements from project stakeholders.	Collect requirements
23. Requirements traceability matrix	A table that traces the origin of the requirements.	Collect requirements
24. Resource breakdown structure	Categorization and type of the project resources..	Estimate activity resources
25. Resource calendars	Shows the availability of resources on the project both physical and HR.	Acquire resources
26. Resource requirements	Description of the number and type of resources needed to complete each work package or activity.	Estimate activity resources
27. Risk register	A list of all the positive and negative risks on a project, along with responses.	Identify risks
28. Risk report	A description of the overall project risks.	Identify risks
29. Schedule data	The information that is used to create the schedule such as who made it, assumptions, and constraints.	Develop schedule
30. Schedule forecasts	A prediction of when the project may be completed based on the current progress of the work.	Control schedule
31. Stakeholder register	A list of all stakeholders, which can include categorization, impact, and communication requirements.	Identify stakeholders
32. Team charter	Guidelines the team should follow on a project. Includes values, decision-making process, acceptable behavior, code of conduct, and etiquette.	Plan resource management
33. Test and evaluation documents	Used to help evaluate the project deliverables when completed.	Manage quality

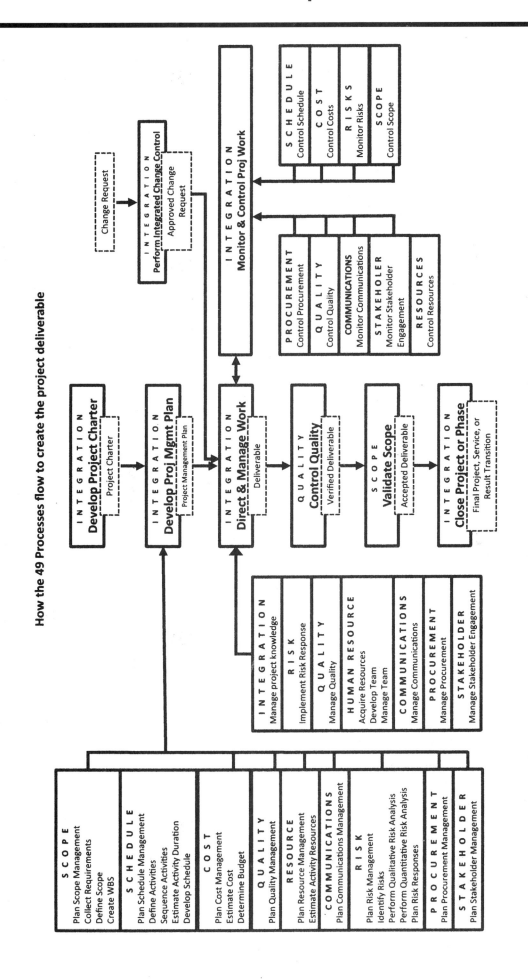

How the 49 Processes flow to create the project deliverable

Study Steps

Studying for this exam will not be easy. I recommend that you spend at least 100 hours of study time on this exam.

Here are some study tips:

- Take this exam very seriously. It is not an easy test to pass.

- Read this guide at least twice.

- Get at least 90% on each of the end-of-chapter quizzes. Keep repeating each one until you understand why the answer is correct while others are wrong. Do not just memorize questions.

- Get over 90% on the mock exam at the end of this book.

- Read the PMBOK® Guide and the PMI Agile Practice Guide at least once. Both of these books comes free with your PMI membership.

- Dedicate study time every week. Try to put in about 6 to 20 hours per week of study time. Studying for an hour every day is much better for retention (and exam success) than trying to cram last minute.

- Do not just memorize the ITTO's; understand what the processes are, and how you can use the ITTO's on the process.

- Do not stop studying for an extended period of time, because it is very easy to forget this material, and you will have to start over again.

- Make flashcards with definitions and ITTO's. You don't need to buy the flashcards. The best flashcards are the ones you make yourself.

- Fill out the PMP exam application on the PMI website (www.pmi.org). You will need to input all of your projects, breaking them down by hours and writing descriptions of them.

- Pre-schedule the PMP exam time. Expect to take an entire day off for this. Between the time it takes to get there, register, take the exam, and check out, it will take you about six hours.

- Schedule the exam for an early morning slot. Don't take the exam in the afternoon. Our brains are not as sharp in the afternoon. Anytime between 8AM and 10AM would be a good start time.

I always recommend pre-scheduling an exam before taking it. I have more than 50 different certifications in IT and Accounting and I consider myself a procrastinator. I would find everything else in the world to do except studying. I would tell myself that I'll study tomorrow and then never get around to it. I don't want this to happen to you.

The only technique I found that works is scheduling the exam and then buy the books to study or attending a class. Buying the book and exam is a sunk cost. This way, I am forced to study for the exam. The date is set, and if I don't study, I might fail and lose my exam fee.

Knowing that you will need to put in at least 60 to 100 hours of study time, you can now decide when would be best for you to schedule the exam. If you work a normal 40-hour week and can spend at least 10-20 hours in the week to study, then schedule it 5-6 weeks ahead. Also, sometimes the testing centers become full quickly, and you might have to wait a few weeks to take the exam. They have even been known to reschedule exams, so always keep an eye out for any communications from the testing center, especially as your exam approaches.

The day before the exam will be very important; here are a few things to do:

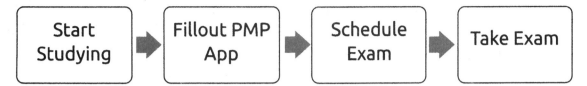

- Review the beginning of this chapter to get used to the formulas and the process table.

- Don't study too much the day before the exam, because you might not retain much of that information.

- Wake up very early. This way, you can be tired the night before the exam and sleep well.

- A good night's sleep is probably your best asset on this (or any) exam. Go to bed early and try to get at least 6-8 hours of sleep. I know this might be hard for some people because of exam anxiety, but you need to find a way. Maybe exercise that day very hard to become tired that night.

- Review your exam center and map out how to get there. You don't want to be late, because you might lose your exam seat. That will count as a failure.

- Get your ID's ready. You will need two forms of identification, one government issued and another with a signature. A driver's license and credit card will be good. Be sure that your name is exactly the same on both.

The morning of the exam:

- Wake up early. Set an alarm if necessary.

- Eat a big enough meal. You will not be able to eat while taking this exam. I personally get fatigued when I am hungry.

- Get to the test site early. Better to be an hour early than be a minute late. Leave your house early just in case of traffic or metro problems.

- Be prepared to be checked in and searched. They will make you put all of your devices into a locker. Then, they will search you with a metal detector. Finally, you will be signed in.

The actual exam. This is it. All of the studying has come down to this point, and here is the actual exam in front of you. Here are some tips for the actual exam:

- Try not to be nervous. I know this is easier said than done, but take a couple of deep breaths and get started.

- They will give you scrap paper and pencil.

- When the exam starts, take the first 5-8 minutes to write down the formulas from the section above, as well as the process chart. This will be very valuable to you. Trust me, when you are at question 178 and almost 4 hours into the exam and they ask for the CV, you might say to yourself, "What is that?!"

- Always ask yourself what a PMBOK® Guide answer would be. It is generally something that is more process-oriented and general. Always evaluate before any step.

- Take breaks. I am telling you, you must take at least one break. Even if you feel that you don't need to, still take at least one. This is very important. The exam will include two breaks, I suggest you take both.

- Technically, you have 77 seconds per question: 230 minutes and 180 questions. Never spend too much time on a question. If it is hard, just answer it, and mark it for review. Never leave a question unanswered. You never know if you will have time to come back to it. The only questions that may take a little longer will be the network diagram questions. This is to be expected.

- When you come to a long question, read the last sentence, glance over the choices, then read the entire question. This is a great tip for saving time on long questions. This way, you will know what they are asking, as you read the question.

- At the end, review the questions you marked. Change the answer only if you are sure about the new choice.

- Submit the exam, and hope for the best.

Celebrate!

Project Code of Ethics and Professional Conduct Questions

1. You are accountable for a large data center project and have requested proposals from several vendors. You will be purchasing $1.2 million worth of networking equipment, a software application, and an ERP solution for the project. Once informed about your upcoming family vacation on an island, one of the vendors offered to let you stay in his Summer cabin on forty acres of land he happens to have on that island. What should you do in this situation?

    A. Decline the offer as it will be considered an integrity issue on the part of the vendor.

    B. Decline the offer as it is an integrity issue and will be considered personal gain.

    C. Accept the offer and also inform the project sponsor about it.

    D. Accept the offer as you do not see any integrity issue or conflict of interest.

2. While discussing the project schedule with the sponsor, both of you recognize that the project is behind schedule and that there is no way to meet the committed deadline. The sponsor asked you not to reveal this fact to the customer in the impending status meeting later on that day. What will be your BEST course of action?

    A. Have a quick chat with the customer and explain your situation.

    B. Request the sponsor to have a conversation with the customer.

    C. Postpone the status meeting.

    D. Explain to the sponsor that it is not ethical to deliberately report incorrect project status to anyone involved with the project.

3. You are working for a consultancy firm that provides PMP exam training and consultancy. You notice that the firm encourages the candidates to be untruthful about their required project management experience and training hours to be eligible to take the test. What will be your MOST appropriate course of action?

    A. Since you are not involved in the registration process, simply ignore what is going on in the organization.

    B. Ask the manager responsible to stop any such unethical practice.

    C. Contact PMI and explain the situation.

    D. Quit your job.

4. You are a senior project manager, and recently you were asked to manage a project to build a brick manufacturing plant. While the team was conducting the feasibility study, you learned that the plant could severely contaminate the air and water in the neighborhood. You became apprehensive that this catastrophic impact could be long-lasting. You discussed your concern with the sponsor and recommended implementation of a robust waste management procedures that will add cost to the project. The sponsor contended that the project should be completed as soon as possible with the defined scope and no extra cost. What will be your BEST course of action in this situation?

    A. Politely refuse to take charge of the project.

    B. Take charge of the project and inform the local residents about the potential negative impact of the manufacturing plant.

    C. Agree with the sponsor.

    D. Take charge of the project and do not disclose any information about the negative impact of the manufacturing plant to the local residents.

5. You have been assigned as a project manager for a project in a country where employees take long lunches and nap-breaks, enjoy six weeks of paid vacation each year, and observe several supplementary holidays that are not offered in your home country. You have been asked by your local team members to authorize the same kind of vacation time and holidays to maintain team equality. What will be your BEST course of action?

A. Inform the foreign team that they must follow the vacation and holiday guidelines of the head office.

B. Be fair and allow the local team to enjoy the same kind of relaxed lifestyle.

C. Treat all the extra vacation days and holidays as schedule constraints in your project.

D. Explore the option of outsourcing this part of the project to some other geographic location.

6. The software project to build a new office application is in progress. While reviewing one of the components, you discover that it does not meet the quality standards of your company. Upon further investigation, you realize that the component does not necessarily need to meet the specified quality standards as it will function well as it is. The team member responsible for the component, mentioned to you that meeting the specified quality standards will be time consuming and pricey. What should be your BEST course of action as a project manager?

A. Accept this particular component, but make sure that the remaining components meet the specified quality standards.

B. Report the concern about the level of quality and seek a solution.

C. Modify the specified quality standards to match the level achieved.

D. Report the component as satisfactory.

7. There are several potential projects in your organization, but the organization needs to select the best project to work on due to limited resources, cash flow, and different strategic objectives and priorities. Higher management asked you to compare these potential projects and find out the best one with the most value based on the project triggers and benefit measurement methods. You are a project manager with several years of experience implementing IT projects, but you are not conversant with project selection methods. What should you do in this situation?

A. Inform higher management that you lack experience and expertise in project selection methods.

B. Do your best and select the project that you think will bring the best value.

C. Politely inform management that you are unable to take the assignment at this time.

D. Seek expert opinion to select the best project.

8. You are replacing a project manager who just left the organization. While reviewing the deliverables and their status, you notice that several deliverables that were reported as completed are still in development. Additionally, management is under the impression that the project is on track when, in fact, it is behind schedule and over budget. What will be your BEST course of action?

A. Politely refuse the project assignment.

B. Revise the status and notify management.

C. Have an urgent meeting with the key stakeholders and ask for suggestions on what to do.

D. Explore crashing the project to bring it back on-track.

9. While finalizing the bi-weekly project status and progress reports, you observe that a few deliverables that were reported as completed are not actually done, and that the team members also did not report the days spent on the activities correctly. Your project statistics and updates become very unrealistic with these wrong estimates given by the team members. What should you do in this kind of situation?

    A. Report the information as it is.

    B. Provide accurate and truthful project information in a timely manner.

    C. Inform the functional managers about the actions of the team members.

    D. Replace the team members who are providing wrong estimates

10. One of your best friends in charge of maintaining customers' finances and investments is working in the same financial institution with you. She shared a secret with you and asked you not to divulge the secret to anyone. She told you that she has been using clients' money to invest in the stock market and has made a substantial amount of money from it. She also asked you to join her so that both of you can make a fortune. What should you do in this kind of situation?

    A. Report your friend to the appropriate authority.

    B. Explore different stock options and find out the best way to make a large amount of money.

    C. Find out if what your friend is doing is really illegal or not.

    D. Ask your friend to stop the illegal activity, but do not mention it to anyone else.

11. You did not utilize all the tools & techniques of risk identification and disregarded a potential risk. The risk shows up during the project planning phase and surprises the team. What kind of response is expected from you as a project manager?

    A. Discuss with the sponsor and seek guidance.

    B. Develop the risk response plan and determine preventive and corrective actions.

    C. Take responsibility and evaluate the impact of the risk item.

    D. Immediately inform the customers about the risk event.

12. You recently found out that one of your best friends has been pretending to be PMP certified. She thinks that the certification is helping her immensely, but she never thought of pursuing it in real life due to the exam's difficulty. What will be your BEST course of action?

    A. Report to your friend's boss.

    B. Hand your friend over to the police immediately.

    C. Encourage your friend to get the real certification.

    D. Contact PMI and report the situation.

13. Your company has been working with numerous financial institutions for several years and has built spectacular relationships with them. Recently you submitted a proposal in response to a bid for a data and disaster center project for one of these financial institutions in which your company has no previous experience and lacks the required expertise. Which of the following is TRUE regarding this situation?

   A. It is a common practice to exaggerate expertise and experience when submitting a proposal for a bid.

   B. You have not violated the PMI code of ethics and professional conduct, but you have violated the procurement code.

   C. There is no violation in this situation.

   D. You have violated the PMI code of ethics and professional conduct.

14. You are one of the members of the proposal evaluation team responsible for evaluating contracts and awarding them to eligible vendors. While reviewing the list of potential vendors, you notice that one of your good friends is a participant in the bidding process. You know that your friend is an expert in his domain and the project will be greatly benefited him, if he is awarded the contract. What will be the BEST course of action in this situation?

   A. Keep silent and continue with the procurement process.

   B. Convince the proposal evaluation team to award your friend the contract.

   C. Inform the sponsor and the evaluation team about your relationship.

   D. Offer your friend some good tips to increase his chance of winning the bid.

15. As a project manager, you are assigned to oversee a network infrastructure project in a foreign country for six months. At the end of the first introductory meeting, all six participants from your team were given exclusive gifts. When you were reluctant to accept the gift, you were told that it is a custom in their country to give this kind of gift to business partners. What will be your BEST course of action?

   A. Decline the gift as accepting it will be considered personal gain in your country.

   B. Decline the gift as accepting it will be considered a conflict of interest in your country.

   C. Accept the gift and inform your management, so that your integrity will not be questioned later on.

   D. Accept the gift as you do not consider it to be a conflict of interest or integrity issue.

16. You are implementing a WIMAX network for one of your clients in a rural area. You recently implemented a similar network for another client and installed several towers and POPs for them throughout the same region. The current client can save a considerable amount of time and money if they can rent the existing infrastructure instead of setting up their own towers and POPs. You have a nondisclosure agreement with the previous client, and you are not supposed to disclose any information on their infrastructure or network architecture. What will be your BEST course of action?

    A. Ignore the nondisclosure agreement, as it is not legally enforceable, and share the network architecture and infrastructure from the previous project.

    B. Install new towers and POPs for the existing customer and ignore the fact that the existing infrastructure can be used for the benefit of both organizations.

    C. Seek guidance from your Project Management Office (PMO).

    D. Have a discussion with your previous client and seek permission to share the information on the existing infrastructure.

17. You are participating in a bid in a foreign country for a company that wants to procure several expensive pieces of hospital equipment. You are told by the procuring organization that you need to obtain a trade license from the local authority and that the entire process will take approximately four weeks. There is only one week left for the bidding, and you cannot wait for four weeks to obtain the trade license. While discussing it with one of the local officials, you discover that you can fast-track the process and obtain the trade license in three days if you pay an "urgent fee" of $750. Which of the following should you consider if the fee is within the approved limit in the budget?

    A. Wait for four weeks if needed, but do not pay the additional fee under any circumstance.

    B. Pay the urgent fee and obtain the license in three days.

    C. Negotiate the urgent fee and try to lower it as much as possible.

    D. Participate in the bidding without the local trade license.

18. Your company just assigned you as a project manager for a large data center project. You were asked by the sponsor to complete the project in six months with $120,000. You soon realize that both the time and cost estimation from higher management is impractical. Your estimation shows that the project could take as long as ten months and that the cost will be at least 20 percent more than the initial estimation. The sponsor tells you that she is considering another project manager to take care of the project in case you do not agree with her time and cost estimations. What will be your BEST course of action?

    A. Excuse yourself from the project.

    B. Document the time and cost constraints and carry on with the project as instructed.

    C. Submit your detailed time and cost estimations and justification to the sponsor.

    D. Have an urgent meeting with the client and explain the situation.

19. You are in charge of a very important, big budget video game project. You have thirteen identified stakeholders and ten team members in the project. You notice that one of the team members who has a major role in the project has been meeting with an anonymous stakeholder to discuss the project details. What should you do in this situation?

    A. Discuss with the team member and express your concern.

    B. Report it to the functional manager.

    C. Have a meeting with the team member and the unidentified stakeholder.

    D. Make sure you continue to keep an eye on the team member.

20. You are overseeing a software project to develop a challenging and innovative video game. One of your friends, who is a connoisseur in this field and has several of his very popular games on the market, has requested you to give him a copy of the game prior to its release, so that he can check it out and provide his feedback. You know his feedback will be valuable to find any defects and improve the game. What should you do in this situation?

    A. Ask your friend to sign a nondisclosure agreement prior to giving him a copy.

    B. Give him a copy of the game, since he is an expert and may provide valuable feedback about the game.

    C. Make sure that your friend will provide you with the required feedback and suggestions prior to giving him a copy of the game.

    D. Decline the request, as the game is the intellectual property of your company.

21. Your company just initiated a project to install a Wi-Fi network in Southeast Asia. One of the clients offers gifts to all your team members and requests you to give his office a dedicated connection with the max bandwidth possible. What should you do in this situation?

    A. Reject the gifts and never communicate with that client again.

    B. Accept the gifts, but refuse to give the dedicated connection.

    C. Reject the gifts, as accepting gifts is a violation of the code of ethics and professional conduct.

    D. Accept the gifts and agree to give the dedicated connection as it will not cost any extra to the project.

22. You are participating in a bid in a foreign country for a company that wants to procure several expensive pieces of hospital equipment. You have meticulously followed the bidding procedure and are expecting to be the most qualified and lowest bidder. One of the representatives of the procuring company contacted you and asked for 10 percent commission on the total price, or they would award the deal to some other vendor. What will be your BEST course of action?

    A. Contact PMI immediately and report the situation.

    B. Negotiate the commission and try to bring it down as much as possible.

    C. Deny the offer and notify your management.

    D. Agree to give 10 percent to secure the deal.

Project Code of Ethics and Professional Conduct Answers

1. **B:** You should decline the offer based on the fact that it will be considered personal gain on your part, and your integrity will be questioned. Option A will not be the correct answer because you are not responsible for the integrity of others.

2. **D:** The best course of action will be to explain to the sponsor that under all circumstances you are obligated to conduct yourself in a truthful manner and report the truth regarding project status. You are also obligated not to deceive others and not to make false or half-true statements. It is not ethical to knowingly report incorrect project status to anyone in the project.

3. **C:** You are obligated to report any violation of the PMI code of ethics and professional conduct to PMI.

4. **A:** One of the mandatory standards in the PMI code of ethics and professional conduct is responsibility. Responsibility is the act of taking ownership of our decisions and admitting our mistakes. As a project manager, you must make decisions based on the best interests of society, public safety, and the environment. It is not advisable to undertake a project that will work against the interests of the public.

5. **C:** One of the mandatory standards in the PMI code of ethics and professional conduct is respect. As a project manager, you should respect personal, ethnic, and cultural differences and avoid engaging in behaviors that might be considered disrespectful. The only valid action will be to treat all extra vacation days and holidays as schedule constraints in your project.

6. **B:** You should report the concern with the level of quality so that the experts can find an appropriate resolution. It would be unethical to modify the specific quality standards and report the component as satisfactory. Making sure that the remaining components will meet the quality standards will not solve the existing problem.

7. **A:** One of the mandatory standards in the PMI code of ethics and professional conduct is honesty. Honesty is the act of communicating and conducting ourselves in a truthful manner, reporting the truth regarding project status, not deceiving others or making false or half-true statements, and being honest about our own experience and expertise. In this particular scenario, you should honestly report your lack of experience and expertise in project selection methods to higher management. Also, as per the PMI code of ethics, you should accept only those assignments that are consistent with your background, experience, skills, and qualifications. Higher management may help you in various ways, including suggesting you seek expert opinions for selecting the project once they are informed about your lack of experience. So, refusing the assignment will not be an appropriate action in this situation.

8. **B:** Since there are changes in project cost and schedule, you should revise the status and update management accordingly before you take any other action. Crashing the project usually adds cost to the project, so it will make things even worse. You cannot simply refuse to manage the project because it is behind schedule and over budget. As a project manager, you should be directing the project instead of asking the stakeholders to do so.

9. **B:** One of the mandatory standards in the PMI code of ethics and professional conduct is honesty. Honesty is the act of communicating and conducting ourselves in a truthful manner, reporting the truth regarding project status, not deceiving others, and not making false or half-true statements. As a project manager, you should always provide accurate and truthful information in a timely manner. It would be unethical to report the wrong project status to anyone in the project. You should discuss with the team members about the negative impact of their actions. If needed, you may need to inform functional managers about the actions of the team members.

10. **A:** You are obligated to report any illegal activity to the appropriate authority.

11. **C:** One of the mandatory standards in the PMI code of ethics and professional conduct is responsibility. Responsibility is the act of taking ownership of our decisions and admitting our mistakes. As a project manager, you must take responsibility for the failure in identifying the risk and evaluate the impact to develop the risk response plan. Once you have the detail on the risk item, you can have a discussion with the customer. Also, you may escalate the risk to the sponsor if the risk is beyond your control.

12. **D:** You are obligated to report any PMI code of ethics and professional conduct violation to PMI.

13. **D:** You have violated the PMI code of ethics and professional conduct. As a project manager, you should be honest about the experience and expertise of your organization.

14. **C:** Since there is a potential conflict of interest, you should discuss the relationship with the sponsor and evaluation team. It will be up to the evaluation team and sponsor to decide whether you should disassociate yourself from the bidding process or not.

15. **C:** You should accept the gift because if you decline, it could severely affect your relationship with the customer. You should also immediately inform your management, so that your integrity will not be questioned later on.

16. **D:** You need to work in the best interest of your client and try to save money and time for them if possible by exploring the option of using the existing infrastructure rather than installing new towers and POPs. Even if the nondisclosure agreement is not legally enforceable, you are ethically bound to comply with it. The best course of action will be to have a discussion with the previous client and seek permission to share the information on the existing infrastructure. Seeking guidance from the PMO will not be essential since approval from the PMO to share the information will not make it acceptable.

17. **B:** In this case, the fee has a valid purpose and should not be considered a bribe. You should pay the urgent fee of $750 and obtain the trade license.

18. **C:** You cannot simply refuse to manage the project because you do not agree with the time and cost estimations of the sponsor. As a project manager, you are expected to present truthful and accurate information regarding time, cost, and other project objectives. So, you should submit your detailed time and cost estimations and justification for the longer duration and additional budget. If your justification is reasonable, the sponsor should agree with your argument. Continuing with the project with unrealistic time and cost expectations will be a recipe for failure. Having an urgent meeting with the client will not be appropriate in this situation.

19. **A:** At first, you should have a discussion with the team member to find out why she is meeting with the unidentified stakeholder. Reporting the incident to the functional manager will not be appropriate until you identify any problem.

20. **D:** You should decline the request as the video game is the intellectual property of your organization.

21. **C:** The client is making a request by offering gifts; thus, you should reject the gifts as it is a violation of the PMI code of ethics and professional conduct. A project manager is expected to be honest and should not engage in dishonest behavior with the intention of personal gain or at the expense of others. If it is customary in that country to offer gifts, you may accept the gift without agreeing to the client's request for a dedicated connection. Not communicating with the specific client may impact the project.

22. **C:** You should never bribe even though it may help you win a project. Your best course of action will be to deny the offer and disclose the incident to higher management.

Chapter 17
Mock Exam

This is the final exam of the book. You should have read this guide at least two times and review my videos in the included e-learning course before trying this exam. It is made to simulate the actual exam. Some of the questions will be hard, and some will be easy. You are expected to get at least 90% before you are ready for the real exam. Take it as many times as you can. Don't just memorize the answers, but try to understand why an answer is correct and others are wrong.

You should expect to spend the entire four hours on this exam. I recommend you do this exam in one shot and not break it up over a few days; this way, you can have the feeling of the real test. You should take two 10-minute breaks after every 60 questions. On the real exam, you will get two 10 minute breaks. The first will be after you completed the first 60 questions and the second will be after you completed the next 60 (at question 120).

1. A project manager managing a video simulator project was informed by one of the team members about a complex problem that can have a drastic negative impact on the project. The project manager immediately defined the cause of the problem by analyzing the problem using a fishbone diagram, identified a solution, and implemented the solution. The project manager recently received a call from the same team member and was informed that the same problem had resurfaced. What did the project manager most likely forget to do?

    A. Validate the solution with the sponsors.

    B. Confirm that the solution actually solved the problem.

    C. Use a Pareto chart.

    D. Identify why the problem occurred.

2. You are overseeing the implementation of a new computer structure at the local hospital. You are currently working on identifying all the internal and external stakeholders who have an interest in your project and can positively or negatively impact your project. While identifying the stakeholders, you realize that stakeholder identification is:

    A. The responsibility of the project sponsor.

    B. To be carried out throughout the project lifecycle.

    C. Not to be done in any phase of the project

    D. To be focused only on stakeholders who will contribute positively to your project.

3. The agile team is having issues estimating how long each of the task would take to complete on the project. What estimating methods should the project manager recommend? (Choose 2)
    A. Bottom-up

    B. T-shirt sizing

    C. Top-down

    D. Planning poker

    E. Parametric

4. Which of the following is NOT true about the fundamental functionality of the Control Quality process?

    A. Implement approved changes to the quality baseline.

    B. Recommend changes, corrective and preventive actions, and defect repairs to Integrated Change Control in order to eliminate non-compliance in the project deliverables.

    C. Ensure that the deliverables of the project comply with relevant quality standards.

    D. Ensure project work is directed toward the completion of the defined scope.

5. You have been assigned as a project manager to implement a new office automation application. Management asks you to make sure that the new application will work on the existing infrastructure and can easily be integrated with other major applications currently running in the organization. This is an example of which one of the following?

    A. Assumptions

    B. Project scope

    C. Constraints

    D. Expectations

6. Which one of the following techniques translates project objectives into tangible deliverables and requirements by improving the project team's understanding of the product?

    A. Product analysis

    B. Alternative generation

    C. Inspection

    D. Decomposition

7. Claims administration is used as a tool & technique in which of the following procurement management processes?

    A. Plan Procurement Management

    B. Conduct Procurements

    C. Control Procurements

    D. Close Project or Phase

8. You are working for a healthcare facility and are overseeing the implementation of a new computer infrastructure and office automation project at the local hospital. You made all the efforts to ensure that a rigorous test was done and the scope was validated prior to any major release in the project. Recently, you made the final delivery to the customer and communicated the successful news to all the relevant members of the project. You were surprised when the customer called to inform you that he was not very happy with the release as it did not support one of his key functionalities and demanded that the feature be added as soon as possible. What should you do first in this kind of situation?

    A. Estimate the time, cost, and resources required to add the feature as specified by the customer.

    B. Have an urgent meeting with the sponsor to discuss the customer's concern.

    C. Inform the customer that the project is delivered and closed and that any addition to the project must be handled as a new project.

    D. Find out the lack in the scope validation and in-house testing procedures to identify the root cause.

9. A project stakeholder is concerned about the lack of communication on the project. They claim no status reports are being sent to them. What should the PM do first to address the stakeholder concerns?

    A. Update the communication management plan to include the stakeholder.

    B. Meet with the stakeholder to assess what report they are looking for then update the communication management plan.

    C. Review the communication management plan to understand the stakeholder concerns.

    D. Immediately send the missing reports to the stakeholder.

10. Based on the network diagram and the following criteria, answer the question below:

Activity B has just been increased by 2 weeks. What will be the critical path for this project?

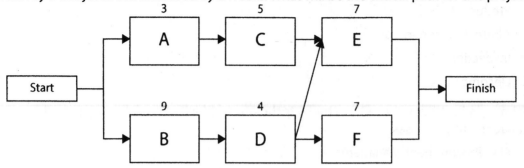

A. 19 weeks

B. 20 weeks

C. 22 weeks

D. 24 weeks

11. Which of the following theories demonstrates that employees who believe their efforts will lead to effective performance and expect to be rewarded for their accomplishments remain productive as rewards meet their expectations?

A. Maslow's Hierarchy of Needs

B. Theory X and Y

C. McClelland's Achievement theory

D. Expectancy theory

12. You have recently been assigned as a project manager for a new and highly complex project to send a satellite into space. There are several stakeholders in the project, and you are working on a communications plan to identify the information and communication needs of the people involved. You do this by determining what needs to be communicated, when, to whom, with what method, in which format, and how frequently. It is extremely important that you develop your communications plan:

A. Evenly throughout the project lifecycle

B. At the earliest stages of the project

C. Upon completion of the project plan

D. During execution

13. What activity can the agile team do to list the reasons for why a particular process was failing during iteration?

A. Fishbone analysis

B. Check-in analysis

C. Short subjects

D. SMART goals

14. The project manager has updated the sponsor with a project report that lists the SPI as being 1.2 and the CPI as .6. The sponsor is very upset and would like the PM to correct this action as soon as possible. What should the project manager do next?

    A. Meet with the team to determine how to fix the project schedule.

    B. Meet with the team to determine how to fix the project budget.

    C. Meet with the team to determine how to bring the project back on schedule and budget.

    D. Informed the sponsor the project is moving along just fine and there is no corrective actions needed.

15. Match the motication description to the theory.

People are Self-led		McGregor's Theory X
Micromanager		McGregor's Theory Y
Hygiene Agents		Ouchi Theory Z
Increasing Employee Loyalty		Herzberg's Theory of Motication

16. Ashley, a senior project manager, recently took over a project to produce a safe and effective drug from another project manager who just left the company. Ashley was surprised to find out that there was no change control board or change control process established for the project. Why is it important to have a robust change control process for any project to be successful?

    A. It will ensure that only stakeholders with significant authority can submit the change requests.

    B. It will minimize the number of changes in the project.

    C. It will ensure that only necessary changes are considered and implemented.

    D. It will maintain the record of all changes for budget tracking purposes.

17. Your sponsor mentioned that the project must be completed within six months and should not exceed $50,000. You should consider this a:

    A. Project assumption

    B. Project constraint

    C. Stakeholder expectation

    D. Project boundary

18. You were given a budget of $3,000, and you spent $2,000. However, you only completed $1,200 worth of work. What do you currently expect the TOTAL project to cost considering your situation?

    A. Not possible to estimate.

    B. $5,000

    C. $6,000

    D. $6,200

19. The project team is working with the customers to write the user stories. The customers have refused as they claim this would add no value to the project. What would be the best step to resolve this?

    a. Have the team write the user stories

    b. At the agile, the project manager writes the user stories

    c. Educate the users why the user stories are valuable

    d. Inform them user stories may not be needed

20. You have received many complaints from your customers indicating that the screens of laptops manufactured at your plant are getting black spots and marks after six months of use. Which of the following tools should your team members use to identify potential causes of this problem?

    A. Flowchart

    B. Statistical sampling

    C. Design of experiments

    D. Ishikawa diagram

21. While reviewing your project schedule, you realize that you have two pending activities that you need to complete as soon as possible. The plan would be for you to set up the development server in the lab and then start coding. But upon further investigation, you find out that you must run the server for 3 days, without failure, before the coding starts. This is an example of:

    A. Lead

    B. Crash

    C. Critical chain

    D. Lag

22. You are utilizing a technique of reconciling the expenditure of funds with the funding limits set for the project. As per the variance between the expenditure of funds and the planned limit, you are trying to reschedule activities to level out the rates of expenditures. This technique is known as:

    A. Funding limit reconciliation

    B. Cost aggregation

    C. Reserve analysis

    D. Fore casting

23. You are overseeing a project to implement an online travel package reservation system that has 6 sponsors and 13 stakeholders. You want to make sure that your project stakeholders will receive the correct version of the product. Which of the following plans will you use to specify how versioning information will be tracked?

    A. Quality management plan

    B. Scope management plan

    C. Change management plan

    D. Configuration management plan

24. Senior management has asked you to shorten your project schedule by 2 months by any means. In order to achieve the target, you added a couple of additional resources to the team and also approved unlimited overtime for the team members. You realize that you are taking the risk of potential conflicts, additional management time, and cost to the project. The technique you are using is:

    A. Crashing

    B. Critical chain

    C. Critical path

    D. Fast-tracking

25. You are overseeing a custom software development project to implement an accounting and financial system for one of your clients. Currently, you are in the process of obtaining the formal acceptance of the completed project scope and associated deliverables from the sponsor, customers, and other stakeholders. This process is closely related to which one of the following?

    A. Control Quality

    B. Manage Stakeholder Engagement

    C. Perform Quality Assurance

    D. Control Risks

26. During the executing stage of a project to develop a cashiering application for a retail customer, a senior stakeholder requested that you slightly modify the project scope to incorporate an additional feature. What will be your first course of action?

    A. Submit the change request to the change control board for their approval or rejection.

    B. Document the change request as per the project scope management plan.

    C. Perform impact analysis on all project objectives such as scope, time, cost, quality, risk, resource, and others.

    D. Deny the request since it is too late in the project life cycle to incorporate any new change.

27. Over the last three weeks, the project team has finally been able to establish a shared vision of what the product would look like when it is complete. This is an example of?

    A. Shared vision

    B. Requirements gathering

    C. Progressive elaboration

    D. Progressive management

28. A project manager is in the Sequence Activities process of identifying and documenting relationships among defined activities and arranging them in the order they must be performed. While in this process, the project manager decides to utilize a Precedence Diagramming Method (PDM) for sequencing the activities. All of the following are true about a precedence diagramming method EXCEPT:

    A. This method creates a schematic display of the sequential and logical relationships of project activities.

    B. It usually shows dependencies and the order in which activities in a project must be performed.

    C. It uses four types of dependency relationships, including finish-to-start.

    D. This diagramming method uses Activity-on-Arrow (AOA) convention, as arrows are used to represent activities and circles show dependencies.

29. You are overseeing a project to build a robot, which will operate on electricity as well as solar power. The robot should have face and voice recognition capability. It should help the owner with daily household activities and keep him or her company. The robot should be able to learn from various experiences, develop its memory, and gradually make more complex decisions on its own. This information should be captured in which of the following documents?

    A. Project scope

    B. Scope baseline

    C. Product scope

    D. Requirements traceability matrix

30. One of your stakeholders is very disheartened about the fact that three of her key recommendations were not implemented in the project. She sends you an e-mail stating that she will not be able to review and approve the user test case document that you sent her as she thinks her feedback really does not matter much. What is your best course of action?

    A. Immediately implement her recommendations.

    B. Remove the stakeholder from the stakeholder register and avoid further communication.

    C. Explain to her that due to time and budget constraints, her recommendations were not implemented, but the team will reassess them in the next release.

    D. Have an urgent meeting with the sponsor to discuss the next strategy.

31. You are managing a software application project to develop an online PMP exam simulator to assist students in practicing exam questions in a similar real-life environment. The team has completed design work, received approval from the technical review team, and initiated coding work. When your management asked what would be the forecast cost of the project, which is the EAC. Which one of the following formulas will you use to get the most accurate Estimate at Completion(EAC)?

    A. EAC = BAC −AC

    B. EAC = AC +EV

    C. EAC=CPI*SPI

    D. EAC =BAC/CPI

32. A new stakeholder has recently been identified for your project. He will be helping team members with data validation and other testings. The stakeholder asks the project manager about the scheduling methodology and tools that will be used in the schedule development. He would also like to know about schedule change control procedures, reporting formats, and frequencies. Which one of the following documents may the project manager refer him to?

    A. Project charter

    B. Stakeholder register

    C. Schedule management plan

    D. Schedule baseline

33. Your team is working on the installation and configuration of a database server. A project manager from another project called to inform you that he is waiting for the completion of the server setup as his team will also be using the server for their testing. You were not aware of this and inform the project manager that the server installation and configuration will be delayed by a few days. What kind of dependency does the other project have on your project?

    A. Discretionary dependency

    B. Mandatory dependency

    C. Internal dependency

    D. External dependency

34. Which of the following is not a principle of agile planning?

    A. Engage the project team

    B. Engage stakeholders

    C. Conduct most of the planning at the beginning

    D. Conduct planning throughout the project

35. In multiphase projects, the projects are usually planned during developing phases that are performed sequentially to ensure proper control of the project and attain the desired product, service, or result. In some cases, it is necessary to accelerate the project life cycle by overlapping project phases. Which of the following is NOT true about this kind of overlapping relationship?

    A. This technique can be applied as a schedule compression technique called "fast-tracking."

    B. This kind of relationship may increase project risks and the potential for conflicts. A subsequent phase can progress before accurate information is available from the previous phase.

    C. In this kind of relationship, a phase is planned at a given time; planning for a subsequent phase is carried out as work progresses on the current phase or deliverables.

    D. This kind of relationship can reduce the ability to develop long-term planning, but it is suitable in an undefined, uncertain, and rapidly changing environment.

36. When following the agile method of scrum, what is each iteration of work call?

    A. Iteration

    B. Sprint

    C. Release

    D. Backlog

37. An organization has decided to move from traditional project management to a hybrid method. The project will start with an agile approach and end with a traditional approach. Where will the deliverables be revived by the customers? (Choose 2)

    A. Validate Scope

    B. Plan Scope Management

    C. Control Scope

    D. Sprint Planning meeting

    E. Sprint Review meeting

38. To calculate the project cost, the project manager utilizes the cost aggregation method by which activity costs are rolled up to the work packages costs; the work packages costs are then rolled up to the "control account" or "cost account" costs and finally to the project cost. At this moment, the project manager is in the final stages of determining the cost baseline for the project and funding requirements. Which process is the project manager working on now?

    A. Plan Cost Management

    B. Estimate Costs

    C. Determine Budget

    D. Control Costs

39. A project manager working for an electric utility company has been assigned to create a new substation that will supply power to a newly developed subdivision. While performing the forecasting analysis, the project manager found that the EAC=$159,000 and became worried to discover that the SPI = 0.74 and the CPI = 0.86. What is the possible reason for this occurrence?

    A. One of the subcontractors needed to be replaced due to poor performance.

    B. An activity with no buffer unexpectedly took longer and required additional manpower to be completed.

    C. The team had to purchase an expensive piece of safety equipment that was not originally planned.

    D. The client made several scope changes.

40. You have been managing a top-secret government project, which has been progressing as planned up until last night. Suddenly, one of your team members called and informed you that an unexpected major problem occurred that was not included in the risk register. The problem will now cost the project an additional amount. What should be your first course of action?

    A. Accept the risk.

    B. Update the risk management plan.

    C. Use management reserves.

    D. Have an urgent meeting with the stakeholders and find out the problem details.

41. Mary is working on the new flooring project and would like to know what document she can use to determine who gave her the requirement to put tiles in the seating area of the office. What document shows the origin of the requirements?

    A. Requirements traceability matrix

    B. Requirement management plan

    C. Scope Statement

    D. Scope Baseline

42. Mark has just spoken with the vendor that supplies all of the raw materials for his project and has learned that it will be delayed by three weeks. He realizes that he cannot complete the scope with the materials. What should Mark do first?

    A. Determine how this would affect other parts of the project

    B. Alert senior management

    C. Alert the customers

    D. Adjust the schedule

43. While working in quality management, you have identified the point where the benefits or revenue from improving quality equals the incremental cost to achieve that quality. Which of the following analyses have you performed?

    A. Cost-Benefit analysis

    B. Root cause analysis

    C. Benchmarking

    D. Quality control analysis

44. A project manager is trying to identify the specific training, coaching, mentoring, assistance, or changes required to improve the team's performance and effectiveness by making formal or informal assessments of the project team's effectiveness. Which of the following is the project manager performing?

    A. Team performance assessment

    B. Project performance appraisal

    C. Observations and conversations

    D. Team-building activities

45. A project manager overseeing a WIMAX deployment project just completed negotiation for three additional resources from different functional areas as well as extra reserve money for her project. During the negotiation, two of the functional managers were very skeptical about the request for additional resources and were reluctant to assign their resources to her project. She attempted to influence the functional managers by using her association with a high-level executive for leverage. Which of the following forms of power is she using in this situation?

    A. Referent

    B. Coercive

    C. Expert

    D. Reward

46. A project manager who was overseeing a construction project negotiated a deal with a tools and equipment rental company for 10 different tools needed for his project. As part of the deal, the rental company will supply all ten pieces of equipment for a total price of $3,000/month for the duration of the project. This is an example of which of the following costs?

    A. Indirect cost

    B. Sunk cost

    C. Opportunity cost

    D. Fixed cost

47. The agile project team has completed the Sprint planning meeting. What would be the output of this meeting?

    A. Product backlog

    B. Sprint backlog

    C. User backlog

    D. Sprint requirements

48. A contract is a formal agreement between two parties, and it is the principal output of procurement management. Which of the following is NOT true about contracts?

    A. Contracts are legally binding and backed by the court system in most countries.

    B. A contract cannot be terminated at any time by the buyer for a cause or convenience.

    C. A contract should help reduce project risks.

    D. A contract is legally binding unless it is in violation of applicable law.

49. Which one of the following is NOT true about issues in a project?

    A. An issue log is a document to record issues that require a solution.

    B. It helps monitor who is responsible for resolving specific problems by a target date.

    C. There should be one owner assigned for each issue reported in the project.

    D. Issues and risks refer to the same thing.

50. In Maslow's Hierarchy of Needs, accomplishment, respect, attention, and appreciation are categorized as:

    A. Physiological

    B. Self-actualization

    C. Esteem

    D. Social

51. You presented your project cost estimates to the sponsor, and she is upset about the inaccuracy of the estimates and demands that the estimates be as accurate as possible. Which of the following techniques will help you most in this situation?

    A. An order of magnitude estimate

    B. A heuristic estimate

    C. A bottom-up estimate

    D. A top-down estimate

52. An organization has recently moved to agile project management and the team is not sure how to estimate the amount of work they can get done in the next sprint. What should the project manager do to help the team?

    A. Conduct training sessions about team velocity

    B. Research and acquire training for the team about team velocity

    C. Ask the sponsor to conduct team training

    D. Hire a new team that knows agile methods

53. This tool & technique is a graphical representation of a process to help analyze how problems occur and also identifies potential process improvement opportunities:

    A. Benchmarking

    B. Root cause analysis

    C. Flowchart

    D. Design of Experiments (DOE)

54. A communications management plan is a subsidiary of the project management plan that can be formal or informal, highly detailed or broadly framed, and is based on the needs of the project. It should include all of the following EXCEPT:

    A. Project communications

    B. Stakeholder communication requirements

    C. Method, time frame, and frequency for the distribution of required information

    D. Glossary of common terms

55. You are responsible for making all kinds of arrangements for your company's annual picnic. You have taken all the necessary actions and have reserved an outdoor park on a particular day. You are now only three days away from the big event, and the weather forecast suggests a light rain shower on the day of the picnic. You bought umbrellas and rented tents just in case you need them. Which of the following risk response strategies are you using in this case?

    A. Acceptance

    B. Mitigation

    C. Avoidance

    D. Transference

56. In the communication process, a basic model of communication that exhibits how information is sent from the sender and how it is received by the receiver has all of the following components EXCEPT:

    A. Sender

    B. Message and a feedback message

    C. Urgency

    D. Noise

57. Steve is a project manager for a power company and is currently supervising a solar panel installation project for a local real estate builder. The project has around fifteen team members and eighteen internal and external stakeholders. One of the team leads sent Steve a status report on his team's deliverables, where he indicated that a major component was completed. Steve is convinced that the team lead was not fully honest in his communication, and the major component is far from being completed. Steve is about to have a meeting with the key stakeholders on the project status. What is the best course of action for Steve in this kind of situation?

    A. Ask the team under the team lead to explain the cause of the discrepancy.

    B. Challenge the team lead on the validity of the report.

    C. Attend the status meeting with the stakeholders and do not mention anything about the major component.

    D. Inform the stakeholders that you need a little more time to verify the information about the major component and will follow up with them shortly.

58. While overseeing a software engineering project, you find that one of the subcontractors failed to deliver on the last three projects. Upon further investigation, you learn that there are several complaints filed against this subcontractor and that they have a very bad reputation in the market. Realizing that it is too big of a risk, you terminate the contract with the subcontractor and instead hire a couple of individuals to work on the components. Which risk response strategy did you use in this situation?

    A. Accept

    B. Transfer

    C. Mitigate

    D. Avoid

59. Which of the following is not one of the Lean Software development principles?

    A. Deliver fast

    B. Empower the team

    C. Empower the project manager

    D. Eliminate waste

60. You are in the Control Risks process of identifying, analyzing, and planning for newly arising risks, taking corrective actions, and overall reviewing the execution and effectiveness of risk responses. All of the following are tools & techniques for Control Risks EXCEPT:

    A. Risk reassessment

    B. Variance and trend analysis

    C. Enhance

    D. Risk audits

61. Agile is an _____ term that is used to refer to different types of iterative development.

    A. Continuous

    B. Set

    C. Umbrella

    D. Predictive

62. One of the customers would like to add a new component to the agile project that would likely increase the functionality of the software. What steps should the customer take when adding this new component?

 A. Fill out a change request form

 B. Ask the agile project manager for permission to add it to the product backlog

 C. Add it to the product backlog

 D. Changes are not allowed on agile projects

63. You are overseeing a large construction project to build a power plant. Your company has purchased a big piece of land close to a mountain and far away from the city for the plant. One of your team members reported to you that while digging the ground, they found some artifacts. Upon initial assessment, you realize that these artifacts have some archaeological significance. What should you do in this situation?

 A. Ask the team members to keep it a secret and collect all the artifacts for the benefit of the project.

 B. This kind of finding is a norm in construction projects; thus, ignore the finding and proceed with the project as per the plan.

 C. Proceed with the project as planned, but inform higher management about the finding.

 D. Stop digging and call the archaeological department to quickly research the findings.

64. An important stakeholder identified a problem with one of the features of a software application your team is working on and submitted a change request. Even though it was out of the project's scope, the change control board has approved the change. What is the BEST action to take next?

 A. Add the risk to the risk register and gather information about its probability and impact.

 B. Disregard any risk at this stage of the project lifecycle.

 C. Have a meeting with the stakeholder to discuss the risk.

 D. Identify what went wrong in the Identify Risks process.

65. One of the values of lean software development is to optimize the whole. What does this value mean?

 A. Ensure the whole project team is available to work

 B. Ensure all problems are treated equally

 C. Deliver products as a whole versus in increments

 D. See the system as more than the sum of all its parts

66. While working on a construction project, you need to find out if any of your team members are available to work during the upcoming weekend. Which one of the following documents will help you the MOST in this situation?

 A. Project team directory

 B. Responsibility Assignment Matrix (RAM)chart

 C. Resource Breakdown Structure(RBS)

 D. Resource calendar

67. When working with the customers on a project to collect the requirements for the scope, what tool should a project manager use to ensure that the deliverable will meet its industry standards?

    A. Benchmarking

    B. Prototypes

    C. Meetings

    D. Scope statements

68. When leading an agile project team, what should be the first step the agile project manager should take?

    A. Determine what software should be used on the project to help them collaborate

    B. Determine where to set up a co-location

    C. Work with the organization management to recruit the most educated members

    D. Learn the team members needs

69. While reviewing the status of your project, you found out the following EV, AC, and PV. Find out the CPI and SPI for the project.

	PV	EV	AC
Month 1	$30,000	$27,000	$25,000

    A. 1.18 and 0.891

    B. 0.891 and 1.18

    C. 1.08 and 0.9

    D. 0.833 and 1.40

70. Your team members have created a requirement document, a project scope statement, and a work breakdown structure. They have identified twenty work packages and completed the WBS dictionary. Some of these team members were also involved in creating the business case and conducting the feasibility study at the early stage of this project. Which one of the following items will the team members work on now?

    A. Help the project manager to develop the schedule.

    B. Create a detailed activity list.

    C. Create a network diagram.

    D. Identify the sequence of the activities.

71. The agile project team has decided to do one of the features of the product backlog. The single feature will take six weeks to complete and will be reviewed by the customer. What actions should the agile project manager take next?

    A. Arrange the workspace for the team members to get started

    B. Inform the customers of the six weeks duration

    C. Inform the team they need to conduct the daily standup meetings

    D. Informed the team six weeks is too long, and they will need to decomposed that feature into smaller increments

72. You created a Change Control Board (CCB) for your project since there is no centralized one in your organization. You also want to follow a robust Integrated Change Control process in your project. Which of the following is NOT a primary goal for performing the Integrated Change Control process?

    A. Prevent unnecessary changes in your project.

    B. Denying changes whenever possible.

    C. Evaluate the possible impacts of the changes in your project.

    D. Managing changes as they occur.

73. One of your hardware vendors sends you an e-mail stating that due to severe weather, she will not be able to deliver the networking equipment on time. You decide to respond to this risk by leasing the required equipment from a local company until yours arrives. Which of the following statements is TRUE?

    A. This is risk avoidance.

    B. This is risk mitigation.

    C. This is risk acceptance.

    D. This is risk exploitation.

74. You are overseeing a twenty-mile railway construction project. You were supposed to spend $10,000 per mile of railway construction and complete the project today, exactly forty weeks from the start of the project. You found out that only 75 percent of the work has been completed. What is your Budget at Completion (BAC)?

    A. $200,000

    B. $150,000

    C. $300,000

    D. $400,000

75. One of the values in the agile manifesto is to respond to change over?

    a. Processes and tools

    b. Comprehensive documentation

    c. Contract negotiation

    d. Following a plan

76. What is the primary method customers will use in order to measure the progress of the agile project?

    A. Percentage-based completion

    B. Working software

    C. Number of iterations

    D. Number releases

77. While managing an agile project, the project team should strive for which of the following?

    A. Simplifying work

    B. Finding the best Kanban software

    C. Creating a change request process

    D. Showing progress of work to customers with daily e-mails

78. You decide to use a combination of tools and techniques to identify risks in your data center project. Which one of the following tools is NOT used for risk identification?

    A. SWOT analysis

    B. Assumptions analysis

    C. Brainstorming

    D. RACI chart

79. Complete Maslow's hierarchy of needs with the terms on the left.

    Safety

    Esteem

    Self-actualization

    Physiological

    Social

80. While overseeing a construction project, you are informed by the site supervisor that the painting team showed up even though the drywall team is not even half done. The painting team lead is not sure when his team is supposed to start the work. Which one of the following is contributing MOST to this issue?

    A. This is due to poor team cohesiveness.

    B. Lack of communication management plan.

    C. A proper work authorization system was not established in the project.

    D. The site supervisor lacks experience.

81. Mark, the project manager, is working on completing the new health system project and discover that someone has added a component that was not in the scope baseline. What is this an example of?

    A. Scope advancement

    B. Scope changes

    C. Scope creep

    D. Change request

82. You are managing a software application project to develop an online PMP exam simulator budgeted for $90,000 to assist students in practicing exam questions in a similar real-life environment. The team has completed design work, received approval from the technical review team, and initiated coding work. When asked by management what you currently expect the project to cost, you think that the costs you have incurred till now are typical for the rest of the project. While reviewing the current status of the project, you found that AC=$30,000 and EV=$35,000. What is your Estimate at Completion (EAC)?

    A. $85,000

    B. $77,586

    C. $90,000

    D. $60,000

83. What is the difference between the product backlog and the iteration backlog?

    A. The product backlog contains the work that the project team will do in the next iteration, and the iteration backlog will contain all the steps needed to complete the work

    B. The product backlog contains all work needed to be completed on the project, and the iteration backlog will contain the steps needed to complete the work

    C. Product backlog contains all work needed to be completed on the project, and the iteration backlog will contain all work that will get done in the next iteration

    D. Product backlog and the iteration backlog will outline the steps needed to manage the product and iteration

84. You are working for a cruise company as a project manager. Your company offers luxury tours to couples at a reasonable price. Currently, the company is considering adding more tours to a few other popular destinations during the holiday season in order to increase traffic and profitability. Which risk response strategy is in use?

    A. Share

    B. Exploit

    C. Accept

    D. Enhance

85. Your organization has outsourced a large portion of the activities of an ERP implementation project to a vendor. According to the contract, the vendor is supposed to review the design and code of any major component with the Technical Review Group (TRG) of your organization. So far, the vendor has completed and deployed three major components without the approval of the TRG team. As a project manager, what should you do in this situation?

    A. Terminate the contract immediately as the vendor has breached the contract.

    B. Stop making payment for the components that were deployed without approval.

    C. Do not worry too much, as the approval of the TRG is not that important.

    D. Issue a default letter to the vendor.

86. After the iteration has completed on an agile project, where will the team inspect the methods they used to build that increments?

    A. Iteration review

    B. Iteration planning

    C. Iteration backlog

    D. Retrospective

87. Which of the following analyses integrates scope, cost, and schedule measures to assess project performance?

    A. Trend analysis

    B. Project presentations and review

    C. Earned value analysis

    D. Variance analysis

88. You are having an issue with one of the manufacturing processes used to create the required parts for routers and switches that your company produces. Due to this major quality problem, only 15 percent of the parts manufactured have been within the control limits set by the Quality Assurance team. Higher management asks you to review the process activities to determine where the process went wrong. Which type of diagram should you use to gather this information?

    A. Control chart

    B. Pareto chart

    C. Scatter diagram

    D. Flowchart

89. As an employee, working conditions, salary, status, and job security matter a lot to you, just like your other coworkers. However, you always feel that you will be more motivated and will contribute more if you are rewarded for your contribution to a project and given the opportunity to grow professionally. Which motivational theory are you referring to?

    A. McGregor's Theory X and Theory Y

    B. Maslow's Hierarchy of Need

    C. Herzberg's Motivation-Hygiene Theory

    D. Dr. William Ouchi's Theory Z

90. While determining the funds needed for your project, you obtained historical information from previous projects as the basis to determine the price per square foot of carpeting. You used this information to calculate the cost of 20,000 square feet of carpeting that is required for the project. Which technique did you use to create the estimate?

    A. Analogous estimating

    B. Three-point estimating

    C. Heuristic estimating

    D. Parametric estimating

91. What is the difference between a release and iteration on an agile project?

    A. A release will contain multiple iterations

    B. An iteration will contain multiple releases

    C. The agile project manager determines what's in a release

    D. The agile project manager determines what's in an iteration

92. You recently completed the SOW detailing the specifications and other requirements for an expensive item you would like to purchase for one of your projects. While working on the SOW, you identified some of the source selection criteria, terms and conditions, and the contract type that you want to use. Also, you put together some documents to solicit proposals from your potential vendors. What tools and techniques will you use in the next process?

    A. Market research, make-or-buy analysis, and expert judgment.

    B. Bidder conference, advertising, and expert judgment.

    C. Procurement audits, procurement negotiations, and records management system.

    D. Contract change control system, procurement performance reviews, and claim administration.

93. An independent team from your organization has identified wasted steps that are not necessary for creating the product for your project. They have recommended a few actions for process improvement and have requested that some of the process documents be updated. Which of the following best describes what is being performed?

    A. They are performing manage quality activity.

    B. They are performing quality control activity.

    C. They are monitoring and controlling activities.

    D. They are directing and managing project work.

94. Place Tuckman's Five Stages in order.

Performing		1
Storming		2
Forming		3
Adjournimg		4
Norming		5

95. Who determines the functionality that will be required in each release of the product increment?

    A. Customer

    B. Agile project manager

    C. Development team

    D. Senior management

96. While overseeing a new wireless media streaming device development project, you notice that your team members are having significant difficulties resolving an issue that they have discovered during unit testing. After working on the issue for a week, the team members identified a number of possible causes for the issue and narrowed it down to two main causes. You asked the team members to determine if there is an interdependency between these two causes that would necessitate further action. Which one of the following tools would be the BEST to use in this situation?

A. Histogram

B. Flowchart

C. Scatter diagram

D. SWOT analysis

97. While working on a project, Bill, the project manager, is currently looking at how the project team is using the physical resources on the project and is worried that they may be using them incorrectly. He has decided to have a meeting with his team to discuss what can be done about this. What process is Bill doing?

A. Acquire Resources

B. Control Resources

C. Control Physical Resources

D. Monitor Resources

98. Mary is currently working on collecting the requirements of a new telephone system project and is worried that her stakeholders might not give her the correct requirements. She speaks to the sponsor, and he tells her to observe the customers as they work to understand the problem with the current system. After doing this process, what process should Mary do next?

A. Create WBS.

B. Define Scope.

C. Develop Scope Statement.

D. Direct and manage project work.

99. While building an agile space, the project manager would like to implement a tool that will allow the team to keep track of the flow of work while limiting the work in progress. What tool best meets these requirements:

A. Gantt chart

B. Kanban development

C. Whiteboard

D. Burndown charts

100. You have just finished negotiation on all terms and conditions of the contract with a selected vendor. As both parties are fully satisfied with the outcome of the negotiation, you started working on a draft official letter of notification of the contract award. Which one of the following processes are you in at this time?

    A. Plan Procurements

    B. Procurement Negotiations

    C. Close Procurements

    D. Conduct Procurements

101. Steve, the project manager for an ERP implementation project, was asked by the client via a change request to delay the implementation of one of the modules by one week. What should Steve do first in this situation?

    A. Instruct the team member responsible for the module to delay the implementation as per the client's request.

    B. Deny the request as it will delay the entire project.

    C. Inform the sponsor about the change request.

    D. Evaluate the impact of the requested change.

102. The use of Kanban development is critical on an agile project because it helps to:

    A. Act as an information radiator

    B. Places limits on who can manipulate the signboard

    C. Allows only people with the right permission to view it

    D. Allows only the agile project manager to edit it.

103. Your company worked on a new video console game for several months and invested a large amount of money in the development of the game. Unfortunately, the game was a flop, as one of the competitors also launched a similar but more sophisticated and higher quality game at the same time your company launched its game. The cost for research and development, patents, manpower, equipment, and intellectual property that your company spent in the development of the game is referred to as:

    A. Sunk costs

    B. Opportunity cost

    C. Depreciation

    D. Law of diminishing returns

104. The project manager, Bill, is currently collecting all of the knowledge the project team has gotten so far on the project. He wants to ensure that it can be used for future activities and maybe future projects. What would be the output of this process?

    A. Lessons learned register

    B. Lessons management system

    C. Project documents updates

    D. Procurement documents updates

105. Mary has completed planning the project and has executed the project. One day, a team member informs her that a major snowstorm is about to hit the city, and it will close down the organization for about three days. This will cause a delay in the project, but luckily Mary and her team have already come up with a response to an event like this. They would all work from home for the next couple of days. Mary decided it is time to set up the remote access software for all the team members to start working from home the next day. What process is Mary doing?

    A. Identity Risk

    B. Plan Risk Response

    C. Implement Risk Response

    D. Control Risk

106. Which of the following is not a servant leadership principle?

    A. Shield the team from interruptions

    B. Remove impediments

    C. Carry food and water

    D. Manage the team schedule.

107. Which of the following is the most critical skill an agile project manager should have?

    A. Management skills

    B. Software skills

    C. Scheduling skills

    D. Soft skills.

108. Which of the following is not considered a waste on an agile project?

    A. Partially done work

    B. Extra features

    C. Value-added processes

    D. Waiting

109. A stakeholder register contains stakeholder classification, identification, and assessment information. It also points out challenges related to working with the stakeholders as well as the project manager's impression of their knowledge, skills, capabilities, and attitude. Which of the following is TRUE regarding the stakeholder register?

    A. It should be accessible to all the team members and stakeholders.

    B. It should be accessible only to the sponsor.

    C. A project manager may publish it with other project documentation or keep it in reserve for personal use only.

    D. It should be accessible only to the PMO.

110. While reviewing the stakeholder engagement assessment matrix, you notice that one of the important stakeholders is in an "unaware" state at the moment and has no clue about what is happening in your project. As this stakeholder can contribute significantly to your project success, you decide to bring him to a "supportive" or "leading" state. Which of the following will help you to achieve your goal with this stakeholder?

    A. Send him regular reports on the project and its benefits.

    B. Offer him a paid vacation in Hawaii in exchange for his support.

    C. Assign top priorities to his expectations, concerns, and issues.

    D. Involve him in some project activities.

111. The higher management in your organization is very averse to risk. While planning the procurement strategy, you would like to make sure that you select the contract type that will have the least risk for the organization. Which of the following contract options will be best in this scenario?

    A. Cost reimbursable

    B. Fixed price economic price adjustment

    C. Fixed price

    D. Time & material

112. You are responsible for delivering a couple of very expensive pieces of equipment to a hospital in a foreign country. As per the agreement, your company is responsible for coordinating moving the equipment all the way to the nineteenth floor of the client's premises. Your local contact informs you that you need to pay a certain fee to the liftman for coordinating the movement of the equipment through the elevator to the specific floor at night time. What should you do in this situation?

    A. Pay the fee.

    B. Have a discussion with the customer and express your concern about the bribe.

    C. Consider the fee a bribe and refuse to pay it.

    D. Hire a local subcontractor to arrange the delivery.

113. What does incremental funding on an agile project mean?

    A. Paying the project team in small increments

    B. Paying the project manager in small increments

    C. Funding the entire project all upfront

    D. Funding the project in small increments as it's releasing features

114. Your management has asked you to lead a team to negotiate and finalize a deal with one of the vendors. While negotiating, you will mainly be focused on all of the following EXCEPT:

    A. Developing a good understanding and relationship with the seller

    B. Obtaining a fair and reasonable price for the product, service, or result

    C. Obtaining the lowest possible price and commitment for the shortest project duration from the vendor

    D. Discovering and dealing with disputes as much as possible prior to contract signing

115. You are overseeing a large data center project and have requested bids from several vendors to procure numerous networking devices such as routers, switches, firewalls, PCs, and servers. You decide to go for the lowest bidder since all the bidders are offering the devices from the same manufacturer. Senior management suggests that you conduct a bidder conference prior to selecting a specific seller. A bidder conference will satisfy which of the following mandatory standards in the PMI code of ethics and professional conduct?

    A. Respect

    B. Honesty

    C. Fairness

    D. Responsibility

116. While reviewing a deliverable due today to the customer, you noticed a technical defect in the deliverable. Upon further inspection, you realize that even though the deliverable fails to meet the project quality standards, it fully satisfies the contractual requirements. You are aware that the customer does not have the domain knowledge and technical expertise to notice the defect. The team member responsible for this deliverable tells you that fixing the defect will be time consuming and superfluous. What is your best course of action?

    A. Contact the customer immediately and inform them that the deliverable will be late due to some unavoidable consequences.

    B. Make sure that the issue is captured in the lessons learned so that future projects can benefit.

    C. Have a discussion with the customer about the issue with the deliverable.

    D. Do not mention anything and get formal acceptance from the customer.

117. Which of the following is mandatory work that must be included in an agile project:

    A. Daily standup meeting

    B. User feedback

    C. Servant leadership

    D. Regulatory compliance

118. You have been managing a top-secret government project, which has been progressing as planned up until last night. Suddenly, one of your team members called and informed you that an unexpected major problem occurred that was not included in the risk register. What should be your first course of action?

    A. Change the scope to exclude the problem.

    B. Update the risk management plan.

    C. Create a workaround.

    D. Create a fallback plan.

119. When managing defects on a project, the agile project manager should be concerned when:

    A. The defects are fixed as soon as they are discovered

    B. The defects are left in the product deliverable and reach the customer

    C. The defects are fixed by the agile team

    D. The defects are analyzed by the agile team

120. It is important to realize that stakeholders play a major role in project success. In order to ensure that stakeholders' expectations are managed properly throughout the life of a project, the project manager needs to do all of the following EXCEPT:

    A. Build trust with the stakeholders.

    B. Resolve conflicts among the stakeholders.

    C. Actively listen to the stakeholders' concerns.

    D. Convey ground rules to the stakeholders.

121. One of the team members informed you that she had identified a design defect that will delay the project by two weeks. You check the risk register and realize that no response plan for this situation has been documented. What action should you take FIRST?

    A. Replace the team member who made a mistake in design.

    B. Call the customer immediately and inform them about the situation.

    C. Contact the sponsor for advice.

    D. Evaluate the impact and brainstorm options with the team members.

122. Which one of the following would most likely result in a change request?

    A. An overall SV of 230.

    B. An overall CV of 50.

    C. A short delay of a critical path activity.

    D. A major delay of a non-critical path activity.

123. Peter is currently working on a software development project. His team is telling him they will take three months to complete the requirements in the sprint backlog. Peter informed them that they need to remove a few of the requirements and get the sprint done in 4 weeks. The team is refusing. What should Peter do?

    A. Listen to the team, as they are the experts and know exactly what they are doing.

    B. Inform them that agile is meant to be done in small increments, and they have to remove some of the requirements and get the sprint done in 4 weeks.

    C. Inform them to get the sprint done in 4 weeks with the current requirements; just hire more people to help with the coding.

    D. Inform the sponsor that the team will be taking 3 months to complete the sprint.

124. What best describes the cost of changes on an agile project?

    A. The cost of change will become incrementally lower as the project progresses

    B. The cost of change will become incrementally higher as the project progresses

    C. The cost of change will not change as the project progresses

    D. There is no cost of change on an agile project

125. You were approaching the end of your project and were asked to release the resources so that they can be assigned to other projects. Before releasing the resources, you want to make sure that you have completed the necessary actions. Which of the following is the correct order of actions that you take during the Closing processes?

    A. Get formal acceptances, write lessons learned, release the team, and close the contract.

    B. Get formal acceptances, release the team, write lessons learned, and close the contract.

    C. Write lessons learned, release the team, get formal acceptances, and close the contract.

    D. Release the team, get formal acceptances, close the contract, and write lessons learned.

126. Your team members have sent you their weekly updates on the deliverables they are working on. While reviewing and scrutinizing updates from the team members, you find out that the CPI=1.1 and SPI=1. What should you do next with the results of your analysis?

    A. Distribute the results to project stakeholders as per your communications management plan.

    B. Since the project is on track, you do not have to do anything at this time.

    C. Find out where you can spend the money that was saved.

    D. Instruct the team members to improve their timing.

127. As an agile project is progressing, which of the following should the project manager not expect to occur?

    A. Issues

    B. Conflicts

    C. Risks

    D. Changing team members during an iteration

128. Which one of the following integration management processes is responsible for implementing process improvement activities?

    A. Direct and Manage Project Work

    B. Monitor and Control Project Work

    C. Develop Project Charter

    D. Perform Integrated Change Control

129. You have been assigned to create a diagram that will demonstrate the logical relationships that exist between activities. You are also asked to display how long the project activities will take. Which of the following methods will you utilize to achieve this goal?

    A. Pareto chart

    B. CPM

    C. Check sheet

    D. PDM

130. When deciding what user stories should get done in the next iteration, what should the project team consider?

    A. How large is the story

    B. How much points the team completed in the past iterations

    C. Which customer wants the story

    D. Which story has the least risks

131. During which specific process does the project manager prevent scope changes from overwhelming the project?

    A. Define Scope

    B. Validate Scope

    C. Control Scope

    D. Perform Integrated Change Control

132. As a project manager, you have managed several projects in your organization. You notice that not all the projects are given the proper support and importance from higher management. You also notice that projects get terminated while in progress due to other higher-priority projects in the organization. You will be managing an IT project soon and want to make sure that your project will get the required support from the performing organization. What will be your best course of action?

    A. Make sure that the project meets the personal objectives of the sponsor.

    B. Communicate the project details and benefits with higher management on a regular basis.

    C. Correlate the need for the project to the organizational strategic objective and goal.

    D. Justify that your project should be the highest-priority project in the organization.

133. While managing an ERP project, you realize the targeted project end date will be delayed by several days. Upon further investigation, you identify some activities that can be performed in parallel. You also realize that you have not fully utilized some of your resources in the project. What will be the BEST course of action in this situation?

    A. Apply leads and lags.

    B. Apply resource leveling.

    C. Apply fast tracking and crashing.

    D. Develop a new project schedule.

134. The user story on an agile project will always contain the value, goal, and?

    A. Requirements

    B. Risks

    C. Change

    D. User type

135. In the data center project that you are managing, you identified several internal and external restrictions or limitations that will affect the performance of a process within the project. Which of the following BEST identifies these issues?

    A. Project assumptions

    B. Project scope

    C. Project requirements

    D. Project constraints

136. After the users have written the user stories, the team will then decomposed the stories into?

    A. Epics

    B. Features

    C. Tasks

    D. Requirements

137. You are currently in the Monitoring and Controlling Project Work process of a networking project that you are overseeing to implement a WIFI network in a rural community. Which of the following tasks will you perform as a part of this process?

    A. Manage the project's vendors closely.

    B. Compare the plan to the actual performance.

    C. Collect requirements from the stakeholders.

    D. Produce the deliverables of the project.

138. Agile project conduct planning at multiple points in time as the scope is refined and change over the project lifecycle. This is known as?

    A. Agile project planning

    B. Progressive planning

    C. Elaborate planning

    D. Rolling wave planning

139. Match the output by process group.

Final Product, Service or Result Transition		Initiating
Quality Metrics		Planning
Project Charter		Executing
Accepted Deliverable		Monitoring and Controlling
Lessons Learned Register		Closing

140. Which of the following is TRUE about stakeholders?

    A. Only the stakeholders who can positively impact the project should be listed in the stakeholder register.

    B. Stakeholder identification is a continuous and sometimes strenuous process.

    C. Change requests from the stakeholder with the most influence should be given the highest priority.

    D. Stakeholders should be given extras in order to meet and exceed their expectations.

141. Which process is MOST closely associated with continuous process improvement?

    A. Perform Qualitative Risk Analysis

    B. Manage quality

    C. Control Quality

    D. Plan Quality Management

142. Planning on an agile project is always considered to be?

    A. Mostly done at the beginning of the project

    B. Approved by the project manager

    C. Approved by the product owner

    D. An ongoing process

143. The cost of developing a product fix is related to which costs of the quality category?

    A. A prevention cost

    B. An internal failure cost

    C. An appraisal cost

    D. An external failure cost

144. Which of the following is considered a norm during agile project planning?

    A. Significant contributions by the agile project manager

    B. The use of outside consultants

    C. Midcourse adjustments

    D. The use of a change control Board.

145. The change control board just approved a change request to modify one of the major deliverables. In which process will this change be implemented?

    A. Perform Integrated Change Control

    B. Monitor and Control Project Work

    C. Close Project or Phase

    D. Direct and Manage Project Work

146. You have been assigned as a project manager for a project expected to last five months. The project has a budget of $450,000 and should be implemented in three different departments in your organization. While reviewing the status of the project after two months, you find that the project is 35 percent complete. Which of the following statements is TRUE about your project?

    A. Your project is on schedule.

    B. Your project is behind schedule.

    C. Your project is ahead of schedule.

    D. You cannot determine if your project is behind or ahead of schedule from the information given.

147. Your organization has enough resources only to work on one of two potential projects and decides to use the Net Present Value (NPV) to assess and select the best project for the organization. Project Alpha has an NPV of $45,000, and Project Beta has an NPV of $60,000. Project Alpha will take 3 years to complete, and Project Beta will take 4 years. What will be the opportunity cost of the project chosen?

    A. $60,000

    B. $45,000

    C. $25,000

    D. $105,000

148. User stories on an agile project should be written by?

    A. Team members

    B. Customers

    C. Agile project manager

    D. Senior management

149. You have been appointed as a project manager in a well-reputed hospital. While working on a project, you find that your employer is violating several codes issued by the local health department. What should be your first action in this situation?

    A. Have a discussion with your employer to find out if they are aware of the violations.

    B. Immediately resign from the company.

    C. Immediately inform the local health department about the violations.

    D. Do not worry about it since it is none of your business.

150. The product owner has requested to be showing how much work there remains to be done on the project. What would be the best agile tool to display this:

    A. Burndown chart

    B. Burnup chart

    C. Velocity chart

    D. Cumulative flow diagram.

151. The agile project team is a global team with members in multiple countries. Which of the following should not be an issue when managing a global agile team:

    A. Time zones

    B. Cultures

    C. Native languages

    D. Virtual meetings.

152. You are a shy project manager struggling with your communication skills. You like to keep to yourself unless you are prompted for your input. On the other hand, Steve is highly regarded by everyone and very well-liked. You consider Steve to be your role model as he is capable of getting others to see his way on many issues. What type of power does Steve possess?

    A. Expert power

    B. Reward power

    C. Referent power

    D. Legitimate power

153. While managing an ERP solution implementation project, you realize that you are not utilizing your resources evenly in the project. You found out that you are using almost all of your resources in some of the work weeks and hardly using any in some other work weeks. You consider moving around some of the activities and resources so that you can utilize your resources evenly throughout the project life cycle. Which of the following techniques are you using?

    A. Fast-tracking

    B. Crashing

    C. Resource leveling

    D. Critical chain

154. Ashley, a senior project manager, recently took over a project to produce a safe and effective drug from another project manager who just left the company. Ashley was surprised to find out that there is no change control board to review, approve, or deny a change request for the project. Upon further investigation, she finds that there is no organizational change control board to manage changes for the entire organization. What should Ashley do in this situation?

    A. Carry on with the change requests without a change control board.

    B. Establish a Change Control Board (CCB) for her project.

    C. Make all the decisions about the requested changes herself with the help of the team members.

    D. Ask the sponsor to approve or deny the change requests.

155. As a project manager, you have collected information about Sabrina, a team member, from multiple sources, including other team members and management staff. You have identified several areas for improvement for Sabrina that you want to discuss with her. You are particularly concerned that Sabrina is having many conflicts with other team members. During the one-on-one meeting, both of you agree on a training program to address the concern of conflicts with other team members. You also make sure that Sabrina understands she needs to submit her status and progress reports at the beginning of every week. Which action are you currently engaged in with Sabrina?

    A. Observation and conversation

    B. Project performance appraisals

    C. Team performance assessment

    D. Conflict management

156. You are having an issue with one of the manufacturing processes being used to create the required parts for routers and switches that your company produces. What should you use to identify the cause of this issue and the effect it may have on your project?

    A. Continuous improvement

    B. Histogram

    C. Ishikawa diagram

    D. Flowchart

157. While working with clients on the final acceptance of the application, you were delighted to find out that the application exceeded the performance criteria specified in the requirement specification approved by the clients. You implemented several features that were not in the project scope to meet and exceed the client's expectations. What can you conclude about the project performance?

    A. The project was a success as it provided features beyond the customers' expectations without any cost and schedule impact.

    B. The project was a success as it exceeded the customers' specified performance criteria.

    C. The project was unsuccessful as it has been gold plated.

    D. The project was a success as it made the clients really happy.

158. You are the project manager overseeing the development of a new console video game. It has 10 components, and 5 team members are working on it. There are 15 stakeholders for this project, and one of the stakeholders is the previous owner of this company. One of the components is of major concern because it is a difficult one to implement. You found out that the soonest you can start working on that component will be early next week, and it will take 10 days to complete. You also found out that as of now, the CPI=.81, and the SPI=1.2. What should be your main concern in this project at this time?

    A. The stakeholder who was the previous owner

    B. Schedule

    C. Number of stakeholders in this project

    D. Cost

159. While managing a WIFI project, you discovered that a few of your team members are not getting along. You also realized that three team members are not sure how to complete their deliverables. All of your team members are working together in the same building. You also set up regular weekly meetings with all the team members in a single meeting room. Which technique will NOT be helpful in this situation?

    A. War room

    B. Training

    C. Reward and recognition

    D. Negotiation

160. Which of the following is a method that will be used to conduct frequent verification and validation that can be done every second on the project?

    A. Pair programming

    B. Unit testing

    C. Integration testing

    D. Acceptance testing.

161. The project team is currently having disagreements about the program and methods they would use to implement a few of the features in the product backlog. What role should the agile project manager be doing during this scenario?

    A. Direct them to a resolution

    B. Coach them to a resolution

    C. Delegate tasks to find a resolution

    D. Inform them the resolution can only be approved by the agile project manager

162. Your sponsor is not very happy about the cost estimate you submitted for a construction project. The sponsor suggested that you come up with an exceptionally accurate cost estimate at your earliest convenience. What will be your best course of action in this situation?

    A. Use the historical information from a similar project and make adjustments for known differences.

    B. Use a rule of thumb estimate.

    C. Perform a cost aggregation for raw materials and labor for each activity in the WBS.

    D. Use the three-point estimates technique.

163. You are overseeing an ERP implementation project that will cost the company $1million and will take three years to complete. Six months into the project, higher management decided to terminate your project as they found an off-the-shelf solution that can be implemented in three months at a fraction of the planned cost. What is the first thing you should do in this situation when your project no longer seems commercially viable for the company?

    A. Conduct scope verification.

    B. Release the team immediately.

    C. Document the lessons learned.

    D. Have an urgent meeting with the sponsor to discuss the situation.

164. What would be an example of a tool agile teams should not be using?

    A. Whiteboard

    B. Task boards

    C. Computer Gantt charts

    D. Kanban board

165. Why is it difficult to have a written contract with an outside consultant when conducting agile projects?

    A. Agile projects has fixed scope

    B. Agile projects has a variable scope

    C. Agile projects has a fixed budget

    D. Agile projects has a variable budget

166. You decided to use a technique called rolling wave planning in your web-based insurance and tax payment application project. Which one of the following may be your key reason for selecting this technique?

    A. To prioritize project activities.

    B. To achieve the appropriate level of detail in each work package at the right time.

    C. To sequence project activities.

    D. To estimate the duration of project activities.

167. Your PMO stipulates that plurality support is the minimum level of support for any major decision in a project. You disagree with a block of supporters on a plan to purchase a piece of expensive equipment for your project. This block is larger than any other in your team, even though it is only 45 percent of the total team. What should you do in this kind of situation?

    A. Have an urgent meeting with the sponsor.

    B. Insist that any major decision should be supported by more than 50 percent of the team.

    C. Do nothing as PMO permits decisions to be made by a plurality, rather than a majority.

    D. Ask PMO to re-evaluate their policy.

168. You have been assigned as a project manager for an ongoing project and asked to provide activity duration estimates as soon as possible. You were surprised to find out that there was no detailed information available on the project. You explored your organizational process assets and identified a few similar projects that had been completed in the past. Which one of the following will be the correct tool to utilize in this kind of situation?

    A. Analogous estimate

    B. Three-point estimate

    C. Heuristic estimate

    D. One point estimate

169. A project manager, Peter, has decided to have a meeting with other project managers in the organization to review the project management processes everyone follows and see if there can be improvements. What term would best describe this?

    A. Project review

    B. Project lessons learned

    C. Project management

    D. Project governance

170. Which of the following statements best describes when releases would be available to the customers?

    A. In weeks

    B. In months

    C. In days

    D. In seconds

171. Mark had just gotten a new job in the organization as a system administrator. His main job is to ensure all the company servers are working properly. Mark's boss has requested that Mark also undertake a new project to upgrade 2 servers. Mark will do that on a part-time basis. What kind of organization is Mark working for?

    A. Functional

    B. Projectized

    C. Strong matrix

    D. Strong functional

172. Workarounds, or unplanned responses to emerging risks that were previously unidentified or accepted, are determined during which risk management process?

    A. Plan Risk Management process

    B. Control Risks process

    C. Plan Risk Responses process

    D. Perform Quantitative Risk Analysis process

173. You identify that there are 36 communication channels in your project. How many members do you have in your team?

    A. 9

    B. 10

    C. 36

    D. 18

174. While identifying risks in your project, your team cannot find any efficient ways to reduce the impact and probability or to insure against one of the risks. The relevant work is integral to the project; thus, you cannot simply remove the work package, and there is no suitable company to outsource the work to either. What is the best course of action in this situation?

    A. Identify ways to transfer the risk.

    B. Accept the risk and have contingency reserves.

    C. Identify ways to avoid the risk.

    D. Keep looking for ways to mitigate the probability and impact of the risk.

175. You notice that you are not utilizing your resources evenly in the project. You want to apply resource leveling by moving some of your activities from the week when you are using many resources to a week when you are hardly using any. Which of the following tools and techniques would be a good choice in this situation?

    A. Network diagram

    B. Responsibility assignment matrix

    C. Organizational breakdown structure

    D. Resource histogram

176. A project manager is using a chart that cross-references team members with the activities or work packages they are to accomplish. Which one of the following is an example of this kind of chart?

    A. Gantt chart

    B. RACI chart

    C. Milestone chart

    D. Flowchart

177. Why would agile projects refuse to use computer models to generate a project schedule?

    A. Schedule can be generated quickly

    B. Schedule can account for risks

    C. Schedule can account for costs

    D. Very little stakeholder interaction.

178. What is defined as a set of functionality that is complete to be useful but small enough not to be an entire project?

    A. Increment

    B. Release

    C. Minimal viable product

    D. Minimal complete product

179. If the work of the project will contain 10 iterations, and the velocity of the team is currently at 14 points. What is the total size of the project in terms of story points?

    A. 150

    B. 130

    C. 140

    D. 110

180. On an Agile project decompose user requirements from the highest level (1) to most detail (4).

    Task

    Stories

    Features

    Epics

    1

    2

    3

    4

Final Exam Answers

1. **B:** Even though the project manager spends a great deal of energy and time preventing problems, there are still problems that need to be resolved. Below is the problem-solving technique:

    – Define the cause of the problem (not just the symptoms)

    – Analyze the problem (cause and effect diagram)

    – Identify solutions

    – Implement the selected solution

    – Review the solution

    – Confirm that the solution solved the problem

    Here the project manager probably forgot to confirm that the solution actually solved the problem.

2. **B:** Stakeholder identification will continue throughout the project lifecycle. As the project proceeds through each phase, additional stakeholders may become involved while others will be released. Stakeholder identification is conducted primarily by the project management team, but some stakeholders may be identified in the project charter. Stakeholders may include people and organizations that may be affected either negatively or positively by the project outcome.

3. **B, D:** T-Shirt sizing and planning poker are both used in agile to estimate how long a task might take to get done.

4. **D:** The Control Quality process is about monitoring specific project results to determine if they comply with relevant quality standards and identifying ways to eliminate causes of unsatisfactory results. Monitoring adherence to the project scope is addressed in the Control Scope process, not in the Control Quality process.

5. **C:** This is an example of constraints. Constraints are limitations that limit the available options for a project.

6. **A:** Product analysis techniques such as product breakdown, systems analysis, system engineering, value engineering, value analysis, functional analysis, and others, may be used to perform a detailed analysis of the product, service, or result. This technique translates project objectives into tangible deliverables and requirements by improving the project team's understanding of the product.

7. **C:** Claims administrations is used as a tool & technique in the Control Procurement process.

8. **C:** Once the project scope has been completed, validated, and final delivery has been made, the project is considered to be completed. Any kind of disputes should be resolved in favor of the customers as much as possible, but the project manager should also be aware that customers are not always right and should resist this kind of situation. Once the project is completed, any addition to the project should be considered as a new project, and a detailed impact analysis should be carried out.

9. **C:** The first step would be to review the communication management plan, to understand what is missing or what needs to be corrected from it.

10. **C:** The current critical path is 20. By increasing B to 11, the new critical path will be 22.

11. **D:** Expectancy theory demonstrates that employees who believe their efforts will lead to effective performance and who expect to be rewarded for their accomplishments, remain productive as rewards meet their expectations.

12. **B:** Plan Communications is included in the planning process, which is generally completed prior to executing. Updates to the project plan, including the communications management plan, will occur during the entire project lifecycle.

13. **A:** A Fishbone analysis is done during the step of generate insight in a retrospective to show the reasons for why something would have failed.

14. **B:** A CPI of 6 means the project is 40% over budget and will need to be corrected.

15.

Micromanager	McGregor's Theory X
People are Self-led	McGregor's Theory Y
Increasing Employee Loyalty	Ouchi Theory Z
Hygiene Agents	Herzberg's Theory of Motication

16. **C:** A robust change control process will ensure that only the necessary changes are considered and implemented. A change control process cannot really help with the number of changes that will be requested in the project as the number of changes depends on how well defined the scope of the project is. Again, all stakeholders, regardless of their authority, should be able to submit change requests.

17. **B:** Constraints are restrictions a project faces, such as limitations on time, budget, scope, quality, schedule, resource, and technology. An imposed deadline and budget are examples of constraints.

18. **B:** Estimate at Completion (EAC)=BAC/CPI

    Here we have BAC=$3,000, AC=$2,000 and EV=$1,200 CPI=EV/AC=1200/2000=.6 So EAC=3000/.6=5,000

19. **C:** When managing an agile project, user stories will produce a lot of value to both the team members and the customers, as such it would be best to educate them on the value of the user stories.

20. **D:** Ishikawa diagram is a tool used for systematically identifying and presenting all the possible causes and sub causes of a particular problem in a graphical format. It can help in quality control by identifying the causes which contributed to a quality problem.

21. **D:** Lag is an inserted waiting time between activities. In this case, there is a 3 day delay before we can start coding.

22. **A:** Funding limit reconciliation is a technique of reconciling the expenditure of funds with the funding limits set for the project. As for the variance between the expenditure of funds and planned limit, the activities can be rescheduled to level out the rates of expenditures.

23. **D:** Configuration management plan describes the different versions and characteristics of the product, service, or result of the project and ensures accuracy and completeness of the description.

24. **A:** Crashing is a technique of adding additional resources to a project activity to complete it in less time. Examples of crashing could include approving overtime, bringing in additional resources, or paying to expedite delivery to activities on the critical path. Crashing does not always produce a viable alternative and may result in increased risk, more management time, and/or cost. Increasing the number of resources may decrease time, but not in a linear amount as activities will often encounter the law of diminishing returns.

25. **A:** You are in the Validate Scope process, which is closely related to the Control Quality process. Both the Control Quality and Validate Scope processes can be performed simultaneously, but Control Quality is usually performed prior to Validate Scope. Control Quality verifies correctness of the work, whereas Validate Scope confirms completeness. Control Quality is focused on measuring specific project results against quality specifications and standards, whereas Validate Scope is mainly focused on obtaining acceptance of the product from the sponsor, customers, and others.

26. **B:** The project manager should document the change request as per the project scope management plan and then submit the change request to the change control board once the impact analysis is completed. The change control board will either approve or deny the request.

27. **C:** Progressive elaboration occurs when more information in detail emerges over time.

28. **D:** The Precedence Diagramming Method (PDM) usually uses the Activity-on-Node (AON) convention where boxes/nodes are used to represent activities and arrows show dependencies.

29. **C:** Product scope describes the features, functions, and physical characteristics that characterize a product, service, or result. On the other hand, project scope describes the work needed to deliver a product, service, or result with the specified features and functions. Product scope may include subsidiary components, and project scope results in a single product, service, or result. Product scope completion, measured against the product requirements to determine successful fulfillment and project scope completion, is measured against the project plan, project scope statement, Work Breakdown Structure (WBS), WBS dictionary, and other elements.

30. **C:** You should proactively work with stakeholders to manage their expectations, address their concerns, and resolve issues.

31. **D.** This question is asking you to find the EAC. All you need to do is BAC/CPI to find the EAC. The rest of the answers are not real ways to get the EAC. Be careful in the exam of fake formulas that may confuse you.

32. **C:** The schedule management plan defines how the project schedule will be planned, developed, managed, executed, and controlled throughout the project life cycle. It serves as guidance for the scheduling process and defines the roles and responsibilities for stakeholders, along with scheduling methodologies, tools, schedule change control procedures, reporting formats, and frequencies.

33. **D:** An external dependency is related to a non-project activity and is considered outside the control of the project team. This is an example of external dependency since the other project manager does not have control over the completion of the server setup, but the project depends on it.

34. **C:** On the traditional project most of the planning is done in the beginning, while agile projects are planned throughout the project with the help of all stakeholders.

35. **C:** In iterative relationships, a phase is planned at a given time; planning for a subsequent phase is carried out as work progresses on the current phase or deliverables. In overlapping relationships, the successor phase can start prior to the completion of the predecessor phase. This approach can be applied as a schedule compression technique called "fast-tracking." This kind of relationship may increase project risk and the potential for conflicts as a subsequent phase progresses before the accurate information is available from the previous phase. This kind of relationship can reduce the ability to develop long-term planning, but it is very suitable in an undefined, uncertain, and rapidly changing environment.

36. **B:** The agile method of scrum calls each increment of work a Sprint.

37. **A, E:** Deliverables are reviewed by the customers in validate scope on a traditional and sprint review meeting in agile.

38. **C:** The project manager is in the process of determining the project budget. The cost baseline and the project funding requirements are outputs of the Determine Budget process.

39. **B:** Both the SPI and CPI are less than one, which suggests that the project is behind schedule and over budget. An activity with no buffer suggests that it is on the critical path. If a critical path activity takes longer and needs more manpower to complete, then it will obviously negatively impact both time and cost. The subcontractor who was replaced may not be working on a critical path activity. Purchasing an expensive piece of equipment will definitely add additional cost, but it will not necessarily add time. The client may add or reduce the scope, so there is a possibility that it will reduce the cost and time.

40. **D:** Your first course of action should be to find out more information about what happened so that you can chose the correct course of action. Meeting with the stakeholders and finding out the details will assist you to address the crisis. Since the problem has occurred, the next thing you should do as a project manager is address the risk. You accept the risk when you have no other option. As a project manager, you would use your available reserves in this kind of situation. The contingency reserves are for "known unknowns;" thus, you use them to pay for risks that you've planned for. You may need to use the management reserves as they are for "unknowns," or problems that you did not plan for, but they showed up anyway. Once the issue is addressed, you may need to reevaluate your risk identification process, look for unexpected effects of the problem, inform management, update the risk management plan, create a fallback plan, and take corrective and preventive actions.

41. **A:** The requirements traceability matrix is an output of the Collect Requirements process and shows the origin of the requirements. It will describe which stakeholder gave the requirement.

42. **A:** The first thing to do when there is a change in the project is to see how it will impact the rest of the project.

43. **A:** A Cost Benefit analysis refers to the point where the benefits or revenue from improving quality equals the incremental cost to achieve that quality.

44. **A:** The goal of team performance assessments is to identify the specific training, coaching, mentoring, assistance, or changes required to improve the team's performance and effectiveness. The project management team makes formal or informal assessments of the project team's effectiveness while team development efforts, such as training, team building, and colocation are implemented. A team's performance is measured against the agreed-upon success criteria, schedule, and budget target.

   The evaluation of a team's effectiveness may include indicators such as:
   - How well the team is performing, communicating, and dealing with conflicts
   - Areas of improvement in skills that will help individuals perform assignments more efficiently and areas of improvement in competencies that will help the team perform better as a team
   - Increased cohesiveness where team members work together to improve the overall project performance by sharing information and experiences openly and helping each other more frequently
   - Reduced staff turnover rate

45. **A:** Referent power is based on referring to someone in a higher position to leverage some of the superior's power. Penalty (coercive/punishment) is predicated on fear and gives the project manager the ability to penalize a team member for not meeting the project goals and objectives. Expert power is based on the knowledge or skill of a project manager on a specific domain. Being the subject matter expert or project management expert will give the project manager substantial power to influence and control team members. Reward power imposes positive reinforcement, and it is the ability of giving rewards and recognition.

46. **D:** This is an example of fixed cost since regardless of how many times the team will use the tools, they will pay $3,000/month.

47. **B:** The output of the Sprint planning meeting is the Sprint backlog, which will outline all work to be done in the next Sprint.

48. **B:** Termination for convenience is a contract clause that permits the buyer to terminate a contract at any time for a cause or convenience. Usually, there will be specific conditions associated with the execution of this clause.

49. **D:** Issues and risks are not the same thing. An issue is an obstacle that threatens project progress and can block the team from achieving its goals. A risk is an uncertain event or condition that may have a positive or negative effect on the project's objective if it occurs.

50. **C:** In Abraham Maslow's Hierarchy of Needs, accomplishment, respect, attention, and appreciation are represented as esteem.

51. **C:** A bottom-up estimate is the most time-consuming and generally the most accurate estimate. In this technique, one estimate per activity is received from the team members. This estimate can be based on expert judgment, historical information, or an educated guess. A rough order of magnitude is an approximate estimate (–25 percent to 75 percent) made without detailed data. It is used during the formative stages for initial evaluation of a project's feasibility. A heuristic estimate is based on a rule of thumb, such as the 80/20 rule. A top-down estimate is usually given to the project manager from the management or the sponsor. This type of estimate measures the project parameters, such as budget, size, complexity, and duration based on the parameters of a previous similar project and historical information. It is usually done during an early phase of the project when not much information is available; thus, it is less accurate even though it is less costly and less time-consuming.

52. **A:** It will be best to get the team the correct training they will need to complete the project

53. **C:** A flowchart helps the project team anticipate and identify where quality problems might occur in a project, which in turn, helps the team develop alternatives when dealing with quality problems.

54. **A:** Project communications is an output of the Manage Communications process. All other items listed are included in the communications management plan.

55. **B:** Mitigation is the specific action that will be taken if threats occur in order to reduce the impact of them.

56. **C:** Urgency is not included in the basic communications model, but should be considered when determining the method of communication to be used.

57. **D:** A project manager should always be truthful in his/her communications and should provide accurate information in a timely manner. A project manager should not deceive others or make misleading half-truths or false statements. None of the options listed in 'A,' 'B,' or 'C' will resolve this issue immediately, and Steve should inform the stakeholder that he needs a little more time to verify the information about the major component and will follow up with him/her shortly when he has an accurate update.

58. **D:** Avoid is the elimination of the threat by eliminating the cause or changing the project management plan. Here you utilized the avoid strategy by terminating the contract with the subcontractor to eliminate the threat to your project.

59. **A:** Empower the project manager is not one of the lean software development principles, the other choices are.

60. **C:** Enhance is a strategy to deal with an opportunity. By influencing the underlying risk triggers, this strategy increases the size, probability, likelihood, and positive impact of an opportunity.

61. **C:** Agile is an umbrella term that is used to refer to different types of iterative development.

62. **C:** When a customer would like to add a change to an agile project, they simply added to the product backlog. That new feature will then be prioritized based on his value in the product backlog.

63. **D:** A project manager should understand the significance of this or to finding and must consult the experts before proceeding further.

64. **A:** Anytime you come across a new risk, the first thing you should do is document it in the risk register and then analyze the impact as well as the probability of that risk. You should not take any further action until you've analyzed the risk.

65. **D:** In lean software development, optimize as a whole is to see a system as more than the sum of its parts.

66. **D:** A resource calendar shows who is and who is not available to work during any given time period. The resource calendar may consider attributes such as experience, skill level, expertise, capabilities, and geographical locations for human resources to identify the best resources and their availability.

67. **A:** Benchmarking is looking at other projects or industry standards to collect the requirements for your project.

68. **D:** The first step in the 12 principles for leading an agile project is to learn the team member's needs.

69. **C:** We know CPI = EV/AC, so CPI = $ 27,000 / $25,000 = 1.08 And SPI = EV/PV, so SPI = $ 27,000 / $30,000 = .9

70. **B:** Once the WBS is created with all the work packages, the team members should work on decomposing the work packages to create the detailed activity list. Network diagram and activity sequencing can be performed only after the activity list is created.

71. **D:** In agile iterations should be no more than one to four weeks. Features that takes longer than should be decomposed into smaller features that can fit within a time-box of one to four weeks.

72. **B:** Some changes in the project are inevitable. A project manager should make sure that the change requests are evaluated and presented to the CCB for review. The project manager should not have the attitude to deny changes whenever possible. The focus of the project manager should be to prevent unnecessary changes, evaluate the impacts, and manage changes as necessary.

73. **B:** Risk mitigation simply means a reduction in the probability and/or impact of an adverse risk event to an acceptable threshold. Leasing the equipment reduces the consequence of the threat in this specific situation.

74. **A:** You have 20 miles to complete at a rate of $10,000/mile. Your budget at completion is 20*10,000 =$200,000.

75. **D:** One of the values in the agile manifesto is responding to changes over following a plan.

76. **B:** One of the agile guiding principles is: "working software is the primary measure of progress."

77. **A:** One of the agile guiding principles is simplicity, the art of maximizing the amount of work not done.

78. **D:** RACI is a type of responsibility assignment matrix chart, which can be used to ensure clear divisions of roles and responsibilities (RACI stands for responsible, accountable, consult, and inform). SWOT analysis, assumption analysis, brainstorming are information gathering techniques and are used to identify risks in the project.

79.

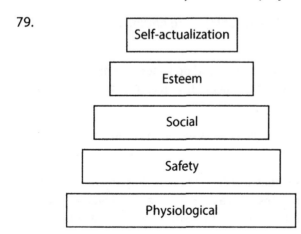

80. **C:** Work authorization system is a formal, documented procedure to describe how to authorize and initiate work in the correct sequence at the appropriate time. The other options listed here could be contributory factors, but most likely a work authorization procedure was either not properly established or not properly followed.

81. **C:** Scope creep is when things are added to the scope and were not in the approved scope baseline.

82. **B:** If CPI or past results are typical or expected to continue, the correct EAC formula is EAC = BAC/CPI. In this case, BAC =$90,000

    CPI=EV/AC=$35,000/$30,000=1.16   EAC=$90,000/1.16=$77,586

83. **C:** The product backlog will contain all the work needed to complete the project, while the iteration backlog will contain the work that will get done in the next iteration.

84. **D:** The cruise company is using the enhance strategy to increase the traffic and profitability. By influencing the underlying risk triggers, this strategy increases the size, probability, likelihood, and positive impact of an opportunity.

85. **D:** Anytime the vendor is not following the instructions stated in the contract, the project manager should inform the vendor that they are in default. Without informing the vendor about the concern and what they are doing wrong, you cannot terminate the contract. You also cannot simply stop any payment.

86. **D:** A retrospective is done after each iteration for the team to inspect and create a plan for improvements to be done in the next iteration.

87. **C:** Earned value analysis is used to integrate scope, cost, and schedule measures to assess project performance. Trend analysis and variance analysis are included in earned value analysis. Variance analysis may include only a comparison of actual performance with one specific baseline. Presentations may be used to deliver information obtained during earned value analysis.

88. **D:** A Flowchart is a graphical representation of a process to help analyze how problems occur and to identify potential process improvement opportunities. There are many styles, but all flowcharts show activities, decision points, the order of processing, points of complexity, and interrelationships between elements in the process.

89. **C:** According to Herzberg, destroying hygiene factors such as working conditions, salary, status, and security can destroy motivation, but improving them under most circum- stances will not improve motivation. The hygiene factors are not sufficient to motivate people, and motivating agents provide the best positive reinforcement. Motivating people is best done by rewarding and letting people grow.

90. **D:** Parametric estimating is a technique that reviews historical data for statistical correlations. Variables are then used to estimate the costs in the current project. For example, if historical information identifies that the flooring installed in a similar project cost$1.50 per square foot, then the 20,000 square feet of flooring required for the new project would cost$30,000. Typically, this technique has been known to produce a high level of accuracy, but it will be costly due to the level of sophistication that is required to implement it. In most cases, the technique is performed when the performing organization conducts many similar projects, historical information is accurate, and the model used for the estimate is scalable.

91. **A:** A release is a part of the product that is pushed all the way to the users and will generally take multiple iterations to complete. The product owner determines the features in a release and the agile project team determines how much work can be done in an iteration.

92. **B:** You just finished the Plan Procurement Management process and should be moving to the next process of Conduct Procurements. In the Conduct Procurement process, you should be obtaining and evaluating seller responses, selecting a seller, and awarding a contract. The tools and techniques you will be using in Conduct Procurement process are bidder conference, advertising, and expert judgment.

93. **A:** Manage Quality is a process to determine if the project activities are complying with organizational and project policies, standards, processes, and procedures. This process is primarily concerned with overall process improvement and does not deal with inspecting the product for quality or measuring defects. The primary focus is on steadily improving the processes and activities undertaken to achieve quality.

94.

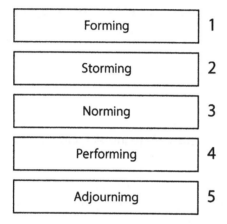

Forming	1
Storming	2
Norming	3
Performing	4
Adjournimg	5

95. **A:** The customers will outline the functionality that will be required in each of the releases not the agile project manager or development team.

96. **C:** A scatter diagram is a tool and technique used in quality management processes to analyze two characteristics of a process and see if there is any interdependency between them. Based on the outcome of the scatter diagram, appropriate actions can be taken to improve quality.

97. **B:** The process of Control Resources is where the project manager will analyze how the physical resources are being used on the project.

98. **B:** Mary is currently in the Collect Requirements process. After you collect the requirements, you would then create the scope statement in the Define Scope process. Choice A would come after you have define the scope. C is a made up choice. D would come after you have finished all the planning process.

99. **B:** The Kanban development is the use of a signboard that is used to help track the work in progress and limit the work in progress.

100. **D:** Conduct Procurements is the process of obtaining seller responses, selecting a seller, and awarding the procurement, usually in the form of a contract. Plan Procurements is the process of documenting project purchasing decisions, specifying the approach, de- fining selection criteria to identify potential sellers, and putting together a procurement management plan. Procurement negotiation is not a process but is a tool & technique used in the Conduct Procurements process. The Close Procurements process is mainly concerned with completing each project procurement.

101. **D:** The very first thing the project manager should do upon receiving a change request is to evaluate the impact on the project objectives, such as scope, time, cost, quality, risk, resources, and others. The change request then should be submitted to the change control board for approval or rejection. Instructing the team member and informing the sponsor of the requested change would not be done prior to evaluating the impact of the requested change. Also, the project manager should make every effort to prevent unnecessary changes in the project as much as possible.

102. **A:** Kanban development is used as an information radiator to allow all customers and team members to visualize the flow of work.

103. **A:** The sunk cost is a retrospective cost that is already paid for a project and often used to describe what is written off from a canceled project as unrecoverable.

104. **A:** The project manager is doing the process of Manage Project Knowledge, which has an output of lessons learned register.

105. **C:** In this question the planning is already done and Mary is just implementing the response they selected in the planning.

106. **D:** Manage the team schedule is not a servant leadership principle, that is more of a traditional project management principle.

107. **D:** Soft skills is important on an agile project due to the constant need to communicate with all stakeholders on the project.

108. **C:** Value-added processes would not be considered waste on a project; all other choices would.

109. **C:** Since a stakeholder register contains sensitive information, a project manager may publish it with other project documentation nor keep it in reserve for personal use only.

110. **D:** Involving the stakeholders in some project activities is a good way to bring them to a supportive or a leading state.

111. **C:** Fixed price contract will be the best option in this case as this type of contract will have less risk for the buyer and most risk for the seller.

112. **A:** You should pay the fee since the fee has a valid purpose and should not be considered a bribe.

113. **D:** Incremental funding is possible on agile projects because it allows the organization to fund the project in small increments as the project is releasing certain features to the customers.

114. **C:** You should always try to have a win-win situation. The lowest possible price and shortest possible duration will put the vendor in an extremely difficult situation and increase the potential for failure. Your main objective of negotiation will be to build trust, obtain a fair and reasonable price that both parties are comfortable with, and uncover the points of conflict and dispute prior to final contract signing.

115. **C:** The bidder conference is also called the contractor conference, vendor conference, or pre-bid conference. It is intended to assure that no seller receives preferential treatment and that all sellers have a clear, common understanding of the procurement (technical requirements, contractual requirements, etc.).The key objective is to provide all potential contractors with the information they need to determine if they would like to continue with the contracting process. The bidder conference will ensure mandatory standard of fairness in the PMI code of ethics and professional conduct by making the opportunity equally available to all qualified vendors.

116. **C:** You should have a discussion with the customer about any issue with the deliverable so that a mutual solution can be identified. Capturing the issue in the lessons learned will not solve the current problem. Issuing the deliverable and getting the formal acceptance will not serve the best interest of the customer.

117. **D:** Regulatory compliance is work that must be implemented on a project due to government regulations. While the other choices are things, we should have on a project they're not mandatory.

118. **C:** Since the problem has occurred, the first thing you should do as a project manager is address the risk by creating a work around. Once the issue is addressed, you may need to re-evaluate you risk identification process, look for unexpected effects of the problem, inform management, update the risk management plan, create a fallback plan, and take corrective and preventive actions.

119. **B:** Defects should not be left in the product deliverable and reach the customers. This will be costly to fix and reduce customer satisfaction.

120. **D:** A project manager should actively listen to the stakeholders' concerns, resolve conflicts among the stakeholders, and build trust. The project manager should convey the ground rules to the team members, not to the stakeholders.

121. **D:** In this kind of situation, you should always find out details of the design defect before you have a discussion about it with the sponsor or the customers. The very first thing you should do is to evaluate the impact of the design defect and have a brainstorming session with the team members on possible solutions.

122. **C:** A short delay of a critical path activity will result in an overall delay of the project duration, so a change request should be created. A major delay of a non-critical path activity may not have any impact on the overall project duration. A project manager can use the contingency reserve to deal with the cost and schedule variances. Fast-tracking and crashing methods can also be used to deal with schedule variance.

123. **B:** Agile is meant to deliver value early to the customers with small increments and sprints has to be done 2-4 weeks. This way, customers can start using the product sooner and give their feedback.

124. **B:** Over the course of an agile project the cost of changes will be incrementally higher as the product goes from requirements into production.

125. **A:** You should not release the team until the lessons learned are documented and added to the organizational process assets as you need their help with the lessons learned. Most contracts have payment terms that allow for some period of time before full payment is required, thus the last thing you do on the project is close the contract.

126. **A:** When the project manager ascertains the current project status, it should be communicated to the project stakeholders as per the communications management plan.

127. **D:** Once an iteration has started it is not advisable for team members to change as this will affect the velocity of the team.

128. **A:** Process improvement activities including corrective actions, preventive actions, and defect repairs, are implemented in the Direct and Manage Project Work process.

129. **B:** Critical Path Method (CPM) is a technique of schedule analysis that evaluates the activities considering activity duration, logical relationship, dependency, leads, lags, assumptions, and constraints to determine the float of each activity and the overall schedule. This method identifies the critical path with the least flexibility and the highest risk so that it can be managed appropriately. The critical path duration is the longest path in the network diagram and the shortest amount of time the project will take to complete.

130. **B:** When determining how much stories can get done in an iteration the team should look at its velocity which is based on how much points they were able to get done in previous iterations.

131. **C:** Control Scope is the process of monitoring the status of the project and product scope, maintaining control over the project by preventing overwhelming scope change requests, and managing changes to the scope baseline. It also assures that underlying causes of all requested changes and recommended corrective actions are understood and processed through the Integrated Change Control Process.

132. **C:** Correlating the need for the project to the organizational strategic objective and goal is the best approach to gain support for the project from the performing organization. Organizational planning can establish the funding and support for the component projects on the basis of specific lines of business, risk categories, and other factors. An organization's strategic goals and objectives are the primary factor guiding investments. Projects, programs, or other related works that contribute the least to the portfolio's strategic objectives may lose the support of the performing organization as soon as there is a higher priority project that is more oriented toward the strategic objective. It is a good idea to meet the personal objectives of the sponsor, but it will not confirm the support from the performing organization. Communicating the project details and benefits will not be sufficient enough to gain support from the performing organization.

133. **C:** Fast-tracking is a schedule compression technique of performing critical path activities in parallel when they were originally planned in series. Crashing is another schedule compression technique of adding additional resources to project critical path activities to complete them more quickly. This technique looks at cost and schedule trade-offs and resources are added either from inside or outside the organization. Since some of the activities in the project can be performed in parallel and resources have not been fully utilized, we can use fast-tracking and crashing in this project.

134. **D:** The user story typically has three parts user type, want/need, and value.

135. **D:** Project constraints specify the limitations and restrictions a project faces, such as limitations on time, budget, scope, quality, schedule, resource, and technology.

136. **C:** Stories are decomposed into tasks.

137. **B:** The Monitoring and Controlling Project Work process usually measures the work results against the plan.

138. **D:** Rolling wave planning is about the scope getting more refined over time as more requirements are learned.

139.

Project Charter	Initiating
Quality Metrics	Planning
Lessons Learned Register	Executing
Accepted Deliverable	Monitoring and Controlling
Final Product, Service or Result Transition	Closing

140. **B:** Stakeholder identification is a continuous and sometimes grueling process as not all stakeholders will be identified during the initiating process. Some of the stakeholders will only be interested in the end product and will get involved in the project at its closing. Stakeholders with both positive and negative influence should be listed in the stakeholder register. All of the stakeholders should be treated equally, and change requests should be prioritized according to project needs. Giving stakeholders extras or gold plating is not a preferred way to meet and exceed stakeholder expectations.

141. **B:** Manage Quality is the process to determine if the project activities are complying with organizational and project policies, standards, processes, and procedures. This process is primarily concerned with overall process improvement and does not deal with inspecting the product for quality or measuring defects. The primary focus is on steadily improving the processes and activities undertaken to achieve quality.

142. **D:** On an agile project, planning is considered to be an ongoing process as customers add features and remove features from the product backlog.

143. **B:** A product fix will require rework and the cost associated with it will fall under the cost of nonconformance internal failure cost category.

144. **C:** Mid-course adjustments are considered the norm on an agile project due to the uncertainty of the project scope is the project is progressing.

145. **D:** An approved change request for corrective actions, preventive actions, and defect repairs will be implemented in the Direct and Manage Project Work process.

146. **B:** The project is 5months long, so every month you are scheduled to complete 20percent of the work. We know PV=BAC*planned % complete

After two months the Planned Value (PV) should be $450,000*40percent=$180,000 We know EV=BAC*actual %complete

After two months you completed 35 percent of the work, so the Earned Value (EV) is $450,000 * 35 percent = $157,500. We know SPI = EV/PV = 157,000 / 180,000 = .872. SPI less than 1 indicates that the project is behind schedule.

147. **B:** We will select Project Beta, since it has a larger NPV. The number of years is irrelevant here since it is already factored into the NPV. We are not selecting Project Alpha, which has a NPV of $45,000. The opportunity cost for the Project Beta will be the value of the project that we did not select or the opportunity that we missed out, in this case Project Alpha.

148. **B:** User stories are written by the customers to help define the shared vision between the team members and the customers.

149. **A:** The best option is to verify your observation by having a discussion with your employer about the violations and learn about the employer's perspective.

150. **A:** A burndown chart displays work that remains to be done.

151. **D:** A virtual meeting is a tool the team will use to communicate and should not be an issue on an agile project, all other choices may pose an issue.

152. **C:** Referent power is based on referring to someone in a higher position to leverage some of the superior's power. This power is also based on the respect or the charismatic personality of the project manager.

153. **C:** Resource leveling is used to produce a resource-limited schedule by letting the schedule slip and cost increase in order to deal with a limited amount of resources, resource availability, and other resource constraints. It can be used when shared or critically required resources are only available at certain times, in limited quantities, or when resources have been over-allocated. We may have several peaks and valleys in our resource histogram. In order to level the resources, evenly utilize them as much as possible, or to keep resource usage at a constant level, we can move some of our activities from the week when we are using many resources to a week when we are hardly using any.

154. **B:** A Change Control Board (CCB) consists of members including stakeholders, managers, project team members, senior management, and other people, and it is responsible for reviewing, approving, or denying change requests. Some organizations have permanent CCB staffed by full-time employees to manage changes for the entire organization, not only for the projects. The project manager should consider establishing a CCB for the project if the organization does not have one.

155. **B:** While performing the project performance appraisals, the project management team meets with the team members and provides feedback about team members' performance and how effectively they are performing their tasks. A 360-degree feedback is used to receive feedback from all directions including peers, superiors, subordinates, and sometimes includes vendors and external contractors.

156. **C:** Ishikawa diagram, or cause and effect diagram, is a tool used to systematically identify and present all the possible causes and sub causes of a particular problem in a graphical format. It can help in quality control by identifying the causes that contributed to a specific quality problem. Cause and effect diagrams are particularly useful for identifying the causes of risks.

157. **C:** The project was unsuccessful as it has been gold plated. We should always focus to meet and exceed customer's expectations by delivering the features and functionalities as per the requirement specification approved by the clients. Gold plating or giving extras to the clients should be avoided by all means.

158. **D:** Your SPI is more than 1, which indicates that you are ahead of schedule, but your CPI is less than 1, which suggests that you are over budget. Cost should be the main concern in this project at this time.

159. **A:** Colocation/war room is a technique of placing many or all of the most active project team members in the same physical location to enhance their ability to perform as a team. Since all the team members are in the same building and having meetings in the same meeting room most of the time already, colocation is not a technique we should be considering in this case. Other techniques listed here will be beneficial to resolve conflict and concern about deliverables.

160. **A:** Pair programming is defined as when one programmer writes the code another inspects the code as it's been written. This leads to the codes being inspected in seconds.

161. **B:** During the storming phase of the Tuckman's letter, the agile project manager should be coaching the team to support constructive disagreement. Let the team find the best methods to resolve their issues.

162. **C:** Cost aggregation describes the bottom-up estimate, which will provide the most accurate estimate in this case. Other estimates such as heuristic and analogous specified in other choices are very quick, but will not produce the most accurate estimate. Three-point estimate is also not the best option in this scenario.

163. **A:** A project can be terminated at any time due to a specific reason or convenience. The project manager should conduct a scope verification to measure the amount of completed work up to the cancellation. All other options can be done once the scope verification is completed and the project manager has the details about the current situation.

164. **C:** Agile tools should be low-tech high touch of which the computerized Gantt chart is not.

165. **B:** Agile project uses the concept of the inverted triangle, in which case the scope changes consistently while the budget and the schedule remain the same. This makes it difficult to write a contract for work that changes as the project is progressing.

166. **B:** Rolling wave planning takes the progressive elaboration approach and plans in great detail current/near term work while future work is planned in a more abstract and less detailed way. During the early strategic planning phase, work packages may be decomposed into less defined milestone levels as all details are not available. At a later date, they will be decomposed into detailed activities. This kind of planning is frequently used in IT and research projects where unknowns tend to be intangibles, but less so in construction projects where unknowns are generally extremely expensive and destructive.

167. **C:** Plurality is a group decision-making technique where a decision is based on the largest block in a group, even if a majority is not achieved. Since PMO permits plurality, you have no option but to agree with the largest block in the group. Asking the PMO to reevaluate their policy will not resolve the problem immediately.

168. **A:** An analogous estimate measures the project parameters, such as budget, size, complexity, and duration based on the parameters of a previous, similar project and historical information. It is usually done during an early phase of the project when not much information is available.

169. **D:** Project governance is used to help improve the processes that are followed on a project.

170. **B:** One release is generally made up of a few iterations, in which case it can take months since each iteration can last one to four weeks.

171. **A:** Companies that do project management on a part-time schedule are usually functional. Notice his main job is still operations.

172. **B:** The project must be in the Control Risks process if risks have occurred. Workarounds are unplanned responses developed to deal with the occurrence of unanticipated risk events that were not included in the risk register.

173. **A:** We know the number of communication channels=n(n−1)/2,where n=number of members in the team So 9(9−1)/2=72/2=36.We have 9 members in the team to have 36 communication channels.

174. **B:** Since the relevant work is integral to the project, you simply cannot remove the work package, nor can you transfer it to a third party. The best approach will be to accept the risk and have a contingency plan to deal with it in case it happens.

175. **D:** A resource histogram is a graphic display that can be used to track resources through a time when shared or critically required resources are only available at certain times, in limited quantities, or when resources have been over-allocated. We may have several peaks and valleys in our resource histogram in the stated situation. In order to level the resources, evenly utilize them as much as possible, or to keep resource usage at a constant level, we can move some of our activities from the week when we are using many resources to a week when we are hardly using any.

176. **B:** A Responsibility Assignment Matrix (RAM) chart cross-references team members with the activities or work packages they are to accomplish. One example of a RAM is a Responsible, Accountable, Consult, and Inform (RACI) chart, which can be used to ensure clear divisions of roles and responsibilities.

177. **D:** One of the reasons not to use computer models in agile is due to the lack of stakeholder interactions, which can lead to poor communications and less customer satisfaction.

178. **C:** A minimal viable product (MVP), refers to a set of functionalities that is complete to be useful, but small enough not to be the entire project.

179. **C:** Total size of the project will be 10 iterations x 14 points = 140 Points.

180.

Epics	1
Features	2
Stories	3
Tasks	4

Acceptance Criteria: A set of conditions that are met before deliverables are accepted by the customers or sponsors.

Activity: A distinct, scheduled portion of work performed during the project. Usually stored on the activity list.

Actual Cost (AC): The actual cost incurred for the work performed on an activity during a specific time period.

Analogous Estimating: A technique for estimating the duration or cost of an activity or a project using historical data from a similar activity or project. Also known as top-down estimating.

Assumption: A factor in the planning processes considered to be true or real without proof or demonstration.

Backward Pass: A critical path method technique for computing the late start and late finish dates by working backward through the schedule model from the project end date.

Baseline: The accepted version of a work product that can be changed using formal change control processes and is used as the basis for comparison to actual results.

Bottom-Up Estimating: A method of estimating project duration or cost by aggregating the estimates of the lower-level components of the work breakdown structure (WBS).

Budget at Completion (BAC): The amount of all budgets established for the work to be performed.

Change Control: A process whereby changes to documents, deliverables, or baselines related with the project are identified, documented, approved, or rejected.

Change Control Board: A formally commissioned group responsible for reviewing, assessing, approving, deferring, or rejecting changes to the project, and for recording and communicating such decisions.

Change Control System: A set of procedures that defines how modifications to the project deliverables and documentation are managed and controlled.

Change Request: A formal proposal to change any document, deliverable, or baseline in the project management plan.

Communications Management Plan: A component of the project management plan that describes how, when, and by whom information will be administered and distributed.

Configuration Management System: A collection of procedures used to track project artifacts and monitor and control changes to these artifacts.

Constraint: A restrictive feature that affects the execution of a project.

Contingency Reserve: Time or money assigned in the schedule or cost baseline for known risks with response strategies.

Corrective Action: A planned activity that restores the performance of the project work with the project management plan.

Cost Baseline: The approved version of work package cost estimates and contingency reserve that can be changed using formal change control procedures.

Cost Management Plan: A component of a project management plan that defines how costs will be planned and controlled.

Cost Performance Index (CPI): A measure of the cost efficiency of budgeted resources expressed as the ratio of earned value to actual cost.

Cost Variance (CV): The amount of budget shortfall or surplus at a given point in time, expressed as the difference between the earned value and the actual cost.

Crashing: A schedule compression technique used to shorten the schedule duration by adding resources. This will generally increase cost on the project.

Critical Chain Method: A schedule method that allows the project team to place buffers on any project schedule path to account for limited resources.

Critical Path: The sequence of activities that represents the longest path through a project, which determines the shortest and longest possible duration. Activities on the critical path have no float.

Critical Path Activity: Any activity on the critical path in a project schedule.

Critical Path Method: A method used to estimate the minimum project duration and determine the amount of scheduling flexibility on the logical network paths within the schedule.

Decomposition: A technique used for dividing and subdividing the project deliverables into smaller, more manageable parts. Also used to subdivide the project activities.

Defect Repair: An intentional activity to modify a nonconforming product or product component.

Deliverable: Deliverable is a part of the product that is presented to the customer or stakeholders for acceptance.

Duration: The total number of work periods required to complete an activity or work breakdown structure component, expressed in hours, days, or weeks.

Early Finish Date: The earliest an activity can finish without delaying the project end date.

Early Start Date: The earliest an activity can start without delaying the project end date

Earned Value (EV): The amount of money worth of work actually accomplished on the project.

Earned Value Management: A methodology that combines scope, schedule, and resource measurements to assess project performance.

Enterprise Environmental Factors: Conditions, not under the immediate control of the team, that influence, constrain, or direct the project.

Estimate at Completion (EAC): The forecast of the total cost of the project at the end based on the current spending rate of the project.

Estimate to Complete (ETC): The amount of money that will be needed to complete the current project based on the current performance.

Fast Tracking: A schedule compression technique in which activities or phases are done in parallel for at least a portion or the their entire duration. This can increase risk on the project.

Finish-to-Finish: A relationship in which a successor activity cannot finish until a predecessor activity has finished.

Finish-to-Start: A relationship in which a successor activity cannot start until a predecessor activity has finished.

Forward Pass: A critical path method technique for calculating the early start and early finish dates by working forward through the schedule.

Functional Organization: An organizational structure in which staff is grouped by areas of specialization and the project manager has limited authority.

Gantt Chart: A bar chart of schedule information where activities are listed. Generally part of the project schedule.

Lag: The amount of time whereby a successor activity will be delayed to a predecessor activity.

Late Finish Date: The latest an activity can finish without delaying the project end date.

Late Start Date: The latest an activity can start without delaying the project end date.

Lead: The amount of time where a successor activity can be started before the predecessor activity finishes.

Lessons Learned: The data gained during a project which shows how project events were addressed or should be addressed in the future for the purpose of improving future performance.

Logical Relationship: A dependency between two activities.

Management Reserve: Time or money that management puts aside in addition to the schedule or cost baseline and issues for unforeseen work that is within the scope of the project. This is not under the control of the project manager and will need an approved change request to access it.

Matrix Organization: An organizational structure in which the project manager shares authority with the functional manager.

Milestone: A significant point or event in a project.

Milestone Schedule: A type of schedule that presents milestones with planned dates.

Most Likely Duration: An estimate of the most probable activity duration that takes into account all of the known variables.

Network Path: A sequence of activities linked by logical relationships in a project schedule network diagram.

Opportunity: A risk that would have a positive effect on one or more project objectives.

Optimistic Duration: An estimate of the shortest activity duration that takes into account all of the known variables.

Organizational Process Assets: Plans, processes, policies, procedures, and knowledge bases specific to and used by the performing organization.

Parametric Estimating: An estimating technique in which an algorithm is used to calculate cost or duration based on historical data and project parameters.

Path Convergence: A relationship in which a schedule activity has more than one predecessor.

Percent Complete: An estimate expressed as a percent of the amount of work that has been completed on an activity.

Performing Organization: An enterprise whose personnel are the most directly involved in doing the work of the project or program.

Pessimistic Duration: An estimate of the longest activity duration that takes into account all of the known variables that could affect performance.

Planned Value (PV): The authorized budget assigned to scheduled work.

Portfolio: Projects and programs, that are grouped together to achieve a strategic business goal.

Portfolio Manager: The person or group assigned by the performing organization to establish, balance, monitor, and control portfolio components in order to achieve strategic business goals.

Precedence Diagramming Method: A technique used for building a schedule in which activities are represented by nodes and are graphically linked by one or more logical relationships to display the sequence in which the activities are to be performed.

Predecessor Activity: An activity that comes before a dependent activity in a schedule.

Preventive Action: An intentional activity that ensures the future performance of the project work is aligned with the project management plan.

Probability and Impact Matrix: A table for diagramming the probability of occurrence of each risk and its impact on project objectives if that risk occurs.

Procurement Management Plan: A component of the project management plan that describes how a team will acquire goods and services from outside of the performing organization.

Product Life Cycle: The series of phases that represent the evolution of a product, from concept through delivery to retirement.

Program: A group of related projects that are managed in a coordinated way to obtain benefits not available from managing them individually.

Program Evaluation and Review Technique (PERT): A technique used to estimate project duration through a weighted average of optimistic, pessimistic, and most likely activity durations.

Program Management: The application of knowledge, skills, tools, and techniques to a program to meet the program requirements and to obtain benefits and control not available by managing projects individually.

Program Manager: The person authorized by the performing organization to lead the team or teams responsible for achieving program objectives.

Progressive Elaboration: The iterative process of increasing the level of detail in a project management plan as greater amounts of information and more accurate estimates become available.

Project: A temporary effort undertaken to create a unique product, service, or result.

Project Calendar: A calendar that identifies working days and shifts that are available for scheduled activities.

Project Charter: A document issued by the project sponsor that formally authorizes the project and provides the project manager with the authority to apply organizational resources to project activities.

Project Life Cycle: The series of phases that a project goes through from its initiation to its closure.

Project Management: The application of knowledge, skills, tools, and techniques to project activities to meet the project requirements.

Project Management Office: A management structure that regulates the project-related governance processes and facilitates the sharing of resources, methodologies, tools, and techniques.

Project Management Plan: The document that defines how the project will be executed, monitored and controlled, and closed.

Project Manager: The person assigned by the performing organization to lead the team that is responsible for achieving the project goals.

Project Phase: A collection of logically related project activities that culminates in the completion of one or more deliverables.

Project Schedule Network Diagram: A graphical representation of the logical relationships among the schedule activities.

Project Scope: The work achieved to deliver a product, service, or result with the specified features and functions.

Project Scope Statement: The explanation of the project scope, major deliverables, assumptions, and constraints.

Projectized Organization: An organizational structure in which the project manager has full authority to assign work and resources.

Quality Management Plan: A component of the project management plan that describes how an organization's quality policies will be implemented.

Requirements Management Plan: A component of the project management plan that describes how requirements will be analyzed, documented, and managed.

Requirements Traceability Matrix: A table that links requirements from their origin to the deliverables that satisfy them.

Residual Risk: The risk that is leftover after risk responses have been implemented.

Resource Breakdown Structure: A ranked representation of resources by category and type.

Resource Calendar: A calendar that identifies the working days and shifts upon which each specific resource is available.

Resource Management Plan: A component of the project management plan that describes the roles and responsibilities of the project team and management of the physical resources on the project.

Resource Leveling: A resource optimization technique in which changes are made to the project schedule to optimize the allocation of resources and which may affect critical path.

Resource Optimization Technique: A technique in which activity start and finish dates are adjusted to balance demand for resources.

Resource Smoothing: A resource optimization technique in which total float are used without affecting the critical path.

Responsibility Assignment Matrix: A grid that shows the project resources assigned to each work package.

Risk: An uncertain event that, if it occurs, has a positive or negative effect on one or more project objectives.

Risk Acceptance: A risk response strategy where the project team decides to acknowledge the risk and not take any action unless the risk occurs.

Risk Appetite: The degree of uncertainty an organization or individual is willing to accept in hope of a reward.

Risk Avoidance: A risk response strategy whereby the project team acts to eradicate the threat or protect the project from its impact.

Risk Breakdown Structure: A ranked representation of risks that is organized according to risk categories.

Risk Category: A group of potential causes of risk.

Risk Enhancement: A risk response strategy where the project team acts to increase the probability of occurrence or impact of an opportunity.

Risk Exploiting: A risk response strategy whereby the project team acts to ensure that an opportunity occurs.

Risk Exposure: A measure of the potential impact of all risks at any given point in time in a project.

Risk Management Plan: A component of the project management plan that describes how risk management activities will be planned and performed.

Risk Mitigation: A risk response strategy whereby the project team acts to reduce the probability of occurrence or impact of a threat.

Risk Register: A register in which outputs of risk management processes are recorded.

Risk Sharing: A risk response strategy where the project team allocates ownership of an opportunity to a third party who is best able to capture the benefit for the project.

Risk Threshold: The level of risk exposure above which risks are addressed and under which risks may be accepted.

Risk Tolerance: The degree of uncertainty that an organization or individual is willing to endure.

Risk Transference: A risk response strategy whereby the project team shifts the impact of a threat to a third party.

Rolling Wave Planning: An iterative planning technique in which the work to be accomplished in the near term is planned in detail, while the work in the future is planned at a higher level.

Schedule Baseline: The approved version of a schedule that can be changed using formal change control procedures and is used as the basis for comparison to actual results. It is part of the project management plan.

Schedule Compression: A method used to shorten the schedule duration without reducing the project scope.

Schedule Management Plan: A component of the project management plan that establishes the criteria and the activities for developing, monitoring, and controlling the schedule.

Schedule Network Analysis: A technique to identify early and late start dates, as well as early and late finish dates, for the unfinished portions of project activities.

Schedule Performance Index (SPI): A measure of schedule efficiency expressed as the fraction of earned value to planned value.

Schedule Variance (SV): A degree of schedule performance expressed as the difference between the earned value and the planned value.

Scope Baseline: The approved version of a scope statement, work breakdown structure (WBS), and its associated WBS dictionary that can be changed using formal change control procedures and is used as the basis for comparison to actual results. It is part of the project management plan.

Scope Creep: The uncontrolled growth to project scope without adjustments to time, cost, and resources.

Scope Management Plan: A component of the project management plan that describes how the scope will be defined, developed, monitored, controlled, and validated.

S-Curve Analysis: A technique used to indicate performance trends by using a graph that displays cumulative costs over a specific time period.

Sponsor: An individual or a group that provides resources and support for the project and is accountable for enabling success.

Stakeholder: An individual, group, or organization that may affect, be affected by, or perceive itself to be affected by a decision, activity, or outcome of a project.

Stakeholder Management Plan: A component of the project management plan that defines how stakeholders will be engaged in project decision making and execution.

Start-to-Finish: A relationship in which a successor activity cannot finish until a predecessor activity has started.

Start-to-Start: A relationship in which a successor activity cannot start until a predecessor activity has started.

Successor Activity: A dependent activity that logically comes after another activity in a schedule.

Threat: A risk that would have a negative effect on one or more project objectives.

Three-Point Estimating: A technique used to estimate cost or duration by applying an average or weighted average of optimistic, pessimistic, and most likely estimates when there is uncertainty with the individual activity estimates.

To-Complete Performance Index (TCPI): A measure of the cost performance that is achieved with the remaining resources in order to meet a specified management goal, expressed as the ratio of the cost to finish the outstanding work to the remaining budget.

Total Float: The amount of time that a schedule activity can be late or extended from its early start date without delaying the project finish date or violating a schedule constraint.

Trigger Condition: An event or situation that indicates that a risk is about to occur.

Variance Analysis: A technique for determining the cause and degree of difference between the baseline and actual performance.

WBS Dictionary: A document that provides detailed deliverable, activity, and scheduling data about each component in the work breakdown structure.

What-If Scenario Analysis: The process of evaluating scenarios in order to predict their effect on project objectives.

Work Breakdown Structure (WBS): A hierarchical decomposition of the total scope of work to be carried out by the project team to accomplish the project objectives and create the deliverables.

Work Package: The work defined at the lowest level of the work breakdown structure for which cost and duration can be estimated and managed.

Workaround: An immediate and temporary response to an issue, for which a prior response had not been planned or was not effective.

Index

D

Online Self-paced PMP Certification Exam Prep Course

Thank you for the purchase of "PMP Exam Prep Simplified". This guide comes with a complementary E-Learning course that will earn you the 35 hours of project management education needed to apply for the PMP certification exam.

Step 1. Log in to your Amazon account and find your orders page.

Step 2. Search for **"PMP Exam Prep Simplified"** and locate the unique 17 digit Amazon order number.

- Take note of this number as it will be used to validate your order.

Step 3. Goto: **https://book.tiapmtraining.com**

- Fill out the form to claim your free course.

TIA
Education
Group

Made in the USA
Coppell, TX
21 April 2021